YOU DECIDE!

Current Debates in Ethics

BRUCE N. WALLER

Youngstown State University

PEARSON

Longman

New York   Boston   San Francisco
London   Toronto   Sydney   Tokyo   Singapore   Madrid
Mexico City   Munich   Paris   Cape Town   Hong Kong   Montreal

Publisher: Priscilla McGeehon
Senior Marketing Manager: Ann Stypuloski
Production Coordinator: Virginia Riker
Cover Design Manager: Nancy Danahy
Cover image courtesy of Getty Images, Inc.
Manufacturing Manager: Mary Fischer

For permission to use copyrighted material, grateful acknowledgment is made to the copyright holders on pp. 332–333, which are hereby made part of this copyright page.

Library of Congress Cataloging-in-Publication Data

You decide! : current debates in ethics / [edited by] Bruce N. Waller.
     p. cm.
ISBN 0-321-5447-8 (alk. paper)
1. Ethics.   I. Waller, Bruce N., 1946–
BJ21.Y68 2005
170--dc22

              2005023543

Please visit our website at http://www.ablongman.com

ISBN 0-321-35447-8

TABLE OF CONTENTS

1. ETHICS AND RELIGION: DOES RELIGION UNDERCUT ETHICS *OR* PROVIDE VITAL SUPPORT FOR ETHICS?   2

Religion Undercuts Ethics

ADVOCATE: James Rachels taught philosophy at the University of Alabama at Birmingham, and his writings have been very influential in ethics, bioethics, and the philosophy of biology. His *Created From Animals: The Moral Implications of Darwinism* (Oxford: Oxford University Press, 1990) is a superb study of the implications of Darwinism.

SOURCE: "God and Human Attitudes," *Religious Studies*, volume 7 (1971): 325–337; reprinted in S. M. Cahn and D. Shatz (eds.), *Contemporary Philosophy of Religion* (New York: Oxford University Press, 1982), pp. 167–181

Religion Provides Vital Support for Ethics

ADVOCATE: George N. Schlesinger taught philosophy at the University of North Carolina at Chapel Hill, and has written extensively on metaphysics, the philosophy of time, the philosophy of science, and philosophy of religion.

SOURCE: *New Perspectives on Old-Time Religion* (Oxford: Oxford University Press, 1988), pp. 79–84

2. REASON, OBJECTIVITY, AND ETHICS: CAN REASON GUIDE US TO OBJECTIVE ETHICAL TRUTHS?   17

Reason Cannot Discover Ethical Truths

ADVOCATE: Bernard Williams was Monroe Deutsch Professor of Philosophy at the University of California, Berkeley, and a Fellow of All Souls College, Oxford.

SOURCE: *Ethics and the Limits of Philosophy* (Cambridge, MA: Harvard University Press, 1985).

Reason Can Discover Ethical Truths

ADVOCATE: Thomas Nagel, University Professor of Philosophy at New York University; author of *The View from Nowhere* (NY: Oxford University Press, 1986)

SOURCE: *The Last Word* (NY: Oxford University Press, 1997).

9. DOES CONTEMPORARY PSYCHOLOGICAL RESEARCH THREATEN VIRTUE THEORY? 173

Virtue Theory is Undercut by Contemporary Psychological Research

ADVOCATE: Gilbert Harman, Stewart Professor of Philosophy at Princeton University; author of *The Nature of Morality* (NY: Oxford University Press, 1977), *Reasoning, Meaning, and Mind* (Oxford: Oxford University Press, 1999), and *Explaining Value and Other Essays in Moral Philosophy* (Oxford: Oxford University Press, 2000).

SOURCE: "Moral Philosophy Meets Social Psychology: Virtue Ethics and the Fundamental Attribution Error," *Proceedings of the Aristotelian Society*, volume 99 (1999): 315–332

Virtue Theory is not Damaged by Contemporary Psychological Research

ADVOCATE: James Montmarquet, Professor of Philosophy at Tennessee State University; author of *Epistemic Virtue and Doxastic Responsibility* (Lanham, MD: Rowman and Littlefield, 1993).

SOURCE: "Moral Character and Social Science Research," *Philosophy*, volume 78 (2003): 355–368

10. IS MORAL PSYCHOLOGY RELEVANT TO MORAL PHILOSOPHY? 191

Moral Psychology Requires Changes in Moral Philosophy

ADVOCATE: Mark L. Johnson, Knight Professor of Liberal Arts and Sciences, Department of Philosophy, University of Oregon; author (with George Lakoff) of *Philosophy in the Flesh: The Embodied Mind and its Challenge to Western Thought* (NY: Basic Books, 1999), and *Moral Imagination: Implications of Cognitive Science for Ethics* (Chicago: University of Chicago Press, 1993)

SOURCE: "How Moral Psychology Changes Moral Theory," from Larry May, Marilyn Friedman, and Andy Clark, eds., *Mind and Morals: Essays on Ethics and Cognitive Science* (Cambridge, MA: MIT Press, 1996): 45–68

Moral Psychology Has Little Effect on Moral Philosophy

ADVOCATE: Virginia Held, Distinguished Professor of Philosophy at the City University Graduate Center of the City University of New York, and a well-known ethicist whose books include *Feminist Morality: Transforming Culture, Society, and Politics* (Chicago: University of Chicago Press, 1993); and *Rights and Goods: Justifying Social Action* (NY: The Free Press, 1984).

SOURCE: "Whose Agenda? Ethics Versus Cognitive Science," from Larry May, Marilyn Friedman, and Andy Clark, eds., *Mind and Morals: Essays on Ethics and Cognitive Science* (Cambridge, MA: MIT Press, 1996): 69–87

13. IS MORALITY RELATIVE TO CULTURE *OR* OBJECTIVELY AND UNIVERSALLY TRUE?   258

Morality is Relative

ADVOCATE: Gilbert Harman, Stewart Professor of Philosophy at Princeton University; author of *The Nature of Morality* (NY: Oxford University Press, 1977), *Reasoning, Meaning, and Mind* (Oxford: Oxford University Press, 1999), and *Explaining Value and Other Essays in Moral Philosophy* (Oxford: Oxford University Press, 2000).

SOURCE: "Is There a Single True Morality?" in David Copp and David Zimmerman, eds., *Morality, Reason, and Truth* (Totawa, NJ: Rowman & Allanheld, 1984)

Morality is Objectively True

ADVOCATE: Carol Rovane, Professor of Philosophy at Columbia University; author of *The Bounds of Metaphysics* (Princeton: Princeton University Press, 1998).

SOURCE: "Earning the Right to Realism or Relativism in Ethics," *Philosophical Issues*, volume 12, Realism and Relativism (2002): 264–285

14. IS CULTURAL RELATIVISM A HELPFUL APPROACH TO ETHICS?   282

Ethical Cultural Relativism Should be Rejected

ADVOCATE: Ruth Macklin, Professor and Head of the Division of Philosophy and History of Medicine, Department of Epidemiology and Population Health, Albert Einstein College of Medicine; member of many important national and international advisory boards and committees, including the U.N. Global Reference Group on HIV/AIDS and Human Rights, the WHO Vaccine Advisory Committee, Council for International Organizations of Medical Sciences (CIOMS), the International Advisory Board on Bioethics of the Pan American Health Organization, and the NIH Recombinant DNA Advisory Committee; author of *Double Standards in Medical Research in Developing Countries* (Cambridge: Cambridge University Press, 2005), and *Enemies of Patients* (NY: Oxford University Press, 1993).

SOURCE: *Against Relativism: Cultural Diversity and the Search for Ethical Universals in Medicine* (NY: Oxford University Press, 1999)

Ethical Cultural Relativism Has Some Advantages

ADVOCATE: Elvin Hatch, Department of Anthropology, University of California Santa Barbara, specializes in the history and theory of cultural anthropology and the study of small communities; among his many works are *Culture and Morality: The Relativity of Values in Anthropology* (NY: Columbia University Press, 1983).

SOURCE: "The Good Side of Relativism," *Journal of Anthropological Research*, volume 53, 1997: 371–381

PREFACE

Contemporary ethical theory is a rich and lively subject, and the debates in this book are intended to represent both the variety and vigor of twenty-first century ethical inquiry. Both champions and critics of major views are represented, together with some indication of the disagreements and arguments both among and within those major perspectives. The debates that follow represent but a sample of the work currently available in ethical theory, and are intended as an intriguing entry into current controversies rather than a survey of contemporary ethics. The goal is not to indicate any final ethical theory, nor even the best available current theory. Instead, this book makes available ongoing inquiries, debates, and discussions of key issues in the study of ethical theory: inquiries and debates that engage the creative and deliberative energies of writers in philosophy, theology, psychology, anthropology, law, and biology.

My home department of philosophy and religious studies at Youngstown State University mixes a rich variety of talents and perspectives in a very supportive and collegial setting. All my colleagues have supplied suggestions, ideas, and encouragement, and I am deeply indebted to Julie Aultmann, Chris Bache, Walter Carvin, Nancy Dawson, Stephanie Dost-Barnhizer, Vince Lisi, Brendan Minogue, Mustansir Mir, Gabriel Palmer-Fernandez, Charles Reid, Tom Shipka, Donna Sloan, J-C Smith, Linda "Tess" Tessier, and Victor Wan-Tatah.

A very special debt of gratitude is owed to our secretary, Joan Bevan, whose warm kindness and amazing efficiency make our department run; and also to Justina Rachella, her very able and cheerful assistant; and to James Sacco, research assistant in Islamic Studies and a wonderful resource for everything related to editing.

The librarians at Y.S.U. have been enormously helpful in tracking down books and articles; special thanks to Ellen Banks, George Heler, Amy Kyle, Jean Romeo, and Kevin Whitfield.

Among my many other faculty colleagues who have offered suggestions and insights are Rebecca Barnhouse, Stephen Flora, Keith Lepak, Dan McNeil, Gary Salvner, Lauren Schroeder, Mark Shutes, Charles Singler, Paul Sracic, Robert Tupaj, Homer Warren, and John White; Bob Weaver was particularly helpful and generous with ideas and sources concerning relativism.

Academic colleagues at other universities have been very helpful in offering ideas for topics and readings, and broadening my understanding of many of the topics covered; among them are Nawal Ammar, Richard Double, George Graham, Bryan Hilliard, Robert Kane, Lia Ruttan, and George Schlesinger.

Thanks to a number of friends who have discussed these and many other issues with me, including Fred Alexander, Luke Lucas, Allen Behsheim, and Jack Raver.

The editorial staff at Pearson Longman have been a delight to work with: always helpful, excellent suggestions, patient guidance, invariably supportive. Special thanks to Priscilla McGeehon and Stephanie Ricotta, and to the special editors for this series, Ted Knight and Jeff Hahn.

Special thanks to my students at Y.S.U., whose enthusiasm for ethics and other areas of philosophy makes my job a delight.

My wife, Mary Newell Waller, has discussed many of these questions with me, been particularly helpful on issues related to psychology, and is always warmly supportive. My sons, Russell and Adam, are my constant source of new ideas, and my greatest joy.

Thanks to the following reviewers who read and commented on earlier drafts of this book.

Sheryl D. Breen
St. Olaf College

Thomas Carroll
Middlesex Community College

Craig Derksen
University of Maryland College Park

Jane M. Drexler
Kent State University-Stark Campus

Michael Eldridge
University of North Carolina at Charlotte

Joan Esposito
Nassau Community College

Daniel Farrell
The Ohio State University

Jon Garthoff
Northwestern University

Joshua Golding
Bellarmine University, Louisville KY

William H. Hardy
Tennessee State University

Bryan Hilliard, Ph.D.
Mississippi University for Women

Dale Jacquette
The Pennsylvania State University

Clarence Sholé Johnson
Middle Tennessee State University

Simon Keller
Boston University

David McNaughton
Florida State University

Steve Odmark
University of Nebraska

Lawrence Pasternack
Oklahoma State University

Thomas Peard
Baker University

Michael Principe
Middle Tennessee State University

Clea Rees
University of California

Dr. Phil Schneider
Coastal Carolina University

H. Peter Steeves
DePaul University

Jason K. Swedene
Lake Superior State University

TO THE STUDENT

There are currently many competing ethical theories, ranging from absolutist views that insist on the existence of fixed, immutable, absolute, universal ethical principles, all the way to views that deny any ethical objectivity whatsoever. Between these two extremes there are ethical theories in abundant variety.

One absolutist view of ethics—a view with a rich history but few current champions—is the **Divine Command theory** of ethics (sometimes called "theological voluntarism"). In this view, moral rules and principles are right if and only if they are commanded by God. If God commands Abraham to slay Isaac, Abraham's beloved son, then killing Isaac is right and good; and if God commands the children of Israel to slaughter every man, woman, and child—and spare not one—in a conquered city, then it is morally wrong to spare a single child from death. In this view, it makes no sense to say that God commands us to love our neighbor *because* that is good; rather, *if* (and only if) God commands it, that *makes* it good. Some people adopt the Divine Command theory because they reason that if God *follows* (rather than dictates) value principles, then that would place limits on God's power. Absent such considerations, however, it is difficult to find points in favor of the Divine Command theory of ethics.

A more plausible absolutist perspective, and one that is much more widely favored, is the **Kantian view.** Immanuel Kant casts a long shadow. Writing during the eighteenth century, Kant developed an ethical system based purely on reason, setting out fundamental principles of ethics that every rational being would understand and approve. In contemporary ethics there are important and insightful philosophers who follow the Kantian model (not in every detail, of course, but on major points), and there are many more who are fierce critics of everything Kantian. In either case, Kant's ethics remains an important landmark.

Though Kantians now come in a variety of shapes and sizes, they share some basic ideas. First, ethical principles must be known through *reason*: they are not known by empirical observation, nor are they based on our feelings or affections, and they can neither be proved nor refuted by any experience, observation, or scientific finding. Second, the principles of ethics must be *universal*: they apply to all rational beings, and they are not relative to culture or country or personality. Third, ethical principles are *objectively true*: if you fail to recognize the true ethical principles, then you are *wrong*, and if two people hold differing principles then at least one person is *mistaken*.

For Kantians, the important thing is the following of principles; in contrast, for **consequentialists** the important consideration is not what principle is honored but what results are accomplished and what *consequences* result. Rather than worrying so much about what principles govern behavior, consequentialists emphasize results: An act is good if it produces the best possible consequences. After all, consequentialists would say, what good is it to follow principles if you don't get good results? Prominent among the consequentialists are the **utilitarians**, who maintain that the best act is the act that produces the greatest balance of pleasure over suffering for *everyone* involved, and this calculation includes both short-term and long-term results. (Actually, not all utilitarians speak of maximizing pleasure over suffering, but that is perhaps the most common—and certainly the best known—version of the utilitarian calculus.)

Another model portrays ethics as an important human artifact. According to **social contract ethics**, we *make*—rather than discover—our ethical system. We make ethics by setting up enforceable agreements among ourselves, agreements covering the basic rights and obligations that we will acknowledge, follow, and support. Another reading of social contract theory treats it as a guide to judging the legitimacy of social and ethical systems of rules: If the rules are rules that we could agree to in setting up a system to govern the behavior of ourselves and others, then the rule system is just.

While Kantian, consequentialist, and contract views—and the controversies among them—have dominated ethical theory for the past century, in recent years two other views have gained considerable following: **virtue theory** and **care ethics**. Virtue theory has a long history, dominating Western ethical thought from the time of Aristotle until well after the Renaissance. Under virtue theory, the key ethical questions revolve around character and character development: What sort of person do I really want to be? What sort of character am I shaping through this act? How can we mold virtuous character in ourselves and others? What kind of community or state is best-suited to the development of virtue in its citizens? During the modern era the ethical focus has shifted away from character and toward questions of rights, obligations, just rewards and deserved punishments. In the last few decades, several ethicists have revived the virtue tradition, emphasizing the larger and longer context in which our acts occur: Rather than asking what act is right or obligatory, they ask what character is best, what habits and activities result in good and bad characters, and how different cultures can facilitate or undercut positive character formation.

Care ethics is a rather loosely defined ethical theory, but it certainly includes an emphasis on affections and feelings, including special relations of friendship and love. Some—but not all—care ethicists hold that feelings are the only source of ethics; and all care ethicists maintain that the exclusive search for universal abstract ethical principles and general rules, known and applied entirely through our rational capacities, is a distorted view of the broader ethical landscape. While champions of care ethics do not deny the importance of rational deliberation in moral decision making, they maintain that ethical theory—particularly Kantian, contract, and utilitarian ethics—has largely confined itself to ethical issues arising among strangers, or in terms of abstract individuals, and has neglected the more intimate ethical sources and concerns. Care ethics is often identified with feminist ethics, and there is no question that feminist theory has contributed a great deal to care ethics, particularly in its contemporary manifestations. But care ethics has a long rich history, and many strands of thought have added to its development.

Another recent position in ethical objectivism is contemporary **moral realism**. Though moral realism encompasses a variety of views, a common factor is the belief that claims of ethical objectivity must be supported by methods analogous to those employed in the empirical sciences (the *real* methods of scientific inquiry, and not some mythic idealized version); and that such ethical inquiries can—or at least eventually *might*—establish objectively true ethical facts.

It might appear that we must choose among these ethical theories; however, when faced with those alternatives, some people choose none of the above. That is, they favor an account of ethics that is fundamentally opposed to all the views so far considered. When asked which ethical theory gives us the correct ethical answers, they reply that none of them do, because there are no objectively or universally true ethical principles. This view takes many forms. Some are relativists, some pragmatists, and some reject ethical objectivity on other grounds.

Among the **ethical nonobjectivists (or ethical relativists)**, there are many who distinguish ethics from other areas of inquiry, such as science; and while they believe that we can have objective scientific knowledge, they deny that ethics can reach objectivity. Such nonobjectivists offer a variety of reasons for that conclusion: They contrast the consensus sometimes reached on scientific questions with the widespread disagreement in ethics. They contrast the operation of scientific methodology with the methods used in ethical inquiry. They claim that we can account for all the phenomena of ethical activity and ethical claims without positing the existence of special objective moral facts, and thus denial of ethical objectivity is a simpler, sounder, and more economical explanation. Or, they emphasize the strong role of feelings in ethics, and argue that science and other realms of objective fact are not so enmeshed in feelings and emotions.

Ethical relativism comes in a variety of forms, but one of the best known is **normative cultural relativism**. Normative cultural relativists hold that there are ethical truths, but such truths apply only within the culture, and not cross-culturally. There are local, cultural ethical truths, but none that are universal. Gilbert Harman favors a form of relativism that focuses on even smaller units: individuals. Individuals may hold ethical beliefs and principles that are near and dear to them, but where basic value conflicts occur among individuals there is no objective means of settling such disputes.

There are significant disagreements among pragmatists, and many pragmatists affirm the existence of objective ethical truth, while some other pragmatists deny it. Both Rorty and Putnam consider themselves pragmatists, but they differ on many points, including the nature of ethics. Putnam rejects *absolute* truths in any realm, but he maintains that we can have genuine objective knowledge, including knowledge of ethical principles. Rorty holds a more skeptical position regarding the existence of objective knowledge, and he rejects claims of objective truth in ethics.

Though understanding the various approaches to ethical theory is useful in examining contemporary controversies, it is important to note that the lines and distinctions among the various ethical theories are not always perfectly clear, and many ethicists are neither doctrinaire proponents of a particular theory nor intransigent opponents of all others. John Rawls, for example, uses social contract theory to develop a Kantian account of fairness and justice; some contemporary Kantians and utilitarians have been much concerned to incorporate greater appreciation of feelings and of personal relationships into their accounts; and some theorists are joining consequentialism with virtue ethics. Thus, the preceding discussion of ethical theories is better regarded as a general guide than a rigid classification. Seen in that light, it may be useful in exploring the basic ethical debates considered in the following pages--basic disputes that explore the essential nature of ethics. Among the fundamental issues: Is ethics an area of objective truth? Must ethical principles apply universally? Will an examination of the sources of our ethical beliefs destroy those beliefs? Are ethical views relative to cultures? Is ethics a matter of discovering the right principles, or developing a better character? Is ethics gender-relative? Does ethics depend on religion? Could psychology or anthropology or biology explain—or even "explain away"–our ethical beliefs? Is the right act purely a matter of principle, or is the rightness of an act determined by its consequences?

One of the most basic ethical questions is whether there is any ethical *truth*, or *ethical objectivity,* and whether ethical truth, if it exists, is analogous to scientific truth; and whether ethical truth would have to be universal (as opposed to being relative to culture, place, or time). This issue is the focus of debates 2, 12, 13, 14, and 15.

Kantians (and utilitarians and contract theorists) focus on obligations, and on what we ought to do—what is the morally *right* act—in various circumstances. Virtue ethics shifts attention away from what specific acts we should perform, and instead concentrates on what character we should strive to develop, the role of the culture and community in fostering good character, and the contribution of moral practices to character development. Debates 8 and 9 examine virtue ethics.

Kantians insist that ethics is an independent enterprise, developed through its own distinctive methods, and therefore ethics cannot be proved, refuted, or explained through the research of other disciplines (such as psychology or biology); and many philosophers who are certainly not Kantians—Virginia Held, for example—join Kantians in asserting the independence of ethics from other disciplines. A number of philosophers, psychologists, anthropologists, and biologists disagree, and maintain that ethics can be better understood, and perhaps should be significantly modified, on the basis of contemporary scientific research. Debates 9, 10, 11, 14, and 15 all are concerned, to various degrees, with that issue. A related question—one that takes up the issue from a very different direction—concerns the relation between religion and ethics, particularly the question of whether ethics is independent of religion, dependent on religion, or (as James Rachels argues) fundamentally inconsistent with traditional religious perspectives. That is the issue in debate 1.

Perhaps the most central issue in contemporary ethical theory is the question of where personal relations of love and friendship and affection fit into the framework of ethics. Kantians tend to place such concerns outside the realm of ethics proper (although there is considerable debate even among Kantians on this issue). Consequentialists (utilitarians) are often accused of leaving no room for personal relationships and affections within their calculations—though many consequentialists dispute that charge. And those who favor the care ethics model often see its greatest strength as its capacity to recognize and fully appreciate the importance of personal relationships, relationships that (care theorists charge) other models neglect, ignore, or even disparage. This issue is central to debates 2, 3, 4, 5, 6, and 7.

All of these questions probe deep into the very nature of ethics, and the arguments are serious and spirited. Perhaps nothing is more central to who we are than our ethical beliefs and outlooks, and the issues debated here are the most central questions of ethics. Participants cover the full spectrum of ethical views, and include philosophers, theologians, anthropologists, psychologists, and biologists. You should find many views you agree with, perhaps more that you reject, and even more that give you an opportunity to think hard about these important and fascinating questions.

YOU DECIDE!

Current Debates in Ethics

ETHICS AND RELIGION: DOES RELIGION UNDERCUT ETHICS *OR* PROVIDE VITAL SUPPORT FOR ETHICS?

RELIGION UNDERCUTS ETHICS

ADVOCATE: James Rachels taught philosophy at the University of Alabama at Birmingham, and his writings have been very influential in ethics, bioethics, and the philosophy of biology. His *Created From Animals: The Moral Implications of Darwinism* (Oxford: Oxford University Press, 1990) is a superb study of the implications of Darwinism.

SOURCE: "God and Human Attitudes," in S. M. Cahn and D. Shatz (eds.), *Contemporary Philosophy of Religion* (NY: Oxford University Press, 1982), pp. 167–181

RELIGION PROVIDES VITAL SUPPORT FOR ETHICS

ADVOCATE: George N. Schlesinger taught philosophy at the University of North Carolina at Chapel Hill, and has written extensively on metaphysics, the philosophy of time, the philosophy of science, and philosophy of religion.

SOURCE: *New Perspectives on Old-Time Religion* (Oxford: Oxford University Press, 1988), pp. 79–84

Are God's commands good because God commands them, or does God command them because they are good? That is, if God commands us to love our neighbor, is that ethically good only because God commands it, or does God command us to love our neighbor because God (in His divine wisdom) recognizes that loving our neighbor is an ethical good? Choosing the latter position implies that God is compelled to follow a standard for goodness existing independently of God. Some believe this position undercuts the supreme power of God, and thus ethics must depend wholly on the will—the commandments—of God. Whatever God commands is good, whatever God forbids is evil, and there is no ethical standard other than God's will.

The *Divine Command Theory* of ethics ("theological voluntarism") wins points for the simplicity of its principles: What is right is whatever God commands. The problem with this view is that it makes God's commandments seem arbitrary: it makes no sense to say that God commands what is good. What if God commanded us to torture children? Would that make the torture of children good? If one replies that God would never command the torture of children, then why not? The most plausible answer seems to be that the torture of children is wrong, and a just God would not order us to do wrong. But that answer presupposes a standard of right and wrong that is independent of God, a standard God recognizes and follows, and that is precisely what the Divine Command theory rejects. Most regard this as a problem for the Divine Command Theory; however, it may be regarded as an advantage by those who insist on the unfathomable nature of God, whose ways are beyond human understanding and to whom we owe abject and unquestioning obedience. More recently, Louis Pojman has proposed another answer: Affirming that God (who is perfectly good) cannot will what is wrong is comparable to saying that God cannot create a square circle. In both cases, Parsons says, we are noting logical impossibilities, not limits on God's power.

If God punishes those who disobey his commandments and rewards those who obey, that will prove nothing about the rightness or wrongness of God's commands. That might make it *expedient* to follow God's commandments, but the same could be said of a ruthless powerful tyrant who orders us to engage in mass murder. Unless we decide to identify what is good as what is expedient for ourselves, then God's rewards and punishments are irrelevant to questions of right and wrong.

In the following two selections, this ancient debate takes a new and interesting twist. James Rachels argues that any ethical view that bases ethical principles on God's commandments would make human ethical behavior impossible. Behaving ethically requires that one act freely and autonomously, and the uncritical following of commandments is not autonomous action. George N. Schlesinger responds that Rachels is basing his critique on a crude concept of religious ethics, and that a deeper understanding of religious devotion reveals a relation between God and ethics that is based on trust and affection rather than abject obedience.

POINTS TO PONDER

➤ Are Rachels and Schlesinger operating with two different concepts of autonomy or free will? What is Rachels' concept of autonomous behavior? Does it match Schlesinger's? Some philosophers and theologians have argued that the only *true* freedom consists in following the Good, with no possibility of going astray. Would Rachels agree? Would Schlesinger? Would you?

➤ Schlesinger's example of the two workers—A, who works from duty, and B, who works from satisfaction—is used in favor of a relation to divinity based on affection rather than duty. But this is an old question: which is better, doing good from duty or doing good through inclination and affection? St. Augustine once advised that we should "Love God, and do as you please," implying that by loving God we would then desire to live well and virtuously. In contrast, Martin Luther maintained that following God was a matter of difficult duty that could not be carried out through feelings of affection. Which view seems more plausible to you? Is the contrast between the views of Augustine and Luther more likely to be based on their different conceptions of God, or of ethics, or of both?

➤ Schlesinger suggests that we might *autonomously* choose to totally and without questioning dedicate ourselves to someone's service or will. If we suppose that the choice to so dedicate ourselves is autonomous, would there remain a question of whether we have autonomously chosen to sacrifice our further autonomy? If you believe that this is a choice to sacrifice your autonomy to another, could that choice be autonomous? That is, could I autonomously choose to become a slave, choose to become nonautonomous?

Ethics and Religion:
Does Religion Undercut Ethics?

James Rachels

> Kneeling down or groveling on the ground, even to express your reverence for heavenly things, is contrary to human dignity.
>
> Kant

It is necessarily true that God (if He exists) is worthy of worship. Any being who is not worthy of worship cannot be God, just as any being who is not omnipotent, or who is not perfectly good, cannot be God. This is reflected in the attitudes of religious believers who recognize that, whatever else God may be, He is a being before whom men should bow down. Moreover, He is unique in this; to worship anyone or anything else is blasphemy. In this paper I shall present an a priori argument against the existence of God which is based on the conception of God as a fitting object of worship. The argument is that God cannot exist, because no being could ever *be* a fitting object of worship.

However, before I can present this argument, there are several preliminary matters that require attention. The chief of these, which will hopefully have some independent interest of its own, is an examination of the concept of worship. In spite of its great importance this concept has received remarkably little attention from philosophers of religion; and when it has been treated, the usual approach is by way of referring to God's awesomeness or mysteriousness: to worship is to "bow down in silent awe" when confronted with a being that is "terrifyingly mysterious." But neither of these notions is of much help in understanding worship. Awe is certainly not the same thing as worship; one can be awed by a performance of *King Lear*, or by witnessing an eclipse of the sun or an earthquake, or by meeting one's favourite film-star, without worshiping any of these things. And a great many things are both terrifying and mysterious that we have not the slightest inclination to worship—I suppose the Black Plague fits that description for many people. The account of worship that I will give will be an alternative to those which rely on such notions as awesomeness and mysteriousness.

Consider McBlank, who worked against his country's entry into the Second World War, refused induction into the army, and was sent to jail. He was active in the "ban the bomb" movements of the fifties; he made speeches, wrote pamphlets, led demonstrations, and went back to jail. And finally, he has been active in opposing the war in Vietnam. In all of this he has acted out of principle; he thinks that all war is evil and that no war is ever justified. I want to make three observations about McBlank's pacifist commitments. (*a*) One thing that is involved is simply his recognition that certain facts are the case. History is full of wars; war causes the massive destruction of life and property; in war men suffer on a scale hardly matched in any other way; the large nations now have weapons which, if used, could destroy the human race; and so on. These are just facts which any normally informed man will admit without argument. (*b*) But of course they are not *merely* facts, which people recognise to be the case in some indifferent manner. They are facts that have special importance to human beings. They form an ominous and threatening backdrop to people's lives—even though for most people they are a backdrop only. But not so for McBlank. He sees the accumulation of these facts as having radical implications for his conduct; he behaves in a very different way from the way he would behave were it not for these facts. His whole style of life is different; his conduct is altered, not just in its details, but in its pattern. (*c*) Not only is his overt behaviour affected; so are his ways of thinking about the world and his place in it. His *self-image* is different. He sees himself as a member of a race with an insane history of self-destruction. He is an opponent of militarism just as he is a father or a musician. When some existentialists say that we "create ourselves" by our choices, they may have something like this in mind.

Thus, there are at least three things that determine McBlank's role as an opponent of war: first, his recognition that certain facts are the case; second, his taking these facts as having important implications for his conduct; and third, his self-image as living his life (at least in part) in response to these facts. My first thesis about worship is that the worshiper has a set of beliefs about God which function in the same way as McBlank's beliefs about war.

First, the worshiper believes that certain things are the case: that the world was created by an all-powerful, all-wise being who knows our every thought and action; that this being, called God, cares for us and regards us as his children; that we are made by him in order to return his love and to live in accordance with his laws; and that, if we do not live in a way pleasing to him, we may be severely punished. Now these beliefs are certainly not shared by all reasonable people; on the contrary, many thoughtful persons regard them as nothing more than mere fantasy. But these beliefs are accepted by religious people, and that is what is important here. I do not say that this particular set of beliefs is definitive of religion in general, or of Judaism or Christianity in particular; it is meant only as a sample of the sorts of belief typically held by religious people in the West. They are, however, the sort of beliefs about God that are required for the business of worshiping God to make any sense.

Second, like the facts about warfare, these are not merely facts which one notes with an air of indifference; they have important implications for one's conduct. An effort must be made to discover God's will both for people generally and for oneself in particular; and to this end, the believer consults the church authorities and the theologians, reads the scripture, and prays. The degree to which this will alter his overt behaviour will depend, first, on exactly what he decides God would have him do, and second, on the extent to which his behaviour would have followed the prescribed pattern in any case.

Finally, the believers recognition of these "facts" will influence his self-image and his way of thinking about the world and his place in it. The world will be regarded as made for the fulfilment of divine purposes; the hardships that befall men will be regarded either as "tests" in some sense or as punishments for sin; and most important, the believer will think of himself as a "Child of God" and of his conduct as reflecting either honour or dishonour upon his Heavenly Father....

Worship is something that is *done*; but it is not clear just *what* is done when one worships. Other actions, such as throwing a ball or insulting one's neighbour, seem transparent enough. But not so with worship: when we celebrate Mass in the Roman Catholic Church, for example, what are we doing (apart from eating a wafer and drinking wine)? Or when we sing hymns in a protestant church, what are we doing (other than merely singing songs)? What is it that makes these acts acts of *worship*? One obvious point is that these actions, and others like them, are ritualistic in character; so, before we can make any progress in understanding worship, perhaps it will help to ask about the nature of ritual.

First we need to distinguish the ceremonial form of a ritual from what is supposed to be accomplished by it. Consider, for example, the ritual of investiture for an English Prince. The Prince kneels; the Queen (or King) places a crown on his head; and he takes an oath: "I do become your liege man of life and limb and of earthly worship, and faith and trust I will bear unto thee to live and die against all manner of folks." By this ceremony the Prince is elevated to his new station; and by this oath he acknowledges the commitments which, as Prince, he will owe the Queen. In one sense the ceremonial form of the ritual is quite unimportant: it is possible that some other procedure might have been laid down, without the point of the ritual being affected in any way. Rather than placing a crown on his head, the Queen might break an egg into his palm (that could symbolise all sorts of things). Once this was established as the procedure to be followed, it would do as well as the other. It would still be the ritual of investiture, so long as it was understood that by the ceremony a Prince is created. The performance of a ritual, then, is in certain respects like the use of language: in speaking, sounds are uttered and, thanks to the conventions of the language, something is said, or affirmed or done, etc.: and in a ritual performance, a ceremony is enacted and, thanks to the conventions associated with the ceremony, something is done, or affirmed, or celebrated, etc.

How are we to explain the point of the ritual of investiture? We might explain that certain parts of the ritual symbolise specific things, for example that the Prince kneeling before the Queen symbolises his subordination to her (it is not, for example, merely to make it easier for her to place the crown on his head). But it is essential that, in explaining the point of the ritual as a whole, we include that a Prince is being created, that he is henceforth to have certain rights in virtue of having been made a Prince, and that he is to have certain duties which he is now acknowledging, among which are complete loyalty and faithfulness to the Queen, and so on. If the listener already knows about the complex relations between Queens, Princes, and subjects, then all we need to tell him is that a Prince is being installed in office; but if he is unfamiliar with this social system, we must tell him a great deal if he is to understand what is going on.

So, once we understand the social system in which there are Queens, Princes, and subjects, and therefore understand the role assigned to each within that system, we can sum up what is happening in the ritual of investiture in this way: someone is being made a Prince, and he is accepting that role with all that it involves. (Exactly the same explanation could be given, *mutatis mutandis*, for the marriage ceremony.)

The question to be asked about the ritual of worship is what analogous explanation can be given of it. The ceremonial form of the ritual may vary according to the customs of the religious community) ; it may involve singing, drinking wine, counting beads, sitting with a solemn expression on one's face, dancing, making a sacrifice, or what-have-you. But what is the point of it?

As I have already said, the worshiper thinks of himself as inhabiting a world created by an infinitely wise, infinitely powerful, perfectly good God; and it is a world in which he, along with other men, occupies a special place in virtue of God's intentions. This gives him a certain role to play: the role of a "Child of God." My second thesis about worship is that in worshiping God one is acknowledging and accepting this role, and that this is the primary function of the ritual of worship. Just as the ritual of investiture derives its significance from its place within the social system of Queens, Princes, and subjects, the ritual of worship gets its significance from an assumed system of relationships between God and men. In the ceremony of investiture, the Prince assumes a role with respect to the Queen and the citizenry; and in worship, a man affirms his role with respect to God.

Worship presumes the superior status of the one worshiped. This is reflected in the logical point that there can be no such thing as mutual or reciprocal worship, unless one or the other of the parties is mistaken as to his own status. We can very well comprehend people loving one another or respecting one another, but not (unless they are misled) worshiping one another. This is because the worshiper necessarily assumes his own inferiority; and since inferiority is an asymmetrical relation, so is worship. (The nature of the "superiority" and "inferiority" involved here is of course problematic; but on the account I am presenting it may be understood on the model of superior and inferior positions within a social system. More on this later.) This is also why *humility* is necessary on the part of the worshiper. The role to which he commits himself is that of the humble servant, "not worthy to touch the hem of His garment." Compared to God's gloriousness, "all our righteousnesses are as filthy rags" (Isaiah 64: 6). So, in committing oneself to this role, one is acknowledging God's greatness and one's

own relative worthlessness. This humble attitude is not a mere embellishment of the ritual: on the contrary, worship, unlike love or respect, *requires* humility. Pride is a sin, and pride before God is incompatible with worshiping him.

On the view that I am suggesting, the function of worship as "glorifying" or "praising" God, which is usually taken to be its primary function, may be regarded as derivative from the more fundamental nature of worship as commitment to the role of God's Child. "Praising" God is giving him the honour and respect due to one in his position of eminence, just as one shows respect and honour in giving fealty to a King.

In short, the worshiper is in this position: He believes that there is a being, God, who is the perfectly good, perfectly powerful, perfectly wise Creator of the Universe; and he views himself as the "Child of God," made for God's purposes and responsible to God for his conduct. And the ritual of worship, which may have any number of ceremonial forms according to the customs of the religious community, has as its point the acceptance of, and commitment to, one's role as God's Child, with all that this involves. If this account is accepted, then there is no mystery as to the relation between the act of worship and the worshiper's other activity. Worship will be regarded not as an isolated act taking place on Sunday morning, with no necessary connection to one's behaviour the rest of the week, but as a ritualistic expression of and commitment to a role which dominates one's whole way of life.

An important feature of roles is that they can be violated; we can act and think consistently with a role, or we can act and think inconsistently with it. The Prince can, for example, act inconsistently with his role as Prince by giving greater importance to his own interests and welfare than to the Queen's; in this case, he is no longer her "liege man." And a father who does not attend to the welfare of his children is not acting consistently with his role as a father (at least as that role is defined in our society), and so on. The question that I want to raise now is, What would count as violating the role to which one is pledged in virtue of worshiping God?

In Genesis there are two familiar stories, both concerning Abraham, that are relevant here. The first is the story of the near-sacrifice of Isaac. We are told that Abraham was "tempted" by God, who commanded him to offer Isaac as a human sacrifice. Abraham obeyed without hesitation: he prepared an altar, bound Isaac to it, and was about to kill him until God intervened at the last moment, saying "Lay not thine hand upon the lad, neither do thou any thing unto him; for now I know that thou fearest God, seeing thou hast not withheld thy son, thine only son from me" (Genesis 22: 12). So Abraham passed the test. But how could he have failed? What was his "temptation"? Obviously, his temptation was to disobey God; God had ordered him to do something contrary to both his wishes and his sense of what would otherwise be right and wrong. He could have defied God; but he did not—he subordinated himself, his own desires and judgments, to God's command, even when the temptation to do otherwise was strongest.

It is interesting that Abraham's record in this respect was not perfect. We also have the story of him bargaining with God over the conditions for saving Sodom and Gomorrah from destruction. God had said that he would destroy those cities because they were so wicked; but Abraham gets God to agree that if fifty righteous men can be found there, then the cities will be spared. Then he persuades

God to lower the number to forty-five, then forty, then thirty, then twenty, and finally ten. Here we have a different Abraham, not servile and obedient, but willing to challenge God and bargain with him. However, even as he bargains with God, Abraham realises that there is something radically inappropriate about it: he says, "Behold now, I have taken upon me to speak unto the Lord, which am but dust and ashes... O let not the Lord be angry..." (Genesis 18: 27, 30).

The fact is that Abraham could not, consistently with his role as God's subject, set his own judgment and will against God's. The author of Genesis was certainly right about this. We cannot recognise any being *as God*, and at the same time set ourselves against him. The point is not merely that it would be imprudent to defy God, since we certainly can't get away with it; rather, there is a stronger, logical point involved—namely, that if we recognise any being *as God*, then we are committed, in virtue of that recognition, to obeying him.

To see why this is so, we must first notice that "God" is not a proper name like "Richard Nixon" but a title like "President of the United States" or "King." Thus, "Jehovah is God" is a nontautological statement in which the title "God" is assigned to Jehovah, a particular being—just as "Richard Nixon is President of the United States" assigns the title "President of the United States" to a particular man. This permits us to understand how statements like "God is perfectly wise" can be logical truths, which is highly problematic if "God" is regarded as a proper name. Although it is not a logical truth that any particular being is perfectly wise, it nevertheless is a logical truth that if any being is God (i.e. if any being properly holds that title) then that being is perfectly wise. This is exactly analogous to saying: although it is not a logical truth that Richard Nixon has the authority to veto congressional legislation, nevertheless it is a logical truth that if Richard Nixon is President of the United States then he has that authority.

To bear the title "God," then, a being must have certain qualifications. He must, for example, be all-powerful and perfectly good in addition to being perfectly wise. And in the same vein, to apply the title "God" to a being is to recognise him as one to be obeyed. The same is true, to a lesser extent, of "King"—to recognise anyone as King is to acknowledge that he occupies a place of authority and has a claim on one's allegiance as his subject. And to recognise any being as God is to acknowledge that he has *unlimited* authority, and an unlimited claim on one's allegiance. Thus, we might regard Abraham's reluctance to defy Jehovah as grounded not only in his fear of Jehovah's wrath, but as a logical consequence of his acceptance of Jehovah *as God*. Camus was right to think that "From the moment that man submits God to moral judgment, he kills Him in his own heart." What a man can "kill" by defying or even questioning God is not the being that (supposedly) *is* God, but *his own conception of that being as God.* That God is not to be judged, challenged, defied, or disobeyed, is at bottom a truth of logic; to do any of these things is incompatible with taking him as One to be worshiped.

So the idea that any being could be *worthy* of worship is much more problematical than we might have at first imagined. For in admitting that a being is worthy of worship we would be recognising him as having an unqualified claim on our obedience. The question, then, is whether there could be such an unqualified claim. It should be noted that the description of a being as all-powerful, all-wise, etc., would not automatically settle the issue; for even while admitting the existence of such an awesome being we might still question whether we should recognise him as having an unlimited claim on our obedience.

In fact, there is a long tradition in moral philosophy, from Plato to Kant, according to which such a recognition could never be made by a moral agent. According to this tradition, to be a moral agent is to be an autonomous or self directed agent; unlike the precepts of law or social custom, moral precepts are imposed by the agent upon himself, and the penalty for their violation is, in Kant's words, "self-contempt and inner abhorrence." The virtuous man is therefore identified with the man of integrity, i.e. the man who acts according to precepts which he can, on reflection, conscientiously approve in his own heart. Although this is a highly individualistic approach to morals, it is not thought to invite anarchy because men are regarded as more or less reasonable and as desiring what we would normally think of as a decent life lived in the company of other men.

On this view, to deliver oneself over to a moral authority for directions about what to do is simply incompatible with being a moral agent. To say "I will follow so-and-so's directions no matter what they are and no matter what my own conscience would otherwise direct me to do" is to opt out of moral thinking altogether; it is to abandon one's role as a moral agent. And it does not matter whether "so and so" is the law, the customs of one's society, or God. This does not, of course, preclude one from seeking advice on moral matters, and even on occasion following that advice blindly, trusting in the good judgment of the adviser. But this is to be justified by the details of the particular case, e.g. that you cannot in that case form any reasonable judgment of your own due to ignorance or inexperience in dealing with the types of matters involved. What is precluded is that a man should, while in possession of his wits, adopt this style of decision-making (or perhaps we should say this style of *abdicating* decision-making) as a general strategy of living, or abandon his own best judgment in any case where he can form a judgment of which he is reasonably confident.

What we have, then, is a conflict between the role of worshiper, which by its very nature commits one to total subservience to God, and the role of moral agent, which necessarily involves autonomous decision-making. The point is that the role of worshiper takes precedence over every other role which the worshiper has—when there is any conflict, the worshiper's commitment to God has priority over any other commitments which he might have. But the first commitment of a moral agent is to do what in his own

heart he thinks is right. Thus the following argument might be constructed:

(a) If any being is God, he must be a fitting object of worship.
(b) No being could possibly be a fitting object of worship, since worship requires the abandonment of one's role as an autonomous moral agent.
(c) Therefore, there cannot be any being who is God....

The above argument will probably not persuade anyone to abandon belief in God—arguments rarely do—and there are certainly many more points which need to be worked out before it can be known whether this argument is even viable. Yet it does raise an issue which is clear enough. Theologians are already accustomed to speaking of theistic belief and commitment as taking the believer "beyond morality," and I think they are right. The question is whether this should not be regarded as a severe embarrassment.

Ethics and Religion:
Religion Provides Vital Support for Ethics

GEORGE N. SCHLESINGER

In an influential article Patrick Nowell-Smith has advanced the claim that religious morality is basically flawed and therefore may appropriately be labelled as 'infantile morality'. He cites Hobbes's phrase 'God who by right, that is by irresistible power, commandeth all things', which he finds repugnant since it equates God's right with his might. In Nowell-Smith's opinion—an opinion shared by most philosophers—for an act to qualify as a moral act, the agent has to perform it because of the intrinsic desirability of that act, and not because of fear of retribution or expectation of reward, or because of any other ulterior motive.

Nowell-Smith explains that the reason why religious morality is essentially infantile is that, first of all, just as a little boy may refrain from pulling his sister's hair not because it hurts her, but because Mummy forbids it (and he is aware that defying her may have painful consequences), so a religious person will refrain from wicked acts not because of their inherent wickedness, but because they violate a Divine command. Secondly, to a child morality is nothing but a curb on his own volition; he is not yet capable of understanding why he must not do certain things he would very much like to do, and so is forced to submit blindly to parental authority. The same is true in religion:

> It is the total surrender of the *will* that is required: Abraham must be prepared to sacrifice Isaac at God's command, and I take this to mean that we must be prepared to sacrifice

our most deeply felt concerns if God should require us to do so. If we dare ask why, the only answer is 'Have faith'; and faith is an essentially heteronomous idea, for it is not a reasoned trust in someone in whom we have good grounds for reposing trust; it is blind faith, utter submission of our own reason and will.

However, a genuinely moral person does not act contrary to his will. His conduct is based on an understanding of what is desirable and what is repugnant. Such an understanding generates the will to act in compliance with the rules of morality, which amount to the required safeguards for proper conduct, ensuring the avoidance of what is bad and the doing of what is good.

Other philosophers, using similar arguments, have gone further to draw the radical conclusion that theism must be false. J. Rachels, for instance, has emphasized that a genuine moral agent is essentially autonomous. However, obedience to divine commands requires the surrendering of one's role as an autonomous moral agent. Religious morality is thus incompatible with genuine morality. Hence Rachels constructs the following compact deductive argument for atheism:

(a) If any being is God, he must be a fitting object of worship.
(b) No being could possibly be a fitting object of worship, since worship requires the abandonment of one's role as an autonomous moral agent.

(c) Therefore, there cannot be any being who is God.

The theist is capable, of course, of defending himself against these attacks. It is interesting to see, however, whether he can do so even if he grants these philosophers all their presuppositions about the nature of ethics. Thus let us not question the assumption that there exists a more or less agreed-upon set of rules that constitutes morality, and that no justification is required to show that these rules are universally binding. Furthermore, we shall also accept it as obvious that an agent who does not act autonomously is at best practising an inferior kind of morality and possibly no morality at all. However, we should not grant any views about religious precepts unless they are reasonable. Now, concerning the question as to what religious morality is, one cannot hope to arrive at the right answer with the aid of any kind of a priori reasoning; it is essential that we acquaint ourselves with the relevant religious teachings. For example, one of the most basic ideas concerning the end to which a pious person must strive, and one that has been emphasized by all religious teachers, is that an individual is to serve God because of the immeasurably great fulfilment and felicity all acts of piety are bound to bestow upon their practitioners. To obey the precepts of religion out of fear of Divine might is an attitude typical of a novice, who as yet has only a very crude understanding of the significance of a God-centred life. Upon a fuller realization of the nature of piety, a person acquires much loftier sentiments and his reverent acts are informed by a spirit of love and of longing for Divine communion. The service of the true worshipper is accompanied by a sense of spiritual self-enhancement and deep fulfilment that is the natural outcome of acts of love and joy. To cite

but one of the many expressions of this idea:

> As the love of God is man's highest happiness and blessedness, and the aim of all human actions, it follows that he alone lives by the Divine law who loves God not from fear of punishment, or from love of any other object... but solely because he has knowledge of God.

It seems therefore sufficient to point out that he who refrains from doing evil for no other reason than his fear of Divine retribution is practising not merely an inferior kind of morality, but, in the view of virtually all religious authorities, also an inferior kind of religion. On the other hand, such a person is still much to be preferred to a complete non-believer, since he has already ascended the first important rung on the ladder leading to salvation, and even if he should rise no further, he—unlike the latter—will at least have the proper restraints to keep him from actually engaging in any wrongdoing.

Once our attention has been drawn to what constitutes a fully realized religious attitude, we are bound to see the mistake of describing all those who obey Divine commands as people who suspend their human autonomy, totally and blindly submitting their will to carry out, robot-like, and in complete ignorance of the whys and wherefores, whatever they are required to do. Suppose a person to whom I owe a very large debt of gratitude, and whom I love and admire greatly, informs me one day that it is imperative for him to get to Washington today, and in view of the airline strike and his inability to drive, he asks me to drive him there. Let us also suppose that because of my anxiety to please my benefactor, I at once cancel all my appointments for the day, inform my son that I shall not attend the school play in which he acts the title role, and so on, and without asking any questions drive to Washington. I do not believe that many would insist that it would have been nobler on my part if, instead of taking off in total ignorance of the purpose of our trip, I had first demanded to be reassured, by being given a full account of what my cherished friend proposed to do in Washington, that there was sufficient reason for this journey.

Also I believe that it would be nonsensical to describe me as one who has acted robot-like, blindly renouncing my autonomy to the will of another. Admittedly I have no idea of the nature of my benefactor's business in the capital, but that is quite irrelevant. What I do know for sure—and this is really what matters—is that he feels his presence is urgently required there, and also that he is a highly judicious person whom I have reason to trust and love. Thus, if I am a decent individual, I shall welcome this opportunity to do something which is beyond any doubt a service to him. Not only are all feelings of being coerced and of surrendering my autonomy totally out of place, but on the contrary I should be expected to be gratified with having made the clear-eyed and fully self-determined decision to carry out my benefactor's wish as promptly and smoothly as possible without subjecting him to an unbecoming interrogation. In a similar fashion, a pious person senses no pressure to which he has to surrender, and feels no coercion, but quite the opposite, will eagerly seek out the opportunity to engage in what to him amounts to the loftiest of all human activities, namely, serving God.

Incidentally, it may be noted that none of the philosophers who have been critical of religious morality are known to have advocated the abolition of punishment for all crimes. Now it is possible to imagine an argument for doing so, since people

who do not steal, embezzle, commit forgery, perjury, armed robbery, or murder, because they recoil from such activities which seem to them reprehensible and ugly, are far superior to those of a juvenile mentality who would eagerly engage in any profitable felony were it not for their fear of legal retribution. The reason is likely to be that sensible citizens regard the suppression of criminal behaviour as vital enough to be prepared themselves to put up with the moral loss resulting from penal legislation, namely, that many will behave decently but not for any lofty motives. Also one might contend that the genuinely upright members of the society will conduct themselves honestly because of their love of justice and virtue; that is, there will be scope for enlightened, uncoerced proper conduct even in the presence of coercive laws.

It is essential also to mention that a truly God-loving person has an additional important motive for behaving ethically. Here, for example, is a brief quotation from the writings of the sixteenth-century theologian Judah Loew: 'The love of people is at the same time a love for God. For when we love one, we necessarily love one's handiwork'. According to this, the pious person will act altruistically, not simply because he feels it to be incumbent upon him to act that way, but out of genuine concern and compassion towards others. These sentiments will have been generated by his primary love of God, which will spill over to affect his feelings toward God's creatures as well. It is natural for a theist to treat every fellow human as his brother or sister, since to him they are all the children of the same Heavenly Father. In addition, in the eyes of the theist, attending to the needs of any human being, who, as he was taught, was created in the image of God, virtually amounts to attending to a Divine need.

Consider now a theist who has selflessly devoted himself to humanitarian works and is constantly concerned with the welfare of others. He does what he does not because of a sense of duty, not because he feels obliged to follow the rules of some ethical system or a code of religious law. His basic motivation is his constant awareness of God's infinite kindness, which sustains him every moment, and in consequence of which his heart is filled with love and gratitude toward his Creator. I do not know precisely how Nowell-Smith or Rachels would characterize the nature of such a person's conduct. It seems to me, however, that there are not many who would look upon such a theist's motives as tarnished, and upon his conduct as undesirable. In fact many people would maintain that he should be regarded as at least as high-minded and noble as someone who believes in no supreme being, is completely devoid of all sympathy or compassion toward strangers, and feels duty-bound to follow the rules of morality solely because of his commitment to a code of ethics.

I admit to my inability to offer a detailed, rigorous justification for the strong feelings I have in this matter. The following story might, however, throw some light on the issue at hand. A and B work hard at what they are paid to do by their employer. A does so out of his awareness of the rules of decency and the belief that a person is duty-bound to put in a full day's work for a full day's pay. He derives no satisfaction from his labour—in fact it is drudgery to him—but he has autonomously chosen to follow the principle never to shirk his responsibilities. B, on the other hand, is completely untutored in matters of the abstract rules of decency; however, because of the immense satisfaction he derives from the creativity involved in carrying out his daily assignments, he keeps at it enthusiastically all day long. Some would argue, perhaps, that A deserves our greater admiration, for his voluntary martyrdom to a theoretical system of work-ethics, than B, who is after all only doing what gives him pleasure—and gets paid for it on top of that. It seems, however, when the time comes to reduce the work-force, the smart manager will fire A and retain B, who is bound to be a more effective labourer, more productive of useful new ideas, and of greater inspiration to his fellow workers. He will be far more valued by those who have the welfare and progress of the company at heart....

THE CONTINUING DEBATE:
Ethics and Religion: Does Religion Undercut Ethics *or* Provide Vital Support for Ethics?

What Is New

R. M. Adams has offered a new model of the relation of God's commandments and ethics. Adams argues that God's commandments are not arbitrary, because they flow from the nature of God and God's nature includes love of His creation. Whether this sets up a prior standard of good ("Is God's nature good?") is a debated question. Process theology, by breaking down the radical God-creation distinction, offers a possible way to defuse the problems generated by the divine command theory of ethics. Both feminist ethics and virtue ethics change the focus of the problem by offering new perspectives on the nature of ethics: Rather than a system of rules (perhaps rules based on divine commands) ethics is concerned with developing virtuous character or with nurturing and protecting relationships of care and trust. Thus, both virtue and care ethics challenge the basic ethical framework of the Divine Command theories of ethics: if ethics is not primarily a matter of following rules, then the problem of where ethical rules come from is no longer a major problem.

Where to Find More

Kai Nielsen is a leading critic of the claim that ethics requires God. See his *Ethics Without God*, Revised Edition (Buffalo, N.Y.: Prometheus Books, 1990); and *Naturalism and Religion* (Amherst, NY: Prometheus Books, 2001). A debate between J. P. Moreland and Kai Nielsen concerning the existence of God contains a chapter on the question of whether ethics requires the existence of God. See *Does God Exist? The Debate Between Theists & Atheists*, by J. P. Moreland and Kai Nielsen (Amherst, NY: Prometheus Books, 1993).

Plato's *Euthyphro* (available in a number of translations and editions) is the classic source for the argument against the Divine Command theory of ethics. Jonathan Berg offers a brief argument for how ethics might be based on religion in, "How Could Ethics Depend on Religion?" in Peter Singer, ed., *A Companion to Ethics* (Oxford: Blackwell, 1991). Philip L. Quinn develops a detailed and sophisticated defense of Divine Command theory in "Divine Command Theory," in Hugh LaFollette, ed., *The Blackwell Guide to Ethical Theory* (Oxford: Blackwell Publishers, 2000). Ton Van Den Beld, "The Morality System With and Without God," *Ethical Theory and Moral Practice*, volume 4 (2001): 383–399, argues that a version of the divine command theory offers the most promising account of the substantive and sometimes costly demands that morality makes on individual persons. Robert Merrihew Adams is one of the most philosophically sophisticated defenders of an essential role for religion in ethics; see his *Finite and Infinite Goods: A Framework for Ethics* (NY: Oxford University Press, 1999).

There are two excellent anthologies on the subject of the relation between religion and ethics: P. Helm, editor, *Divine Commands and Morality* (Oxford: Oxford University Press, 1981); and G. Outka and J. P. Reeder, Jr., eds, *Religion and Morality: A Collection of Essays* (Garden City/New York: Anchor/Doubleday, 1973). *A Companion to Philosophy of Religion*, edited by Philip L. Quinn and Charles Taliaferro, is a wide-ranging collection of very good articles, including many on the relation between religion and ethics.

An anthology that offers insightful new perspectives on religion as well as its relation to ethics is Teresa Elwas, editor, *Women's Voices: Essays in Contemporary Feminist Theology* (London: Marshall Pickering, 1992). *From a Broken Web: Separation, Sexism, and Self,* by C. Keller, is an interesting combination of feminist and process theology approaches.

An excellent and very clear discussion of the questions surrounding religion and ethics can be found in Chapter 13 of Michael Peterson, William Hasker, Bruce Reichenbach, and David Basinger, *Reason & Religious Belief: An Introduction to the Philosophy of Religion*, Second Edition (NY: Oxford University Press, 1998).

REASON, OBJECTIVITY, AND ETHICS: CAN REASON GUIDE US TO OBJECTIVE ETHICAL TRUTHS?

REASON CANNOT DISCOVER ETHICAL TRUTHS

ADVOCATE: Bernard Williams was Monroe Deutsch Professor of Philosophy at the University of California, Berkeley, and a Fellow of All Souls College, Oxford.

SOURCE: *Ethics and the Limits of Philosophy* (Cambridge, MA: Harvard University Press, 1985)

REASON CAN DISCOVER ETHICAL TRUTHS

ADVOCATE: Thomas Nagel, University Professor of Philosophy at New York University; author of *The View from Nowhere* (NY: Oxford University Press, 1986)

SOURCE: *The Last Word* (NY: Oxford University Press, 1997)

Thomas Nagel and Bernard Williams are grappling with what is perhaps the central ethical issue of the last two and a half millennia. In Plato's *Republic*, Thrasymachus asserts that "the just is nothing else than the advantage of the stronger." There are no objective moral principles, he argues, and might makes right. Socrates takes up the challenge, arguing that principles of ethics and justice can be established by reason (and only by reason). This debate has raged ever since, taking many forms: Can reason discover ethical truths, or must they be revealed by God? Are ethical truths known by reason, or is ethics based on our emotions and affections (or our intuitions, or perhaps our empirical experience)? Can reason reveal ethical truths, or is the notion of objective ethical truth an illusion? For modern philosophy, the defining figures in the continuing controversy are Immanuel Kant, who argued that objective universal ethical truths can be known purely and exclusively by reason; and David Hume, who maintained that ethics is derived solely from our feelings. In this debate, Thomas Nagel follows in the Kantian tradition while Williams champions a position more like Hume's. The basic question that divides them is this long-contested issue: If we are guided by *reason* and function as rational beings, does that in itself presuppose substantive ethical principles (such as an obligation of impartiality among ourselves and other rational beings)?

The campaign to establish universal objective moral truths takes a variety of forms. The Kantian approach does not start with a quest for moral truth that we somehow discover as an end result of our inquiries; rather, Kantians maintain that the very process of practical reasoning involves or presupposes substantive moral principles and obligations that apply to all who use practical reason: Moral obligations, in other words, are inherent in the practical reasoning process itself. That basic Kantian claim is the pivot point for the debate between Williams and Nagel.

POINTS TO PONDER

➤ Bernard Williams denies that rational deliberation can establish an impartial ethical standpoint that respects the interests of all persons, because—Williams argues—practical deliberation is a personal process of deciding about my own preferences (and is distinct from factual deliberation concerning the world, which *does* involve impartial rational deliberation). Is there (contrary to Williams' claims) an essential element of impartiality in personal practical deliberation? That is, could it be argued that impartiality is an essential element of *all* rational deliberation?

➤ Thomas Nagel asserts that "someone who abandons or qualifies his basic methods of moral reasoning on historical or anthropological grounds alone is nearly as irrational as someone who abandons a mathematical belief on other than mathematical grounds.... Moral considerations occupy a position in the system of thought that makes it illegitimate to subordinate them completely to anything else." Thus in Nagel's view, biology or psychology or anthropology might lead us to modify some of our moral beliefs (for example, learning more about chimpanzees might lead us to believe we are morally obligated to change our treatment of them); but those disciplines could never legitimately lead us to abandon or modify our methods of moral reasoning. Do you agree? Can you think of any possible scientific finding that could cause you to radically revise your basic perspective on the nature of morality and moral deliberation?

➤ Nagel argues that when psychological (or other scientific) accounts give a causal explanation for our moral beliefs, it is always possible to step back and look impersonally at our moral principles *in light of* the new information about their origin; and from that new broader perspective, we can always ask whether we now have good reason for believing in those moral principles. Thus scientific research could never destroy our belief in objective morality, since it is always open to us to take account of that research, reflect upon it, and (with the new information in hand) make a rational decision about what moral principles it is now most reasonable to hold. Of course, at some point we might give up and decide that scientific accounts have undermined all reasonable belief in the rational objectivity of our moral beliefs; but, according to Nagel, "to give up would be nothing but moral laziness." Do you agree? Could there come a point (following several levels of debunking causal explanation of why we hold what we thought were rationally derived moral principles) at which it would be *unreasonable* (rather than "morally lazy") to claim that at a higher reflective level we can still make an objectively reasonable moral evaluation?

Reason, Objectivity, and Ethics: Reason Cannot Discover Ethical Truths

Bernard Williams

There is a... project that tries... to start from the ground up.... It starts from a very abstract conception of rational agency. It still tries to give an answer to Socrates' question, though a minimal one. It gives the answer to each agent, merely because the agent can ask the question. Hence its answers are more abstract and less determinately human than those in the Aristotelian style. This type of argument yields, if anything, general and formal principles to regulate the shape of relations between rational agents. These are the concerns of Kant.

This may seem a surprising thing to say. Kant's name is associated with an approach to morality in which, it is often supposed, there can be no *foundations* for morality at all. He insisted that morality should be "autonomous," and that there could be no reason for being moral. A simple argument shows why, in the Kantian framework, this must be so. Any reason for being moral must be either a moral or a nonmoral reason. If it is moral, then it cannot really be a reason for being moral, since you would have to be already inside morality in order to accept it. A nonmoral reason, on the other hand, cannot be a reason for being *moral*; morality requires a purity of motive, a basically moral intentionality (which Kant took to be obligation), and that is destroyed by any nonmoral inducement. Hence there can be no reason for being moral, and morality presents itself as an unmediated demand, a categorical imperative.

It is specifically *morality* that Kant introduces.... Kant's outlook indeed re-

quires that there be no reason for morality, if that means a motivation or inducement for being moral, but it does not imply that morality has no foundations. Kant thought that we could come to understand why morality should rightly present itself to the rational agent as a categorical demand. It was because rational agency itself involved accepting such a demand, and this is why Kant described morality in terms of laws laid down by practical reason for itself.

In his extraordinary book *The Groundwork of the Metaphysic of Morals,*... he tries to explain how this can be. I do not want to try to set out the argument, however, by directly expounding Kant. That would involve many special problems of its own. I shall treat his outlook as the destination rather than the route and shall develop in the first place an argument that will be simpler and more concrete than Kant's....

Is there anything that rational agents necessarily want? That is to say, is there anything they want (Or would want if they thought hard enough about it) merely as part or precondition of being agents?

When they are going to act, people necessarily want, first of all, some outcome: they want the world to be one way rather than another. You can want an outcome without wanting to produce that outcome—you might prefer that the outcome merely materialize. Indeed, there are some cases in which the outcome you want will count only if you do not directly produce it (you want her to fall in love with you). But, in direct contrast to that possibility, in many cases you essentially want not only the outcome, but to produce the outcome. To put it another way (a way that is complicated but still conceals some complications), the outcome you want itself includes the action that your present deliberation will issue in your doing.

We do not merely want the world to contain certain states of affairs (it is a deep error of consequentialism to believe that this is all we want). Among the things we basically want is to act in certain ways. But even when we basically want some state of affairs, and would be happy if it materialized, we know that we do not live in a magical world, where wanting an outcome can make it so. Knowing, therefore, that it will not come about unless we act to produce it, when we want an outcome we usually also want to produce it.... Moreover, we do not want it merely to *turn out* that we produced it; we want these thoughts of ours to produce it. The wants involved in our purposive activities thus turn out to be complex. At the very least, what we want is that the outcome should come about because we wanted it, because we believed certain things, and because we acted as we did on the basis of those wants and beliefs. Similar considerations apply to keeping things that we want to keep.

This adds up, then, to the following: on various occasions we want certain outcomes; we usually want to produce those outcomes; we usually want to produce them in a way that expresses our want to produce them. Obviously enough, on those occasions we do not want to be frustrated, for instance by other people. Reflecting on all this, we can see that we have a general, dispositional, want not to be frustrated, in particular by other people.

We have a general want, summarily put, for freedom....

It is not enough, though, for this freedom merely that we should not be frustrated in doing whatever it is we want to do. We might be able to do everything we wanted, simply because we wanted too little. We might have unnaturally straitened or impoverished wants. This consideration shows that we have another general want, if an indeterminate one: we want (to put it vaguely) an adequate range of wants.

It does not follow from all this that we want our choices to be as little limited as possible, by anything or anyone. We do not want our freedom to be limitless. It may seem to follow, but to accept it would be to leave out another vital condition of rational agency. Some things, clearly, are accessible to an agent at a given time and others are not. Moreover, what is accessible, and how easily, depends on features both inside and outside the agent. He chooses, makes up plans, and so on, in a world that has a certain practicable shape, in terms of where he is, what he is, and what he may become. The agent not only knows this is so (that is to say, he is sane), but he also knows, on reflection, that it is necessary if he is indeed going to be a rational agent. Moreover, he cannot coherently think that in an ideal world he would not need to be a rational agent. The fact that there are restrictions on what he can do is what requires him to be a rational agent, and it also makes it possible for him to be one; more than that, it is also the condition of his being some particular person, of living *a* life at all. We may think sometimes that we are dismally constrained to be rational agents, and that in a happier world it would not be necessary. But that is a fantasy (indeed it is *the* fantasy).

Similar conditions apply to the agent's knowledge. Acting in a particular situation, he must want his plans not to go wrong through ignorance or error. But even in that particular case, he does not want to know everything, or that his action should have no unintended consequences. Not to know everything is, once more, a condition of having a life—some things are unknown, for instance, because they will form one's future. If you cannot coherently want to know everything, then you also cannot coherently want never to be in error. They are not the same thing (omniscience is not the same as infallibility), but there are many connections between them. For one thing, as Karl Popper has always emphasized, you must make errors, and recognize them, if you are going to extend such knowledge as you have.

These last considerations have concerned things a rational agent does not need to want, indeed needs not to want, as a condition of being such an agent. They assume him or her to be a finite, embodied, historically placed agent....

As rational agents, then, we want what I have summarily called freedom, though that does not mean limitless freedom. Does this commit us to thinking that our freedom is a good and that it is a good thing for us to be free? One path leading to this conclusion would be to say that when an agent wants various particular outcomes, he must think that those various outcomes are good. Then he would be bound to think that his freedom was a good thing, since it was involved in securing those outcomes.

Is it true that if we want something and purposively pursue it, then we think of our getting that thing as good? This is a traditional doctrine, advanced in Plato's *Meno* and hallowed in a saying of scholastic philosophy, *omne appetitum appetitur sub specie boni*, everything pursued is pursued as being something good. It seems to me not true. In any ordinary understanding of *good*, surely, an extra step is taken if you go from saying that you want something or have decided to pursue it to saying that it is good, or (more to the point) that it is good that you should have it. The idea of something's being good imports an idea, however minimal or hazy, of a perspective in which it can be acknowledged by more than one agent as good. An agent who merely has a certain purpose may of course think that his purpose is good, but he does not have to. The most he would commit himself to merely by having a purpose would presumably be that it would be good *for him* if he succeeded in it, but must even this much be involved? Even this modest claim implies a perspective that goes somewhere beyond the agent's immediate wants, to his longer-term interests or well-being. To value something, even relatively to your own interests, as you do in thinking that it would be better "for me," is always to go beyond merely wanting something. I might indeed come to put all the value in my life into the satisfaction of one desire, but if I did, it would not simply be because I had only one desire. Merely to have one desire might well be to have no value in my life at all; to find all the value in one desire is to have just one desire that *matters* to me.

Even if we give up the traditional doctrine, however, so that I do not have to see everything I want as good, it might still be true that I should see my freedom as good. "Good for me," I suggested, introduces some reference to my interests or well-being that goes beyond my immediate purposes, and my freedom is one of my fundamental interests. So perhaps I must regard my own freedom as a good. But if so, I must not be misled into thinking that my freedom constitutes a good, period. This would be so only if it were a good, period, that I should be a rational agent, and there is no reason why others should assent to that. In fact, it is not even clear that *I* have to assent to it. This begins to touch on some deeper questions about my conception of my own existence.

Everything said so far about the basic conditions and presuppositions of rational action seems to be correct. The argument that tries to provide a foundation for morality attempts to show that, merely because of those conditions, each agent is involved in a moral commitment. Each agent, according to this argument, must think as follows. Since I necessarily want my basic freedom, I must be opposed to courses of action that would remove it. Hence I cannot agree to any arrangement of things by which others would have the right to remove my basic freedom. So when I reflect on what arrangement of things I basically need, I see that I must claim a *right* to my basic freedom. In effect, I must lay it down as a rule for others that they respect my freedom. I claim this right solely because I am a rational agent with purposes. But if this fact alone is the basis of my claim, then a similar fact must equally be the basis of such a claim by others. If, as I suppose, I legitimately and appropriately think that they should respect my freedom, then I must recognize that they legitimately and appropriately think that I should respect their freedom. In moving from my need for freedom to "they ought not to interfere with me," I must equally move from their need to "I ought not to interfere with them."

If this is correct, then each person's basic needs and wants commit him to stepping into morality, a morality of rights and duties, and someone who rejects that step will be in a kind of pragmatic conflict with himself. Committed to being a rational agent, he will be trying to reject the commitments necessarily involved in that. But is the argument correct? Its very last step—that if in my case rational agency alone is the ground of a right to noninterference, then it must be so in the case of other people—is certainly sound. It rests on the weakest and least contestable version of a "principle of universalizability," which is brought into play simply by *because* or *in virtue of.* If a particular consideration is really enough to establish a conclusion in my case, then it is enough to establish it in anyone's case. That must be so if enough is indeed enough. If the conclusion that brings in morality does not follow, it must be because of an earlier step. Granted that the original claims are correct about a rational agent's wants and needs, the argument must go wrong when I first assert my supposed right.

It is useful to consider what the agent might say in thinking out his claims. It could be put like this:

> I have certain purposes.
>
> I need freedom to pursue these or any other purposes.
>
> So, I need freedom.
>
> I prescribe: let others not interfere with my freedom.

Call the one who is thinking this, the agent A. Assume for the moment that we know what a "prescription" is, and call this prescription of A's, Pa. Then A also thinks

> Pa is reasonable,

where what this means is that Pa is reasonably related to his, A's, being a rational agent. A can of course recognize that another agent, say B, can have thoughts just like his own. He knows, for instance, that

> B prescribes: let A not interfere with my freedom,

and, calling B's prescription Pb, the principle of universalizability will require A to agree that

Pb is reasonable.

It may look as if he has now accepted B's prescription as reasonable in the sense of making some claim on himself. This is what the argument to morality requires. But A has not agreed to this. He has agreed only that *Pb* is reasonable in the same sense that *Pa* is, and what this means is only that *Pb* is reasonably related to B's being a rational agent—that is to say, B is as rational in making his prescription as A is rational in making his. It does not mean that B would be rational in accepting *Pa* (or conversely) if in accepting it he would be committing himself not to interfere with A's freedom.

The same point comes out in this: one could never get to the required result, the entry into the ethical world, just from the consideration of the *should* or *ought* of rational agency itself, the *should* of the practical question. The reasons that B has for doing something are not in themselves reasons for another's doing anything. The *should* of practical reason has, like any other, a second and a third person, but these forms merely represent my perspective on your or his interests and rational calculations, the perspective of "if I were you." Considering in those terms what B should do, I may well conclude that he should interfere with my freedom.

But can I "prescribe" this for him? What does it mean? Certainly I do not want him to interfere with my freedom. But does this, in itself, generate any prescription that leads to obligations or rights? The argument suggests that if I do not prescribe that others ought not to interfere with my freedom, I shall be logically required to admit that they *may* interfere with it—which I do not want to do. What the argument claims is that I must either give them the right to interfere with my freedom or withold that

right from them. The argument insists, in effect, that if I am to be consistent, I must make a rule to the effect that others should not interfere with my freedom, and nothing less than this rule will do. But the rule, of course, just because it is a general rule, will equally require me not to interfere with their freedom.

But why must I prescribe any rule? If I am in the business of making rules, then clearly I will not make one enjoining others to interfere with my freedom, nor will I make one permitting them to do so. But there is another possibility: I do not regard myself as being in this business, and I make no rule either way. I do not have to be taken as giving permission. If there is a system of rules, then no doubt if the rules are silent on a certain matter (at least if the rules are otherwise wide enough in their scope), that fact can naturally be taken to mean permission. The law, like other sovereign agencies, can say something by remaining silent. But if there is no law, then silence is not meaningful, permissive, silence: it is simply silence. In another sense, of course, people "may" interfere with my freedom, but that means only that there is no law to stop, permit, or enjoin. Whether they "may" means they "can" depends on me and what I can do. As the egoist Max Stirner put it: "The tiger that assails me is in the right, and I who strike him down am also in the right. I defend against him not my *right*, but *myself*."

I can also ask why, if I am going to prescribe that much, I should not more ambitiously prescribe that no one interfere with whatever particular purposes I may happen to have. I *want* the success of my particular projects, of course, as much as anything else, and I want other people not to interfere with them. Indeed, my need for basic freedom was itself derived from that kind of want. But the argument is certainly not going to allow me to pre-scribe for all my particular wants.

The argument depends on a particular conception of the business of making rules, a conception that lies at the heart of the Kantian enterprise. If I were in a position to make any rules I liked and to enforce them as an instrument of oppres-sion, then I could make a law that suited my interests and attacked the competing interests of others. No one else would have a reason to obey such a law, except the rea-son I gave him. But the laws we are con-sidering in these arguments are not that kind of law, have no external sanction, and respond to no inequalities between the parties. They are *notional* laws. The question "what law could I make?" then becomes "what law could I make that I could reasonably expect others to accept?" When we reflect on the fact that everyone asks it from an equal position of power-lessness—since these are laws for a king-dom where power is not an issue—we see that the question could equally be "what law could I accept?" and so, finally, "what laws should there be?"

If this is the question, asked in such a spirit, for such a kingdom, then we can see why its answer should be on the lines of Kant's fundamental principle of action, the Categorical Imperative of morality, which… requires you to "act only on that maxim through which you can at the same time will that it should become a universal law." But the problem immedi-ately becomes: Why should one adopt such a picture? Why should I think of my-self as a legislator and—since there is no distinction—at the same time a citizen of a republic governed by these notional laws? This remains a daunting problem, even if one is already within ethical life and is considering how to think about it. But it is a still more daunting problem when this view of things is being de-

manded of any rational agent. The argu-ment needs to tell us what it is about ra-tional agents that requires them to form this conception of themselves as, so to speak, abstract citizens.

It might be thought that the question answers itself because, simply as rational agents, there is nothing else for them to be, and there is no difference among them. But to arrive at the model in this way would be utterly unpersuasive. We are concerned with what any given person, however powerful or effective he may be, should reasonably do as a rational agent, and this is not the same thing as what he would reasonably do if he were a rational agent *and no more*. Indeed, that equation is unintelligible, since there is no way of being a rational agent and no more. A more sensible test would be to ask what people should reasonably do if they did not know anything about themselves ex-cept that they were rational agents; or, again, what people should do if they knew more than that, but not their own particu-lar powers and position. This is an inter-esting test for some things; in particular, it is a possible test for justice, and in that role it can be proposed to those with a concern for justice. But it is not a persua-sive test for what you should reasonably do if you are not already concerned with justice. Unless you are already disposed to take an impartial or moral point of view, you will see as highly unreasonable the proposal that the way to decide what to do is to ask what rules you would make if you had none of your actual advantages, or did not know what they were.

The Kantian project, if it is to have any hope, has to start farther back. It has to be, in a vital way, more like Kant's own project than the argument I have just out-lined. The argument started from what rational agents need, and while what it said about that was true, it was not enough to lead each agent into morality. Kant started from what in his view rational agents essentially *were*. He thought that the moral agent was, in a sense, a rational agent and no more, and he presented as essential to his account of morality a particular metaphysical conception of the agent, according to which the self of moral agency is what he called a "noumenal" self, outside time and causality, and thus distinct from the concrete, empirically determined person that one usually takes oneself to be....

What we are looking for... is an argument that will travel far enough into Kant's territory to bring back the essential conclusion that a rational agent's most basic interests must coincide with those given in a conception of himself as a citizen legislator of a notional republic; but does not bring back the more extravagant metaphysical luggage of the noumenal self. The argument might go something like this. We have already agreed that the rational agent is committed to being free, and we have said something about what is required for that freedom. But we have not yet reached a deep enough understanding of what that freedom must be. The idea of a rational agent is not simply the third-personal idea of a creature whose behavior is to be explained in terms of beliefs and desires. A rational agent acts *on* reasons, and this goes beyond his acting in accordance with some regularity or law, even one that refers to beliefs and desires. If he acts *on* reasons, then he must not only be an agent but reflect on himself as an agent, and this involves his seeing himself as one agent among others. So he stands back from his own desires and interests, and sees them from a standpoint that is not that *of* his desires and interests. Nor is it the standpoint of anyone else's

desires and interests. That is the standpoint of impartiality. So it is appropriate for the rational agent, with his aspiration to be genuinely free and rational, to see himself as making rules that will harmonize the interests of all rational agents.

In assessing this line of argument, it is important to bear in mind that the kind of rational freedom introduced by it is manifested, according to Kant, not only in decisions to act but also in theoretical deliberation, thought about what is true. It is not merely freedom as an agent—the fact (roughly speaking) that what I do depends on what I decide—that leads to the impartial position, but my reflective freedom as a thinker, and this applies also to the case of factual thought. In both cases, Kant supposed, I am not merely caused to arrive at a conclusion: I can stand back from my thoughts and experiences, and what otherwise would merely have been a cause becomes *a consideration for me*. In the case of arriving by reflection at a belief, the sort of item that will be transmuted in this way will be a piece of evidence, or what I take to be evidence: it might for instance be a perception. In the case of practical deliberation, the item is likely to be a desire, a desire which I take into consideration in deciding what to do. In standing back from evidence, or from my desires, so that they become considerations in the light of which I arrive at a conclusion, I exercise in both cases my rational freedom. When, in the practical case, I adopt the standpoint outside my desires and projects, I may endorse my original desires, as in the factual case I may endorse my original disposition to believe. If I do this my original desire may in the outcome be my motive for action (though someone who uses this picture would naturally say that on some occasions what I eventually do will be motivated by none of the desires I originally had, but is radically produced by my reflection.)

The fact that Kant's account of rational freedom is meant to apply to factual deliberation as much as to practical brings out what is wrong with the Kantian argument. What it says about reflection does indeed apply to factual deliberation, but it does so because factual deliberation is not essentially first-personal. It fails to apply to practical deliberation, and to impose a necessary impartiality on it, because practical deliberation is first-personal, radically so, and involves an *I* that must be more intimately the *I* of my desires than this account allows.

When I think about the world and try to decide the truth about it, I think *about the world*, and I make statements, or ask questions, which are about it and not about me. I ask, for instance,

Is strontium a metal?

or confidently say to myself

Wagner never met Verdi.

Those questions and assertions have first-personal shadows, such as

I wonder whether strontium is a metal,

or

I believe that Wagner never met Verdi.

But these are derivative, merely reflexive counterparts to the thoughts that do not mention me. I occur in them, so to speak, only in the role of one who has this thought....

What should I think about this question?

where that has the same effect as

What is the truth about this question?

is again a case in which *I* occurs only derivatively: the last question is the primary one.

Because of this, the *I* of this kind is also impersonal. The question,

What should I think about this question?

could as well be

What should anyone think about this question?

This is so, even when it means

What should I think about this on the evidence I have?

This must ask what anyone should think about it on that evidence. Equally, what anyone truly believes must be consistent with what others truly believe, and anyone deliberating about the truth is committed, by the nature of the process, to the aim of a consistent set of beliefs, one's own and others'.

It is different with deliberation for action. Practical deliberation is in every case first-personal, and the first person is not derivative or naturally replaced by *anyone*. The action I decide on will be mine, and (on the lines of what was said earlier about the aims of action) its being mine means not just that it will be arrived at by this deliberation, but that it will involve changes in the world of which I shall be empirically the cause, and of which these desires and this deliberation itself will be, in some part, the cause. It is true that I can stand back from my desires and reflect on them, and this possibility can indeed be seen as part of the rational freedom at which any rational agent aims. This goes somewhat beyond the considerations about freedom and intentionality acknowledged earlier in the discussion, but it still does not give the required result in relation to morality. The *I* of the reflective practical deliberation is not required to take the result of anyone else's properly conducted deliberation as a datum, nor be committed from the outset to a harmony of everyone's deliberations—that is to say, to making a rule from a standpoint of equality. Reflective deliberation about the truth indeed brings in a standpoint that is impartial and seeks harmony, but this is because it seeks truth, not because it is reflective deliberation, and those features will not be shared by deliberation about what to do simply because it too is reflective. The *I* that stands back in rational reflection from my desires is still the *I* that has those desires and will, empirically and concretely, act; and it is not, simply by standing back in reflection, converted into a being whose fundamental interest lies in the harmony of all interests. It cannot, just by taking this step, acquire the motivations of justice.

Indeed, it is rather hard to explain why the reflective self, if it is conceived as un- committed to all particular desires, should have a concern that any of them be satisfied. The reflective self of theoretical or factual deliberation has a unity of interest with prereflective belief: each in its way aims at truth, and this is why the pre-reflective disposition to believe yields so easily, in the standard case, to corrective reflection. But on the model we are considering there is not an identity of interest between the reflective practical self and any particular desires, my own or others'. It is unclear, then, why the reflective self should try to provide for the satisfaction of those desires. This is just another aspect of the mistake that lies in equating, as this argument does, reflection and detachment....

What has been shown... I believe, is that there is no route to the impartial standpoint from rational deliberation alone.

Reason, Objectivity, and Ethics:
Reason Can Discover Ethical Truths

THOMAS NAGEL

I take it for granted that the objectivity of moral reasoning does not depend on its having an external reference. There is no moral analogue of the external world—a universe of moral facts that impinge on us causally. Even if such a supposition made sense, it would not support the objectivity of moral reasoning. Science, which this kind of reifying realism takes as its model, doesn't derive its objective validity from the fact that it starts from perception and other causal relations between us and the physical world. The real work comes after that, in the form of active scientific reasoning, without which no amount of causal impact on us by the external world would generate a belief in Newton's or Maxwell's or Einstein's theories, or the chemical theory of elements and compounds, or molecular biology.

If we had rested content with the causal impact of the external world on us, we'd still be at the level of sense perception. We can regard our scientific beliefs as objectively true not because the external world causes us to have them but because we are able to *arrive at* those beliefs by methods that have a good claim to be reliable, by virtue of their success in selecting among rival hypotheses that survive the best criticisms and questions we can throw at them. Empirical confirmation plays a vital role in this process, but it cannot do so without theory.

Moral thought is concerned not with the description and explanation of what happens but with decisions and their justification. It is mainly because we have no comparably uncontroversial and well-developed methods for thinking about morality that a subjectivist position here is more credible than it is with regard to science. But just as there was no guarantee at the beginnings of cosmological and scientific speculation that we humans had the capacity to arrive at objective truth beyond the deliverances of sense-perception—that in pursuing it we were doing anything more than spinning collective fantasies—so there can be no decision in advance as to whether we are or are not talking about a real subject when we reflect and argue about morality. The answer must come from the results themselves. Only the effort to reason about morality can show us whether it is possible—whether, in thinking about what to do and how to live, we can find methods, reasons, and principles whose validity does not have to be subjectively or relativistically qualified.

Since moral reasoning is a species of practical reasoning, its conclusions are desires, intentions, and actions, or feelings and convictions that can motivate desire, intention, and action. We want to know how to live, and why, and we want the answer in general terms, if possible. Hume famously believed that because a 'passion' immune to rational assessment must underly every motive, there can be no such thing as specifically practical reason, nor specifically moral reason either. That is false, because while 'passions' are the source of some reasons, other passions or desires are themselves motivated and/or justified by reasons that do not depend on still more basic desires. And I would contend that either the question whether one should have a certain desire or the question whether, given that one has that desire, one should act on it, is always open to rational consideration.

The issue is whether the procedures of justification and criticism we employ in such reasoning, moral or merely practical, can be regarded finally as just something we do—a cultural or societal or even more broadly human collective practice, within which reasons come to an end. I believe that if we ask ourselves seriously how to respond to proposals for contextualization and relativistic detachment, they usually fail to convince. Although it is less clear than in some of the other areas we've discussed, attempts to get entirely outside of the object language of practical reasons, good and bad, right and wrong, and to see all such judgments as expressions of a contingent, nonobjective perspective will eventually collapse before the independent force of the first-order judgments themselves.

Suppose someone says, for example, "You only believe in equal opportunity because you are a product of Western liberal society. If you had been brought up in a caste society or one in which the possibilities for men and women were radically unequal, you wouldn't have the moral convictions you have or accept as persuasive the moral arguments you now accept." The second, hypothetical sentence is probably true, but what about the first—specifically the "only"? In general, the fact that I wouldn't believe something if I hadn't learned it proves nothing about the status of the belief or its grounds. It may be impossible to explain the learning without invoking the content of the belief itself, and the reasons for its truth; and it may be clear that what I have learned is

such that even if I hadn't learned it, it would still be true. The reason the genetic fallacy is a fallacy is that the explanation of a belief can sometimes confirm it.

To have any content, a subjectivist position must say more than that my moral convictions are my moral convictions. That, after all, is something we can all agree on. A meaningful subjectivism must say that they are *just* my moral convictions—or those of my moral community. It must *qualify* ordinary moral judgments in some way, must give them a self-consciously first-person (singular or plural) reading. That is the only type of antiobjectivist view that is worth arguing against or that it is even possible to disagree with.

But I believe it is impossible to come to rest with the observation that a belief in equality of opportunity, and a wish to diminish inherited inequalities, are merely expressions of our cultural tradition. True or false, those beliefs are essentially objective in intent. Perhaps they are wrong, but that too would be a nonrelative judgment. Faced with the fact that such values have gained currency only recently and not universally, one still has to try to decide whether they are right—whether one ought to continue to hold them. That question is not displaced by the information of contingency: The question remains, at the level of moral content, whether I would have been in error if I had accepted as natural, and therefore justified, the inequalities of a caste society, or a fairly rigid class system, or the orthodox subordination of women. It can take in additional facts as material for reflection, but the question of the relevance of those facts is inevitably a moral question: Do these cultural and historical variations and their causes tend to show that I and others have less reason than we had supposed to favor equality of opportunity? Presentation of an array of historically and culturally conditioned attitudes, including my own, does not disarm first-order moral judgment but simply gives it something more to work on—including information about influences on the formation of my convictions that may lead me to change them. But the relevance of such information is itself a matter for moral reasoning—about what are and are not good grounds for moral belief.

When one is faced with these real variations in practice and conviction, the requirement to put oneself in everyone's shoes when assessing social institutions—some version of universalizability—does not lose any of its persuasive force just because it is not universally recognized. It dominates the historical and anthropological data: Presented with the description of a traditional caste society, I have to ask myself whether its hereditary inequalities are justified, and there is no plausible alternative to considering the interests of all in trying to answer the question. If others feel differently, they must say why they find these cultural facts relevant—why they require some qualification to the objective moral claim. On both sides, it is a moral issue, and the only way to defend universalizability or equal opportunity against subjectivist qualification is by continuing the moral argument. It is a matter of understanding exactly what the subjectivist wants us to give up, and then asking whether the grounds for those judgments disappear in light of his observations.

In my opinion, someone who abandons or qualifies his basic methods of moral reasoning on historical or anthropological grounds alone is nearly as irrational as someone who abandons a mathematical belief on other than mathematical grounds. Even with all their uncertainties and liability to controversy and distortion, moral considerations occupy a position in the system of human thought that makes it illegitimate to subordinate them completely to anything else. Particular moral claims are constantly being discredited for all kinds of reasons, but moral considerations per se keep rising again to challenge in their own right any blanket attempt to displace, defuse, or subjectivize them.

This is an instance of the more general truth that the normative cannot be transcended by the descriptive. The question "What should I do?" like the question "What should I believe?" is always in order. It is always possible to think about the question in normative terms, and the process is not rendered pointless by any fact of a different kind—any desire or emotion or feeling, any habit or practice or convention, any contingent cultural or social background. Such things may in fact guide our actions, but it is always possible to take their relation to action as an object of further normative reflection and ask, "How should I act, given that these things are true of me or of my situation?"

The type of thought that generates answers to this question is practical reason. But, further, it is always possible for the question to take a specifically moral form, since one of the successor questions to which it leads is, "What should anyone in my situation do?"—and consideration of that question leads in turn to questions about what everyone should do, not only in this situation but more generally.

Such universal questions don't always have to be raised, and there is good reason in general to develop a way of living that makes it usually unnecessary to raise them. But if they are raised, as they always can be, they require an answer of the appropriate kind—even though the answer may be that in a case like this one may do as one likes. They cannot be ruled out of order by pointing to something more fundamental—psychological, cultural, or biological—that brings the request for justification to an end. Only a justification can bring the request for justifications to an end. Normative questions in general are not undercut or rendered idle by anything, even though particular normative answers may be. (Even when some putative justification is exposed as a rationalization, that implies that something else could be said about the justifiability or nonjustifiability of what was done.)

The point of view to defeat, in a defense of the reality of practical and moral reason, is in essence the Humean one. Although Hume was wrong to say that reason was fit only to serve as the slave of the passions, it is nevertheless true that there are desires and sentiments prior to reason that it is not appropriate for reason to evaluate—that it must simply treat as part of the raw material on which its judgments operate. The question then arises how pervasive such brute motivational data are, and whether some of them cannot perhaps be identified as the true sources of those grounds of action which are usually described as reasons. Hume's theory of the "calm" passions was designed to make this extension, and resisting it is not a simple matter—even if it is set in the context of a minimal framework of practical rationality stronger than Hume would have admitted.

If there is such a thing as practical reason, it does not simply dictate particular actions but, rather, governs the *relations* among actions, desires, and beliefs—just as theoretical reason governs the relations among beliefs and requires some specific material to work on. Prudential rationality, requiring uniformity in the weight accorded to desires and interests situated at different times in one's life, is an example—and the example about which Hume's skepticism is most implausible,

when he says it is not contrary to reason "to prefer even my own acknowledged lesser good to my greater, and have a more ardent affection for the former than the latter." Yet Hume's position always seems a possibility, because whenever such a consistency requirement or similar pattern has an influence on our decisions, it seems possible to represent this influence as the manifestation of a systematic second-order desire or calm passion, which has such consistency as its object and without which we would not be susceptible to this type of "rational" motivation. Hume need then only claim that while such a desire (for the satisfaction of one's future interests) is quite common, to lack it is not contrary to reason, any more than to lack sexual desire is contrary to reason. The problem is to show how this misrepresents the facts.

The fundamental issue is about the order of explanation, for there is no point in denying that people have such second-order desires: the question is whether they are sources of motivation or simply the manifestation in our motives of the recognition of certain rational requirements. A parallel point could be made about theoretical reason. It is clear that the belief in modus ponens, for example, is not a rationally ungrounded *assumption* underlying our acceptance of deductive arguments that depend on modus ponens: Rather, it is simply a recognition of the validity of that form of argument.

The question is whether something similar can be said of the "desire" for prudential consistency in the treatment of desires and interests located at different times. I think it can be and that if one tries instead to regard prudence as simply a desire among others, a desire one happens to have, the question of its appropriateness inevitably reappears as a normative question, and the answer can only be given in terms of the principle itself. The normative can't be displaced by the psychological.

If I think, for example, "What if I didn't care about what would happen to me in the future?" the appropriate reaction is not like what it would be to the supposition that I might not care about movies. True, I'd be missing something if I didn't care about movies, but there are many forms of art and entertainment, and we don't have to consume them all. Note that even this is a judgment of the *rational acceptability* of such variation—of there being no reason to regret it. The supposition that I might not care about my own future cannot be regarded with similar tolerance: It is the supposition of a real failure—the paradigm of something to be regretted—and my recognition of that failure does not reflect merely the antecedent presence in me of a contingent second-order desire. Rather, it reflects a judgment about what is and what is not relevant to the justification of action against a certain factual background.

Relevance and consistency both get a foothold when we adopt the standpoint of decision, based on the total circumstances, including our own condition. This standpoint introduces a subtle but profound gap between desire and action, into which the free exercise of reason enters. It forces us to the idea of the difference between doing the right thing and doing the wrong thing (here, without any specifically ethical meaning as yet)—given our total situation, *including* our desires. Once I see myself as the subject of certain desires, as well as the occupant of an objective situation, I still have to decide what to do, and that will include deciding what justificatory weight to give to those desires.

This step back, this opening of a slight space between inclination and decision, is the condition that permits the operation of reason with respect to belief as well as with respect to action, and that poses the demand for generalizable justification. The two kinds of reasoning are in this way parallel. It is only when, instead of simply being pushed along by impressions, memories, impulses, desires, or whatever, one stops to ask "What should I do?" or "What should I believe?" that reasoning becomes possible—and, having become possible, becomes necessary. Having stopped the direct operation of impulse by interposing the possibility of decision, one can get one's beliefs and actions into motion again only by thinking about what, in light of the circumstances, one should do.

The controversial but crucial point, here as everywhere in the discussion of this subject, is that the standpoint from which one assesses one's choices after this step back is not just first-personal. One is suddenly in the position of judging what one ought to do, against the background of all one's desires and beliefs, in a way that does not merely flow from those desires and beliefs but *operates* on them—by an assessment that should enable anyone else also to see what is the right thing for you to do against that background.

It is not enough to find some higher order desires that one happens to have, to settle the matter: such desires would have to be placed among the background conditions of decision along with everything else. Rather, even in the case of a purely self-interested choice, one is seeking the right answer. One is trying to decide what, given the inner and outer circumstances, *one should do*—and that means not just what *I* should do but what *this person* should do. The same answer should be given to that question by anyone to whom the data are presented, whether or not he is in your circumstances and shares your desires. That is what gives practical reason its generality.

The objection that has to be answered, here as elsewhere, is that this sense of unconditioned, nonrelative judgment is an illusion—that we cannot, merely by stepping back and taking ourselves as objects of contemplation, find a secure platform from which such judgment is possible. On this view whatever we do, after engaging in such an intellectual ritual, will still inevitably be a manifestation of our individual or social nature, not the deliverance of impersonal reason—for there is no such thing.

But I do not believe that such a conclusion can be established a priori, and there is little reason to believe it could be established empirically. The subjectivist would have to show that all purportedly rational judgments about what people have reason to do are really expressions of rationally unmotivated desires or dispositions of the person making the judgment—desires or dispositions to which normative assessment has no application. The motivational explanation would have to have the effect of *displacing* the normative one—showing it to be superficial and deceptive. It would be necessary to make out the case about many actual judgments of this kind and to offer reasons to believe that something similar was true in all cases. Subjectivism involves a positive claim of empirical psychology.

Is it conceivable that such an argument could succeed? In a sense, it would have to be shown that all our supposed practical reasoning is, at the limit, a form of rationalization. But the defender of practical reason has a general response to all psychological claims of this type. Even when some of his actual reasonings are convincingly analyzed away as the expression of merely parochial or personal inclinations, it will in general be reasonable for him to add this new information to the body of his beliefs about himself and then step back once more and ask, "What, in light of all this, do I have reason to do?" It is logically conceivable that the subjectivist's strategy might succeed by exhaustion; the rationalist might become so discouraged at the prospect of being once again undermined in his rational pretensions that he would give up trying to answer the recurrent normative question. But it is far more likely that the question will always be there, continuing to appear significant and to demand an answer. To give up would be nothing but moral laziness.

More important, as a matter of substance I do not think the subjectivist's project can be plausibly carried out. It is not possible to give a debunking psychological explanation of prudential rationality, at any rate. For suppose it is said, plausibly enough, that the disposition to provide for the future has survival value and that its implantation in us is the product of natural selection. As with any other instinct, we still have to decide whether acting on it is a good idea. With some biologically natural dispositions, both motivational and intellectual, there are good reasons to resist or limit their influence. That this does not seem the right reaction to prudential motives (except insofar as we limit them for moral reasons) shows that they cannot be regarded simply as desires that there is no reason to have. If they were, they wouldn't give us the kind of reasons for action that they clearly do. It will never be reasonable for the rationalist to concede that prudence is just a type of consistency in action that he happens, groundlessly, to care about, and that he would have no reason to care about if he didn't already.

The null hypothesis—that in this unconditional sense there are no reasons—is acceptable only if from the point of view of detached self-observation it is superior to the alternatives; and as elsewhere, I believe it fails that test.

Bernard Williams is a prominent contemporary representative of the opposite view. In chapter 4 of *Ethics and the Limits of Philosophy*, he argues that reflective practical reason, unlike reflective theoretical reason, always remains first-personal: One is always trying to answer the question "What shall (or should) *I* do?" and the answer must derive from something internal to what he calls one's "motivational set." Williams says that in theoretical reasoning, by contrast, while it is true that one is trying to decide what to believe, the question "What should I believe?" is in general replaceable by a substantive question which need make no first-person reference: a question like "Did Wagner ever meet Verdi?" or "Is strontium a metal?" This means that the pursuit of freedom through the rational, reflective assessment of the influences on one's beliefs leads, in the theoretical case, to the employment of objective, non-first-personal standards. To decide what to believe, I have to decide, in light of the evidence available to me, and by standards that it would be valid for anyone to use in drawing a conclusion from that evidence, what is probably true.

But Williams holds that in deciding what to do, even if I try to free myself from the blind pressures of my desires and instincts by reflecting on those influences and evaluating their suitability as reasons for action, such reflection will never take me outside of the domain of first-personal thought. Even at my most reflective, it will still be a decision about what I should do and will have to be based on *my* reflective assessment of my motives and reasons. To believe that at some point I will reach a level of reflection where I can consider truly objective reasons, valid for any-

one, that reveal what *should be done* by this person in these circumstances, is to deceive myself. In the practical domain, there is no such standpoint of assessment.

It has to be admitted that phenomenologically, the subjectivist view is more plausible in ethics than in regard to theoretical reason. When I step back from my practical reasonings and ask whether I can endorse them as correct, it is possible to experience this as a move to a deeper region of myself rather than to a higher universal standpoint. Yet at the same time there seems to be no limit to the possibility of asking whether the first-personal reasoning I rely on in deciding what to do is also objectively acceptable. It always seems appropriate to ask, setting aside that the person in question is oneself, "What ought to happen? What is the right thing to do, in this case?"

That the question can take this form does not follow merely from the fact that it is always possible to step back from one's present intentions and motives and consider whether one wishes to change them. The fact that the question "What should I do?" is always open, or reopenable, is logically consistent with the answer's always being a first-personal answer. It might be, as Williams believes, that the highest freedom I can hope for is to ascend to higher order desires or values that are still irreducibly my own—values that determine what kind of person I as an individual wish to be—and that all apparently objective answers to the question are really just the first person masquerading as the third. But do values really disappear into thin air when we adopt the external point of view? Since we can reach a *descriptive* standpoint from which the first person has vanished and from which one regards oneself impersonally, the issue is whether at that point description outruns evaluation. If it does not, if evaluation of some sort keeps pace with it, then we will finally have to evaluate our conduct from a non-first-person standpoint.

Clearly, description can outrun some evaluations. If I don't like shrimp, there simply is no higher order evaluation to be made of this preference. All I can do is to observe that I have it; and no higher order value seems to be involved when it leads me to refrain from ordering a dish containing shrimp or to decline an offer of shrimp when the hors d'oeuvres are passed at a cocktail party. However external a view I may take of the preference, I am not called on either to defend it or to endorse it: I can just accept it. But there are other evaluations, by contrast, that seem at least potentially to be called into question by an external, descriptive view, and the issue is whether those questions always lead us finally to a first-person answer.

Suppose I reflect on my political preferences—my hope that candidate X will not win the next presidential election, for example. What external description of this preference, considered as a psychological state, is consistent with its stability? Can I regard my reasons for holding it simply as facts about myself, as my dislike of shrimp is a fact about myself? Or will any purely descriptive observation of such facts give rise to a further evaluative question—one that cannot be answered simply by a reaffirmation that this is the kind of person I am?

Here, as elsewhere, I don't think we can hope for a decisive proof that we are asking objective questions and pursuing objective answers. The possibility that we are deceiving ourselves is genuine. But the only way to deal with that possibility is to think about it, and one must think about it by weighing the plausibility of the debunking explanation against the plausibility of the ethical reasoning at which it is aimed. The claim that, at the most objec-tive level, the question of what we should do becomes meaningless has to compete head-to-head with specific claims about what in fact we should do, and their grounds. So in the end, the contest is between the credibility of substantive ethics and the credibility of an external psychological reduction of that activity....

The first step on the path to ethics is the admission of *generality* in practical judgments. That is actually equivalent to the admission of the existence of reasons, for a reason is something one person can have only if others would also have it if they were in the same circumstances (internal as well as external). In taking an objective view of myself, the first question to answer is whether I have, in this generalizable sense, any reason to do anything, and a negative answer is nearly as implausible as a negative answer to the analogous question of whether I have any reason to believe anything. Neither of those questions—though they are, to begin with, about me—is essentially first-personal, since they are supposed not to depend for their answers on the fact that I am asking them.

It is perhaps less impossible to answer the question about practical reasons in the negative than the question about theoretical reasons. (And by a negative answer, remember, we mean the position that there *are* no reasons, not merely that I have no reason to believe, or do, anything rather than anything else—the skeptical position, which is also universal in its grounds and implications.) If one ceased to recognize theoretical reasons, having reached a reflective standpoint, it would make no sense to go on having beliefs, though one might be unable to stop. But perhaps action wouldn't likewise become senseless if one denied the existence of practical reasons: One could still be moved by impulse and habit, without thinking that what one did was justified in any sense—even by one's inclinations—in a way that admitted generalization.

However, this seems a very implausible option. It implies, for example, that none of your desires and aversions, pleasures and sufferings, or your survival or death, give you any generalizable reason to do anything—that all we can do from an objective standpoint is to observe, and perhaps try to predict, what you *will* do. The application of this view to my own case is outlandish: I can't seriously believe that I have *no reason* to get out of the way of a truck that is bearing down on me in the street—that my motive is a purely psychological reaction not subject to rational endorsement. Clearly I have a reason, and clearly it is generalizable.

The second step on the path to familiar moral territory is the big one: the choice between agent-relative, essentially egoistic (but still general) reasons and some alternative that admits agent-neutral reasons or in some other way acknowledges that each person has a noninstrumental reason to consider the interests of others. It is possible to understand this choice partly as a choice of the way in which one is going to value oneself and one's own interests. It has strong implications in that regard.

Morality is possible only for beings capable of seeing themselves as one individual among others more or less similar in general respects—capable, in other words, of seeing themselves as others see them. When we recognize that although we occupy only our own point of view and not that of anyone else, there is nothing cosmically unique about it, we are faced with a choice. This choice has to do with the relation between the value we naturally accord to ourselves and our fates from our own point of view, and the attitude we take toward these same things when viewed from the impersonal standpoint

that assigns to us no unique status apart from anyone else.

One alternative would be not to "transfer" to the impersonal standpoint in any form those values which concern us from the personal standpoint. That would mean that the impersonal standpoint would remain purely descriptive and our lives and what matters to us as we live them (including the lives of other people we care about) would not be regarded as mattering at all if considered apart from the fact that they are ours, or personally related to us. Each of us, then, would have a system of values centering on his own perspective and would recognize that others were in exactly the same situation.

The other alternative would be to assign to one's life and what goes on in it some form of impersonal as well as purely perspectival value, not dependent on its being one's own. This would then imply that everyone else was also the subject of impersonal value of a similar kind.

The agent-relative position that all of a person's reasons derive from his own interests, desires, and attachments means that I have no reason to care about what happens to other people unless what happens to them matters to me, either directly or instrumentally. This is compatible with the existence of strong derivative reasons for consideration of others—reasons for accepting systems of general rights, and so forth—but it does not include those reasons at the ground level. It also means, of course, that others have no reason to care about what happens to me—again, unless it matters to them in some way, emotionally or instrumentally. All the practical reasons that any of us have, on this theory, depend on what is valuable *to us*.

It follows that we each have value only to ourselves and to those who care about us. Considered impersonally, we are valueless and provide no intrinsic reasons for concern to anyone. So the egoistic answer to the question of what kinds of reasons there are amounts to an assessment of oneself, along with everyone else, as *objectively worthless*. In a sense, it doesn't matter (except to ourselves) what happens to us: Each person has value only *for himself*, not *in himself*.

Now this judgment, while it satisfies the generality condition for reasons, and while perfectly consistent, is in my opinion highly unreasonable and difficult to honestly accept. Can you really believe that objectively, it doesn't matter whether you die of thirst or not—and that your inclination to believe that it does is just the false objectification of your self-love? One could really ask the same question about anybody else's dying of thirst, but concentrating on your own case stimulates the imagination, which is why the fundamental moral argument takes the form, "How would you like it if someone did that to you?" The concept of reasons for action faces us with a question about their content that it is very difficult to answer in a consistently egoistic or agent-relative style....

THE CONTINUING DEBATE:
Reason, Objectivity, and Ethics: Can Reason Guide Us to Objective Ethical Truths?

What Is New

Nagel states that "in the end, the contest [over rational moral objectivity] is between the credibility of substantive ethics and the credibility of an external psychological reduction of that activity." Thus debates 9 and 10, which examine some specific attempts to use psychological research to undermine or at least modify some elements of ethics, have direct relevance to the issues raised in this debate: Such appeals to psychological research to modify ethical methodology or moral principles are an attempt to accomplish what Nagel claims cannot be done. The claims concerning evolutionary biology and its influence on ethics (debate 11), the questions concerning the impact of anthropological research for ethics (debate 14), and the material on interpretation of ethics as ideology (debate 15) are also relevant—and are in some respects a challenge—to Nagel's position.

Where to Find More

Among Bernard Williams' many important works (in addition to *Ethics and the Limits of Philosophy*) are *Moral Luck* (Cambridge: Cambridge University Press, 1981); *Shame and Necessity* (Berkeley: University of California Press, 1993); and *Making Sense of Humanity* (Cambridge: Cambridge University Press, 1995).

In addition to *The Last Word* and *The View from Nowhere*, Thomas Nagel's major works include *Mortal Questions* (London: Cambridge University Press, 1979); *Equality and Partiality* (Oxford: Oxford University Press, 1991), and *Concealment and Exposure* (Oxford: Oxford University Press, 2002). Though Nagel represents the Kantian position in this debate, many of his views are quite different from those of Kant—see, in particular, Nagel's *The View from Nowhere*.

Among Kant's classic works on ethics are *Groundwork of the Metaphysic of Morals*, trans. H. J. Paton, as *The Moral Law* (London: Hutchinson, 1953); *Critique of Practical Reason*, trans. L. W. Beck (Indianapolis: Bobbs-Merrill, 1977); and *Religion Within the Limits of Reason Alone*, trans. T. M. Greene and H. H. Hudson (NY: Harper and Row, 1960).

Excellent works on Kant's ethics include Lewis White Beck's *A Commentary on Kant's Critique of Practical Reason* (Chicago: University of Chicago Press, 1960); and Onora O'Neill, *Constructions of Reason: Explorations of Kant's Practical Philosophy* (Cambridge: Cambridge University Press, 1989). A fascinating brief challenge to Kant's ethical system is Rae Langton's "Maria von Herbert's Challenge to Kant," which can be found in Peter Singer, editor, *Ethics* (Oxford: Oxford University Press, 1994).

Many outstanding contemporary philosophers follow—to at least some degree—the Kantian tradition in ethics. A small sample would include Kurt Baier, *The Moral Point of View* (Ithaca, NY: Cornell University Press, 1958); Alan Donagan, *The Theory of Morality* (Chicago: University of Chicago Press, 1977); and Alan Gewirth, *Reason and Morality* (Chicago: University of Chicago Press, 1978); Stephen Darwall, *Impartial Reason* (Ithaca, NY: Cornell University Press, 1983) and *Philosophical Ethics*

(Boulder, CO: Westview Press, 1998); Onora O'Neill, *Constructions of Reason: Explorations of Kant's Practical Philosophy* (Cambridge: Cambridge University Press, 1989); Marcia W. Baron, *Kantian Ethics Almost Without Apology* (Ithaca, NY: Cornell University Press, 1995); and Christine Korsgaard, *Creating the Kingdom of Ends* (Cambridge: Cambridge University Press, 1996).

Kantian ethics can seem cold and austere. For a more engaging perspective on Kantian ethics, see Thomas E. Hill, Jr., a Kantian who writes with clarity and charm in *Respect, Pluralism, and Justice: Kantian Perspectives* (Oxford: Oxford University Press, 2000); and *Human Welfare and Moral Worth: Kantian Perspectives* (Oxford: Oxford University Press, 2002).

David Hume has two classic works on ethics and emotions (though both works also contain much more). The first is *A Treatise of Human Nature*, originally published in 1738. A good edition is by L. A. Selby-Bigge (Oxford: Clarendon Press, 1978). The second is *An Inquiry Concerning Human Understanding*, originally published in 1751. A good edition is L. A. Selby-Bigge's *Hume's Enquiries*, 2nd ed. (Oxford: Clarendon Press, 1902).

Kai Nielsen, *Why Be Moral?* (Buffalo, NY: Prometheus Books,1989) is a very readable defense of nonobjectivist ethics based in emotions.

IS ETHICS BASED ON A SOCIAL CONTRACT?

SOCIAL CONTRACT THEORY OFFERS THE BEST GROUNDS FOR ETHICS

ADVOCATE: David Gauthier is Distinguished Service Professor of Philosophy and Senior Research Fellow at the Center for Philosophy of Science at the University of Pittsburgh. His *Morals by Agreement* (Oxford: Oxford University Press, 1986) is widely regarded as one of the most significant and influential contemporary works on social contract theory.

SOURCE: "Why Contractarianism?" from Peter Vallentyne, editor, *Contractarianism and Rational Choice: Essays on David Gauthier's Morals By Agreement* (New York: Cambridge University Press, 1991), pages 15–30

SOCIAL CONTRACT THEORY IS AN INADEQUATE ACCOUNT OF ETHICS

ADVOCATE: Jean Hampton was Professor of Philosophy at the University of California, Davis. She was the author of *Hobbes and the Social Contract Tradition* (Cambridge: Cambridge University Press, 1986) and (with Jeffrie Murphy) *Forgiveness and Mercy* (Cambridge: Cambridge University Press, 1988).

SOURCE: "Two Faces of Contractarian Thought," from Peter Vallentyne, editor, *Contractarianism and Rational Choice: Essays on David Gauthier's Morals By Agreement* (New York: Cambridge University Press, 1991), pages 31–55

Social contract theorists start by proposing that mankind's earliest existence was in a "state of nature" with no laws nor restraints—a "war of all against all," where life is "nasty, brutish, and short," and the only rule is to do unto others *before* they do unto you. After a time people in this condition recognize that it is in their own individual best interests to contract with one another for a more peaceful, law-abiding, and rights-recognizing existence. Of course there was not literally a time when everyone suspended murder and mayhem and sat together drawing up a social contract. Social contract theory is neither history nor anthropology; rather, it offers a model for judging when the rules of a society or state are just and fair. If—as a self-interested contractor—you would agree to accept a set of rules, then those rules are reasonably just.

There have been two major developments in contemporary social contract theory. First, John Rawls used social contract theory to develop an account of "justice as fairness," in which he considered what rules of social justice we would approve from "behind the veil of ignorance". That is, suppose you will be born into a society as a human being with the standard needs and desires of our species, but you know nothing else about your position or characteristics or capacities. You have no idea of your gender, race, ethnic group; whether you will be lazy or industrious, bright or dull, athletic or clumsy, poor or privileged. From behind this veil of ignorance, what social rules would you favor? Rawls' social contract theory pushes us to think hard about what rules and systems we would regard as fair and just, if we set aside our biases of race, gender, privilege, inherited wealth, special interests, and individual talents.

David Gauthier, whose work is the focus of our readings, brings a new twist to social contract theory by his very effective use of the Prisoner's Dilemma. Suppose that Alice and Barbara have been caught with stolen money. The police suspect they were the robbers, but can't prove it. If both keep quiet, each will serve a two-year sentence. Alice and Barbara are in separate cells and unable to communicate. Each is offered the same deal: If Alice squeals on her friend, and Barbara keeps silent, Alice's sentence will be reduced to one year; Barbara will be sentenced to ten years. If you both talk, you'll both be convicted for the robbery, but your cooperation will net each of you a five-year sentence. Being a self-interested criminal, Alice reaches a quick conclusion: "If I keep quiet, the best I can get is a two-year sentence, assuming that Barbara also keeps her mouth shut. But if that rat squeals on me, I'll get ten. If I talk, the best I can get is a one-year sentence, and the worst is five years. Whether Barbara talks or clams up, my best bet is to talk." The problem is, Barbara is thinking the same thing. They both talk, and both get five-year sentences. If they could have reliably cooperated, both would have been better off. The moral of the story is simple but important: There are circumstances when my individual interests are best served by cooperating rather than seeking the maximum benefits I could gain individually. As a purely self-interested individual, social cooperation—even involving personal sacrifices—is my best policy. And that is sufficient cooperative foundation to build a social contract society.

POINTS TO PONDER

➤ In constructing his moral system, Gauthier starts from an assumption of rationally self-interested nonmoral beings. Some critics consider this too austere: Humans are, after all, a profoundly social species. What advantages or disadvantages are there in Gauthier's starting point?

➤ Gauthier proposes his social contract morality as a means of "resolving morality's foundational crisis." Does such a crisis exist?

➤ Hampton claims that traditional contract theory (such as Hobbes' theory) embraces a "radical individualism" that "goes too far in trying to represent us as radically separate from others." The United States, founded on a social contract model, has a strongly individualistic, "make it on your own or suffer the consequences" social structure (for example, the U.S. is the only developed country that does not provide health care for all its citizens). Has social contract thinking shaped U.S. "rugged individualism"?

➤ Hampton's key criticism is that Gauthier's moral system is not as purely individualistic as Gauthier supposes. Is that a legitimate criticism? If it is, what effect would that have on Gauthier's moral system?

Social Contract Theory:
The Best Ground for Ethics

DAVID GAUTHIER

Morality faces a foundational crisis. Contractarianism offers the only plausible resolution of this crisis. These two propositions state my theme. What follows is elaboration.

Nietzsche may have been the first, but he has not been alone, in recognizing the crisis to which I refer. Consider these recent statements. "The hypothesis which I wish to advance is that in the actual world which we inhabit the language of morality is in... [a] state of grave disorder... we have—very largely, if not entirely—lost our comprehension, both theoretical and practical, of morality" (Alasdair MacIntyre). "The resources of most modern moral philosophy are not well adjusted to the modern world" (Bernard Williams). "There are no objective values.... [But] the main tradition of European moral philosophy includes the contrary claim" (J. L. Mackie). "Moral hypotheses do not help explain why people observe what they observe. So ethics is problematic and nihilism must be taken seriously... An extreme version of nihilism holds that morality is simply an illusion.... In this version, we should abandon morality, just as an atheist abandons religion after he has decided that religious facts cannot help explain observations" (Gilbert Harman).

I choose these statements to point to features of the crisis that morality faces. They suggest that moral language fits a world view that we have abandoned—a view of the world as purposively ordered. Without this view, we no longer truly understand the moral claims we continue to make. They suggest that there is a lack of fit between what morality presupposes—objective values that help explain our behavior, and the psychological states—desires and beliefs—that, given our present world view, actually provide the best explanation. This lack of fit threatens to undermine the very idea of a morality as more than an anthropological curiosity. But how could this be? How could morality *perish*?

To proceed, I must offer a minimal characterization of the morality that faces a foundational crisis. And this is the morality of justified constraint. From the standpoint of the agent, moral considerations present themselves as constraining his choices and actions, in ways independent of his desires, aims, and interests. Later, I shall add to this characterization, but for the moment it will suffice. For it reveals clearly what is in question—the ground of constraint. This ground seems absent from our present world view. And so we ask, what reason can a person have for recognizing and accepting a constraint that is independent of his desires and interests? He may agree that such a constraint would be *morally* justified; he would have a reason for accepting it *if* he had a reason for accepting morality. But what justifies paying attention to morality, rather than dismissing it as an appendage of outworn beliefs? We ask, and seem to find no answer....

We have, ready to hand, an alternative mode for justifying our choices and actions. In its more austere and, in my view, more defensible form, this is to show that choices and actions maximize the agent's expected utility, where utility is a measure of considered preference. In its less austere version, this is to show that choices and actions satisfy, not a subjectively defined requirement such as utility, but meet the agent's objective interests. Since I do not believe that we have objective interests, I shall ignore this latter. But it will not matter. For the idea is clear; we have a mode of justification that does not require the introduction of moral considerations.

Let me call this alternative nonmoral mode of justification, neutrally, deliberative justification. Now moral and deliberative. rative justification are directed at the same objects—our choices and actions. What if they conflict? And what do we say to the person wlo offers a deliberative justification of his choices and actions and refuses to offer any other? We can say, of course, that his behavior lacks *moral* justification, but this seems to lack any hold, unless he chooses to enter the moral framework. And such entry, he may insist, lacks any deliberative justification, at least for him.

If morality perishes, the justificatory enterprise, in relation to choice and action, does not perish with it. Rather, one mode of justification perishes, a mode that, it may seem, now hangs unsupported. But not only unsupported, for it is difficult to deny that deliberative justification is more clearly basic, that it cannot be avoided insofar as we are rational agents, so that if moral justification conflicts with it, morality seems not only unsupported but opposed by what is rationally more fundamental.

Deliberative justification relates to our deep sense of self. What distinguishes human beings from other animals, and provides the basis for rationality, is the capacity for semantic representation. You can, as your dog on the whole cannot, represent a state of affairs to yourself, and consider in particular whether or not it is the case,

and whether or not you would want it to be the case. You can represent to yourself the contents of your beliefs, and your desires or preferences. But in representing them, you bring them into relation with one another. You represent to yourself that the Blue Jays will win the World Series, and that a National League team will win the World Series, and that the Blue Jays are not a National League team. And in recognizing a conflict among those beliefs, you find rationality thrust upon you. Note that the first two beliefs could be replaced by preferences, with the same effect.

Since in representing our preferences we become aware of conflict among them, the step from representation to choice becomes complicated. We must, somehow, bring our conflicting desires and preferences into some sort of coherence. And there is only one plausible candidate for a principle of coherence—a maximizing principle. We order our preferences, in relation to decision and action, so that we may choose in a way that maximizes our expectation of preference fulfillment. And in so doing, we show ourselves to be rational agents, engaged in deliberation and deliberative justification. There is simply nothing else for practical rationality to be.

The foundational crisis of morality thus cannot be avoided by pointing to the existence of a practice of justification within the moral framework, and denying that any extramoral foundation is relevant. For an extramoral mode of justification is already present, existing not side by side with moral justification, but in a manner tied to the way in which we unify our beliefs and preferences and so acquire our deep sense of self. We need not suppose that this deliberative justification is itself to be understood foundationally. All that we need suppose is that moral justification does not plausibly survive conflict with it.

In explaining why we may not dismiss the idea of a foundational crisis in morality as resulting from a misplaced appeal to a philosophically discredited or suspect idea of foundationalism, I have begun to expose the character and dimensions of the crisis. I have claimed that morality faces an alternative, conflicting, deeper mode of justification, related to our deep sense of self, that applies to the entire realm of choice and action, and that evaluates each *action* in terms of the reflectively held concerns of its *agent*. The relevance of the agent's concerns to practical justification does not seem to me in doubt. The relevance of anything else, except insofar as it bears on the agent's concerns, does seem to me very much in doubt. If the agent's reflectively endorsed concerns, his preferences, desires, and aims, are, with his considered beliefs, constitutive of his self-conception, then I can see no remotely plausible way of arguing from their relevance to that of anything else that is not similarly related to his sense of self. And, indeed, I can see no way of introducing anything as relevant to practical justification except through the agent's self-conception. My assertion of this practical individualism is not a conclusive argument, but the burden of proof is surely on those who would maintain a contrary position. Let them provide the arguments—if they can.

Deliberative justification does not refute morality. Indeed, it does not offer morality the courtesy of a refutation. It ignores morality, and seemingly replaces it. It preempts the arena of justification, apparently leaving morality no room to gain purchase. Let me offer a controversial comparison. Religion faces—indeed, has faced—a comparable foundational crisis. Religion demands the worship of a divine being who purposively orders the universe. But it has confronted an alternative mode of explanation. Although the emergence of a cosmological theory based on efficient, rather than teleological, causation provided warning of what was to come, the supplanting of teleology in biology by the success of evolutionary theory in providing a mode of explanation that accounted in efficient-causal terms for the *appearance* of a purposive order among living beings, may seem to toll the death knell for religion as an intellectually respectable enterprise. But evolutionary biology and, more generally, modern science do not refute religion. Rather they ignore it, replacing its explanations by ontologically simpler ones. Religion, understood as affirming the justifiable worship of a divine being, may be unable to survive its foundational crisis. Can morality, understood as affirming justifiable constraints on choice independent of the agent's concerns, survive?

There would seem to be three ways for morality to escape religion's apparent fate. One would be to find, for moral facts or moral properties, an explanatory role that would entrench them prior to any consideration of justification. One could then argue that any mode of justification that ignored moral considerations would be ontologically defective. I mention this possibility only to put it to one side. No doubt there are persons who accept moral constraints on their choices and actions, and it would not be possible to explain those choices and actions were we to ignore this. But our explanation of their behavior need not commit us to their view. Here the comparison with religion should be straightforward and uncontroversial. We could not explain many of the practices of the religious without reference to their beliefs. But to characterize what a religious person is doing as, say, an act of worship, does not commit us to supposing that an object of worship actually exists, though it does commit us to supposing that she believes such an object to exist. Similarly, to characterize what a moral agent is doing as, say, fulfilling a duty does not commit us to supposing that there are any duties, though it does commit us to supposing that he believes that there are duties. The skeptic who accepts neither can treat the apparent role of morality in explanation as similar to that of religion. Of course, I do not consider that the parallel can be ultimately sustained, since I agree with the religious skeptic but not with the moral skeptic. But to establish an explanatory role for morality, one must first demonstrate its justificatory credentials. One may not assume that it has a prior explanatory role.

The second way would be to reinterpret the idea of justification, showing that, more fully understood, deliberative justification is incomplete, and must be supplemented in a way that makes room for morality. There is a long tradition in moral philosophy, deriving primarily from Kant, that is committed to this enterprise. This is not the occasion to embark on a critique of what, in the hope again of achieving a neutral characterization, I shall call universalistic justification. But critique may be out of place. The success of deliberative justification may suffice. For theoretical claims about its incompleteness seem to fail before the simple practical recognition that it works. Of course, on the face of it, deliberative justification does not work to provide a place for morality. But to suppose that it must, if it is to be fully adequate or complete as a mode of justification, would be to assume what is in question, whether moral justification is defensible.

If, independent of one's actual desires, and aims, there were objective values, and if, independent of one's actual purposes, one were part of an objectively purposive order, then we might have reason to insist on the inadequacy of the deliberative framework. An objectively purposive order would introduce considerations relevant to practical justification that did not depend on the agent's self-conception. But the supplanting of teleology in our physical and biological explanations closes this possibility, as it closes the possibility of religious explanation.

I turn then to the third way of resolving morality's foundational crisis. The first step is to embrace deliberative justification, and recognize that morality's place must be found within, and not outside, its framework. Now this will immediately raise two problems. First of all, it will seem that the attempt to establish any constraint on choice and action, within the framework of a deliberation that aims at the maximal fulfillment of the agent's considered preferences, must prove impossible. But even if this be doubted, it will seem that the attempt to establish a constraint *independent of the agent's preferences,* within such a framework, verges on lunacy. Nevertheless, this is precisely the task accepted by my third way. And, unlike its predecessors, I believe that it can be successful; indeed, I believe that my recent book, *Morals by Agreement,* shows how it can succeed.

... Let me sketch briefly those features of deliberative rationality that enable it to constrain maximizing choice. The key idea is that in many situations, if each person chooses what, given the choices of the others, would maximize her expected utility, then the outcome will be mutually disadvantageous in comparison with some alternative—everyone could do better. Equilibrium, which obtains when each person's action is a best response to the others' actions, is incompatible with (Pareto-)optimality, which obtains when no one could do better without someone else doing worse. Given the ubiquity of such situations, each person can see the benefit, to herself, of participating with her fellow in practices requiring each to refrain from the direct endeavor to maximize her own utility, when such mutual restraint is mutually advantageous. No one, of course, can have reason to accept any unilateral constraint on her maximizing behavior; each benefits from, and only from, the constraint accepted by her fellows. But if one benefits more from a constraint on others than one loses by being constrained oneself, one may have reason to accept a practice requiring everyone, including oneself, to exhibit such a constraint. We may represent such a practice as capable of gaining unanimous agreement among rational persons who were choosing the terms on which they would interact with each other. And this agreement is the basis of morality.

Consider a simple example of a moral practice that would command rational agreement. Suppose each of us were to assist her fellows only when either she could expect to benefit herself from giving assistance, or she took a direct interest in their well-being. Then, in many situations, persons would not give assistance to others, even though the benefit to the recipient would greatly exceed the cost to the giver, because there would be no provision for the giver to share in the benefit. Everyone would then expect to do better were each to give assistance to her fellows, regardless of her own benefit or interest, whenever the cost of assisting was low and the benefit of receiving assistance considerable. Each would thereby accept a constraint on the direct pursuit of her own concerns, not unilaterally, but given a like acceptance by others. Reflection leads us to recognize that those who belong to groups whose members adhere to such a practice of mutual assistance enjoy benefits in interaction that are denied to others. We may then represent such a practice as rationally acceptable to everyone.

This rationale for agreed constraint makes no reference to the content of anyone's preferences. The argument depends simply on the *structure* of interaction, on the way in which each person's endeavor to fulfill her own preferences affects the fulfillment of everyone else. Thus, each person's reason to accept a mutually constraining practice is independent of her particular desires, aims and interests, although not, of course, of the fact that she has such concerns. The idea of a purely rational agent, moved to act by reason alone, is not, I think, an intelligible one. Morality is not to be understood as a constraint arising from reason alone on the fulfillment of nonrational preferences. Rather, a rational agent is one who acts to achieve the maximal fulfillment of her preferences, and morality is a constraint on the manner in which she acts, arising from the effects of interaction with other agents.

Hobbes's Foole now makes his familiar entry onto the scene, to insist that however rational it may be for a person to agree with her fellows to practices that hold out the promise of mutual advantage, yet it is rational to follow such practices only when so doing directly conduces to her maximal preference fulfillment. But then such practices impose no real constraint. The effect of agreeing to or accepting them can only be to change the expected payoffs of her possible choices, making it rational for her to choose what in the absence of the practice would not be utility maximizing. The practices would offer only true prudence, not true morality.

The Foole is guilty of a twofold error. First, he fails to understand that real acceptance of such moral practices as assisting one's fellows, or keeping one's promises, or telling the truth is possible only among those who are disposed to comply with them. If my disposition to comply extends only so far as my interests or concerns at the time of performance, then you will be the real fool if you interact with me in ways that demand a more rigorous compliance. If, for example, it is rational to keep promises only when so doing is directly utility maximizing, then among persons whose rationality is common knowledge, only promises that require such limited compliance will be made. And opportunities for mutual advantage will be thereby forgone.

Consider this example of the way in which promises facilitate mutual benefit. Jones and Smith have adjacent farms. Although neighbors, and not hostile, they are also not friends, so that neither gets satisfaction from assisting the other. Nevertheless, they recognize that, if they harvest their crops together, each does better than if each harvests alone. Next week, Jones's crop will be ready for harvesting; a fortnight hence, Smith's crop will be ready. The harvest in, Jones is retiring, selling his farm, and moving to Florida, where he is unlikely to encounter Smith or other members of their community. Jones would like to promise Smith that, if Smith helps him harvest next week, he will help Smith harvest in a fortnight. But Jones and Smith both know that in a fortnight, helping Smith would be a pure cost to Jones. Even if Smith helps him, he has nothing to gain by returning the assistance, since neither care for Smith nor, in the circumstances, concern for his own reputation, moves him. Hence, if Jones and Smith know that Jones acts straightforwardly to maximize the fulfillment of his preferences, they know that he will not help Smith. Smith, therefore, will not help Jones even if Jones pretends to promise assistance in return. Nevertheless, Jones would do better could he make and keep such a promise—and so would Smith.

The Foole's second error, following on his first, should be clear; he fails to recognize that in plausible circumstances persons who are genuinely disposed to a more rigorous compliance with moral practices than would follow from their interests at the time of performance can expect to do better than those who are not so disposed. For the former, constrained maximizers as I call them, will be welcome partners in mutually advantageous cooperation, in which each relies on the voluntary adherence of the others, from which the latter, straightforward maximizers, will be excluded. Constrained maximizers may thus expect more favorable opportunities than their fellows. Although in assisting their fellows, keeping their promises, and complying with other moral practices, they forgo preference fulfillment that they might obtain, yet they do better overall than those who always maximize expected utility, because of their superior opportunities.

In identifying morality with those constraints that would obtain agreement among rational persons who were choosing their terms of interaction, I am engaged in rational reconstruction. I do not suppose that we have actually agreed to existent moral practices and principles. Nor do I suppose that all existent moral practices would secure our agreement, were the question to be raised. Not all existent moral practices need be justifiable—need be ones with which we ought willingly to comply. Indeed, I do not even suppose that the practices with which we ought willingly to comply need be those that would secure our present agreement. I suppose that justifiable moral practices are those that would secure our agreement ex ante, in an appropriate premoral situation. They are those to which we should have agreed as constituting the terms of our future interaction, had we been, per impossible, in a position to decide those terms. Hypothetical agreement thus provides a test of the justifiability of our existent moral practices.

Many questions could be raised about this account, but here I want to consider only one. I have claimed that moral practices are rational, even though they constrain each person's attempt to maximize her own utility, insofar as they would be the objects of unanimous ex ante agreement. But to refute the Foole, I must defend not only the rationality of agreement, but also that of compliance, and the defense of compliance threatens to preempt the case for agreement, so that my title should be "Why Constraint?" and not "Why Contractarianism?" It is rational to dispose oneself to accept certain constraints on direct maximization in choosing and acting, if and only if so disposing oneself maximizes one's expected utility. What then is the relevance of agreement, and especially of hypothetical agreement? Why should it be rational to dispose oneself to accept only those constraints that would be the object of mutual agreement in an appropriate premoral situation, rather than those constraints that are found in our existent moral practices? Surely it is acceptance of the latter that makes a person welcome in interaction with his fellows. For compliance with existing morality will be what they expect, and take into account in choosing partners with whom to cooperate.

I began with a challenge to morality—how can it be rational for us to accept its constraints? It may now seem that what I have shown is that it is indeed rational for us to accept constraints, but to accept them whether or not they might be plausibly considered moral. Morality, it may

seem, has nothing to do with my argument; what I have shown is that it is rational to be disposed to comply with whatever constraints are generally accepted and expected, regardless of their nature. But this is not my view.

To show the relevance of agreement to the justification of constraints, let us assume an ongoing society in which individuals more or less acknowledge and comply with a given set of practices that constrain their choices in relation to what they would be did they take only their desires, aims, and interests directly into account. Suppose that a disposition to conform to these existing practices is prima facie advantageous, since persons who are not so disposed may expect to be excluded from desirable opportunities by their fellows. However, the practices themselves have, or at least need have, no basis in agreement. And they need satisfy no intuitive standard of fairness or impartiality, characteristics that we may suppose relevant to the identification of the practices with those of a genuine morality. Although we may speak of the practices as constituting the morality of the society in question, we need not consider them morally justified or acceptable. They are simply practices constraining individual behavior in a way that each finds rational to accept.

Suppose now that our persons, as rational maximizers of individual utility, come to reflect on the practices constituting their morality. They will, of course, assess the practices in relation to their own utility, but with the awareness that their fellows will be doing the same. And one question that must arise is: Why these practices? For they will recognize that the set of actual moral practices is not the only possible set of constraining practices that would yield mutually advantageous, optimal outcomes. They will recognize the possibility of alternative moral orders. At this point it will not be enough to say that, as a matter of fact, each person can expect to benefit from a disposition to comply with existing practices. For persons will also ask themselves: Can I benefit more, not from simply abandoning any morality, and recognizing no constraint, but from a partial rejection of existing constraints in favor of an alternative set? Once this question is asked, the situation is transformed; the existing moral order must be assessed, not only against simple noncompliance, but also against what we may call alternative compliance.

To make this assessment, each will compare her prospects under the existing practices with those she would anticipate from a set that, in the existing circumstances, she would expect to result from bargaining with her fellows. If her prospects would be improved by such negotiation, then she will have a real, although not necessarily sufficient, incentive to demand a change in the established moral order. More generally, if there are persons whose prospects would be improved by renegotiation, then the existing order will be recognizably unstable. No doubt those whose prospects would be worsened by renegotiation will have a clear incentive to resist, to appeal to the status quo. But their appeal will be a weak one, especially among persons who are not taken in by spurious ideological considerations, but focus on individual utility maximization. Thus, although in the real world, we begin with an existing set of moral practices as constraints on our maximizing behavior, yet we are led by reflection to the idea of an amended set that would obtain the agreement of everyone, and this amended set has, and will be recognized to have, a stability lacking in existing morality.

The reflective capacity of rational agents leads them from the given to the agreed, from existing practices and principles requiring constraint to those that would receive each person's assent. The same reflective capacity, I claim, leads from those practices that would be agreed to, in existing social circumstances, to those that would receive ex ante agreement, premoral and presocial. As the status quo proves unstable when it comes into conflict with what would be agreed to, so what would be agreed to proves unstable when it comes into conflict with what would have been agreed to in an appropriate presocial context. For as existing practices must seem arbitrary insofar as they do not correspond to what a rational person would agree to, so what such a person would agree to in existing circumstances must seem arbitrary in relation to what she would accept in a presocial condition.

What a rational person would agree to in existing circumstances depends in large part on her negotiating position vis-à-vis her fellows. But her negotiating position is significantly affected by the existing social institutions, and so by the currently accepted moral practices embodied in those institutions. Thus, although agreement may well yield practices differing from those embodied in existing social institutions, yet it will be influenced by those practices, which are not themselves the product of rational agreement. And this must call the rationality of the agreed practices into question. The arbitrariness of existing practices must infect any agreement whose terms are significantly affected by them. Although rational agreement is in itself a source of stability, yet this stability is undermined by the arbitrariness of the circumstances in which it takes place. To escape this arbitrariness, rational persons will revert from actual to hypothetical agreement, considering what practices they would have agreed to from an initial position not structured by existing institutions and the practices they embody.

The content of a hypothetical agreement is determined by an appeal to the equal rationality of persons. Rational persons will voluntarily accept an agreement only insofar as they perceive it to be equally advantageous to each. To be sure, each would be happy to accept an agreement more advantageous to herself than to her fellows, but since no one will accept an agreement perceived to be less advantageous, agents whose rationality is a matter of common knowledge will recognize the futility of aiming at or holding out for more, and minimize their bargaining costs by coordinating at the point of equal advantage. Now the extent of advantage is determined in a twofold way. First, there is advantage internal to an agreement. In this respect, the expectation of equal advantage is assured by procedural fairness. The step from existing moral practices to those resulting from actual agreement takes rational persons to a procedurally fair situation, in which each perceives the agreed practices to be ones that it is equally rational for all to accept, given the circumstances in which agreement is reached. But those circumstances themselves may be called into question insofar as they are perceived to be arbitrary—the result, in part, of compliance with constraining practices that do not themselves ensure the expectation of equal advantage, and so do not reflect the equal rationality of the complying parties. To neutralize this arbitrary element, moral practices to be fully acceptable must be conceived as constituting a possible outcome of a hypothetical agreement under circumstances that are unaffected by social institutions that themselves lack full acceptability. Equal rationality demands consideration of external circumstances as well as internal procedures.

But what is the practical import of this argument? It would be absurd to claim that mere acquaintance with it, or even acceptance of it, will lead to the replacement of existing moral practices by those that would secure presocial agreement. It would be irrational for anyone to give up the benefits of the existing moral order simply because he comes to realize that it affords him more than he could expect from pure rational agreement with his fellows. And it would be irrational for anyone to accept a long-term utility loss by refusing to comply with the existing moral order, simply because she comes to realize that such compliance affords her less than she could expect from pure rational agreement. Nevertheless, these realizations do transform, or perhaps bring to the surface, the character of the relationships between persons that are maintained by the existing constraints, so that some of these relationships come to be recognized as coercive. These realizations constitute the elimination of false consciousness, and they result from a process of rational reflection that brings persons into what, in my theory, is the parallel of Jürgen Habermas's ideal speech situation. Without an argument to defend themselves in open dialogue with their fellows, those who are more than equally advantaged can hope to maintain their privileged position only if they can coerce their fellows into accepting it. And this, of course, may be possible. But coercion is not agreement, and it lacks any inherent stability.

Stability plays a key role in linking compliance to agreement. Aware of the benefits to be gained from constraining practices, rational persons will seek those that invite stable compliance. Now compliance is stable if it arises from agreement among persons each of whom considers both that the terms of agreement are sufficiently favorable to herself that it is rational for her to accept them, and that they are not so favorable to others that it would be rational for them to accept terms less favorable to them and more favorable to herself. An agreement affording equally favorable terms to all thus invites, as no other can, stable compliance.

In defending the claim that moral practices, to obtain the stable voluntary compliance of rational individuals, must be the objects of an appropriate hypothetical agreement, I have added to the initial minimal characterization of morality. Not only does morality constrain our choices and actions, but it does so in an impartial way, reflecting the equal rationality of the persons subject to constraint. Although it is no part of my argument to show that the requirements of contractarian morality will satisfy the Rawlsian test of cohering with our considered judgments in reflective equilibrium, yet it would be misleading to treat rationally agreed constraints on direct utility maximization as constituting a morality at all, rather than as replacing morality, were there no fit between their content and our pretheoretical moral views. The fit lies, I suggest, in the impartiality required for hypothetical agreement.

The foundational crisis of morality is thus resolved by exhibiting the rationality of our compliance with mutual, rationally agreed constraints on the pursuit of our desires, aims, and interests. Although bereft of a basis in objective values or an objectively purposive order, and confronted by a more fundamental mode of justification, morality survives by incorporating itself into that mode. Moral considerations have the same status, and the same role in explaining behavior, as the other reasons acknowledged by a rational

deliberator. We are left with a unified account of justification, in which an agent's choices and actions are evaluated in relation to his preferences—to the concerns that are constitutive of his sense of self. But since morality binds the agent independently of the particular content of his preferences, it has the prescriptive grip with which the Christian and Kantian views have invested it.

In incorporating morality into deliberative justification, we recognize a new dimension to the agent's self-conception. For morality requires that a person have the capacity to commit himself, to enter into agreement with his fellows secure in the awareness that he can and will carry out his part of the agreement without regard to many of those considerations that normally and justifiably would enter into his future deliberations. And this is more than the capacity to bring one's desires and interests together with one's beliefs into a single coherent whole. Although this latter unifying capacity must extend its attention to past and future, the unification it achieves may itself be restricted to that extended present within which a person judges and decides. But in committing oneself to future action in accordance with one's agreement, one must fix at least a subset of one's desires and beliefs to hold in that future. The self that agrees and the self that complies must be one. "Man himself must first of all have become *calculable, regular, necessary*, even in his own image of himself, if he is to be able to stand security for *his own future*, which is what one who promises does!"

In developing "*the right to make promises*," we human beings have found a contractarian bulwark against the perishing of morality.

Social Contract Theory:
Inadequate Account of Ethics

JEAN HAMPTON

Although Hobbes's masterpiece *Leviathan* is primarily concerned with presenting a contract argument for the institution of a certain kind of state (one with an absolute sovereign), if one looks closely, one also sees a sketch of a certain kind of contractarian approach to morality, which has profoundly influenced contemporary moral theorists such as Gauthier.

Hobbes's approach to morality does not assume there are natural moral laws or natural rights that we discern through the use of our reason or intuition. It is not an approach that assumes there is a naturally good object in the world (such as Aristotle's *Summmum Bonum*) that moral action serves and that people ought to pursue. It is not an approach that explains moral action as "natural," for example, as action generated by powerful other-regarding sentiments; Hobbes did not believe that such sentiments were very important or powerful in human life. And it is not an approach that justifies morality as a set of laws commanded by God—although Hobbes believed that his moral imperatives were *also* justified as commands of God. Using his contractarian method, he seeks to define the nature and authority of moral imperatives by reference to the desires and reasoning abilities of human beings, so that regardless of their religious commitments, all people will see that they have reason to act morally. So without repudiating the divine origin of the laws, Hobbes invokes contract language in order to develop an entirely *human* justification of morality....

Let me simply state here the features of what I take to be the Hobbesian moral theory....

1. What is valuable is what a person desires, not what he ought to desire (for no such prescriptively powerful object exists); and rational action is action that achieves or maximizes the satisfaction of desire (where it is a fact that the desire for self-preservation is our primary desire, and that human beings are, by and large, mutually unconcerned).

2. Moral action is rational for a person to perform if and only if such action advances his interests.

3. Morality is, in part, a body of causal knowledge about what human actions lead to peace, an end which it is common knowledge people desire and which they can all share, so that such actions are rational for them and "mutually agreeable." (This precept rests on the Hobbesian belief that people are not self-sufficient, and that they are roughly equal in strength and mental ability.)

4. Peace producing action is only individually rational to perform (hence only moral action) when there is a convention in the community that people perform such action (so that I know that if I behave cooperatively, then others will do so too, and vice versa). These conventions comprise the institution of morality in our society. The rationality of perform-

ance is, however, subject to two provisos:

Proviso 1: In order to be moral, an action must be not only peace producing and performed in the knowledge that others are willing to do so, but also an action that involves no net loss for the agent.

Proviso 2: Human beings are not, as a group, rational enough to be able to institute moral conventions, and hence must create a sovereign who can use his power to generate them.

5. Defining justice or equitable treatment in situations of conflict is done by considering what principles of justice the people involved "could agree to" or "what they would be unreasonable to reject," where the reasonableness of rejection is determined by a calculation comparing the benefits and costs of accepting an arbitrator's resolution with the benefits and costs of resorting to violence to resolve the conflict. An impartial judge, therefore, arbitrates according to the principle "to each according to his threat advantage in war."

... Let us reflect, for a moment, on the interesting features and strengths of a moral theory with this structure. Consider, first of all, that the Hobbesian approach relies on a very strong conception of individuality. According to Hobbes, cooperative social interaction is presented neither as inevitable nor as something that people value for its own sake, but rather as something that asocially defined individuals find instrumentally valuable given their primary (nonsocially defined) desires. To think that cooperative behavior needs to be encouraged and justified, so that we

must be *persuaded* to behave socially toward one another, is to believe that, even if society has some affect on us, it does not determine our fundamental or "intrinsic" nature as human beings, which is a nature that "dissociates us, and renders us apt to invade and destroy one another" (*Leviathan* 13, 10, 62).

Moreover, notice that there are two quite different ways in which this moral contractarian theory uses the notion of agreement. Features 2 and 3 capture the idea that the behavior enjoined by Hobbes's laws of nature is "agreeable," that is, that such action helps to secure the most-desired objects and/or states of affairs for each individual. Feature 5 captures the idea for which moral contractarians are famous; namely, that certain features of morality (e.g., fair resolution of conflict) can be understood as the *object* of agreement. However, there is connection, in Hobbes's theory, between the latter way of using agreement and the former. To resolve conflicts via the use of arbitrators and agreement procedures is to resolve them peacefully and with much less cost to the parties than more violent resolution procedures. Hobbes commends the use of arbitrators as individually rational for disputants, and warns the arbitrators that their usefulness to the disputants depends on the extent to which their peaceful resolution is more acceptable than going to war to resolve the dilemma. It is therefore conducive to self preservation to use a cooperative agreement procedure to resolve conflict, so that defining moral behavior through agreement is itself, for Hobbes, a mutually agreeable—that is, mutually self-preserving—behavior.

But perhaps most important of all, we should appreciate that all five features of Hobbes's moral view fit into a moral theory that is committed to the idea that morality is a *human-made institution,* which is justified only to the extent that it effectively furthers human interests. That is, Hobbes seeks to explain the *existence* of morality in society by appealing to the convention-creating activities of human beings, while arguing that the *justification* of morality in any human society depends upon how well its moral conventions serve individuals' desires.

In fact, there is a connection between Hobbes's contractarian approach to the state and this approach to morality. His decision to justify absolute sovereignty by reference to what people "could agree to" in a prepolitical society is an attempt to explain and legitimate the state's authority by appealing neither to God nor to any natural features of human beings that might be thought to explain the subordination of some to others, but solely to the needs and desires of the people who will be subjects of political realms. In the same manner, he insists that existing moral rules have power over us because they are social conventions for behavior (where Hobbes would also argue that these conventions only exist because of the power of the sovereign).

But Hobbes does not assume that existing conventions are, in and of themselves, justified. By considering "what we *could* agree to" if we had the chance to reappraise and redo the cooperative conventions in our society, we are able to determine the extent to which our present conventions are "mutually agreeable" and so *rational* for us to accept and act on. So Hobbes's moral theory invokes both actual agreements (i.e., conventions) and hypothetical agreements (which involve considering what conventions would be "mutually agreeable") at different points in his theory; the former are what he believes our moral life consists of; the latter are what he believes our moral life *should* consist of—that is, what our actual moral life should model. The contractarian methodology is useful in defining and justifying morality for one who believes that morality is man-made because considering what moral laws "people could agree to" (as well as what laws they have agreed to) is a way of confirming *that* morality is man-made, and a way of appraising how well the present institution serves the powerful self-regarding interests that virtually all of us have.

Note that this way of cashing out the language of hypothetical agreement makes the agreement-talk only a kind of metaphor, and not a device that reveals, in and of itself, the nature of morality or justice. What rational agents could all agree to is the securing of an object and/or state of affairs, the benefits of which they could all share and for which there is a rational argument using premises that all rational agents would take as a basis for deliberation. Hence, to determine what these agents "could all agree to," one must perform a deduction of practical reason, something that Hobbes believes he has done in Chapters 14 and 15 of *Leviathan*.

Hence, the notion of contract or agreement does not do justificational work *by itself* in the Hobbesian moral theory. What we "could agree to" has moral force for Hobbes not because make-believe promises in hypothetical worlds have any binding force, but because this sort of agreement is a device that *reveals* the way in which the agreed-upon outcome is rational for all of us. The justificational force of this kind of contract theory is therefore carried within, but derived from sources other than, the contract or agreement in the theory.

There was enormous interest in this Hobbesian understanding of morality in the seventeenth century by both detractors and supporters alike....

In the latter half of the twentieth century, we find renewed enthusiasm for this approach and a sustained interest in developing it further. And I suspect that the source of the enthusiasm comes from contemporary philosophers' attraction to the most important and fundamental feature of this approach, the presumption that morality is a human creation....

The contemporary theory that most completely realizes the Hobbesian approach and that develops it in important ways is presented by David Gauthier in *Morals by Agreement*, where he attempts to "validate the conception of morality as a set of rational, impartial constraints on the pursuit of individual interest." Every one of the features of Hobbes's moral theory is embraced in some fashion by Gauthier. On his view, moral behavior is rational and mutually advantageous behavior (features 1 and 2) that will lead to a cooperative state of affairs that is desired by everyone (feature 3), assuming of course, that they are equal in rationality and technology, when (and only when) people become disposed to engage in such behavior on a widespread basis (i.e., when a convention to behave cooperatively exists—feature 4). Gauthier also argues that resolution of conflict by such individuals should proceed via principles arrived at by considering the outcome of a hypothetical bargain among equals (feature 5). The people in this theory are quite clearly determinate individuals, who are defined prior to the morality that their contractual agreement is supposed to justify. While Gauthier does not explicitly say,... that the constraints traditionally endorsed as "moral" in human societies are human inventions, that idea, as well as the idea that these constraints can be "reinvented" to better serve human purposes, appears to be the assumption behind his philosophical project, which aims to show what conventions people *would* agree to if they were the sort of perfectly rational people we are all striving to become.

However, what makes Gauthier's moral contractarianism so interesting is the way in which it develops certain features of Hobbes's moral theory to produce not only a more sophisticated moral theory than Hobbes's own, but also one that is more palatable to twentieth-century moral theorists. Consider again feature 4 of Hobbes's theory: that it would only be rational to act cooperatively if others are disposed to do so. In general, Hobbes seems to be right that cooperative situations have a game-theoretic structure such that people are rational to act cooperatively together, but irrational to act cooperatively alone. Yet sometimes cooperation is surely going to have a Prisoner's Dilemma structure, so that even when others are disposed to cooperate, the individual agent is still rational *not* to cooperate. This suggests that the correct moral attitude is one that says, in essence: "I will cooperate with others, when they are willing to do so, except in situations where, by not cooperating, I can gain benefits from them with impunity," but this attitude is hardly what one would call "moral." [David] Hume explicitly worries about this problem when he discusses the "sensible knave" who has exactly the attitude I have just described:

> And though it is allowed that, without a regard to property, no society could subsist; yet according to the imperfect way in which human affairs are conducted, a sensible knave, in particular incidents, may think that an act of iniquity or infidelity will make a considerable addition to his fortune, without causing any considerable breach in the social

union or confederacy. That *honesty is the best policy*, may be a good general rule, but is liable to many exceptions; and he, it may perhaps be thought, conducts himself with most wisdom, who observes the general rule, and takes advantage of all the exceptions.

The knave is essentially saying that he will cooperate if and only if it is utility maximizing for him to do so, and thus will be prepared not to do so in situations, such as the Prisoner's Dilemma, despite the existence of a moral convention to perform the cooperative act in that sort of situation. And what does Hume say to this sensible knave? Essentially nothing. Given the difficulties that Hobbes himself had providing an answer to the same knavish question, we see that it is difficult for anyone who embraces the Hobbesian approach to morality to persuade someone who has no natural sentiments against exploitation of his fellow man not to exploit them when he can do so with impunity. Yet such a person is very far from being moral.

Gauthier attempts, however, to answer the knave, inspired by a line of argumentation that he believes Hobbes suggests (but does not develop adequately) in an attempt to answer the "foole"—who offers roughly the same challenge as Hume's knave. It is rational, says Gauthier, for people to become "disposed" to cooperate in such situations (assuming, however, that a sufficient number of others will become similarly disposed). By doing so, they become "constrained maximizers" rather than knavish "straightforward maximizers," where the former are people who pursue their advantage but who do so respecting a constraint against exploitative noncooperation in Prisoner's Dilemmas, where they have good reason to believe

that their partners are inclined to cooperate. Such people are willing to forego benefit in Prisoner's Dilemmas; hence, they are not straightforwardly maximizing utility. Yet they have chosen to be disposed to act in this way because they have determined that they can amass more utility by having this disposition than by not having it. A constrained maximizer refrains from taking advantage of any person who is also disposed to constrain his maximizing behavior because "he is not the sort of person that is disposed to do that sort of thing." That is the "moral" attitude that the sensible knave lacks. But the constrained maximizer has that "moral" attitude because of a prior determination that it is individually utility maximizing to have it. So, true to Hobbesian principles, Gauthier is arguing that moral behavior is utility maximizing and, in the long run, behavior that involves no net cost.

Contemporary Hobbesians and Humeans would certainly *want* to embrace Gauthier's argument if they could. It offers them a way to explain how collectively rational cooperative action that involves forgoing exploitative opportunities, but which is not dangerous, is also *individually rational* for the agent. But I am not so sure that they can embrace it. First, the idea that one could "will" to be disposed to act as Gauthier describes is dubious if one accepts Hobbesian psychology, and perhaps just as dubious on more plausible contemporary psychological theories. Second, it remains to be seen whether or not Gauthier's argument that it is rational to become disposed to act as a constrained maximizer actually succeeds. If Peter Danielson is right..., it is rational to adopt the more "knavish" cooperative attitude called "reciprocal cooperation," which differs from Gauthier's constrained maximization in that it directs us, to exploit (rather than cooperate with) unconditional cooperators. Finally, it might he even more rational only to *pretend* to be disposed to cooperate in either Gauthier's or Danielson's sense, ready to exploit others whenever one can do so with impunity.

The jury is, therefore, still out on the question of whether constrained maximization is rational for individuals to adopt. But other of Gauthier's modifications of Hobbes's project face what seem to be even more serious difficulties. For example, Gauthier argues that Hobbes was wrong to think that we could not establish moral conventions voluntarily, and that we need a sovereign to make their creation possible (although he admits that a limited political power would be needed to handle those among us who are not rational). Not only are most people able to constrain their maximizing tendencies for long-term gain on his view, but they are also able to recognize and act from principle of acquisition that will provide a rational starting point for further agreement on the terms of cooperation. This principle is what Gauthier calls the "Lockean Proviso"—which directs that one is to acquire goods in a way that leaves no one worse off; and the principle defining fair terms of cooperation that rationally proceeds from a bargain based on this proviso is what Gauthier calls the principle of "minimax relative concession" (hereafter the MRC principle), which essentially directs that the parties are to accept that outcome that is the result of their making equal concessions to one another in the bargaining process.

It may appear that Hobbes has no equivalent of the proviso or the MRC principle since, in his view, there is no way that people could develop a peaceful method of acquiring or dividing goods outside of civil society. But this is not quite so; as we saw, he does consider the

kind of principle that an arbitrator (were such a thing possible in the state of nature) would be rational to use in resolving disputes about the acquisition or the division of goods: "to each according to his threat advantage in war." Clearly, there is a big difference between this principle and Gauthier's cooperative rules! Is either theorist's argument for his approach effective?

James Buchanan comes down on the side of Hobbes. Imagine, says Buchanan, a state of nature in which people are competing for some scarce good *x*:

> Each would find it advantageous to invest effort, a "bad," in order to secure the good *x*. Physical strength, cajolery, stealth—all these and other personal qualities might determine the relative abilities of the individuals to secure and protect for themselves quantities of *x*... as a result of the actual or potential conflict over the relative proportions of *x* to be finally consumed, some "natural distribution" will come to be established.

It is this "natural distribution" that then becomes the baseline for any further contractual agreements. And it is that distribution that then "defines the individual" for purposes of future bargaining.

This future bargaining should occur, according to Buchanan, because everyone has a motive for resolving disputes and allocating goods peacefully given the substantial costs of predation and defense. Successful resolution of conflict through peaceful means would free up the resources used in warfare, and any agreement reached regarding the distribution of these resources, or any portions of the good *x* not appropriated, will proceed from the natural distribution. What Buchanan does not notice is that the natural distribution also generates the principle to be used in the peaceful resolution of these sorts of competitive conflicts: it is the principle "to each according to what he would have received in war." Consider the following passage from *Leviathan*:

> *if a man be trusted to judge between man and man,* it is a precept of the law of nature, *that he deale Equally between them.* For without that, the controversies of men cannot be determined but by War. He therefore that is partial in judgement, doth what in him lies, to deter men from the use of Judges, and Arbitrators; and consequently (against the fundamental Law of Nature) is the cause of War. (*Leviathan* 15, 23–4, 77)

Hobbes is saying here that an arbitrator in a dispute must beware not to be "partial" in his resolution of the conflict or else the parties will ignore his resolution and go to war to resolve their dispute. But the knowledge that warfare may be deemed rational by the parties if the outcome is not to their liking will affect how the arbitrator resolves the conflict. He must try, as far as possible, to mimic the distribution of the goods or the resolution of the conflict that the parties believe warfare between them will likely effect (assuming that each would stop short of attempting to kill the other). To do otherwise would be to risk one party deciding, "I won't accept this resolution: I can get more if I go to war." Of course, there are costs to going to war that are not involved in accepting an arbitrator's resolution of the conflict, so that even if the arbitrator got the resolution wrong, he might be close enough to the division each thinks warfare would effect such that no party would feel it was

worth the cost of warfare to try to get more. On the other hand, one or both of them may be vainglorious and believe (falsely) that he can win a fight over the other and wrest away everything that he wants, in which case there is no way the arbitrator can resolve their dispute that both will find acceptable. But when both are at least fairly realistic in assessing their powers, the arbitrators can peacefully decide conflicts between them using the maxim "To each according to his threat advantage in a conflict between them."

Gauthier argues that the initial bargaining position is misidentified with the noncooperative outcome, and although his argument is directed at Buchanan, it would clearly apply to Hobbes as well. Why, Gauthier asks, should people behave in a way that maintains the effects of predation after it has been banned?

> Were agreement to lapse, then what might I expect? Buchanan depends on the threat implicit in the natural distribution to elicit compliance. But a return to the natural distribution benefits no one. The threat is unreal. What motivates compliance is the absence of coercion rather than the fear of its renewal.

Gauthier is, I believe, trying to make the following point. If people have decided to enter a world in which their interactions are cooperative rather than coercive, then coercive power and the goods that this power has amassed no longer define the parties' bargaining positions; instead, it is their power as cooperators that determines their clout in the bargain, as the MRC principle is meant to represent. If Buchanan and Hobbes reply that past coercers can threaten a return to predation and warfare unless they get them, then Gauthier will counter that such a return is extremely expensive for them, so expensive that it would be a threat they would never feel they could carry out. Not only would they lose the resources that had been freed up by the ban on predation, but they would also give up any productive returns that those freed-up resources may have been able to yield in cooperative investments with others. Gauthier argues that distribution according to predative power should be abandoned, and that initial distribution rationally proceeds according to the Lockean Proviso, while the results of further cooperation should be distributed by the market or, when the market fails, according to the MRC principle.

But Buchanan and Hobbes can defend their claim that predative power should still be understood as the foundation of the parties' bargaining on distribution of a cooperative surplus. Imagine a world in which predation has gone on for some time. The predators would certainly prefer to the MRC principle the Hobbesian "warfare threat advantage" principle, which would give every party at least what she would have gotten in the state of war, plus some of the resources that previously went into predation and defense. The predators would point out that no one would lose, and everyone would gain, from this deal, although the weak would not gain as much from this principle as they would from MRC. But why should the weak, who may have considerable cooperative potential, go along with this deal? Doesn't such potential generate a new threat advantage, so that the result of the agreement will be (loosely) "To each according to his production in the cooperative endeavour"? I want to propose that the strong may have a strategy for ensuring that it does not by invoking the very notion of commitment that Gauthier himself thought so powerful in his answer

to the knave. The strong would be rational to turn the situation into a two-move game and use what game theorists call a "precommitment strategy," which is essentially just the same as Gauthier's technique of "constraining oneself for gain." On the first move they would perform two actions. They would:

(a) make a threat to reassemble the means of war for as long as it took to persuade the noncompliers to go along with the threat-advantage principle;

and then they would

(b) dispose themselves to keep their threats no matter how expensive it is to do so.

The second move would be made by the weak. What is their rational response to the first move of the strong? Clearly, they would find it utility maximizing to accept the threat-advantage principle rather than to hold out for a principle more favorable to them. Hence, by transforming the situation into a two-move game and using the first move to make a threat that they would then commit themselves to keep, the strong would be able to insist on ensuring that the structure of future mutual cooperation respects their past predative power.

In response, Gauthier could try to contend that this kind of two-move strategy would be unavailable to the people in his bargaining situation. For example, he might argue that insofar as the weak are perfectly rational, they would know that this strategy would be rational for the strong, and would do their best to block it. But precisely because they *are* weak, blocking this strategy might be difficult. Indeed, it is difficult for Gauthier to *prove* that the weak could block it. His bargaining situation is so sparsely described and highly idealized that we can find nothing in the structure of that situation to rule out this kind of precommitment strategy by the strong, so that it seems possible for both the starting point and the results of a Gauthierian initial contract to be alarmingly Hobbesian.

These remarks make me appear strangely unappreciative of Gauthier's attempt to mount a plausible neo-Hobbesian moral theory. It seems that I am commending to contemporary contractarian, the meanest and most unappealing aspects of Hobbes's approach to justice and property. But those mean and unappealing aspects are quite clearly and strongly linked with Hobbes's requirement that moral action involve no net loss to the agent. There are no free giveaways or free rides on Hobbes's theory; you get what it is in your interest to get and what it is in others' interest to let you have. The results of this kind of thinking are not, I think, very attractive. Contemporary Hobbesians like Gauthier try to accept the self-interested underpinnings of the theory but dress up or deny the conclusions that Hobbes claims they force one to draw. I have attempted to suggest in these remarks that Hobbes is right to insist on them. I suspect that if Gauthier or other theorists sympathetic to the structure of Hobbesian theory long for "nicer" principles of morality and justice than those that Hobbes develops they need to find a non-Hobbesian foundation for them. And as I now discuss, there are signs that Gauthier himself suspects this is so.

Consider what many have found a particularly ugly side to Hobbesian morality: its radical individualism. Recall that the people in Hobbes's or Gauthier's contracting world are fully developed, asocially defined individuals. But when *Leviathan* was originally published some readers were

shocked by the idea that the nature of our ties to others was interest-based. Aristotelian critics contended that Hobbes's theory goes too far in trying to represent us as radically separate from others. Their worries are also the worries of many twentieth-century critics. Do not our ties to our mothers and fathers, our children and our friends define, at least in part, who we are? Isn't it true that our distinctive tastes, projects, interests, characteristics, and skills are defined by and created within a social context? So how can a moral theory that does not take this into account be an accurate representation of our moral life? It would seem that we *must* bring into our moral theory noninstrument ties with others that are not based on our affections because it is through such ties that we *become* individuals....

Hobbes would either not understand or else resist the claims of our social definition. But Gauthier, a member of our place and time, accepts them, and this has strange consequences for his moral theory. Gauthier is moved by the criticism that it is unfair to use allocation procedures such as the market, to distribute goods in circumstances where the society permits—even encourages—one class of people to prevent development in another class of people of those talents that allow one to do well in a system using that allocation procedure. Thus, he suggests that we see his contract on the fair terms of cooperation not as an agreement among determinate, already defined, individuals, but as an agreement at a hypothetical "Archimedean Point" among "protopeople"—people who have a certain genetic endowment and who are concerned to select principles that will structure their society such that they will develop well:

The principles chosen from the Archimedean point must therefore provide that each person's expected share of the fruits of social interaction be related, not just to what he actually contributes, since his actual contribution may reflect the contingent permissions and prohibitions found in any social structure, but *to the contributions he would make* in that social structure most favorable to the actualization of his capacities and character traits, and to the fulfillment of his preferences, provided that this structure is a feasible alternative meeting the other requirements of the Archimedean choice. (My emphasis)

No longer does Gauthier's contract talk presume fully determinate individuals, and no longer is the object of any contract a principle for the resolution of conflict among individuals. Now the contract methodology is used to choose principles that are "for" the structuring of the social system that plays a profound role in structuring individuals. Like Rawls, Gauthier is declaring that the first order of moral business is the definition of social justice.

This is not a benign addition to Gauthier's Hobbesian moral theory: it is an addition that essentially destroys its character as a Hobbesian theory. Of course, it undermines the individualism of the original Hobbesian theory; many will think that this is no great loss. But it was that individualism that much of the rest of the theory presupposed. Consider, for example, that a Hobbesian theory answers the "Why be moral?" question with the response, "Because it is in your interest to be so." But that answer no longer makes sense in a contract theory designed to pursue the nature of social justice using protopeople. Suppose the results of that theory call for a more egalitarian distribution of resources and opportunities open to talents that society will attempt to develop in all its members. If I am a white male in a society that accords white males privileged opportunities to develop talents that will allow them to earn well, then why is it rational for me to pursue a restructuring of social institutions in which this is no longer true?

Indeed, given that their development has already taken place, *why is it even rational for adult minority members or females to support this restructuring?* All of these people are already "made." Restructuring the social world such that it does a fairer job of creating future generation of individuals is a costly and other-regarding enterprise. Why should these determinate individuals be rational to undertake it, given its cost, unless they just happened to be affected by sympathy for other members of their race or caste or sex, and so enjoyed the struggle? But the nontuistic perspective Gauthier encourages his bargainers to take encourages them to discount any benefits to others from their actions. So assuming the Hobbesian/Gauthierian theory of rationality, what it would be rational for "proto-me" to agree to in some extrasocietal bargain seems to have little bearing on what it is rational for "determinate-me" to accept now.

It is because the self-interest of *determinate* individuals does not seem sufficient to explain the commitment to the results of a bargain among *protopeople* that one wonders whether Gauthier's eventual interest in defining fair principles for the development of individual talents in a social system betrays a commitment to the intrinsic value of the individuals themselves. And it is the idea that individuals have intrinsic value that is missing from the Hobbesian approach. It has not been sufficiently appreciated, I believe, that by answering the "Why be moral?" question by invoking self-interest in the way that

Hobbes does, one makes not only cooperative action, but the human beings with whom one will cooperate merely of *instrumental value*; and this is an implicit feature of Hobbes's moral theory that is of central importance. Now Hobbes is unembarrassed by the fact that in his view, "The *Value*, or WORTH of a man, is as of all other things, his Price; that is to say, so much as would be given for the use of his Power: and therefore is not absolute; but a thing dependent on the need and judgement of another" (*Leviathan* 10, 16, 42). But this way of viewing people is not something that we, or even Gauthier, can take with equanimity. In the final two chapters of his book, Gauthier openly worries about the fact that the reason why we value moral imperatives on this Hobbesian view is that they are instrumentally valuable to us in our pursuit of what we value. But note *why* they are instrumentally valuable: in virtue of our physical and intellectual weaknesses that make it impossible for us to be self-sufficient, we need the cooperation of others to prosper. If there were some way that we could remedy our weaknesses and become self-sufficient, for example, by becoming a superman or superwoman, or by using a Ring of Gyges to make ourselves invisible and so steal from the stores of others with impunity, then it seems we would no longer value or respect moral constraints because they would no longer

be useful to us—unless we happened to like the idea. But in this case sentiment, rather than reason, would motivate kind treatment. And without such sentiment, people would simply be "prey" for us.

Even in a world in which we are not self-sufficient, the Hobbesian moral theory gives us no reason to respect those with whom we have no need of cooperating, or those whom we are strong enough to dominate, such as old people, or the handicapped, or retarded children whom we do not want to rear, or people from other societies with whom we have no interest in trading. And I would argue that this shows that Hobbesian moral contractarianism fails in a very serious way to capture the nature of morality. *Regardless* of whether or not one can engage in beneficial cooperative interactions with another, our moral intuitions push us to assent to the idea that one owes that person respectful treatment simply in virtue of the fact that he or she is a *person*. It seems to be a feature of our moral life that we regard a human being, whether or not she is instrumentally valuable, as always intrinsically valuable. Indeed, to the extent that the results of a Hobbesian theory are acceptable, this is because one's concern to cooperate with someone whom one cannot dominate leads one to behave in ways that mimic the respect one ought to show her simply in virtue of her worth as a human being....

THE CONTINUING DEBATE:
Is Ethics Based on a Social Contract?

What Is New

While social contract theory—especially in the forms developed by Rawls and Gauthier—is a major focus of contemporary ethical theory, it is also a favorite target for some ethical theorists, particularly those who favor care ethics, or feminist ethics. The issue of whether social contract ethics promotes an overly narrow perspective that neglects important personal elements of ethical relations is currently much debated.

Where to Find More

Thomas Hobbes' *Leviathan*, the classic source for social contract theory, is available from Bobbs-Merrill (Indianapolis: 1958); it was originally published in 1651. John Locke's *Second Treatise on Government* was originally published in 1690; an accessible edition is Indianapolis: Bobbs-Merrill, Library of Liberal Arts, 1952. Rousseau's *Social Contract (Du Contrat Social)* was originally published in 1762; it is available in an edition edited by R. Masters (NY: St. Martin's Press, 1978).

A very interesting non-western, non-European perspective on the social contract is offered by the Constitution of the Iroquois Confederacy. For a discussion of the development of the Iroquois social contract, and the influence of the Iroquois Confederation on the writing of the United States Constitution, see Bruce E. Johansen, *Forgotten Founders: Benjamin Franklin, the Iroquois and the Rationale for the American Revolution* (Ipswich, MA: Gambit Publishers, 1982). An account of the development of the Iroquois social contract, and a link to the remarkably detailed and progressive agreement itself, can be found at the World Civilizations Website at Washington State University, at *http://www.wsu.edu:8080/~dee/CULAMRCA/IRLEAGUE.HTM.* The Iroquois constitution is also available at *http://Tuscaroras.com*

Discussions of social contract theory tradition include Jean Hampton, *Hobbes and the Social Contract Tradition* (Cambridge: Cambridge University Press, 1986); and P. Riley, *Will and Political Legitimacy: A Critical Exposition of Social Contract Theory in Hobbes, Locke, Rousseau, Kant, and Hegel* (Cambridge, MA: Harvard University Press, 1982).

Probably the best known philosophical book of the late twentieth century presenting an updated version of social contract theory is John Rawls, *A Theory of Justice* (London: Oxford University Press, 1971). Robert Nozick, in *Anarchy, State and Utopia* (NY: Basic Books, 1974) develops a well-known opposing view to Rawls' position. David Gauthier, *Morals by Agreement* (Oxford: Oxford University Press, 1986), is a very interesting contemporary version of social contract theory. See Peter Vallentyne, ed., *Contractarianism and Rational Choice: Essays on David Gauthier's Morals By Agreement* (NY: Cambridge University Press, 1991) for excellent discussion of Gauthier's work.

There is an extensive literature critiquing social contract theory from the care ethics perspective. See particularly Carole Pateman, *The Sexual Contract* (Stanford: Stanford University Press, 1988), who argues that contract theory preserves patriarchal domination rather than opening a path to freedom and equality. Virginia Held, *Feminist Morality: Transforming Culture, Society, and Politics* (Chicago: Chicago

University Press, 1993), claims that social contract theory reduces individuals to "economic man," and neglects the full rich range of human relationships. Eva Feder Kittay, *Love's Labor* (NY: Routledge, 1999), raises objections based on who is left out of social contract considerations.

There are several good web sources that discuss social contract theory. See *The Internet Encyclopedia of Philosophy*, *http://www.ut.edu/s/soc-cont.htm*; the *Stanford Encyclopedia of Philosophy*, *http://plato.stanford.edu/entries/contractarianism*; and also see "game theory and ethics" in *Stanford Encyclopedia of Philosophy*, *http://plato.stanford. edu/entries/game-ethics*.

CAN CONSEQUENTIALISM MAKE ROOM FOR FRIENDSHIP?

CONSEQUENTIALISM LEAVES NO ROOM FOR FRIENDSHIP

ADVOCATE: Michael Stocker, Irwin and Marjorie Guttag Professor of Ethics and Political Philosophy, Syracuse University; author of *Plural and Conflicting Values* (Oxford: Oxford University Press, 1989) and *Valuing Emotions* (Cambridge: Cambridge University Press, 1996).

SOURCE: : "The Schizophrenia of Modern Ethical Theories," *Journal of Philosophy*, volume 73 (1976): 453–466

CONSEQUENTIALISM CAN ACCOMMODATE THE VALUE OF FRIENDSHIP

ADVOCATE: Peter Railton, John Stephenson Perrin Professor of Philosophy, University of Michigan; author of *Facts, Values, and Norms: Essays Toward a Morality of Consequence* (Cambridge: Cambridge University Press, 2003).

SOURCE: "Alienation, Consequentialism, and the Demands of Morality," *Philosophy and Public Affairs*, volume 13, number 2 (1984): 134–171

Consequentialism is the broad ethical view that what makes an act right or wrong is primarily or exclusively its *consequences*. It is usually contrasted with Kantian (sometimes called deontological) ethical theories, which hold that the rightness of an act is determined by basic rules or principles. Why is it wrong to tell a lie? The consequentialist offers a simple answer: Telling lies causes people to get hurt; honesty produces better results, greater happiness, less suffering. The Kantian rejects such consequentialist calculations: Lying is wrong because it violates a basic ethical principle. Fortunately, telling the truth is usually beneficial; but even if telling lies produced more overall pleasure or better consequences, it would still be wrong.

Though there is some disagreement about the exact dimensions of utilitarian ethics, a rough definition of utilitarianism is: a consequentialist theory according to which the right act is that act which maximizes utility. (Consequentialism is the broader category, and not all consequentialists are utilitarians; for example, a consequentialist might favor acts producing the greatest knowledge or virtue or godliness, regardless of whether those goals have or lack utility.)

Though consequentialism seems simple and straightforward, it swiftly leads to difficult questions that divide consequentialists. Perhaps the most basic division is between Act (or "direct") and Rule ("indirect") utilitarians. Act utilitarians (like Railton) believe that each act must be evaluated for the best overall consequences; rule utilitarians believe that some rules (such as "keep your promises") have positive overall consequences, and that we should therefore adopt those rules (on consequentialist grounds) and follow the rules in our individual behavior. A second issue for utilitarians concerns exactly what *consequences* we should seek. *Hedonistic* utilitarians seek to maximize pleasure and minimize suffering; *pluralistic* utilitarians (like Railton) believe there are a variety of good consequences that cannot be reduced to the maximizing of pleasure; and *preference* utilitarians seek to maximize the satisfaction of preferences (whatever those preferences are). A third utilitarian distinction is between objective and subjective views. Objective utilitarians (including Railton) believe that the right act is the act that actually produces the best consequences, while subjective utilitarians hold that the right act is the act one reasonably believes (perhaps mistakenly) will produce optimum consequences.

Though there are many criticisms of utilitarian ethics, perhaps the one that currently draws the most attention is that utilitarian ethics is coldly impersonal, and that it undervalues or ignores the close personal and family relationships that are central to a healthy and wholesome ethical life. In particular, consequentialism seems to imply that we should calculate the best overall consequences for everyone, without playing favorites; and that means we should not give special consideration to our family and friends. Suppose that two people are drowning; one is your spouse, and the other a stranger. Whom should you save? You might run the consequentialist calculations and conclude that you should save your spouse; but if that is your thought process, then (in the famous phrase of Bernard Williams) you have had "one thought too many." If your beloved spouse is in peril, then the bonds of affection demand your immediate devotion to that person's welfare. Calculating which rescue would produce the best consequences is fundamentally incompatible with acting from special relations of affection and devotion. If you explain your heroic rescue effort to your beloved in terms of "I rescued you because I calculated that such an act would produce the best consequences," you are likely to severely damage the loving relationship. Likewise, "I visited you in the hospital because I calculated that would produce the greatest overall utility" seems much less satisfactory than simply "I visited you because you are my friend, and I care about you." Thus utilitarian ethics is sometimes criticized as an impersonal, austere ethics that devalues friendship and affection, and Michael Stocker enlarges that criticism to argue that utilitarian ethics alienates us from our most basic personal commitments. Peter Railton examines whether utilitarianism can answer that criticism.

POINTS TO PONDER

➢ Michael Stocker considers restricting utilitarianism to the public impersonal sphere, and using another ethical model for personal relationships. He rejects that solution because it "would pose severe difficulties of integration within ethical theory." What would be the nature of those difficulties, and are they insurmountable?

➢ Peter Railton favors what he calls *sophisticated* consequentialism, in which the consequentialist may make use of nonconsequentialist approaches to ethics. If someone objected that this is no longer consequentialism at all, could Railton successfully answer that criticism?

➢ Could Stocker accept the version of consequentialism favored by Railton, or would he still regard it as alienating?

Consequentialism Leaves No Room for Friendship

Michael Stocker

Modern ethical theories, with perhaps a few honorable exceptions, deal only with reasons, with values, with what justifies. They fail to examine motives and the motivational structures and constraints of ethical life. They not only fail to do this, they fail as ethical theories by not doing this....

One mark of a good life is a harmony between one's motives and one's reasons, values, justifications. Not to be moved by what one values—what one believes good, nice, right, beautiful, and so on—bespeaks a malady of the spirit. Not to value what moves one also bespeaks a malady of the spirit. Such a malady, or such maladies, can properly be called *moral schizophrenia*—for they are a split between one's motives and one's reasons. (Here and elsewhere, 'reasons' will stand also for 'values' and 'justifications'.)

An extreme form of such schizophrenia is characterized, on the one hand, by being moved to do what one believes bad, harmful, ugly, abasing; on the other, by being disgusted, horrified, dismayed by what one wants to do. Perhaps such cases are rare. But a more modest schizophrenia between reason and motive is not, as can be seen in many examples of weakness of the will, indecisiveness, guilt, shame, self-deception, rationalization, and annoyance with oneself.

At the very least, we should be moved by our major values and we should value what our major motives seek. Should, that is, if we are to lead a good life. To repeat, such harmony is a mark of a good life. Indeed, one might wonder whether human life—good or bad—is possible without some such integration.

This is not, however, to say that in all cases it is better to have such harmony. It is better for us if self-seeking authoritarians feel fettered by their moral upbringing; better, that is, than if they adopt the reason of their motives. It would have been far better for the world and his victims had Eichmann not wanted to do what he thought he should do.

Nor is this to say that in all areas of endeavor such harmony is necessary or even especially conducive to achieving what is valued. In many cases, it is not. For example, one's motives in fixing a flat tire are largely irrelevant to getting under way again. (In many such cases, one need not even value the intended outcome.)

Nor is this even to say that in all "morally significant" areas such harmony is necessary or especially conducive to achieving what is valued. Many morally significant jobs, such as feeding the sick, can be done equally well pretty much irrespective of motive. And, as Ross, at times joined by Mill, argues, for a large part of ethics, there simply is no philosophical question of harmony or disharmony between value and motive: you can do what is right, obligatory, your duty no matter what your motive for so acting. If it is your duty to keep a promise, you fulfill that duty no matter whether you keep the promise out of respect for duty, fear of losing your reputation, or whatever. What motivates is irrelevant so far as rightness, obligatoriness, duty are concerned.

Notwithstanding the very questionable correctness of this view so far as rightness, obligatoriness, duty are concerned, there remain at least two problems. The first is that even here there is still a question of harmony. What sort of life would people have who did their duties but never or rarely wanted to? Second, duty, obligation, and rightness are only one part—indeed, only a small part, a dry and minimal part—of ethics. There is the whole other area of the values of personal and interpersonal relations and activities; and also the area of moral goodness, merit, virtue. In both, motive is an essential part of what is valuable; in both, motive and reason must be in harmony for the values to be realized.

For this reason and for the reason that such harmony is a mark of a good life, any theory that ignores such harmony does so at great peril. Any theory that makes difficult, or precludes, such harmony stands, if not convicted, then in need of much and powerful defense. What I shall now argue is that modern ethical theories—those theories prominent in the English-speaking philosophical world—make such harmony impossible.

CRITICISM OF MODERN ETHICS

Reflection on the complexity and vastness of our moral life, on what has value, shows that recent ethical theories have by far over-concentrated on duty, rightness, and obligation. This failure—of overconcentrating—could not have been tolerated but for the failure of not dealing with motives or with the relations of motives to values. (So too, the first failure supports and explains the second.) In this second failure, we find a far more serious defect of modern ethical theories than such over-concentration: they necessitate a schizophrenia between reason and motive in vitally important and pervasive areas of value, or alternatively they allow us the

harmony of a morally impoverished life, a life deeply deficient in what is valuable. It is not possible for moral people, that is, people who would achieve what is valuable, to act on these ethical theories, to let them comprise their motives. People who do let them comprise their motives will, for that reason, have a life seriously lacking in what is valuable.

These theories are, thus, doubly defective. As ethical theories, they fail by making it impossible for a person to achieve the good in an integrated way. As theories of the mind, of reasons and motives, of human life and activity, they fail, not only by putting us in a position that is psychologically uncomfortable, difficult, or even untenable, but also by making us and our lives essentially fragmented and incoherent.

The sort of disharmony I have in mind can be brought out by considering a problem for egoists, typified by hedonistic egoists. Love, friendship, affection, fellow feeling, and community are important sources of personal pleasure. But can such egoists get these pleasures? I think not— not so long as they adhere to the motive of pleasure-for-self.

The reason for this is not that egoists cannot get together and decide, as it were, to enter into a love relationship. Surely they can (leaving aside the irrelevant problems about deciding to do such a thing). And they can do the various things calculated to bring about such pleasure: have absorbing talks, make love, eat delicious meals, see interesting films, and so on, and so on.

Nonetheless, there is something necessarily lacking in such a life: love. For it is essential to the very concept of love that one care for the beloved, that one be prepared to act for the sake of the beloved. More strongly, one must care for the beloved and act for that person's sake as a final goal; the beloved, or the beloved's welfare or interest, must be a final goal of one's concern and action.

To the extent that my consideration for you—or even my trying to make you happy—comes from my desire to lead an untroubled life, a life that is personally pleasing for me, I do not act for your sake. In short, to the extent that I act in various ways toward you with the final goal of getting pleasure—or, more generally, good—for myself, I do not act for your sake.

When we think about it this way, we may get some idea of why egoism is often claimed to be essentially lonely. For it is essentially concerned with external relations with others, where, except for their effects on us, one person is no different from, nor more important, valuable, or special than any other person or even any other thing. The individuals as such are not important, only their effects on us are; they are essentially replaceable, anything else with the same effects would do as well. And this, I suggest, is intolerable personally. To think of yourself this way, or to believe that a person you love thinks of you this way, is intolerable. And for conceptual, as well as psychological, reasons it is incompatible with love.

It might be suggested that it is rather unimportant to have love of this sort. But this would be a serious error. The love here is not merely modern-romantic or sexual. It is also the love among members of a family, the love we have for our closest friends, and so on. Just what sort of life would people have who never "cared" for anyone else, except as a means to their own interests? And what sort of life would people have who took it that no one loved them for their own sake, but only for the way they served the other's interest?

Just as the notion of doing something for the sake of another, or of caring for the person for that person's sake, is essential for love, so too is it essential for friendship and all affectionate relations. Without this, at best we could have good relations, friendly relations. And similarly, such caring and respect is essential for fellow feeling and community.

Before proceeding, let us contrast this criticism of egoism with a more standard one. My criticism runs as follows: Hedonistic egoists take their own pleasure to be the sole justification of acts, activities, ways of life; they should recognize that love, friendship, affection, fellow feeling, and community are among the greatest (sources of) personal pleasures. Thus, they have good reason, on their own grounds, to enter such relations. But they cannot act in the ways required to get those pleasures, those great goods, if they act on their motive of pleasure-for-self. They cannot act for the sake of the intended beloved, friend, and so on; thus, they cannot love, be or have a friend, and so on. To achieve these great personal goods, they have to abandon that egoistical motive. They cannot embody their reason in their motive. Their reasons and motives make their moral lives schizophrenic.

The standard criticism of egoists is that they simply cannot achieve such nonegoistical goods, that their course of action will, as a matter of principle, keep them from involving themselves with others in the relevant ways, and so on. This criticism is not clearly correct. For there may be nothing inconsistent in egoists' adopting a policy that will allow them to forget, as it were, that they are egoists, a policy that will allow and even encourage them to develop such final goals and motives as caring for another for that person's own sake. Indeed, as has often been argued, the wise egoist would do just this.

Several questions should be asked of this response: would the transformed person still be an egoist? Is it important, for the defense of egoism, that the person remain an egoist? Or is it important only that the person live in a way that would be approved of by an egoist? It is, of course, essential to the transformation of the person from egoistical motivation to caring for others that the person-as-egoist lose conscious control of him/herself. This raises the question of whether such people will be able to check up and see how their transformed selves are getting on in achieving egoistically approved goals. Will they have a mental alarm clock which wakes them up from their nonegoistical transforms every once in a while, to allow them to reshape these transforms if they are not getting enough personal pleasure—or, more generally, enough good? I suppose that this would not be impossible. But it hardly seems an ideal, or even a very satisfactory, life. It is bad enough to have a private personality, which you must hide from others; but imagine having a personality that you must hide from (the other parts of) yourself. Still, perhaps this is possible. If it is, then it seems that egoists may be able to meet this second criticism. But this does not touch my criticism: that they will not be able to embody their reason in their motives; that they will have to lead a bifurcated, schizophrenic life to achieve what is good.

This might be thought a defect of only such ethical theories as egoism. But consider those utilitarianisms which hold that an act is right, obligatory, or whatever if and only if it is optimific in regard to pleasure and pain (or weighted expectations of them). Such a view has it that the only good reason for acting is pleasure vs. pain, and thus should highly value love, friendship, affection, fellow feeling, and community. Suppose, now, you embody this utilitarian reason as your motive in your actions and thoughts toward some-

one. Whatever your relation to that person, it is necessarily not love (nor is it friendship, affection, fellow feeling, or community). The person you supposedly love engages your thought and action not for him/herself, but rather as a source of pleasure....

Just as egoism and the above sort of utilitarianism necessitate a schizophrenia between reason and motive—and just as they cannot allow for love, friendship, affection, fellow feeling, and community—so do current rule utilitarianisms. And so do current deontologies.

What is lacking in these theories is simply—or not so simply—the person. For, love, friendship, affection, fellow feeling, and community all require that the other person be an essential part of what is valued. The person—not merely the person's general values nor even the person-qua-producer-or-possessor-of-general-values—must be valued. The defect of these theories in regard to love, to take one case, is not that they do not value love (which, often, they do not) but that they do not value the beloved. Indeed, a person who values and aims at simply love, that is, love-in-general or even love-in-general-exemplified-by-this-person "misses" the intended beloved as surely as does an adherent of the theories I have criticized.

The problem with these theories is not, however, with *other*-people-as-valuable. It is simply—or not so simply—with *people*-as-valuable. Just as they would do *vis-à-vis* other people, modern ethical theories would prevent each of us from loving, caring for, and valuing ourself—as opposed to loving, caring for, and valuing our general values or ourself-qua-producer-or-possessor-of-general-values. In these externality-ridden theories, there is as much a disappearance or nonappearance of the self as of other people. Their externality-ridden universes of what is intrinsically valuable are not solipsistic; rather, they are devoid of all people.

It is a truism that it is difficult to deal with people as such. It is difficult really to care for them for their own sake. It is psychically wearing and exhausting. It puts us in too open, too vulnerable a position. But what must also be looked at is what it does to us—taken individually and in groups as small as a couple and as large as society—to view and treat others externally, as essentially replaceable, as mere instruments or repositories of general and non-specific value; and what it does to us to be treated, or believe we are treated, in these ways.

At the very least, these ways are dehumanizing. To say much more than this would require a full-scale philosophical anthropology showing how such personal relations as love and friendship are possible, how they relate to larger ways and structures of human life, and how they—and perhaps only they—allow for the development of those relations which are constitutive of a human life worth living: how, in short, they work together to produce the fullness of a good life, a life of eudaimonia....

At this point, it might help to restate some of the things I have tried to do and some I have not. Throughout I have been concerned with what sort of motives people can have if they are to be able to realize the great goods of love, friendship, affection, fellow feeling, and community. And I have argued that, if we take as motives, embody in our motives, those various things which recent ethical theories hold to be ultimately good or right, we will, of necessity, be unable to have those motives. Love, friendship, affection, fellow feeling, and community, like many other states

and activities, essentially contain certain motives and essentially preclude certain others; among those precluded we find motives comprising the justifications, the goals, the goods of those ethical theories most prominent today. To embody in one's motives the values of current ethical theories is to treat people externally and to preclude love, friendship, affection, fellow feeling, and community—both with others and with oneself. To get these great goods while holding those current ethical theories requires a schizophrenia between reason and motive.

I have not argued that if you have a successful love relationship, friendship,..., then you will be unable to achieve the justifications, goals, goods posited by those theories. You can achieve them, but not by trying to live the theory directly. Or, more exactly, to to the extent that you live the theory directly, to that extent you will fail to achieve its goods....

It might be expected that, in those areas explicitly concerned with motives and their evaluation, ethical theories would not lead us into this disharmony or the corresponding morally defective life. And to some extent this expectation is met. But even in regard to moral merit and demerit, moral praise- and blameworthiness, the moral virtues and vices, the situation is not wholly dissimilar. Again, the problem of externality and impersonality, and the connected disharmony, arises.

The standard view has it that a morally good intention is an essential constituent of a morally good act. This seems correct enough. On that view, further, a morally good intention is an intention to do an act for the sake of its goodness or rightness. But now, suppose you are in a hospital, recovering from a long illness. You are very bored and restless and at loose ends when Smith comes in once again. You are now convinced more than ever that he is a fine fellow and a real friend—taking so much time to cheer you up, traveling all the way across town, and so on. You are so effusive with your praise and thanks that he protests that he always tries to do what he thinks is his duty, what he thinks will be best.... It is not essentially because of you that he came to see you, not because you are friends, but because he thought it was his duty....

Surely there is something lacking here—and lacking in moral merit or value. The lack can be sheeted home to two related points: again, the wrong sort of thing is said to be the proper motive; and, in this case at least, the wrong sort of thing is, again, essentially external.

SOME QUESTIONS AND CONCLUDING REMARKS

I have assumed that the reasons, values, justifications of ethical theories should be such as to allow us to embody them in our motives and still act morally and achieve the good. But why assume this? Perhaps we should take ethical theories as encouraging indirection—getting what we want by seeking something else: e.g., some say the economic well-being of all is realized, not by everyone's seeking it but by everyone's seeking his/her own well-being....

It may not be very troubling to talk about indirection in such large-scale and multi-person matters as the economics of society. But in regard to something of such personal concern, so close to and so internal to a person as ethics, talk of indirection is both implausible and baffling. Implausible in that we do not seem to act by indirection, at least not in such areas as love, friendship, affection, fellow feeling, and community. In these cases, our motive has to do directly with the loved one, the friend,..., as does our reason. In doing something for a loved child or parent, there is no need to appeal to, or even

think of, the reasons found in contemporary ethical theories. Talk of indirection is baffling, in an action- and understanding-defeating sense, since, once we begin to believe that there is something beyond such activities as love which is necessary to justify them, it is only by something akin to self-deception that we are able to continue them.

One partial defense of these ethical theories would be that they are not intended to supply what can serve as both reasons and motives; that they are intended only to supply indices of goodness and rightness, not determinants. Formally, there may be no problems in taking ethical theories this way. But several questions do arise. Why should we be concerned with such theories, theories that cannot he acted on? Why not simply have a theory that allows for harmony between reason and motive? A theory that gives determinants? And indeed, will we not need to have such a theory? True, our pre-analytic views might be sufficient to judge among index theories; we may not need a determinant theory to pick out a correct index theory. But will we not need a determinant theory to know why the index is correct, why it works, to know what is good about what is so indexed?

Another partial defense of recent theories would be that, first, they are concerned almost entirely with rightness, obligation, and duty, and not with the whole of ethics; and, second, that within this restricted area, they do not suffer from disharmony or schizophrenia. To some extent this defense, especially its second point, has been dealt with earlier. But more should be said. It is perhaps clear enough by now that recent ethicists have ignored large and extremely important areas of morality—e.g., that of personal relations and that of merit. To this extent, the first point of the defense is correct.

What is far from clear, however, is whether these theories were advanced only as partial theories, or whether it was believed by their proponents that duty and so on were really the whole, or at least the only important part, of ethics.

We might be advised to forget past motivation and belief, and simply look at these theories and see what use can be made of them. Perhaps they were mistaken about the scope and importance of duty and so on. Nonetheless they could be correct about the concepts involved. In reply, several points should be made. First, they were mistaken about these concepts, as even a brief study of supererogation and self-regarding notions would indicate. Second, these theories are dangerously misleading; for they can all too readily be taken as suggesting that all of ethics can be treated in an external, legislation-model, index way…. Third, the acceptance of such theories as partial theories would pose severe difficulties of integration within ethical theory. Since these theories are so different from those concerning, e.g., personal relations, how are they all to be integrated? Of course, this third point may not be a criticism of these theories of duty, but only a recognition of the great diversity and complexity of our moral life.

In conclusion, it might be asked how contemporary ethical theories come to require either a stunted moral life or disharmony, schizophrenia. One cluster of (somewhat speculative) answers surrounds the preeminence of duty, rightness, and obligation in these theories. This preeminence fits naturally with theories developed in a time of diminishing personal relations; of a time when the ties holding people together and easing the frictions of their various enterprises were less and less affection; of a time when commercial relations superseded family (or family-like) relations; of a time of growing individual-ism. It also fits naturally with a major concern of those philosophers: legislation. When concerned with legislation, they were concerned with duty, rightness, obligation…. When viewing morality from such a legislator's point of view, taking such legislation to be the model, motivation too easily becomes irrelevant. The legislator wants various things done or not done; it is not important why they are done or not done; one can count on and know the actions, but not the motives. (This is also tied up with a general devaluing of our emotions and emotional possibilities—taking emotions to be mere feelings or urges, without rational or cognitive content or constraint; and taking us to be pleasure-seekers and pain-avoiders—forgetting or denying that love, friendship, affection, fellow feeling, and desire for virtue are extremely strong movers of people.) Connected with this is the legislative or simply the third-person's-eye view, which assures us that others are getting on well if they are happy, if they are doing what gives them pleasure, and the like….

Why have I said that contemporary ethics suffers from schizophrenia, bifurcation, disharmony? Why have I not claimed simply that these theories are mistaken in their denomination of what is good and bad, right- and wrong-making? For it is clear enough that, if we aim for the wrong goal, then (in all likelihood) we will not achieve what we really want, what is good, and the like. My reason for claiming more than a mere mistake is that the mistake is well reasoned; it is closely related to the truth, it bears many of the features of the truth. To take only two examples (barring bad fortune and bad circumstances), good activity does bring about pleasure; love clearly benefits the lover. There is, thus, great plausibility in taking as good what these theories advance as good. But when we try to act on the theories, try to embody their reasons in our motives—as opposed to simply seeing whether our or others' lives would be approved of by the theories—then in a quite mad way, things start going wrong. The personalities of loved ones get passed over for their effects, moral action becomes self-stultifying and self-defeating. And perhaps the greatest madnesses of all are—and they stand in a vicious interrelation—first, the world is increasingly made such as to make these theories correct; and, second, we take these theories to be correct and thus come to see love, friendship, and the like only as possible, and not very certain, sources of pleasure or whatever. We mistake the effect for the cause and when the cause-seen-as-effect fails to result from the effect-seen-as-cause, we devalue the former, relegating it, at best, to good as a means and embrace the latter, wondering why our chosen goods are so hollow, bitter, and inhumane.

Consequentialism Can Accommodate the Value of Friendship

Peter Railton

INTRODUCTION

Living up to the demands of morality may bring with it alienation—from one's personal commitments, from one's feelings or sentiments, from other people, or even from morality itself. In this article I will discuss several apparent instances of such alienation, and attempt a preliminary assessment of their bearing on questions about the acceptability of certain moral theories. Of special concern will be the question whether problems about alienation show consequentialist moral theories to be self-defeating.

I will not attempt a full or general characterization of alienation. Indeed, at a perfectly general level alienation can be characterized only very roughly as a kind of estrangement, distancing, or separateness (not necessarily consciously attended to) resulting in some sort of loss (not necessarily consciously noticed). Rather than seek a general analysis I will rely upon examples to convey a sense of what is involved in the sorts of alienation with which I am concerned....

JOHN AND ANNE AND LISA AND HELEN

To many, John has always seemed a model husband. He almost invariably shows great sensitivity to his wife's needs, and he willingly goes out of his way to meet them. He plainly feels great affection for her. When a friend remarks upon the extraordinary quality of John's concern for his wife, John responds without any self-indulgence or self-congratulation. "I've al- ways thought that people should help each other when they're in a specially good position to do so. I know Anne better than anyone else does, so I know better what she wants and needs. Besides, I have such affection for her that it's no great burden—instead, I get a lot of satisfaction out of it. Just think how awful marriage would be, or life itself, if people didn't take special care of the ones they love."...

Lisa has gone through a series of disappointments over a short period, and has been profoundly depressed. In the end, however, with the help of others she has emerged from the long night of anxiety and melancholy. Only now is she able to talk openly with friends about her state of mind, and she turns to her oldest friend, Helen, who was a mainstay throughout. She'd like to find a way to thank Helen, since she's only too aware of how much of a burden she's been over these months, how much of a drag and a bore, as she puts it. "You don't have to thank me, Lisa," Helen replies, "you deserved it. It was the least I could do after all you've done for me. We're friends, remember? And we said a long time ago that we'd stick together no matter what. Some day I'll probably ask the same thing of you, and I know you'll come through. What else are friends for?"...

WHAT'S MISSING?

What is troubling about the words of John and Helen? Both show stout character and moral awareness. John's remarks have a benevolent, consequentialist cast, while Helen reasons in a deontological language of duties, reciprocity, and respect. They are not self-centered or without feeling. Yet something seems wrong.

The place to look is not so much at what they say as what they don't say. Think, for example, of how John's remarks might sound to his wife. Anne might have hoped that it was, in some ultimate sense, in part for *her* sake and the sake of their love as such that John pays such special attention to her. That he devotes himself to her because of the characteristically good consequences of doing so seems to leave her, and their relationship as such, too far out of the picture—this despite the fact that these characteristically good consequences depend in important ways on his special relation to her. She is being taken into account by John, but it might seem she is justified in being hurt by the way she is being taken into account. It is as if John viewed her, their relationship, and even his own affection for her from a distant, objective point of view—a moral point of view where reasons must be reasons for any rational agent and so must have an impersonal character even when they deal with personal matters. His wife might think a more personal point of view would also be appropriate, a point of view from which "It's my wife" or "It's Anne" would have direct and special relevance, and play an unmediated role in his answer to the question "*Why* do you attend to her so?"

Something similar is missing from Helen's account of why she stood by Lisa. While we understand that the specific duties she feels toward Lisa depend upon particular features of their relationship, still we would not be surprised if Lisa finds Helen's response to her expression of gratitude quite distant, even chilling. We need not question whether she has strong feeling for Lisa, but we may wonder at how that feeling finds expression in Helen's thinking.

John and Helen both show alienation: there would seem to be an estrangement between their affections and their rational, deliberative selves; an abstract and universalizing point of view mediates their reponses to others and to their own sentiments. We should not assume that they have been caught in an uncharacteristic moment of moral reflection or after-the-fact rationalization; it is a settled part of their characters to think and act from a moral point of view. It is as if the world were for them a fabric of obligations and permissions in which personal considerations deserve recognition only to the extent that, and in the way that, such considerations find a place in this fabric....

THE MORAL POINT OF VIEW

Perhaps the lives of John and Anne or Helen and Lisa would be happier or fuller if none of the alienation mentioned were present. But is this a problem for *morality?* If, as some have contended, to have a morality is to make normative judgments from a moral point of view and be guided by them, and if by its nature a moral point of view must exclude considerations that lack universality, then any genuinely moral way of going about life would seem liable to produce the sorts of alienation mentioned above. Thus it would be a conceptual confusion to ask that we never be required by morality to go beyond a personal point of view, since to fail ever to look at things from an impersonal (or nonpersonal) point of view would be to fail ever to *be* distinctively moral—not immoralism, perhaps, but amoralism. This would not be to say that there are not other points of view on life worthy of our attention, or that taking a moral point of view is always appropriate—one could say that John and Helen show no moral defect in thinking so impersonally, although they do moralize to excess. But the fact that a particular morality requires us to take an impersonal point of view could not sensibly be held against it, for that would be what makes it a morality at all.

This sort of position strikes me as entirely too complacent. First, we must somehow give an account of practical reasoning that does not merely multiply points of view and divide the self—a more unified account is needed. Second, we must recognize that loving relationships, friendships, group loyalties, and spontaneous actions are among the most important contributors to whatever it is that makes life worthwhile; any moral theory deserving serious consideration must itself give them serious consideration. As William K. Frankena has written, "Morality is made for man, not man for morality." Moral considerations are often supposed to be overriding in practical reasoning. If we were to find that adopting a particular morality led to irreconcilable conflict with central types of human well-being—as cases akin to John's and Helen's have led some to suspect—then this surely would give us good reason to doubt its claims....

Should we say at this point that the lesson is that we should give a more prominent role to the value of non-alienation in our moral reasoning? That would be too little too late: the problem seems to be the way in which morality asks us to look at things, not just the things it asks us to look at....

REDUCING ALIENATION IN MORALITY

Let us now move to morality proper. To do this with any definiteness, we must have a particular morality in mind. For various reasons, I think that the most plausible sort of morality is consequentialist in form, assessing rightness in terms of contribution to the good. In attempting to sketch how we might reduce alienation in moral theory and practice, therefore, I will work within a consequentialist framework....

Of course, one has adopted no morality in particular even in adopting consequentialism unless one says what the good is. Let us, then, dwell briefly on axiology. One mistake of dominant consequentialist theories, I believe, is their failure to see that things other than subjective states can have intrinsic value. Allied to this is a tendency to reduce all intrinsic values to one—happiness. Both of these features of classical utilitarianism reflect forms of alienation. First, in divorcing subjective states from their objective counterparts, and claiming that we seek the latter exclusively for the sake of the former, utilitarianism cuts us off from the world in a way made graphic by examples such as that of the experience machine, a hypothetical device that can be programmed to provide one with whatever subjective states he may desire. The experience machine affords us decisive subjective advantages over actual life: few, if any, in actual life think they have achieved all that they could want, but the machine makes possible for each an existence that he cannot distinguish from such a happy state of affairs. Despite this striking advantage, most rebel at the notion of the experience machine. As Robert Nozick and others have pointed out, it seems to matter to us what we actually *do* and *are* as well as how life *appears* to us. We see the point of our lives as bound up with the world and other people in ways not captured by subjectivism, and our sense of loss in contemplating a life tied to an experience machine, quite literally alienated from the surrounding world, suggests where subjectivism has gone astray. Second, the reduction of all goals to the purely abstract goal of happiness or pleasure, as in hedonistic utilitarianism, treats all other goals instrumentally. Knowledge or friendship may promote happiness, but is it a fair characterization of our commitment to these goals to say that this is the only sense in which they are ultimately valuable? Doesn't the insistence that there is an abstract and uniform goal lying behind all of our ends bespeak an alienation from these particular ends?

Rather than pursue these questions further here, let me suggest an approach to the good that seems to me less hopeless as a way of capturing human value: a pluralistic approach in which several goods are viewed as intrinsically, non-morally valuable—such as happiness, knowledge, purposeful activity, autonomy, solidarity, respect, and beauty. These goods need not be ranked lexically, but may be attributed weights, and the criterion of rightness for an act would be that it must contribute to the weighted sum of these values in the long run....

Consider, then, Juan, who, like John, has always seemed a model husband. When a friend remarks on the extraordinary concern he shows for his wife, Juan characteristically responds: "I love Linda. I even *like* her. So it means a lot to me to do things for her. After all we've been through, it's almost a part of me to do it." But his friend knows that Juan is a principled individual, and asks Juan how his marriage fits into that larger scheme. After all, he asks, it's fine for Juan and his wife to have such a close relationship, but what about all the other, needier people Juan could help if he broadened his horizon still further? Juan replies, "Look, it's a better world when people can have a relationship like ours—and nobody could if everyone were always asking themselves who's got the most need. It's not easy to make things work in this world, and one of the best things that happens to people is to have a close relationship like ours. You'd make things worse in a hurry if you broke up those close relationships for the sake of some higher goal. Anyhow, I know that you can't always put family first. The world isn't such a wonderful place that it's OK just to retreat into your own little circle. But still, you need that little circle. People get burned out, or lose touch, if they try to save the world by themselves. The ones who can stick with it and do a good job of making things better are usually the ones who can make that fit into a life that does not make them miserable. I haven't met any real saints lately, and I don't trust people who think they *are* saints."

If we contrast Juan with John, we do not find that the one allows moral considerations to enter his personal life while the other does not. Nor do we find that one is less serious in his moral concern. Rather, what Juan recognizes to be morally required is not by its nature incompatible with acting directly for the sake of another. It is important to Juan to subject his life to moral scrutiny—he is not merely stumped when asked for a defense of his acts above a personal level, he does not *just* say "Of course I take care of her, she's my wife!" or "It's Linda" and refuse to listen to the more impersonal considerations raised by his friend. It is consistent with what he says to imagine that his motivational structure has a form akin to that of the sophisticated hedonist, that is, his motivational structure meets a counterfactual condition: while he ordinarily does not do what he does simply for the sake of doing what's right, he would seek to lead a different sort of life if he did not think his were morally defensible. His love is not a romantic submersion in the other to the exclusion of worldly responsibilities, and to that extent it may be said to involve a degree of alienation from Linda. But this does not seem to drain human value from their relationship. Nor need one imagine that Linda would be saddened to hear Juan's words the way Anne might have been saddened to overhear the remarks of John.

Moreover, because of his very willingness to question his life morally, Juan avoids a sort of alienation not sufficiently discussed—alienation from others, beyond one's intimate ties. Individuals who will not or cannot allow questions to arise about what they are doing from a broader perspective are in an important way cut off from their society and the larger world. They may not be troubled by this in any very direct way, but even so they may fail to experience that powerful sense of purpose and meaning that comes from seeing oneself as part of something larger and more enduring than oneself or one's intimate circle. The search for such a sense of purpose and meaning seems to me ubiquitous—surely much of the impulse to religion, to ethnic or regional identification (most strikingly, in the "rediscovery" of such identities), or to institutional loyalty stems from this desire to see ourselves as part of a more general, lasting, and worthwhile scheme of things....

Let us now distinguish two kinds of consequentialism. *Subjective consequentialism* is the view that whenever one faces a choice of actions, one should attempt to determine which act of those available would most promote the good, and should then try to act accordingly. One is behaving as subjective consequentialism requires—that is, leading a *subjectively consequentialist life*—to the extent that one uses and follows a distinctively consequentialist mode of decision making, consciously aiming at the overall good and conscientiously using the best available information with the greatest possible rigor. *Objective consequentialism* is the view that

the criterion of the rightness of an act or course of action is whether it in fact would most promote the good of those acts available to the agent. Subjective consequentialism,... is a view that prescribes following a particular mode of deliberation in action; objective consequentialism,... concerns the outcomes actually brought about, and thus deals with the question of deliberation only in terms of the tendencies of certain forms of decision making to promote appropriate outcomes. Let us reserve the expression *objectively consequentialist act (or life)* for those acts (or that life) of those available to the agent that would bring about the best outcomes.... Let us say that a *sophisticated consequentialist* is someone who has a standing commitment to leading an objectively consequentialist life, but who need not set special stock in any particular form of decision making and therefore does not necessarily seek to lead a subjectively consequentialist life. Juan, it might be argued (if the details were filled in), is a sophisticated consequentialist, since he seems to believe he should act for the best but does not seem to feel it appropriate to bring a consequentialist calculus to bear on his every act.

Is it bizarre, or contradictory, that being a sophisticated consequentialist may involve rejecting subjective consequentialism? After all, doesn't an adherent of subjective consequentialism also seek to lead an objectively consequentialist life? He may, but then he is mistaken in thinking that this means he should always undertake a distinctively consequentialist deliberation when faced with a choice. To see his mistake, we need only consider some examples.

It is well known that in certain emergencies, the best outcome requires action so swift as to preclude consequentialist deliberation. Thus a sophisticated consequentialist has reason to inculcate in himself certain dispositions to act rapidly in obvious emergencies. The disposition is not a mere reflex, but a developed pattern of action deliberately acquired....

There are somewhat more intriguing examples that have more to do with psychological interference than mere time efficiency: the timid, put-upon employee who knows that if he deliberates about whether to ask for a raise he will succumb to his timidity and fail to demand what he actually deserves; the self-conscious man who knows that if, at social gatherings, he is forever wondering how he should act, his behavior will be awkward and unnatural, contrary to his goal of acting naturally.... People can learn to avoid certain characteristically self-defeating lines of thought... and the sophisticated consequentialist may learn that consequentialist deliberation is in a variety of cases self-defeating, so that other habits of thought should be cultivated.

The sophisticated consequentialist need not be deceiving himself or acting in bad faith when he avoids consequentialist reasoning. He can fully recognize that he is developing the dispositions he does because they are necessary for promoting the good. Of course, he cannot be *preoccupied* with this fact all the while, but then one cannot be preoccupied with anything without this interfering with normal or appropriate patterns of thought and action.

To the list of cases of interference we may add John, whose all-purpose willingness to look at things by subjective consequentialist lights prevents the realization in him and in his relationships with others of values that he would recognize to be crucially important....

CONTRASTING APPROACHES

The seeming "indirectness" of objective consequentialism may invite its confusion with familiar indirect consequentialist theories, such as rule-consequentialism. In fact, the subjective/objective distinction cuts across the rule/act distinction, and there are subjective and objective forms of both rule- and act-based theories. Thus far, we have dealt only with subjective and objective forms of act-consequentialism. By contrast, a *subjective rule*-consequentialist holds (roughly) that in deliberation we should always attempt to determine which act, of those available, conforms to that set of rules general acceptance of which would most promote the good; we then should attempt to perform this act. An *objective rule*-consequentialist sets actual conformity to the rules with the highest acceptance value as his criterion of right action, recognizing the possibility that the best set of rules might in some cases—or even always—recommend that one not perform rule-consequentialist deliberation.

Because I believe this last possibility must be taken seriously, I find the objective form of rule-consequentialism more plausible. Ultimately, however, I suspect that rule-consequentialism is untenable in either form, for it could recommend acts that (subjectively or objectively) accord with the best set of rules even when these rules are *not* in fact generally accepted, and when as a result these acts would have devastatingly bad consequences.... Hence, the arguments in this article are based entirely upon act-consequentialism.

Indeed, once the subjective/objective distinction has been drawn, an act-consequentialist can capture some of the intuitions that have made rule- or trait-consequentialism appealing. Surely part of the attraction of these indirect consequentialisms is the idea that one should have certain traits of character, or commitments to persons or principles, that are sturdy enough that one would at least sometimes refuse to forsake them even when this refusal is known to conflict with making some gain—perhaps small—in total utility. Unlike his subjective counterpart, the objective act-consequentialist is able to endorse characters and commitments that are sturdy in just this sense.

To see why, let us first return briefly to one of the simple examples.... A sophisticated act-consequentialist may recognize that if he were to develop a standing disposition to render prompt assistance in emergencies without going through elaborate act-consequentialist deliberation, there would almost certainly be cases in which he would perform acts worse than those he would have performed had he stopped to deliberate, for example, when his prompt action is misguided in a way he would have noticed had he thought the matter through. It may still be right for him to develop this disposition, for without it he would act rightly in emergencies still less often—a quick response is appropriate much more often than not, and it is not practically possible to develop a disposition that would lead one to respond promptly in exactly those cases where this would have the best results. While one can attempt to cultivate dispositions that are responsive to various factors which might indicate whether promptness is of greater importance than further thought, such refinements have their own costs and, given the limits of human resources, even the best cultivated dispositions will sometimes lead one astray. The objective act-consequentialist would thus recommend cultivating dispositions that will sometimes lead him to violate his own criterion of right action. Still, he will not, as a trait-consequentialist would, shift his criterion and say that an act is right if it stems from the traits it would be best overall to have (given the limits of what is humanly achievable, the balance of costs and benefits, and so on). Instead, he continues to believe that an act may stem from the dispositions it would be best to have, and yet be wrong (because it would produce worse consequences than other acts available to the agent in the circumstances).

This line of argument can be extended to patterns of motivation, traits of character, and rules. A sophisticated act-consequentialist should realize that certain goods are reliably attainable—or attainable at all—only if people have well-developed characters; that the human psyche is capable of only so much self-regulation and refinement; and that human perception and reasoning are liable to a host of biases and errors. Therefore, individuals may be more likely to act rightly if they possess certain enduring motivational patterns, character traits, or *prima facie* commitments to rules in addition to whatever commitment they have to act for the best. Because such individuals would not consider consequences in all cases, they would miss a number of opportunities to maximize the good; but if they were instead always to attempt to assess outcomes, the overall result would be worse, for they would act correctly less often.

We may now strengthen the argument to show that the objective act-consequentialist can approve of dispositions, characters, or commitments to rules that are sturdy in the sense mentioned above, that is, that do not merely supplement a commitment to act for the best, but sometimes override it, so that one knowingly does what is contrary to maximizing the good. Consider again Juan and Linda, whom we imagine to have a commuting marriage. They normally get together only every other week, but one week she seems a bit depressed and harried, and so he decides to take an extra trip in order to be with her. If he did not travel, he would save a fairly large sum that he could send OXFAM to dig a well in a drought-stricken village. Even reckoning in Linda's uninterrupted malaise, Juan's guilt, and any ill effects on their relationship, it may be that for Juan to contribute the fare to OXFAM would produce better consequences overall than the unscheduled trip. Let us suppose that Juan knows this, and that he could stay home and write the check if he tried. Still, given Juan's character, he in fact will not try to perform this more beneficial act but will travel to see Linda instead. The objective act-consequentialist will say that Juan performed the wrong act on this occasion. Yet he may also say that if Juan had had a character that would have led him to perform the better act (or made him more inclined to do so), he would have had to have been less devoted to Linda. Given the ways Juan can affect the world, it may be that if he were less devoted to Linda his overall contribution to human well-being would be less in the end, perhaps because he would become more cynical and self-centered. Thus it may be that Juan should have (should develop, encourage, and so on) a character such that he sometimes knowingly and deliberately acts contrary to his objective consequentialist duty. Any other character, of those actually available to him, would lead him to depart still further from an objectively consequentialist life. The issue is not whether staying home would *change* Juan's character—for we may suppose that it would not—but whether he would in fact decide to stay home if he had that character, of those available, that would lead him to perform the most beneficial overall sequence of acts....

ALIENATION FROM MORALITY

By way of conclusion, I would like to turn to alienation from morality itself, the experience (conscious or unconscious) of morality as an external set of demands not rooted in our lives or accommodating to our perspectives. Giving a convincing answer to the question "Why should I be moral?" must involve diminishing the extent that morality appears alien.

Part of constructing such an answer is a matter of showing that abiding by morality need not alienate us from the particular commitments that make life worthwhile, and in the previous sections we have begun to see how this might be possible within an objective act-consequentialist account of what morality requires. We saw how in general various sorts of projects or relationships can continue to be a source of intrinsic value even though one recognizes that they might have to undergo changes if they could not be defended in their present form on moral grounds. And again, knowing that a commitment is morally defensible may well deepen its value for us, and may also make it possible for us to feel part of a larger world in a way that is itself of great value. If our commitments are regarded by others as responsible and valuable (or if we have reason to think that others should so regard them), this may enhance the meaning or value they have for ourselves, while if they are regarded by others as irresponsible or worthless (especially, if we suspect that others regard them so justly), this may make it more difficult for us to identify with them or find purpose or value in them. Our almost universal urge to rationalize our acts and lives attests our wish to see what we do as defensible from a more general point of view....

These remarks about the role of general perspectives in individual lives lead us to what I think is an equally important part of answering the question "Why should I be moral?": reconceptualization of the terms of the discussion to avoid starting off in an alienated fashion and ending up with the result that morality still seems alien....

Morality may be conceived of as in essence selfless, impartial, impersonal. To act morally is to subordinate the self and all contingencies concerning the self's relations with others or the world to a set of imperatives binding on us solely as rational beings. We should be moral, in this view, because it is ideally rational. However, morality thus conceived seems bound to appear as alien in daily life....

As a start, let us begin with individuals situated in society, complete with identities, commitments, and social relations. What are the ingredients of such identities, commitments, and relations? When one studies relationships of deep commitment—of parent to child, or wife to husband—at close range, it becomes artificial to impose a dichotomy between what is done for the self and what is done for the other. We cannot decompose such relationships into a vector of self-concern and a vector of other concern, even though concern for the self and the other are both present. The other has come to figure in the self in a fundamental way—or, perhaps a better way of putting it, the other has become a reference point of the self. If it is part of one's identity to be the parent of Jill or the husband of Linda, then the self has reference points beyond the ego, and that which affects these reference points may affect the self in an unmediated way.

These reference points do not all fall within the circle of intimate relationships, either. Among the most important constituents of identities are social, cultural, or religious ties—one is a Jew, a Southerner, a farmer, or an alumnus of Old Ivy. Our identities exist in relational, not absolute space, and except as they are fixed by reference points in others, in society, in culture, or in some larger constellation still, they are not fixed at all....

A system of available, shared meanings would seem to be a precondition for sustaining the meaningfulness of individual lives in familiar sorts of social arrangements. Moreover, in such arrangements identity and self-significance seem to depend in part upon the significance of others to the self. If we are prepared to say that a sense of meaningfulness is a precondition for much else in life, then we may be on the way to answering the question "Why should I be moral?" for we have gone beyond pure egocentrism precisely by appealing to facts about the self.... By adopting a non-alienated starting point—that of situated rather than presocial individuals—and by showing how some of the alienation associated with bringing morality to bear on our lives might be avoided, perhaps we have reduced the extent to which morality seems alien to us by its nature.

THE CONTINUING DEBATE:
Can Consequentialism Make Room for Friendship?

What Is New

Utilitarian ethics originated in concern for large public and political issues (what policies should the government adopt, what is the best way of distributing resources), and some utilitarians are trying to refocus there, with less attempt to make utilitarianism a theory of personal or family ethics. Whether that distinction can be preserved—after all, when we devote our resources to our families, we choose not to use them to alleviate hunger abroad—is a debated question.

In addition to the utilitarian distinctions already discussed—Act/Rule, Hedonist/Pluralist/Preference, and Subjective/Objective—contemporary utilitarians also distinguish between *maximizing* and *satisficing* (Michael Slote's term) forms of consequentialism: Most utilitarians have held that the right act is the act which produces the *maximum* utility; but satisficing utilitarians argue that maximizing utility makes demands that are too strong, and our obligation is to insure that our acts have positive consequences rather than the best possible consequences. Another issue concerns *whose* consequences must be considered in the utilitarian calculation. Jeremy Bentham maintained that the pleasure and suffering of *all* sentient creatures must be included, a position followed by Peter Singer; however, some utilitarians place restrictions.

Where to Find More

The classic utilitarian writings are Jeremy Bentham, *An Introduction to the Principles of Morals and Legislation* (London: 1823) and John Stuart Mill, *Utilitarianism* (London:1863). Perhaps the most influential contemporary utilitarian, and certainly one of the most readable, is Peter Singer. His *Writings on an Ethical Life* (NY: HarperCollins, 2000) is the work of a philosopher thinking carefully about ethical obligations, and sincerely striving to live his life by his utilitarian principles.

For a critique of utilitarian ethics, see Samuel Scheffler, *The Rejection of Consequentialism* (Oxford: Clarendon Press, 1982). An excellent debate on utilitarian ethics can be found in J. J. C. Smart and Bernard Williams, *Utilitarianism: For and Against* (Cambridge: Cambridge University Press, 1973). Bernard Williams' influential criticisms of utilitarianism can also be found in "Persons, Character, and Morality," in Bernard Williams, *Moral Luck* (Cambridge: Cambridge University Press, 1981). Robert Nozick's pleasure machine argument (directed against one form of utilitarianism, and discussed by Railton) is found in *Anarchy, State, and Utopia* (NY: Basic Books, 1974), starting on page 42. A response to Nozick—along with other interesting essays on utilitarianism—can be found in Fred Feldman, *Utilitarianism, Hedonism, and Desert* (Cambridge: Cambridge University Press, 1997); see especially the essay "Two Questions About Pleasure."

Robert E. Goodin, "Utility and the Good," in Peter Singer, editor, *A Companion to Ethics* (Oxford: Blackwell, 1991), offers a particularly clear account of the view that utilitarianism is best considered as a guide to public and legislative (rather than personal) ethics. See also Philip Pettit, "Consequentialism," in the same volume, for an excellent brief examination of contemporary consequentialism.

Michael Slote's conception of "satisficing consequentialism" can be found in "Satisficing Consequentialism," *Proceedings of the Aristotelian Society*, volume 58 (1984); and *Common-Sense Morality and Consequentialism* (London: Routledge and Kegan Paul, 1985).

Elinor Mason, "Do Consequentialists Have One Thought Too Many?" *Ethical Theory and Moral Practice*, volume 2 (1999), responds to some of the arguments by Williams and Stocker.

Among the many excellent anthologies on consequentialism and utilitarianism are Amartya Sen and Bernard Williams, editors, *Utilitarianism and Beyond* (Cambridge: Cambridge University Press, 1982); Samuel Scheffler, editor, *Consequentialism and its Critics* (Oxford: Clarendon Press, 1988); Philip Pettit, *Consequentialism* (Aldershot, Hants: Dartmouth, 1993); Brad Hooker, Elinor Mason, and Dale E. Miller, editors, *Morality, Rules, and Consequences: A Critical Reader* (Lanham, MD: Rowman & Littlefield, 2000); and Stephen Darwall, *Consequentialism* (Malden, MA: Blackwell, 2003).

Three Methods of Ethics: A Debate, by Marcia W. Baron, Philip Pettit, and Michael Slote (NY: Oxford University Press, 1993) is a well-argued debate among thoughtful and capable champions of Kantian, consequentialist, and virtue ethics.

For more on the question of ethics and alienation, and more on Railton's views on this subject, see debate 15.

Walter Sinnott-Armstrong provides an excellent account of contemporary consequentialism in the online *Stanford Encyclopedia of Philosophy*; go to *http://plato. stanford.edu/entries/consequentialism*.

5 MORALITY: UNIVERSAL PRINCIPLES OF JUSTICE *OR* SPECIFIC CARING RELATIONSHIPS?

CARING RELATIONSHIPS CAN TAKE PRECEDENCE

ADVOCATE: Virginia Held, Distinguished Professor of Philosophy at the City University Graduate Center of the City University of New York, and a well-known ethicist whose books include *Feminist Morality: Transforming Culture, Society, and Politics* (Chicago: University of Chicago Press, 1993); and *Rights and Goods: Justifying Social Action* (NY: The Free Press, 1984).

SOURCE: "Caring Relations and Principles of Justice," *Controversies in Feminism*, edited by James P. Sterba (Lanham, MD: Rowman & Littlefield Publishers, 2001): 67–81.

JUSTICE AND CARE OPERATE TOGETHER

ADVOCATE: Claudia Card, Emma Goldman Professor of Philosophy, University of Wisconsin; author of *The Unnatural Lottery: Character and Moral Luck* (Philadelphia: Temple University Press, 1996) and *The Atrocity Paradigm: A Theory of Evil* (NY: Oxford University Press, 2002); editor of *On Feminist Ethics and Politics* (Lawrence, KS: University Press of Kansas, 1999).

SOURCE: "Particular Justice and General Care," *Controversies in Feminism*, edited by James P. Sterba (Lanham, MD: Rowman & Littlefield Publishers, 2001): 99–105.

This is a distinctly new version of the controversy that has continued since David Hume and Immanuel Kant (and long before), and is also represented in Debate 2. On one side are those who view ethics as a rule-governed enterprise that depends primarily or even *exclusively* on our rational deliberative powers (whether the rules are given by pure reason or through utilitarian calculations). On the other side are ethicists who maintain that ethical behavior is primarily—though not exclusively—guided by our feelings (such as affection, care, pity, friendship). In this particular version of the debate, however, the positions taken are considerably more subtle and nuanced.

For those like Virginia Held, who emphasize the importance of caring and affection, the important questions cannot be resolved by making space for special caring relations within the rules of impartial justice. From the care ethics perspective, this distorts the nature of the special relations of love and care and friendship we have with family and friends. These are relations that cannot be represented accurately in terms of general rules and principles, because the special particularity of the relations is part of their very nature. A system that makes all of ethics a matter of impartial rules involves the systematic neglect of a vital part of our ethical lives. On the other side, ethicists such as Martha Nussbaum grant the importance of caring, but insist on the special importance of universal principles of justice that govern even our caring relationships; without such principles, it is too easy for caring relationships to become exploitative and for family structures to be autocratic and demeaning.

Virginia Held recognizes the importance of impartial justice, but challenges the view that the requirements of impartial justice should always take precedence over special commitments to friends and family; and she emphasizes that caring relationships cannot be adequately understood or fully appreciated using exclusively the language of rights and justice. Claudia Card agrees with Held that we cannot automatically give preference to impartial justice demands over the concerns of particular friendships and affections, though she is not convinced that such concerns cannot be part of a larger conception of justice; and in particular, Card raises doubts about drawing any clear line between care ethics and principles of justice.

POINTS TO PONDER

➤ Suppose that we are convinced by Virginia Held that special relations of friendship and affection should *sometimes* override principles of impartial justice. Obviously there could be some cases where we still thought that rules of impartial justice *should* override any special consideration for friends and family: It would be wrong to rig an election for my sister, wrong to provide an alibi for a friend whom we discover is a serial killer. Does that imply, then, that we must have some higher order principle of impartial justice to guide us in weighing the limits of special partiality?

➤ Imagine a defender of impartial rationalist ethics—in a debate with Virginia Held. The impartial retionalist asserts that his view does not deny the importance of personal relationships, and acknowledges that in some circumstances it is legitimate to be partial toward one's friends and loved ones (perhaps in showing them special affection or doing special favors for them). But, he argues, when there is a conflict between the demands of impartial justice and the feelings of affection and partiality, then justice must always take precedence. Thus, he continues, my view offers a well-ordered ethical system, that gives us clear guidance when we face moral quandaries. Your position, he says to Held, leaves us with moral dilemmas and no clear means of resolving them. Suppose that Held replies: That's quite true; but that's an advantage of my position, not a flaw. Ethical decision-making is *not* as neat and rational as your impartialist rationality represents it to be.

At that point in the discussion, is there anything further that either side could say to convince the other?

➤ *Suppose* that it is true, as Held claims, that ethical decisions cannot always be reached in a neat, precise, and decisive manner. Would *you* find that pleasing or distressing?

➤ When considering the ethical issues surrounding particular relationships of affection and friendship, Claudia Card prefers to characterize them as issues of "particular justice" rather than as distinctive issues of "care ethics" (the designation preferred by Held). What is the significance of that difference? Is it merely terminological?

Caring Relationships Can Take Precedence

VIRGINIA HELD

THE CONTROVERSY

The question of whether impartial, universal, and rational moral principles must always be given priority over other possible grounds for moral motivation continues to provoke extensive debate. David Velleman has recently added his defense of Kantian ethics to those offered by others against recent challenges to the priority of impartial rules. The challenges have come from Bernard Williams, among others, and especially from certain advocates of a feminist ethic of care….

Velleman concentrates on the case that Bernard Williams discusses, originally put forward by Charles Fried and much discussed since, of whether a man may justifiably save his wife rather than a stranger, if he can save only one. Williams suggests that if the man stops to think about whether universal principles could permit him to give special consideration to his wife rather than treating both persons impartially, the man is having "one thought too many." Velleman argues that Kantian principles would include, not deny, that we have special responsibilities for the members of our families and that these can be consistently universalized, so there need be no conflict here. One commentator, Thomas Hill, changed the example to avoid any sexist stereotypes involved, but agreed with the defense of Kantian impartiality against this kind of attack. Harry Frankfurt, another commentator, gave more support to Williams's critique, but none of the three addressed the feminist versions of the challenge to Kantian principles, which resemble Williams's in some respects and differ from it in others.

Williams's arguments are presented from the point of view of a man with a set of projects, the sorts of projects that make life worth living for this man. The image, like its Kantian alternative, is still that of an individual deliberator. Williams pits the individual's particular goals—to live life with his wife or, in another case, to be a painter—against the individual's rational and impartial moral principles, and he doubts that the latter should always have priority. Williams disputes the view that our particular projects must always be constrained by universal principles requiring that we should only pursue what universal principles permit. If a man's life would be worth living only if he put, for example, his art ahead of his universalizable moral obligations to his family, Williams is not willing to give priority to his moral obligations. In the example of the man and the drowning others, the man's wife may be his project, but the dilemma is posed in terms of an individual's own particular goals versus his universal moral obligations. At a formal level it remains within the traditional paradigm of egoism versus universalism. Williams is unwilling to yield the claims of the ego, especially those that enable it to continue to be the person it is, to the requitements of universalization. But he does not reject the traditional way of conceptualizing the alternatives. Like Thomas Nagel in *The Possibility of Altruism*, and most other philosophers before him, the problem is seen as pitting the claims of an individual ego against those of impartial rules.

The feminist challenge to Kantian moralities does require a change in this paradigm. It does not pit an individual ego against universal principles, but considers a particular relationship between persons, a caring relationship, and questions whether it should always yield to universal principles of justice. It sees the relationship as not reducible to the individual projects of its members. When universal principles conflict with the claims of relationships, the feminist challenge disputes that the principles should always have priority. The feminist critique of liberalism as moral theory and of Kantian morality gives us reason to doubt that, in terms of how the debate has been framed, justice should always have priority over care.

In his new book, *Justice as Impartiality*, Brian Barry devotes a considerable portion of Chapter 10 to the feminist critique of impartiality. He attributes it to misunderstandings. Thoroughly disparaging the work of Lawrence Kohlberg, the psychologist of moral development criticized by Carol Gilligan, Barry blames Kohlberg for the confusions that he thinks are responsible for the feminist critique of impartiality. Barry fails to see that much of what feminist moral philosophers have written about feminist morality and the ethics of care has little to do with Kohlberg, but does have a great deal to do with the kind of justice as impartiality defended by Barry.

Barry advocates what he formulates as second-order impartiality. This kind of impartiality requires that the moral and legal rules of a society be such that they are "capable of attaining the... assent of all" taken as free and equal individuals. This does not require or imply first-order

impartiality, the kind of impartiality that dictates that we should not be partial to our own friends and family members. Barry argues that as long as we can all accept the rules, these rules can, of course, permit us to give special consideration to our friends and families.

Barry points out that most second-order impartiality theories, such as John Rawls's theory of justice, are designed for judging institutions, not the actions of persons in personal situations, and for judging institutions in "nearly just" societies. This renders them of little use for recommending actions in the context of the seriously unjust conditions of currently existing institutions. According to Barry, there can be second-order impartiality theories that support the morality of breaking some bad laws rather than merely waiting for them to change. Thus, his arguments for impartiality are an improvement over many others. But Barry supports the position of impartialists generally in holding that justice, now formulated as second-order impartiality, always has priority over considerations of care, not just in legal but in all moral contexts. In Barry's view, care can justifiably be the basis of choice only after the demands of justice as impartiality have been met. He argues that there can be no genuine conflicts between the rules of justice and considerations of care: they deal with different matters. We are morally obligated to fulfill the requirements of impartiality, and then, we can be moved as we choose by our feelings for friends and family.

This interpretation of the issues side-steps rather than addresses the arguments of many defenders of the ethics of care. The latter question the priority of justice as impartiality (including second-order impartiality) and are not willing to relegate care to an optional choice about preferences once all the requirements of justice have been satisfied. These advocates of care deny that we are simply talking about different matters; they hold that those who defend the priority of justice and those advocating an ethic of care are, at least sometimes, both talking about the same topic—morality—and are disagreeing about it. The debates have often seen the issues as being about which kind of approach would be better for a given problem: the approach of justice or the approach of care? And they reject the view that considerations of care are appropriate only in personal relations after the rules of justice have decided them to be permissible. Questions of care can appropriately arise in public as well as personal contexts, and we can wonder at fundamental levels whether we should always treat people as if the liberal assumptions of impartial justice take priority in our dealings with them. Sometimes the points of view of care and of justice provide different moral evaluations of and recommendations for the same problems and matters. When they do, we need to choose between them rather than simply talking past each other.

Stephen Darwall is another philosopher who has tried to address the challenge presented by feminist ethics. He finds that the ethics of care usefully calls attention to the actual relationships that are such an important part of our lives. But he denies that the ethics of care really presents an alternative opposed to the moralities of impartial universal principles, the moralities of Kant and utilitarianism. He argues that we arrive at the basic idea of utilitarianism, "that everyone's welfare matters and matters equally," by thinking about why we value an actual particular child who engages our attention. We realize that it is because the particular child we care about is "someone with a conscious life that can be affected for good or ill," and that the sympathy we

feel for a particular child is something we can feel for any other. Similarly, according to Darwall, Kantian respect for persons "involves recognizing an individual's dignity or value in himself, but it is grounded in features that a person shares with any other moral agent." Hence, we extend to all persons the kind of respect we can recognize that an individual we know deserves. To Darwall, then, the ethics of care is a "supplement" to "morality as conceived by the moderns," but both aim at the same ideas of equal concern and respect.

This interpretation, like Barry's, fails to recognize the challenge to moralities of universal, impartial principles that the ethics of care, or Bernard Williams, present. And to an advocate of an ethic of care, Darwall's interpretation of what it is in our child that leads us to value or respect him is rather questionable in terms of descriptive persuasiveness. What a parent may value in her child may well not be what makes this child like every other, but the very particular relationship that exists between them such that she is the mother of this child, and this particular person is her child. If we think of how we would respond to the question "Why do you care about this child?" asked perhaps by an official of a hypothetical regime threatening to take the child for adoption by more favored parents, or for a scientific experiment authorized by the regime, we are probably more likely to imagine our response being "because she is my child" than "because she has a conscious life, like all children." This does not mean that we associate our child with our property, thinking of her as belonging to us, or thinking of ourselves as individuals who own our children as well as our property. Nor does it mean we think the reasons the government should or should not take our child are like the reasons it should or should not appropriate our property. The relationship we have with our child is very different from the relationship we have to our property. We might favor policies that would allow governments to appropriate significant amounts and kinds of property in ways that would be fair, yet strongly oppose policies that would sever bonds with our children, even if they would be fair.

In elaborating the reasons that the two kinds of cases are different, we might refer to the conscious life of our child and all other children, or to Kantian principles against treating persons as means. But the relationship between a particular child and a particular parent is a more plausible source of the valuing of each by the other than are the features they share with all other children and parents. And so if the moral recommendations grounded on this relationship ever conflict with the moral recommendations derived from universal moral principles, the problem of which has priority remains, despite Darwall's efforts to dissolve it.

DIFFERENCES AMONG FEMINISTS

Martha Nussbaum is another philosopher who argues for liberal universalism against the ethics of care; she believes that the kind of liberalism for which she argues will be better for women than care ethics and should be embraced by feminists. She acknowledges that some of the feminist critique of liberalism can conflict with what she sees as the "norms of reflective caring that are preferred by liberalism." The latter norms would demand that love or attachment be based on an uncoerced choice from a position of equality, whereas an ethic of care recognizes that many of our attachments cannot or need not be based on such choice. A most obvious example is that no child can choose her parents, who are for many years more powerful than she. Though Nussbaum does not acknowledge it, many defenders

of an ethic of care favor reflective care over blind care, but they part company with Nussbaum in not seeing care primarily in terms of individual interest or choice, as does Nussbaum. Nussbaum cites Nel Noddings's description of the maternal paradigm of care and writes: "Liberalism says, let them give themselves away to others—provided that they so choose in all freedom. Noddings says that this is one thought too many—that love based on reflection lacks some of the spontaneity and moral value of true maternal love." To Nussbaum, such a view does present a challenge to the Kantian liberalism she defends. But she thinks the position of the ethics of care should be rejected; she thinks it is bad for women. Her reasons, in my view, are based on too limited a view of the ethics of care, a view that identifies it unduly with its earliest formulations.

Many feminists who criticize the liberal individualist view of persons do not deny, as Martha Nussbaum implies, the importance of rights for women who lack them. When women are denied, as they are in many parts of the world, an equal share of the food or education available to a family, when women are subject to marital rape and domestic violence, extending liberal rights to women is, of course, enormous progress. So is it when, as is still widely the case in the United States, women receive equal shares of basic necessities but are still expected and pressured to make greater sacrifices for their children than are men. The point that feminists often make, however, is that the progress should not stop with equal rights and that the liberal individualist way of formulating the goals of morality is one-sided and incomplete. Nussbaum claims that "what is wrong with the views of the family endorsed by [many liberals] is not that they are too individualist, but that they are not individualist enough" because they do not extend liberal individualism to gender relations within the family as Nussbaum thinks they should. Contrary to Nussbaum's characterization of them, however, most feminists, including those who defend an ethic of care, agree with her that various individual rights should be extended to gender relations in the family. The right not to be assaulted, for instance, should protect women and children in the family, and women should assert rights to a more equitable division of labor in the household. But those who advocate an ethic of care have a very different view from liberal individualists of what gender relations, relations between children and parents, relations of friendship, and human relations generally, should be like even when these rights are extended to those previously left out from the protections they provide.

The feminist critique of liberalism that a view such as Nussbaum's misses is the more fundamental one that turning everyone into a complete liberal individual leaves no one adequately attentive to relationships between persons, whether they be caring relations within the family or social relations holding communities together. It is possible for two strangers to have a so-called "relation" of equality between them, with nothing at all to bind them together into a friendship or a community. Liberal equality doesn't itself provide or concern itself with the more substantial components of relationship. It is in evaluating and making recommendations for the latter that an ethic of care is most appropriate. As many feminists argue, the issues for moral theory are less a matter of justice versus care than of how to appropriately integrate justice and care, or care and justice if we are wary of the traditional downgrading and marginalizing of care. And it is not satisfactory to think of care, as it is conceptualized by lib-eral individualism, as a mere personal preference an individual may choose or not. Neither is it satisfactory to think of caring relationships as merely what rational individuals may choose to care about as long as they give priority to universal, and impartial, moral principles.

Marilyn Friedman calls attention to when partiality is or is not morally valuable. "Personal relationships," she writes, "vary widely in their moral value. The quality of a particular relationship is profoundly important in determining the moral worth of any partiality which is necessary for sustaining that relationship." Partiality toward other white supremacists on the part of a white supremacist, for instance, does not have moral worth. When relationships cause harm, or are based on such wrongful relations as that of master and slave, we should not be partial toward them. But when a relationship has moral worth, such as a caring relationship between parents and children, or a relation of trust between friends and lovers clearly may have, the question of the priority, or not, of impartiality can arise. And as moralities of impartial rules so easily forget, and as Friedman makes clear, "close relationships call… for personal concern, loyalty, interest, passion, and responsiveness to the uniqueness of loved ones, to their specific needs, interests, history, and so on. In a word, personal relationships call for attitudes of partiality rather than impartiality."

Evaluating the worth of relationships does not mean that universal norms have priority after all. It means that from the perspective of justice, some relationships are to be judged unjustifiable often to the point that they should be ended to the extent possible, although this is often a limited extent. (For instance, we will never stop being the sibling of our siblings, or the ex-friend or ex-spouse of the friends or spouse with whom we have broken a relation). But once a relationship can be deemed to have value, moral issues can arise as to whether the claims of the relationship should or should not be subordinated to the perspective of justice. And that is the issue I am examining. Moreover, the aspects of a relationship that make it a bad relationship can often be interpreted as failures to appropriately care for particular others, rather than only as violations of impartial moral rules. Certainly, avoiding serious moral wrongs should take priority over avoiding trivial ones, and pursuing highly important moral goods should take priority over pursuing insignificant ones. But this settles nothing about caring relations versus impartial moral rules, now that we know enough to reject the traditional view that what men do in public life is morally important while what women do in the household is morally trivial. Some caring relations are of the utmost importance, morally as well as causally—human beings cannot flourish or even survive without them—while some of the requirements of impartial moral rules are relatively insignificant. And sometimes it is the reverse.

The practice of partiality, as Friedman well argues, cannot be unqualified.

> When many families are substantially impoverished, then [various] practices of partiality further diminish the number of people who can achieve well-being, integrity, and fulfillment through close relationships. Partiality, if practiced by all, untempered by any redistribution of wealth or resources, would appear to lead to the integrity and fulfillment of only some persons....

But this only shows, as defenders of the ethics of care usually agree, that partiality and the values of caring relationships are not the only values of concern to morality. The social conventions through which partiality is practiced need to be evaluated and justified, and impartial moral principles can be relevant in doing so. But a morality of impartial principles will be incomplete and unsatisfactory if it stops with impartial evaluations of what individuals are forbidden or permitted to do. Morality needs to evaluate relationships of care themselves, showing, for instance, how shared consideration, sensitivity, and trustworthiness enhance them and increase their value, while also showing how they can degenerate into mere occasions for individuals to pursue their own interests, or to reluctantly fulfill the duties imposed on individuals by impartial rules. When relationships are valuable ones, moral recommendations based on them may conflict with moral recommendations that would be made from the point of view of impartiality.

A LOOK AT SOME CASES

Let me now try to examine in greater detail what is at issue between an ethic of care and a morality built on impartiality, and why a satisfactory feminist morality should not accept the view that universal, impartial, liberal moral principles of justice and right should always be accorded priority over the concerns of caring relationships, which include considerations of trust, friendship, and loyalty. The argument needs to be examined both at the level of personal relationships and at the level of social policy. Advocates of an ethic of care have argued successfully against the view that care—within the bounds of what is permitted by universal principles—is admirable in personal relations, but that the core value of care is inappropriate for the impersonal relations of strangers and citizens. I will explore issues of both kinds.

Consider, first, the story of Abraham. It has been discussed by a number of defenders of an ethic of care who do not agree with the religious and moral teaching that Abraham made the right decision when be chose to obey the command of God and kill his infant son. (That God intervened later to prevent the killing is not relevant to an evaluation of Abraham's decision for anyone but a religious consequentialist). From the perspective of an ethic of care, the relationship between child and parent should not always be subordinated to the command of God or of universal moral rules. But let's consider a secular case in which there is a genuine conflict between impartialist rules and the parent-child relation. Barry's and Darwall's attempts to reshape the Bernard Williams and the feminist problems so that there is no conflict merely deal with a different kind of case and fail to address the question of what has priority when there is a conflict.

Suppose the father of a young child is by profession a teacher with a special skill in helping troubled young children succeed academically. Suppose now that on a utilitarian calculation of how much overall good will be achieved, he determines that, from the point of view of universal utilitarian rules, he ought to devote more time to his work, staying at his school after hours and so on, letting his wife and others care for his own young child. But he also thinks that from the perspective of care, he should build his relationship with his child, developing the trust and mutual consideration of which it is capable. Even if the universal rules allow him some time for family life, and even if he places appropriate utilitarian value on developing his relationship with his child—the good it will do the child, the pleasure it will give him, the good it will enable the child to do in the future, etc.—the calculation still

comes out, let's say, as before: he should devote more time to his students. But the moral demands of care suggest to him that he should spend more time with his child.

I am constructing the case in such a way that it is not a case of the kind Barry suggests where impartial moral rules that all can accept permit us to favor our own children, within bounds set by impartial rules. Rather, I am taking a case where the impartial rules that all could accept direct the father to spend more time practicing his profession, but considerations of care urge him to spend more time with his child. It is a case where the perspective of impartiality and the perspective of care are in conflict....

The argument for impartiality might go something like this: Reasoning as an abstract agent, I should act on moral rules that all could accept from a perspective of impartiality. Those rules recommend that we treat all persons equally, including our children, with respect to exercising our professional skills, and that when we have special skills we should use them for the benefit of all persons equally. For example, a teacher should not favor his own child if his child happens to be one of his students. And if one has the abilities and has had the social advantages to become a teacher, one should exercise those skills when they are needed, especially when they are seriously needed.

But the father in my example also considers the perspective of care. From this perspective his relationship with his child is of enormous and irreplaceable value. He thinks that out of concern for this particular relationship he should spend more time with his child. He experiences the relationship as one of love and trust and loyalty, and thinks in this case that he should subordinate such other considerations as exercising his professional skills to this relationship. He thinks he should free himself to help his child feel the trust and encouragement his development will require, even if this conflicts with impartial morality.

He reflects on what the motives would be in choosing between the alternatives. For one alternative, the motive would be: because universal moral rules recommend it. For the other, the motive would be: because this is my child and I am the father of this child and the relationship between us is no less important than universal rules. He reflects on whether the latter can be a moral motive and concludes that it can in the sense that he can believe it is the motive he ought to act on. And he can do this without holding that every father ought to act similarly toward his child. He can further conclude that if Kantian and utilitarian moralities deny that such a motive can be moral, then they have mistakenly defined the moral to suit their purposes, and, by arbitrary fiat, excluded whatever might challenge their universalizing requirements. He may have read Annette Baier's discussion of the possible tendency of women to resist subordinating their moral sensitivities to autonomously chosen Kantian rules. Baier writes:

> What did Kant, the great prophet of autonomy, say in his moral theory about women? He said they were incapable of legislation, not fit to vote, that they needed the guidance of more 'rational' males. Autonomy was not for them; it was only for first-class, really rational persons.... But where Kant concludes 'so much the worse for women,' we can conclude 'so much the worse for the male' fixation on the special skill of drafting legislation, for the bureaucratic mentality of rule-worship, and for the male exaggeration of the importance of independence over mutual interdependence.

The father in my example may think fathers should join mothers in paying more attention to relationships of care and in resisting the demands of impartial rules when they are excessive.

From the perspective of all, or everyone, perhaps particular relationships should be subordinated to universal rules. But from the perspective of particular persons in relationships, it is certainly meaningful to ask: Why must we adopt the perspective of all and everyone when it is a particular relationship that we care about at least as much as "being moral" in the sense required by universal rules? This relationship, we may think, is central to the identities of the persons in it. It is relationships between people, such as in families, which allow persons to develop and to become aware of themselves as individuals with rights. And it is relationships between people that sustain communities within which moral and political rights can be articulated and protected. Perhaps the perspective of universal rules should be limited to the domain of law, rather than expected to serve for the whole of morality. Then, in my example, the law should require gender fairness in parental leaves. Beyond this, it might allow persons with professional skills to work more or fewer hours as they choose, but the case as I developed it was to consider the moral decision that would still face the father in question after the law had spoken. Even if the law permitted him to work less, would it be what he morally ought to do? From the perspective of universal impartial utilitarian rules, the answer is no. But, from the perspective of care, the answer is yes. And it is this moral issue I am trying to explore. What I am arguing is that in the ethics of care, the moral claims of caring are no less valid than the moral claims of impartial rules. This is not to say that considerations of impartiality are unimportant; it does deny that they should always have priority. This makes care ethics a challenge to liberalism as a moral theory, not a mere supplement.

THE REACH OF JUSTICE

The concern expressed by liberals such as Nussbaum that every person is a separate entity with interests that should not be unduly subordinated to the "good of the community" can be matched by a defender of care who maintains that relationships of care should not be unduly subordinated to universal rules conferring equal moral rights and obligations and designed for contexts of conflict. The law and legalistic approaches should be limited to an appropriate domain, not expanded to the whole of human life and morality....

"Liberalism," Nussbaum writes, "holds that the flourishing of human beings taken one by one is both analytically and normatively prior to the flourishing" of any group. But Marxian and other arguments that human beings are social beings show how artificial such assumptions are, as we see how the material and experiential realities of any individual's life are fundamentally tied to those of others, and how the social relations in which persons are enmeshed are importantly constitutive of their "personhood." Feminist arguments that take into account the realities of caretaker/child relationships show how misleading this liberal individualist assumption is, ignoring as it does how, for any child to become a liberal individual, it must have been enmeshed in the caring social relations of caretakers and children for many years. The adult liberal individual regarding himself as "separate" is formed as well by innumerable social

bonds of family, friendship, professional association, citizenship, and the like. Certainly we can decide that for certain contexts, such as a legal one, we will make the assumption that persons are liberal individuals. But we should never lose sight of the limits of the context for which we think this may be an appropriate assumption, nor of how unsatisfactory an assumption it is for more complete conceptions of "persons."...

Children do not develop adequately when others merely go through the motions of meeting their basic needs; children need to experience social relations of trust and caring. Arguably, then, caring relations are in some sense normatively prior to individual well-being in families. But the priority is not just developmental or causal. Without the social relations within which people constitute themselves as individuals, they do not have the individuality the liberal seeks. At the level of larger groups, persons do not constitute themselves into political or social entities unless social relations of trust and loyalty tie members together into a collectivity of some kind.... Arguably, then, social relationships of persons caring enough about one another to respect them as fellow members of a community are normatively prior to individuals being valued as holders of individual rights, or to citizenship in a liberal state, and the like. And perhaps gradually, the community within which such ties must be developed so that members can be respected as having human rights is the global, human community.

We might conclude, then, that what has priority are relationships of care or fellow-feeling within which we seek rules that can be agreed on by all for treating each other with equal concern and respect and for those kinds of issues where impartial rules will be appropriate, recognizing that much that has moral value in both personal and political life is "beyond jus- tice." Such a view denies that the rules of impartial morality always have priority, and that we ought only to pursue what other values these rules permit. The out- look within the context of law is that law "covers" all behavior, allowing whatever it does not forbid, and demanding compli- ance on all that it does forbid. The view that moral rules of impartiality always take priority over considerations of care expands this outlook to the whole of morality. But we generally recognize a dis- tinction between law and morality, and can well argue that morality has normative priority. Then, at the moral level, on my argument we have good reasons not to give priority to moral rules of impartiality, but to acknowledge the claims of caring relations as no less fundamental. This view argues that, at the moral level, justice is one value among others, not always the highest value. Care and its related values of relationship and trust are no less im- portant.

Susan Mendus, discussing Bernard Williams's argument about the man saving his wife, writes that the force of the argu- ment is "that it is not merely impractical and politically inexpedient to force this extension of the scope of impartiality: it is also, and crucially, a deformation of con- cepts such as love and friendship, which are what they are precisely because they are not underpinned by completely justifi- catory explanations. In the example of the man saving his wife, willingness to pose the justificatory question is, in part, an ac- ceptance of this deformed model." This way of putting the point assumes that "justification" can only be in terms of im- partial rules, whereas a broader concept of justification might not be limited to just

such forms. But from the perspective of an ethic of care, Mendus is entirely right to argue that accepting the demand to apply rules of impartiality is, in many cases of love and friendship and caring relations, to accept a "deformed model" of these.

MODELS OF MORALITY

At the level of morality, we need to decide which "models" are appropriate for which contexts....

An ethic of care suggests that the prior- ity of justice is at best persuasive for the legal-judicial context. It might also suggest that calculations of general utility are at best appropriate for some choices about public policy. A moral theory is still needed to show us how, within the relat- edness that should exist among all persons as fellow human beings, and that does exist in many personal contexts and nu- merous group ones, we should apply the various possible models. We will then be able to see how we should apply the legal- judicial model of impartiality to given ranges of issues, or the utilitarian model of concern for the general welfare to another range of issues, all the time recognizing other issues, such as those that can be seen most clearly among friends and within families and in cases of group solidarity, for which these models are inappropriate or inadequate. And we will see how the model of caring relations can apply and have priority in some contexts, and how it should not be limited to the personal choices made by individuals after they have met all the requirements of justice. A comprehensive moral theory would show, I believe, how care and its related values are not less important than justice. Whether they are more important remains to be argued, but not in this paper.

Justice and Care Operate Together

CLAUDIA CARD

Are there cases in which we must decide, ethically, whether to prioritize justice over care or to prioritize care over justice? Professor Held finds that there are and argues that, at least sometimes, we ought to prioritize care. She has in mind cases in which the demands of a particular relationship, such as a parent-child relationship, collide with those of universal rules. My discussion is directed to her argument's presupposition that ethical concerns of care lie outside the scope of justice, and that concerns of justice lie outside the scope of care.

It is difficult to compare care ethics with justice because of the relative imprecision of philosophical accounts of care ethics. Justice has a longer and fuller academic philosophical history than care ethics. The requirements of care ethics are less clear, even if it is sometimes clear what caring for someone requires, or what someone needs for basic well-being, or what a relationship requires to survive or thrive. Whereas principles of justice have been elaborated in detail, the requirements of care ethics tend to be left at an intuitive level. Or, conclusions are drawn about what care requires in particular cases without a clear rationale for why care requires that rather than something else. How does care ethics determine which needs one ought to respond to and in which ways one ought to respond? Perhaps care ethics is not only about responding to needs.

If it is difficult to compare care ethics with justice, it is also true, because of narrow but common assumptions about what justice requires, that relationships between justice and care can seem clearer than they should. Justice is often assumed to be impartial and universal, as though "impartial justice" and "universal justice" were redundancies. Justice, Kantian ethics, and impartial rules are sometimes lumped together, as though they were more or less the same. Yet Kant's ethics includes what Kant called "duties of virtue" as well as his "duties of justice." Kant understands justice as pertaining only to what is appropriately enforceable. His duties of virtue include such unenforceable matters as gratitude. But even justice narrowly understood (as pertaining to the enforceable) requires more than consistency and impartiality in the application of rules. It matters what the rules are. Justice requires more than can be captured even by carefully formulated principles and rules. As Aristotle noted, equity is a kind of justice that eludes codification in rules, and we need equity for those inevitable cases in which correct applications of the rules (no matter how well designed they are) fail to yield a just solution.

Justice has many strands, some very general and others very particular. A principle of formal justice requires us to treat relevantly similar cases in relevantly similar ways. It directs that we apply rules consistently. But it does not tell us what rules to have. Other principles of justice, such as those put forward and defended by John Rawls, are framed as bases for justifying or evaluating general rules (such as those of a political constitution or legislation). Yet as Joel Feinberg argued long ago, justice is also a matter of responding to personal deserts. Justice is not concerned only with impartiality and universality. It is also concerned with treating particular individuals as they deserve, where what they deserve is a less formal matter than their entitlements (rights) or even qualifications as determined by general rules. Feinberg claimed that the bases of desert are characteristics of the deserving individual or something that the deserving individual has done. Yet what a particular individual deserves is often deserved from a particular other. When that is the case, it seems to me that the desert is often (although not always) grounded in a relationship between them, such as friendship. Justice grounded in deserts is particular justice, by contrast with the justice grounded in universal or impartial principles applying to everyone alike.

Particular justice has received less attention in ethical theory than universal and impartial justice. John Rawls presents his principles of justice (as Kant does his Categorical Imperative) as imposing limits on the legitimate pursuit of goals. They serve as filters or "side-constraints," scruples. Considerations of care, on the other hand, may seem to set goals for us: the pursuit of human well-being, the maintenance of relationships. But deserts may also impose scruples on the pursuit of goals. The particular justice of being responsive to deserts may also be a way of caring that is better understood as a kind of scrupulousness than as the pursuit of certain goals.

The view of justice as imposing scruples and of care as setting goals could account for a common view, to which Professor Held objects, that justice and care are compatible in the following way: once the requirements of justice are met, we are permitted to act on considerations of care. This view may seem to reduce care ethics to matters of personal preference, optional deeds. Yet, one could understand care as imposing requirements also, but requirements that do not come into play until general principles of justice are satisfied. This appears to be Kant understanding. His duty to help others is presented as "imperfect." Imperfect duties, he says, must always yield to perfect ones in cases of conflict between them, and duties of justice are perfect. On that understanding we have a lexical ordering of justice and care, one that prioritizes justice systematically over care. Professor Held's view is that care is not always simply optional and that it would be wrong to order its requirements lexically in that way with respect to justice.

I agree that the claims of particular relationships (such as friendships) are not always optional or reducible to matters of personal preference. Such relationships impose genuine responsibilities (obligations, although usually not correlated with rights). Although I am not yet persuaded that such responsibilities lie outside the scope of justice, I do find it plausible that no lexical ordering of universal justice and particular justice will withstand scrutiny.

Sometimes the demands of a particular relationship or a person for whom one cares can be momentous, as Professor Held notes, whereas a conflicting demand based on a general moral rule may be relatively trivial. One may have to break a promise to meet someone for coffee, for example, in order to render aid to a seriously injured person or just to "be there" for a partner in crisis. Keeping the promise may be naturally understood as a requirement of justice. But isn't the requirement to aid the injured party, or to be there for one's partner, also a demand of justice?

Lest one object that such a case simply illustrates a conflict between two general rules (keep promises and aid those in trouble), let me vary the case so as to particularize the demand for care more. Suppose that keeping a promise not to reveal secret conflicts with the demands of loyalty to a friend, because you have learned, since you made the promise, how seriously knowledge of that secret could affect your friend's welfare. It may not be obvious what you should do. But it is possible that the promise will not release you, even though the reason you were asked to keep the secret is relatively trivial, whereas the potential impact on your friend of the knowledge of that secret is momentous. If your friend's future welfare would be seriously endangered by not knowing the secret, breaking the promise could be the right thing to do. Does this mean that care would triumph over justice? Or was what your friend deserved from you a more important demand of justice? Couldn't it be unjust (to your friend and to the relationship between you) to be a stickler about promises here?

Deserts of punishment and reward are paradigms of justice. But these are not the only morally significant kinds of deserts. People can also deserve trust and loyalty. Betrayal of a friend can be deeply unjust even if no promise was made. If the demands of a particular relationship or individual can be articulated in terms of what that person or relationship deserves from us, then, even though the same demands might also be articulated in the language of care, it is misleading to say that we confront a conflict between justice and care. Some demands of justice (those based on deserts) can be in conflict with others (those based on impartial rules).

Although failing to treat others as they deserve is a paradigm of injustice, it need not take the form of violating rights. People often deserve rewards, for example, but seldom have a right to them. Although sometimes rights and deserts may be interchangeable, they are not always. Following Feinberg's distinctions, deserts more often tend to be relatively informal, in contrast with entitlements (rights) and eligibilities (meeting minimum qualifications). Deserts elude codification in rules—desert of gratitude, for example. Where deserts are relatively informal in this way, it is sometimes more natural to speak of being unfair to someone than to use the language of injustice. Yet the values may be the same. Whether we call it injustice to someone or unfairness to someone, we are honoring what makes an individual special, rather than what all individuals have in common. Where there is no enforcement or even codification of the appropriate conduct, it takes a stronger, more developed, more nuanced sense of justice to do what is required.

Aristotle presented justice as giving each their due. "What is due" did not mean, "what one has a right to." Aristotle appears to have had no conception of rights. "Due" appears to mean something like "deserved." What our children deserve from us is different from what our parents or lovers deserve. We cannot talk about Aristotelian justice without also talking about relationships—not just in an abstract logical sense, but relationships in the sense of connections. Aristotle observes that "friendship and justice... seem to be concerned with the same objects and exhibited between the same persons"; that "the claims of justice differ too; the duties of parents to children and those of brothers to each other are not the same, nor those of comrades and those of fellow citizens"; and that "the injustice increases by being exhibited towards those who are friends in a fuller sense; e.g., it is a more terrible thing to defraud a comrade than a fellow citizen, more terrible not to help a brother than a stranger." He continues, saying that "the demands of justice also seem to increase with the intensity of the friendship, which implies that friendship and justice exist between the same persons and have an equal extension." These remarks may seem difficult to reconcile with his earlier observation that "when men are friends they have no need of justice" unless we take it that "needing justice" in that context means "needing enforcement." But he goes on to note that when people are just, they need friendship as well and "the truest form of justice is thought to be a friendly quality." These observations suggest that relationships underlie justice and determine its scope.

Although Feinberg claimed that deserts are based on some characteristic of the deserving person, or on something that person has done, I would point out that deserts often seem grounded more generally in the relationship between the deserving person and the person or persons from whom certain kinds of treatment are deserved. Friends deserve our loyalty, not simply on the basis of their characteristics as individuals or even on the basis of what they have done simply as individuals, but because they are our friends—at least, if they are good friends (or, perhaps, friends in good standing). Benefactors deserve our gratitude; being someone's benefactor—befriending someone—is being in a certain kind of relationship to that person. Repentant wrongdoers may sometimes deserve forgiveness. Rescuers may deserve praise. A lover may deserve one's trust. Because failing to treat people as they deserve can be unjust to them, justice has a wider scope than that of rights. It is not merely a legal or legalistic concept.

These responses—loyalty, gratitude, forgiveness, praise, trust—are also instances of caring, are they not? If so, they show that caring is wider in scope than caretaking, care giving, or benevolence. Loyalty might require caretaking on some occasions, but I can be loyal on other occasions simply by refusing to betray someone. Caring is often a matter of taking an appropriately supportive or appreciative attitude toward someone, one that shows that you value that person or your relationship with that person in a certain way. Fred Berger argued that gratitude is important because it shows that we value our benefactor not just as a source of our own welfare. Such responses are not deserved by just anyone from just anyone else. They are particularized. They demonstrate concern and appreciation for the individual. They share emotive elements commonly associated with caring. As with caring, generally, it can be difficult to specify what particular acts, if any, are required for having the appropriate response.

Not all responsiveness to deserts exemplifies caring; arguably, for example, responsiveness to desert of punishment and blame do not. But responsiveness to many kinds of deserts that Feinberg classified as "non-polar"—the kinds mentioned above: gratitude, loyalty, trust, forgiveness—does exhibit behavior that is also naturally recognized as caring behavior, and such responsiveness may be essential to the maintenance of relationships such as friendships.

In her "Look at Some Cases," Professor Held comments briefly on the story in Genesis 22 of God's testing Abraham by asking him to sacrifice his son Isaac, a case much discussed by proponents of care ethics. She then presents at greater length her own case of a father who has special skills that could help many other children besides his own, but only at the cost of his leaving the care of his own child largely to others. Regarding Abraham, she notes that "the relationship between parent and child should not always be subordinated to the command of God or of universal moral rules." Yet it seems arbitrary to regard

Abraham's relationship with God as giving only the side of justice and not care, and to regard Abraham's relationship with Isaac as giving the side of care but not justice. If there is obvious justice on either side, is it not in the obligation not to kill? Kierkegaard found the claims of universality on the side of not killing when he presented God's demand as a "teleological suspension of the ethical." Actually, Abraham is caught between two special relationships: with God and with Isaac. God tests Abraham's trust, and Isaac trusts Abraham. Insofar as God deserves Abraham's trust, and Isaac deserves to be able to trust Abraham, there are demands of particular justice on both sides. There is also a demand of universal justice on the side of not killing.

Professor Held's case of the father who has special skills in helping troubled young children succeed academically shows, I think, something very wrong with a utilitarian conception of justice. It also illustrates how difficult it can be to identify what appropriate care requires for all those who may make claims on one's care. The father's child has special claims on his attention. Unless he has already accepted a position of responsibility for the care of other children, it is not unjust favoritism to give special attention to his own child rather than others (when he cannot do both). It might be difficult for him to decide whether to take on the responsibility to care for other children where no one else who had the requisite skills was readily available. But saving others the inconvenience of having to look elsewhere for those skills, perhaps at some expense, need not be sufficient to justify his acceding to their demand. He could justifiably refuse on the grounds of his prior commitment to his family. If securing someone else with the requisite skills proved costly (or even impossible), the

responsibility would not be simply the father's. The other children's needs are, presumably, the responsibility of a wider community. A problem with utilitarianism is that it distributes responsibility too expediently.

But, further, in this kind of case, as in Abraham's case, there are demands of care on both sides. Corresponding claims of justice argue each way. On one side is what a particular individual, your child, deserves from you, the parent. On the other is the general demand to help others where you can do so without excessive cost. Care is deserved on one side but also demanded on the other (even if not deserved by the other children from this father). To represent only one side as that of care oversimplifies care ethics. Presumably it is not Professor Held's view that, in general, from the point of view of care ethics, the claims of particular relationships (such as fatherhood) always take precedence over the needs of strangers. Yet no rationale is provided for why they do so here. Pointing out that the child is the father's own, as an answer to that question, only suggests that, from the point of view of care, special relationships always take priority. Yet that is not plausible. On the other hand, within the idea of justice, we have a case in which the son's particular deserts are pitted against a more general rule of helping those in need, particular justice against universal justice. To present only the claims of universal justice as "the side of justice" is to suggest, inevitably, that universal claims always win out over particular ones from the perspective of justice. Yet that is also implausible.

The case of the father who has skills reminds me of another case, somewhat similar but also different, documented in Jung Chang's narrative of the Cultural Revolution, *Wild Swans: Three Daughters of China*. Her father, as a public official, refused to take advantage of his access to medical supplies to bring home more than the allotted share of medications for his own family, who needed them badly. He refused on the grounds that doing that sort of thing was just the kind of corruption that had caused so many problems with public life in China. At first, the mother could not understand his attitude, and he could not understand how she could expect him to do such a thing. But eventually, they came to understand each other's point of view without abandoning their own values and principles.

Jung Chang's father, in my opinion, did the right thing. He was not a less caring parent for having so acted. As a public official, he had public responsibilities as well as private ones, and he was not being asked in his public capacity to make his family sacrifice more than other families were expected to do. Other families deserved to receive their share, just as his family deserved his special concerns. But the validity of his special concerns did not mean that his family deserved more than their fair share or that in respecting others' shares, he cared less than he should have for his own family.

It may be tempting to describe the case of Jung Chang's father as pitting care (for his own family) against justice (in administering the rules for distributing medicines) and say that, in contrast with Professor Held's case, here is one where justice wins out over care. Yet, again, I find this misleading, because there is justice on both sides and there are concerns of care on both sides, albeit particularized on the one side and generalized on the other.

The reader by now may be asking what difference it makes which language we use (that of justice or that of care) to describe these conflicts, as long as we appreciate that such conflicts arise and that there is no lexical ordering of values that will yield the right answer in every case. What difference does it make whether we label the demands of particular relationships those of "care" or those of "particular justice"? As long as we find care on both sides, or as long as we find justice on both sides, perhaps it does not matter which language we use. It is important, however, to recognize that there are importantly similar values at work on both sides of such conflicts. In particular relationships, we may be more likely to appreciate those values in a lively way if the relationship engages us positively and if it is especially vital to our well-being. On the other hand, if we have come to take particular relationships for granted and if we self-consciously identify with a more public role (and the more formal relationships that define it), it may be easier to appreciate the values at stake in universal claims. In either case, the likelihood or ease of our appreciation of the relevant values does not, in itself, carry ethical weight. Feminist criticism of ethical theories that pay insufficient attention to the values at stake in particular relationships could exploit the concept of justice to make that point.

THE CONTINUING DEBATE:
Morality: Universal Principles of Justice *or* Specific Caring Relationships?

What Is New

Care ethics focuses on particular experiences and personal relationships, arguing that these have been neglected and devalued by the traditional emphasis on impersonal universal principles of justice and obligation. The personal orientation of care ethics raises the issue of relativism, leading to questions of whether care ethics sacrifices universal objectivity and thus loses its right to critique and condemn local cultural practices that subordinate women. In one line of response, Laurie Shrage embraces ethical cultural relativism as a means of appreciating the experiences of women in other cultures and of forging new political programs of change. In contrast, Martha Nussbaum holds that principles of objective impartial justice are essential for challenging the oppressive cultures and customs that perpetuate injustice toward women.

Where to Find More

Bernard Williams' work—discussed and critiqued by Virginia Held—can be found in *Moral Luck: Philosophical Papers 1973–80* (Cambridge: Cambridge University Press, 1981); see also debate 2. The views of Brian Barry, another target of Held's, are in his *Justice as Impartiality* (Oxford: Oxford University Press, 1995). Stephen Darwall's impartialist position is presented in *Impartial Reason* (Ithaca, NY: Cornell University Press, 1983), and *Philosophical Ethics* (Boulder, CO: Westview Press, 1998).

Nel Noddings' work has been influential in both philosophy and education; see her *Caring: A Feminine Approach to Ethics and Moral Education* (Berkeley, CA: University of California Press, 1984); and *Educating Moral People: A Caring Alternative to Character Education* (NY: Teachers College Press, 2002). Annette C. Baier is a clear and cogent writer on this topic, who is particularly insightful in placing care ethics in a larger philosophical perspective: see her *Moral Prejudices* (Cambridge, MA: Harvard University Press, 1994). Among the best advocates of care ethics is Lawrence A. Blum, *Friendship, Altruism and Morality* (London: Routledge & Kegan Paul, 1980).

Laurie Shrage's relativist care ethics is available in *Moral Dilemmas of Feminism* (NY: Routledge, 1994). Martha Nussbaum's case for the importance of critical objective standards for condemning oppressive cultures is developed in Martha Nussbaum and Amartya Sen, eds., *The Quality of Life* (Oxford: Clarendon Press, 1993); Martha Nussbaum and Jonathan Glover, *Women, Culture and Development: A Study of Human Capabilities* (Oxford: Calrendon Press, 1995); and Martha Nussbaum, "In Defense of Universal Values," in *Controversies in Feminism*, edited by James P. Sterba (Lanham, MD: Rowman & Littlefield Publishers, 2001): 3–23. A good review of contemporary feminist ethics is provided by Samantha Brennan, "Recent Work in Feminist Ethics," *Ethics*, volume 109 (July 1999): 858–893.

An excellent collection of articles and debates is found in *Controversies in Feminism*, edited by James P. Sterba (Lanham, MD: Rowman & Littlefield Publishers, 2001). Some other fine anthologies include Claudia Card, ed., *On Feminist Ethics and Politics* (Lawrence: University Press of Kansas, 1999); Peggy DesAutels and Joanne Waugh, eds., *Feminists Doing Ethics* (Lanham, MD: Rowman & Littlefield,

2001); and Samantha Brennan, ed., *Feminist Moral Philosophy* (Calgary, Alberta: University of Calgary Press, 2002).

The article by Judy Whipps on "Pragmatist Feminism" in the *Stanford Encyclopedia of Philosophy* is excellent, particularly the historical material; it is available at *http://plato.stanford.edu/entries/femapproach-pragmatism.*

See also the Where to Find More sections in debate 4 and debate 7.

6 DO MORAL OBLIGATIONS ALWAYS TAKE PRECEDENCE?

WE SHOULD LIMIT THE DEMANDS OF MORALITY

ADVOCATE: Susan Wolf, Edna J. Koury Professor of Philosophy at University of North Carolina at Chapel Hill; author of *Freedom Within Reason* (NY: Oxford University Press, 1990).

SOURCE: "Moral Saints," *Journal of Philosophy*, Volume 79, number 8 (August 1982): 419–439.

FOLLOWING THE STRONGEST DEMANDS OF MORALITY IS A WORTHWHILE GOAL

ADVOCATE: Catherine Wilson, Professor of Philosophy, University of British Columbia; author of *Moral Animals: Ideals and Constraints in Moral Theory* (Oxford: Oxford University Press, 2004).

SOURCE: "On Some Alleged Limitations to Moral Endeavor," *The Journal of Philosophy*, Volume 90, number 6 (June 1993): 275–289.

There's an old joke among those who wish to follow a religious tradition, but would rather not follow its moral precepts and prohibitions too closely: "If God had wanted us to keep ten commandments, He would have given us twenty." The humor stems from its rejection of an unstated basic assumption that most people hold concerning ethical principles: That is, that you are supposed to follow them, and follow them completely and to the highest degree possible. Of course we often fail; but if we do, we have fallen short perfection, and what we *should* do—from the moral perspective—is strive for the highest degree of moral behavior we can achieve. A modest amount of wine aids the digestion, enhances the flavor of your food, and increases your dining pleasure; but it's certainly possible to have too much. But that doesn't apply to virtue or moral goodness: You can't be too good; you can't practice virtue to excess. Or so it seems. But it is precisely that assumption that Susan Wolf calls into question: Striving to live a good moral life is certainly worthwhile; but even with morality, there can be too much of a good thing.

Wolf's essay lays bare an idea that finds considerable popular support, but that philosophers and ethicists are reluctant to acknowledge: Morality may be nice in moderation, but most people wouldn't really want to live an ideal moral life. Jesus of Nazareth taught we should sell all our possessions, and give the money to the poor; and from a utilitarian perspective, perhaps that would yield the greatest overall balance of pleasure over suffering (certainly it would produce an overall better result than my buying a new car and adding a jacuzzi to my deck); but I'm not sure I really want to be *that* morally upright. A modest contribution to some relief fund seems to be about as moral as I really want to be, though I am happy to applaud those who aspire to "moral sainthood." Still, I may feel a twinge of guilt at my significantly submaximum commitment to moral perfection.

Wolf is not merely trying to eliminate our residual guilt at not striving for moral perfection; rather, her claim that "moral sainthood" is not even a worthwhile ideal is designed to pose a profound challenge to the basic ideas of some prominent ethical theories. In particular, she argues that ethics too often neglects or even disparages the conditions essential for living a rich and satisfying human life.

Catherine Wilson does not come to the defense of the Kantian and utilitarian positions which Wolf criticizes; rather, Wilson probes into what she sees as the underlying assumptions—the unrecognized "ideology"—beneath Wolf's view. In considering Wilson's criticisms, two questions arise: Are there in fact such ideological assumptions behind the position taken by Wolf? If so, are the assumptions illegitimate?

POINTS TO PONDER

> ➤ Susan Wolf notes that a life of "moral sainthood" has its drawbacks. But then, few of us are in any significant danger of becoming moral saints. To the contrary, most of us struggle to be morally decent. Does the fact that we are very unlikely come anywhere close to moral sainthood diminish the significance of Wolf's essay?

> ➤ Wolf states that "I have not meant to condemn the moral saint or the person who aspires to become one." However, she does insist that there are other life goals than being "maximally morally good," and that these goals are also legitimate aspirations. One person may aspire to write a great novel, another to become a splendid marathoner, and a third strives to become a moral saint. It sounds odd, but is there anything objectionable in Wolf's position?

> ➤ Catherine Wilson maintains that ethics should make us somewhat uncomfortable with our position of privilege, and should challenge our comfortable acceptance of a "life style" of luxurious and aggressive consumption (particularly in light of widespread poverty and misery). *Is* that the proper role of ethics? Or should ethics aim at formulating standards for minimally decent behavior within the culture and cultural values in which we live?

> ➤ Wilson's criticisms obviously are focused against the easy acceptance of a luxurious consumer lifestyle; but would she have any difficulty accommodating the special valuing of personal relationships and personal goals? Does her position make moral sainthood a mandatory goal?

We Should Limit the Demands of Morality

SUSAN WOLF

I don't know whether there are any moral saints. But if there are, I am glad that neither I nor those about whom I care most are among them. By *moral saint* I mean a person whose every action is as morally good as possible, a person, that is, who is as morally worthy as can be. Though I shall in a moment acknowledge the variety of types of person that might be thought to satisfy this description, it seems to me that none of these types serve as unequivocally compelling personal ideals. In other words, I believe that moral perfection, in the sense of moral saintliness, does not constitute a model of personal well-being toward which it would be particularly rational or good or desirable for a human being to strive.

Outside the context of moral discussion, this will strike many as an obvious point. But, within that context, the point, if it be granted, will be granted with some discomfort. For within that context it is generally assumed that one ought to be as morally good as possible and that what limits there are to morality's hold on us are set by features of human nature of which we ought not to be proud. If, as I believe, the ideals that are derivable from common sense and philosophically popular moral theories do not support these assumptions, then something has to change. Either we must change our moral theories in ways that will make them yield more palatable ideals, or, as I shall argue, we must change our conception of what is involved in affirming a moral theory.

In this paper, I wish to examine the notion of a moral saint, first, to understand what a moral saint would be like and why such a being would be unattractive, and, second, to raise some questions about the significance of this paradoxical figure for moral philosophy. I shall look first at the model(s) of moral sainthood that might be extrapolated from the morality or moralities of common sense. Then I shall consider what relations these have to conclusions that can be drawn from utilitarian and Kantian moral theories. Finally I shall speculate on the implications of these considerations for moral philosophy.

MORAL SAINTS AND COMMON SENSE

Consider first what, pretheoretically, would count for us—contemporary members of Western culture—as a moral saint. A necessary condition of moral sainthood would be that one's life be dominated by a commitment to improving the welfare of others or of society as a whole. As to what role this commitment must play in the individual's motivational system, two contrasting accounts suggest themselves to me which might equally be thought to qualify a person for moral sainthood.

First, a moral saint might be someone whose concern for others plays the role that is played in most of our lives by more selfish, or, at any rate, less morally worthy concerns. For the moral saint, the promotion of the welfare of others might play the role that is played for most of us by the enjoyment of material comforts, the opportunity to engage in the intellectual and physical activities of our choice, and the love, respect, and companionship of people whom we love, respect, and enjoy. The happiness of the moral saint, then, would truly lie in the happiness of others, and so he would devote himself to others gladly, and with a whole and open heart.

On the other hand, a moral saint might be someone for whom the basic ingredients of happiness are not unlike those of most of the rest of us. What makes him a moral saint is rather that he pays little or no attention to his own happiness in light of the overriding importance he gives to the wider concerns of morality. In other words, this person sacrifices his own interests to the interests of others, and feels the sacrifice as such.

Roughly, these two models may be distinguished according to whether one thinks of the moral saint as being a saint out of love or one thinks of the moral saint as being a saint out of duty (or some other intellectual appreciation and recognition of moral principles). We may refer to the first model as the model of the Loving Saint; to the second, as the model of the Rational Saint.

The two models differ considerably with respect to the qualities of the motives of the individuals who conform to them. But this difference would have limited effect on the saints' respective public personalities. The shared content of what these individuals are motivated to be—namely, as morally good as possible—would play the dominant role in the determination of their characters. Of course, just as a variety of large-scale projects, from tending the sick to political campaigning, may be equally and maximally morally worthy, so a variety of characters are compatible with the ideal of moral sainthood. One moral saint may be more or less jovial, more or less garrulous, more or less athletic than another. But, above all, a moral saint must have and cultivate those qualities which are apt to allow him to treat others as justly and kindly as possible. He will have the standard moral virtues to a nonstandard degree. He will be patient, considerate, even-tempered, hospitable, charitable in thought as well as in deed. He will be very reluctant to make negative judgments of other people. He will be careful not to favor some people over others on the basis of properties they could not help but have.

Perhaps what I have already said is enough to make some people begin to regard the absence of moral saints in their lives as a blessing. For there comes a point in the listing of virtues that a moral saint is likely to have where one might naturally begin to wonder whether the moral saint isn't, after all, too good—if not too good for his own good, at least too good for his own well-being. For the moral virtues, given that they are, by hypothesis, *all* present in the same individual, and to an extreme degree, are apt to crowd out the nonmoral virtues, as well as many of the interests and personal characteristics that we generally think contribute to a healthy, well-rounded, richly developed character.

In other words, if the moral saint is devoting all his time to feeding the hungry or healing the sick or raising money for Oxfam, then necessarily he is not reading Victorian novels, playing the oboe, or improving his backhand. Although no one of the interests or tastes in the category containing these latter activities could be claimed to be a necessary element in a life well lived, a life in which *none* of these possible aspects of character are developed may seem to be a life strangely barren....

An interest in something like gourmet cooking will be, for different reasons, difficult for a moral saint to rest easy with. For it seems to me that no plausible argument can justify the use of human resources involved in producing a *paté de ca-*

nard en croûte against possible alternative beneficent ends to which these resources might be put. If there is a justification for the institution of haute cuisine, it is one which rests on the decision *not* to justify every activity against morally beneficial alternatives, and this is a decision a moral saint will never make....

A moral saint will have to be very, very nice. It is important that he not be offensive. The worry is that, as a result, he will have to be dull-witted or humorless or bland.

This worry is confirmed when we consider what sorts of characters, taken and refined both from life and from fiction, typically form our ideals. One would hope they would be figures who are morally good—and by this I mean more than just not morally bad—but one would hope, too, that they are not just morally good, but talented or accomplished or attractive in nonmoral ways as well. We may make ideals out of athletes, scholars, artists—more frivolously, out of cowboys, private eyes, and rock stars. We may strive for Katharine Hepburn's grace, Paul Newman's "cool"; we are attracted to the high-spirited passionate nature of Natasha Rostov; we admire the keen perceptiveness of Lambert Strether. Though there is certainly nothing immoral about the ideal characters or traits I have in mind, they cannot be superimposed upon the ideal of a moral saint. For although it is a part of many of these ideals that the characters set high, and not merely acceptable, moral standards for themselves, it is also essential to their power and attractiveness that the moral strengths go, so to speak, alongside of specific, independently admirable, nonmoral ground projects and dominant personal traits.

When one does finally turn one's eyes toward lives that are dominated by explicitly moral commitments, moreover, one finds oneself relieved at the discovery of idiosyncrasies or eccentricities not quite in line with the picture of moral perfection. One prefers the blunt, tactless, and opinionated Betsy Trotwood to the unfailingly kind and patient Agnes Copperfield; one prefers the mischievousness and the sense of irony in Chesterton's Father Brown to the innocence and undiscriminating love of St. Francis.

It seems that, as we look in our ideals for people who achieve nonmoral varieties of personal excellence in conjunction with or colored by some version of high moral tone, we look in our paragons of moral excellence for people whose moral achievements occur in conjunction with or colored by some interests or traits that have low moral tone. In other words, there seems to be a limit to how much morality we can stand....

Moreover, there is something odd about the idea of morality itself, or moral goodness, serving as the object of a dominant passion in the way that a more concrete and specific vision of a goal (even a concrete *moral* goal) might be imagined to serve. Morality itself does not seem to be a suitable object of passion. Thus, when one reflects, for example, on the Loving Saint easily and gladly giving up his fishing trip or his stereo or his hot fudge sundae at the drop of the moral hat, one is apt to wonder not at how much he loves morality, but at how little he loves these other things. One thinks that, if he can give these up so easily, he does not know what it is to truly love them. There seems, in other words, to be a kind of joy which the Loving Saint, either by nature or by practice, is incapable of experiencing. The Rational Saint, on the other hand, might retain strong nonmoral and concrete desires—he simply denies himself the opportunity to act on them. But this is no less troubling. The Loving Saint one might suspect of missing a piece of perceptual machinery, of being blind to some of what the world has to offer. The Rational Saint, who sees it but foregoes it, one suspects of having a different problem—a pathological fear of damnation, perhaps, or an extreme form of self-hatred that interferes with his ability to enjoy the enjoyable in life.

In other words, the ideal of a life of moral sainthood disturbs not simply because it is an ideal of a life in which morality unduly dominates. The normal person's direct and specific desires for objects, activities, and events that conflict with the attainment of moral perfection are not simply sacrificed but removed, suppressed, or subsumed. The way in which morality, unlike other possible goals, is apt to dominate is particularly disturbing, for it seems to require either the lack or the denial of the existence of an identifiable, personal self....

The moral saint, may, by happy accident, find himself with nonmoral virtues on which he can capitalize morally or which make psychological demands to which he has no choice but to attend. The point is that, for a moral saint, the existence of these interests and skills can be given at best the status of happy accidents—they cannot be encouraged for their own sakes as distinct, independent aspects of the realization of human good.

It must be remembered that from the fact that there is a tension between having any of these qualities and being a moral saint it does not follow that having any of these qualities is immoral. For it is not part of common-sense morality that one ought to be a moral saint. Still, if someone just happened to want to be a moral saint, he or she would not have or encourage these qualities, and, on the basis of our common-sense values, this counts as a reason *not* to want to be a moral saint....

The fact that the moral saint would be without qualities which we have and which, indeed, we like to have, does not in itself provide reason to condemn the ideal of the moral saint. The fact that some of these qualities are good qualities, however, and that they are qualities we *ought* to like, does provide reason to discourage this ideal and to offer other ideals in its place. In other words, some of the qualities the moral saint necessarily lacks are virtues, albeit nonmoral virtues, in the unsaintly characters who have them. The feats of Grocho Marx, Reggie Jackson, and the head chef at Lutèce are impressive accomplishments that it is not only permissible but positively appropriate to recognize as such. In general, the admiration of and striving toward achieving any of a great variety of forms of personal excellence are character traits it is valuable and desirable for people to have. In advocating the development of these varieties of excellence, we advocate nonmoral reasons for acting, and in thinking that it is good for a person to strive for an ideal that gives a substantial role to the interests and values that correspond to these virtues, we implicitly acknowledge the goodness of ideals incompatible with that of the moral saint. Finally, if we think that it is *as* good, or even better for a person to strive for one of these ideals than it is for him or her to strive for and realize the ideal of the moral saint, we express a conviction that it is good not to be a moral saint.

MORAL SAINTS AND MORAL THEORIES

I have tried so far to paint a picture—or, rather, two pictures—of what a moral saint might be like, drawing on what I take to be the attitudes and beliefs about morality prevalent in contemporary, common-sense thought. To my suggestion that common-sense morality generates conceptions of moral saints that are unattractive or otherwise unacceptable, it is open to someone to reply, "so much the worse for common-sense morality." After all, it is often claimed that the goal of moral philosophy is to correct and improve upon common-sense morality, and I have as yet given no attention to the question of what conceptions of moral sainthood, if any, are generated from the leading moral theories of our time.

A quick, breezy reading of utilitarian and Kantian writings will suggest the images, respectively, of the Loving Saint and the Rational Saint. A utilitarian, with his emphasis on happiness, will certainly prefer the Loving Saint to the Rational one, since the Loving Saint will himself be a happier person than the Rational Saint. A Kantian, with his emphasis on reason, on the other hand, will find at least as much to praise in the latter as in the former. Still, both models, drawn as they are from common sense, appeal to an impure mixture of utilitarian and Kantian intuitions. A more careful examination of these moral theories raises questions about whether either model of moral sainthood would really be advocated by a believer in the explicit doctrines associated with either of these views.

Certainly, the utilitarian in no way denies the value of self-realization. He in no way disparages the development of interests, talents, and other personally attractive traits that I have claimed the moral saint would be without. Indeed, since just these features enhance the happiness both of the individuals who possess them and of those with whom they associate, the ability to promote these features both in oneself and in others will have considerable positive weight in utilitarian calculations.

This implies that the utilitarian would not support moral sainthood as a universal ideal. A world in which everyone, or even a large number of people, achieved moral sainthood—even a world in which they *strove* to achieve it—would probably contain less happiness than a world in which people realized a diversity of ideals involving a variety of personal and perfectionist values. More pragmatic considerations also suggest that, if the utilitarian wants to influence more people to achieve more good, then he would do better to encourage them to pursue happiness-producing goals that are more attractive and more within a normal person's reach.

These considerations still leave open, however, the question of what kind of an ideal the committed utilitarian should privately aspire to himself. Utilitarianism requires him to want to achieve the greatest general happiness, and this would seem to commit him to the ideal of the moral saint.

One might try to use the claims I made earlier as a basis for an argument that a utilitarian should choose to give up utilitarianism. If, as I have said, a moral saint would be a less happy person both to be and to be around than many other possible ideals, perhaps one could create more total happiness by not trying too hard to promote the total happiness. But this argument is simply unconvincing in light of the empirical circumstances of our world. The gain in happiness that would accrue to oneself and one's neighbors by a more well-rounded, richer life than that of the moral saint would be pathetically small in comparison to the amount by which one could increase the general happiness if one devoted oneself explicitly to the care of the sick, the downtrodden, the starving, and the homeless. Of course, there may be psychological limits to the extent to which a person can devote himself to such things without going crazy. But the utilitarian's individual limitations would not thereby become a positive feature of his personal ideals....

Still, the criticisms I have raised against the saint of common-sense morality should make some difference to the utilitarian's conception of an ideal which neither requires him to abandon his utilitarian principles nor forces him to fake an interest he does not have or a judgment he does not make. For it may be that a limited and carefully monitored allotment of time and energy to be devoted to the pursuit of some nonmoral interests or to the development of some nonmoral talents would make a person a better contributor to the general welfare than he would be if he allowed himself no indulgences of this sort. The enjoyment of such activities in no way compromises a commitment to utilitarian principles as long as the involvement with these activities is conditioned by a willingness to give them up whenever it is recognized that they cease to be in the general interest.

This will go some way in mitigating the picture of the loving saint that an understanding of utilitarianism will on first impression suggest. But I think it will not go very far. For the limitations on time and energy will have to be rather severe, and the need to monitor will restrict not only the extent but also the quality of one's attachment to these interests and traits. They are only weak and somewhat peculiar sorts of passions to which one can consciously remain so conditionally committed. Moreover, the way in which the utilitarian can enjoy these "extra-curricular" aspects of his life is simply not the way in which these aspects are to be enjoyed insofar as they figure into our less saintly ideals.

The problem is not exactly that the utilitarian values these aspects of his life only as a means to an end, for the enjoyment he and others get from these aspects are not a means to, but a part of, the general happiness. Nonetheless, he values these things only because of and insofar as they *are* a part of the general happiness. He values them, as it were, under the description 'a contribution to the general happiness'. This is to be contrasted with the various ways in which these aspects of life may be valued by nonutilitarians. A person might love literature because of the insights into human nature literature affords. Another might love the cultivation of roses because roses are things of great beauty and delicacy. It may be true that these features of the respective activities also explain why these activities are happiness-producing. But, to the nonutilitarian, this may not be to the point. For if one values these activities in these more direct ways, one may not be willing to exchange them for others that produce an equal, or even a greater amount of happiness. From that point of view, it is not because they produce happiness that these activities are valuable; it is because these activities are valuable in more direct and specific ways that they produce happiness....

The Kantian believes that being morally worthy consists in always acting from maxims that one could will to be universal law, and doing this not out of any pathological desire but out of reverence for the moral law as such. Or, to take a different formulation of the categorical imperative, the Kantian believes that moral action consists in treating other persons always as ends and never as means only. Presumably, and according to Kant himself, the Kantian thereby commits himself to some degree of benevolence as well as to the rules of fair play. But we surely would not will that *every* person become a moral saint, and treating others as ends hardly requires bending over backwards to protect and promote their interests. On one interpretation of Kantian doctrine, then, moral perfection would be achieved simply by unerring obedience to a limited set of side-constraints. On this interpretation, Kantian theory simply does not yield an ideal conception of a person of any fullness comparable to that of the moral saints I have so far been portraying.

On the other hand, Kant does say explicitly that we have a duty of benevolence, a duty not only to allow others to pursue their ends, but to take up their ends as our own. In addition, we have positive duties to ourselves, duties to increase our natural as well as our moral perfection. These duties are unlimited in the degree to which they *may* dominate a life. If action in accordance with and motivated by the thought of these duties is considered virtuous, it is natural to assume that the more one performs such actions, the more virtuous one is. Moreover, of virtue in general Kant says, "it is an ideal which is unattainable while yet our duty is constantly to approximate to it". On this interpretation, then, the Kantian moral saint, like the other moral saints I have been considering, is dominated by the motivation to be moral....

On the second interpretation of Kant, the Kantian moral saint is, not surprisingly, subject to many of the same objections I have been raising against other versions of moral sainthood. Though the Kantian saint may differ from the utilitarian saint as to *which* actions he is bound to perform and which he is bound to refrain from performing, I suspect that the range of activities acceptable to the Kantian saint will remain objectionably restrictive.... As the utilitarian could value his activities and character traits only insofar as they fell under the description of 'contributions to the general happiness', the Kantian would have to value his activities and character traits insofar as they were

manifestations of respect for the moral law. If the development of our powers to achieve physical, intellectual, or artistic excellence, or the activities directed toward making others happy are to have any moral worth, they must arise from a reverence for the dignity that members of our species have as a result of being endowed with pure practical reason. This is a good and noble motivation, to be sure. But it is hardly what one expects to be dominantly behind a person's aspirations to dance as well as Fred Astaire, to paint as well as Picasso, or to solve some outstanding problem in abstract algebra, and it is hardly what one hopes to find lying dominantly behind a father's action on behalf of his son or a lover's on behalf of her beloved.

Since the basic problem with any of the models of moral sainthood we have been considering is that they are dominated by a single, all-important value under which all other possible values must be subsumed, it may seem that the alternative interpretation of Kant, as providing a stringent but finite set of obligations and constraints, might provide a more acceptable morality. According to this interpretation of Kant, one is as morally good as can be so long as one devotes some limited portion of one's energies toward altruism and the maintenance of one's physical and spiritual health, and otherwise pursues one's independently motivated interests and values in such a way as to avoid overstepping certain bounds....

Even this more limited understanding of morality, if its connection to Kant's views is to be taken at all seriously, is not likely to give an unqualified seal of approval to the nonmorally directed ideals I have been advocating. For Kant is explicit about what he calls "duties of apathy and self-mastery"—duties to ensure that our passions are never so strong as to interfere with calm, practical deliberation, or so deep as to wrest control from the more disinterested, rational part of ourselves. The tight and self-conscious rein we are thus obliged to keep on our commitments to specific individuals and causes will doubtless restrict our value in these things, assigning them a necessarily attenuated place.

A more interesting objection to this brand of Kantianism, however, comes when we consider the implications of placing the kind of upper bound on moral worthiness which seemed to count in favor of this conception of morality. For to put such a limit on one's capacity to be moral is effectively to deny, not just the moral necessity, but the moral goodness of a devotion to benevolence and the maintenance of justice that passes beyond a certain, required point. It is to deny the possibility of going morally above and beyond the call of a restricted set of duties. Despite my claim that all-consuming moral saintliness is not a particularly healthy and desirable ideal, it seems perverse to insist that, were moral saints to exist, they would not, in their way, be remarkably noble and admirable figures. Despite my conviction that it is as rational and as good for a person to take Katharine Hepburn or Jane Austen as her role model instead of Mother Theresa, it would be absurd to deny that Mother Theresa is a morally better person....

A moral theory that does not contain the seeds of an all-consuming ideal of moral sainthood thus seems to place false and unnatural limits on our opportunity to do moral good and our potential to deserve moral praise. Yet the main thrust of the arguments of this paper has been leading to the conclusion that, when such ideals are present, they are not ideals to which it is particularly reasonable or healthy or desirable for human beings to aspire....

If the above remarks are understood to be implicitly critical of the views on the content of morality which seem most popular today, an alternative that naturally suggests itself is that we revise our views about the content of morality.... Such a change in approach involves substantially broadening or replacing our contemporary intuitions about which character traits constitute moral virtues and vices and which interests constitute moral interests. If, for example, we include personal bearing, or creativity, or sense of style, as features that contribute to one's *moral* personality, then we can create moral ideals which are incompatible with and probably more attractive than the Kantian and utilitarian ideals I have discussed. Given such an alteration of our conception of morality, the figures with which I have been concerned above might, far from being considered to be moral saints, be seen as morally inferior to other more appealing or more interesting models of individuals.

This approach seems unlikely to succeed, if for no other reason, because it is doubtful that any single, or even any reasonably small number of substantial personal ideals could capture the full range of possible ways of realizing human potential or achieving human good which deserve encouragement and praise. Even if we could provide a sufficiently broad characterization of the range of positive ways for human beings to live, however, I think there are strong reasons not to want to incorporate such a characterization more centrally into the framework of morality itself. For, in claiming that a character trait or activity is morally good, one claims that there is a certain kind of reason for developing that trait or engaging in that activity. Yet, lying behind our criticism of more conventional conceptions of moral sainthood, there seems to be a recognition that among the immensely valuable traits and activities that a human life might positively embrace are some of which we hope that, if a person does embrace them, he does so *not* for moral reasons. In other words, no matter how flexible we make the guide to conduct which we choose to label "morality," no matter how rich we make the life in which perfect obedience to this guide would result, we will have reason to hope that a person does not wholly rule and direct his life by the abstract and impersonal consideration that such a life would be morally good....

If we are not to respond to the unattractiveness of the moral ideals that contemporary theories yield either by offering alternative theories with more palatable ideals or by understanding these theories in such a way as to prevent them from yielding ideals at all, how, then, are we to respond? Simply, I think, by admitting that moral ideals do not, and need not, make the best personal ideals.... Given the empirical circumstances of our world, it seems to be an ethical fact that we have unlimited potential to be morally good, and endless opportunity to promote moral interests. But this is not incompatible with the not-so-ethical fact that we have sound, compelling, and not particularly selfish reasons to choose not to devote ourselves univocally to realizing this potential or to taking up this opportunity.

Thus, in one sense at least, I am not really criticizing either Kantianism or utilitarianism. Insofar as the point of view I am offering bears directly on recent work in moral philosophy, in fact, it bears on critics of these theories who, in a spirit not unlike the spirit of most of this paper, point out that the perfect utilitarian would be flawed in this way or the perfect Kantian flawed in that. The assumption lying behind these claims, implicitly or explicitly, has been that the recognition of these flaws shows us something wrong with utilitarianism as opposed to Kantianism, or something wrong with Kantianism as opposed to utilitarianism, or something wrong with both of these theories as opposed to some nameless third alternative. The claims of this paper suggest, however, that this assumption is unwarranted. The flaws of a perfect master of a moral theory need not reflect flaws in the intramoral content of the theory itself.

MORAL SAINTS AND MORAL PHILOSOPHY

In pointing out the regrettable features and the necessary absence of some desirable features in a moral saint, I have not meant to condemn the moral saint or the person who aspires to become one. Rather, I have meant to insist that the ideal of moral sainthood should not be held as a standard against which any other ideal must be judged or justified, and that the posture we take in response to the recognition that our lives are not as morally good as they might be need not be defensive. It is misleading to insist that one is *permitted* to live a life in which the goals, relationships, activities, and interests that one pursues are not maximally morally good. For our lives are not so comprehensively subject to the requirement that we apply for permission, and our nonmoral reasons for the goals we set ourselves are not excuses, but may rather be positive, good reasons which do not exist *despite* any reasons that might threaten to outweigh them. In other words, a person may be *perfectly wonderful* without being *perfectly moral*....

The claims of this paper do not so much conflict with the content of any particular currently popular moral theory as they call into question a metamoral assumption that implicitly surrounds discussions of moral theory more generally.

Specifically, they call into question the assumption that it is always better to be morally better.

The role morality plays in the development of our characters and the shape of our practical deliberations need be neither that of a universal medium into which all other values must be translated nor that of an ever-present filter through which all other values must pass. This is not to say that moral value should not be an important, even the most important, kind of value we attend to in evaluating and improving ourselves and our world. It is to say that our values cannot be fully comprehended on the model of a hierarchical system with morality at the top....

Justice and Care Operate Together

CATHERINE WILSON

The problem of affluence is neatly summarized by Thomas Nagel. "The bill for two," he observes,

> in a moderately expensive New York restaurant equals the annual per capita income of Bangladesh. Every time I eat out, not because I have to but just because I feel like it, the same money could do noticeably more good if contributed to famine relief. The same could be said of many purchases of clothing, wine, theater tickets, vacations, gifts, books, records, furniture, stemware, etc. It adds up both to a form of life and to quite a lot of money.

Nagel, who has long been concerned with the problem of altruism, confesses that he does not know quite what to make of this observation. He does not believe that his current manner of life can really be justified, and he does not think it is immune from criticism. Yet he also does not think it is obvious that he should not engage in this form of life, or that certain kinds of moral argument have shown that he is in the wrong insofar as he does. Perhaps, he says, he might be converted to another way of living "by a leap of self-transcendence." But because the life after the event would be so different from the life before, it is not, strictly speaking, to be envisioned from his present point of views. Alternatively, he says, one might aim for or hope for a political rather than a personal solution to the problem of unequal distribution of goods.

Although he formulates the problem as an urgent and troubling one, the effect of Nagel's text—in the context of the book of which it is a part—is to diminish its urgency. For Nagel shows himself ready in this book to treat the problem of affluence and responsibility as a particular case of a general nonconvergence between subjective views of the world and an objective view, a nonconvergence to which he assigns a positive rather than a negative value. And here we meet with an extraordinary feature of contemporary moral philosophy: one so striking that it deserves discussion, namely, its thoroughgoing rejection of the idea that philosophical enlightenment entails a detachment from worldly goods and worldly pleasures....

One reads passages such as the one quoted from Nagel with a sense of unease. It takes only a few degrees of philosophical distance to ask oneself in this connection whether the objects and pursuits deemed meritorious in what Thorstein Veblen referred to almost a century ago as "pecuniary society" really are so; whether the codes of this society correspond to actual meanings? What about those wineglasses and theater tickets? And what are we to say when it is philosophers themselves who implicitly endorse the right to these things and the way of life of which they are part by finding an irreconcilable difference between subjective and objective points of view? Following Karl Mannheim, the founder of the sociology of knowledge, we may well suppose that the intelligentsia of a society, especially its philosophers, are the people whose task it is to produce an interpretation of life for that society, and that what the new moral philosophers are doing is producing such an interpretation. Now, according to Mannheim, an ideology is produced when a "ruling group becomes so interest-bound that they cannot see facts which would undermine their sense of domination; they obscure the real condition of society to themselves and others and thereby stabilize it." We have thus to ask whether the designation of certain spheres of activity and experience as protected regions which are above, beyond, and perhaps beneath the reach of impersonal theories of justice might not constitute an ideology of academicians who are now, in a way they have never been before, part of a materially favored class.

THE DECLINE OF IMPERSONAL THEORIES

The earlier trends in ethics to which the work we have been considering may be seen as a response were socio-legal in tenor, broad in scale, and redistributionist in their slant: John Rawls dominated the former era with *A Theory of Justice*, published in 1971. To show the endpoints of the scale between impartial justice ethics and the ethos of private pursuits which Nagel's passage invokes, we may consider the positions taken by Peter Singer in an article published almost twenty years ago and by Susan Wolf in 1982.

In "Famine, Affluence and Morality," Singer argued that the affluence of the richer nations and their unwillingness to devote more than a fraction of their gross national product—about 1%—to aid to other countries, in which people were suffering from hunger, cold, climactic catastrophes, and overpopulation was wrong. It was also wrong for individuals, not just nations, to devote so little of their own income to charity. The right thing to do, he

said, was, in effect, to forgo the glassware, the theater tickets, the new outfits, the vacation, and just give the money one would have spent on those things to a relief organization. It was both possible and morally obligatory to compare the percentage of one's income spent on the nonnecessities of life with the percentage spent to provide these necessities for others who do not have them. Psychologically, he admitted, it is difficult to care about people on the other side of the world experiencing a famine or another catastrophe, but it is morally wrong nevertheless to ignore them.

A position orthogonal to this one was adopted by Wolf, who spoke out daringly in favor of private and even wasteful activities. Wolf did not even try to redefine morality in such a way as to make it accord better with experience; she rejected the pursuit of moral perfection in any terms. In "Moral Saints," she considered the appearance of wrongness produced by affluence and argued that it was illusory. She willingly conceded that "no plausible argument can justify the use of human resources involved in producing paté de canard en croûte against possible beneficent ends to which these resources might be put." Yet, she said, it is not right to reproach the diner on paté de canard, and this diner need not maintain a defensive posture with respect to this pleasure. For morality—in the sense in which it would require us to sacrifice ourselves for others—is not the only value, the one to which every other good must be sacrificed. And she went on to describe other projects, which consume time and money, the participation in which precludes time exercise of charity, which are worthy and appropriate for human beings. We need to recognize the value, she insisted, of "the normal person's direct and specific desires for objects, activities, and events that conflict with the attainment of moral perfection."

The unrestrained pursuit of moral excellence would, Wolf said, even make it impossible to be excellent in the broader sense. There were accordingly both positive and negative sides to her paper. Part of it was spent painting sainthood, which she interpreted as the dedication of all one's resources and energies to helping others, in an undesirable light. Saints were portrayed as overly focused, self-righteous, and narrow. The suggestion was that the whole-hearted giving oneself over to projects of relieving other people's suffering would have a strangely dehumanizing effect; we should be in awe of people who managed to do this but it would be unpleasant to be forced into social intimacy with them, for we nonsaints would have no common ground with them. The rest of the article was spent painting a picture of a good or wonderful life. This life is characterized by variety, enjoyment, and the improvement of abilities and talents; the author mentions reaching Victorian novels, playing the oboe, improving one's backhand, gourmet cooking, watching old comedies, eating caviar, and cello playing, as its possible constituents. The emphasis here is on pursuits and activities, rather than, as in Nagel's chapter, the accumulation of personal and transitory experiences; however, in both cases, one is not being pejorative in pointing out that some typical enjoyments of upper-middle class people furnish the domain.

The difficulty with Singer's paper, which left it vulnerable to challenges such as Wolf's, was that it seemed to bring us up against the limits of philosophy as a discursive mode. It could not bring about the effect in the reader that its content mandated. Even in the context of the early 1970s concern with social justice, it seemed prophetic, utopian. The reaction of the reader was to concede that there was a great deal to what Singer had said, that the good arguments were all on his side, but one felt that Singer had claimed the moral high ground and issued an ultimatum, though one without threats or enticements. The paper was, as a text, unpersuasive, for Singer did not even acknowledge our pre-existing local and partialist concerns. In ignoring what people actually care about—the protection of their children and themselves from the more brutal aspects of existence; the cultivation of their talents and interests; and the beautification of themselves, their houses, their environments—he succeeded in portraying only a system of redistribution that could be imposed by a philosopher king. And, like Rawls, he regarded the private emotions of pity and shame as irrelevant to the question of public justice.

Singer's response would have been at the time to say that the philosopher's role is just to point out contradictions and entailments, such as the obligation to charity necessitated by impartialist concepts of justice, which he took for granted. Rhetoric and psychology belong to a different department. Such are the limits of philosophy. Interestingly, Wolf too believes in the limits to philosophy: she does not believe that philosophy can *justify* selfish or inconsequential pursuits, and she claims that justifying them is not what she is doing. Rather, she is taking a meta-ethical stance, and making a meta-ethical claim, viz., that "the posture we take in response to the recognition that our lives are not as morally good as possible need not be defensive." According to Wolf, no philosophical theory can tell us how important moral goodness is as against other forms of goodness, or how much time, effort, and money we ought to devote to other-directed moral pursuits as against selfish, pleasurable pursuits. Thus, where

Singer failed to take into account some obvious limits of philosophical argument, Wolf seems to be positing and even welcoming the limits to argument.

THE FACT OF DIVIDED LOYALTIES

One may be convinced by what Wolf says and convinced as a result that Singer's conclusions about what we ought to do are erroneous. In such a case one may nevertheless be dissatisfied with "Moral Saints" for reasons other than the cogency of its argument: one may, for example, believe that asceticism is part of the philosopher's role, and that, whatever she does as a private person, it is wrong for a philosopher to abandon her role in this way. Such disapproval would, however, tend to lend strength to Wolf's implicit contention that the way in which philosophers have often wanted to talk about morality makes them guilty of hypocrisy. Alternatively, however, one might believe that Wolf's claim to be able to speak from outside a moral perspective, from a perspective which recognizes morality as merely one human good among others, is unjustified. If, as I shall try to show, this is in fact the case, then Singer and other philosophers who insist on the need for sweeping revisions to ordinary life in the name of morality have not been answered.

First, though, a word on benign and necessary hypocrisies. In the historian Paul Veyne's illuminating and increasingly cited study of the psychology of divided loyalties—*Did the Greeks Believe in Their Myths?*—he argued that the Greeks did, in some sense, believe in their myths, but that they left off using them where their interest in believing them ended. This pattern of partial allegiance is, he thinks, universal. We live, Veyne argues, in a number of different worlds at once, or rather we live lives that are characterized by various programs—aesthetic, moral, religious,

practical, social. Normally, the question of the consistency or inconsistency of these programs does not arise, but sometimes a convulsive effort at consistency is made. (Religious cults provide an obvious example: for the Massachusetts Puritans, for example, constant surveillance and proofing of the thoughts, language, dress, behavior, etc., of oneself, one's children, one's servants, and one's neighbors for their conformity to religious prescripts was an obligation.) But in most places and at most times, life is not like this: our minds are Balkanized but peaceful.

Every special subject—religion, morality, art, and politics—on Veyne's account, has its proponents who claim that it is the alpha and omega of human existence. They argue that it constitutes the highest reality, or the deepest level of analysis, or the most urgent spring of conduct. The moralist says that every human action must be assigned to the category of the morally permitted, obligatory, or proscribed; the theologian says that everything serves and glorifies a god or disobeys his rules. The politician says that all actions are important in so far as they maintain or threaten political ideals and institutions. The aesthete says that only the fascinating, the marvellous, the complicated, or the unfathomable, have enduring value. But whatever these spokespeople say, real life is not like this. At any given moment, each special subject is relatively unimportant; each occupies only a narrow band in the quotidian spectrum.

So it may be that an ethics of the impersonal sort is a cultural icon that serves for cultural orientation without being fully operational at every moment. On parade days—in moments of great indignation or conflict—morality might come, in full dress as it were, into play, and permit the subject to articulate his opposition or think his situation through in a way he could not otherwise. If this is how things are, then the unease prompted by "Moral Saints" is perhaps a function of the fact that, for these worthy cultural icons to serve us well, they cannot be positively identified as such....

IMMANENCE AS A VALUE

It is one thing to take exception to "Moral Saints" because the author has exposed morality as an idol, thereby producing a general relief, but also a certain discomfort, while failing to give a better foundation for the idea of a wonderful life. It is quite another to take exception to it on the grounds that the literature of partiality and personal projects really constitutes a defense of a life of leisure and privilege, and that part of its constituting such a defense involves the inclusion of a specific statement to the effect that it is not a defense. If it really is a defense posing as a proof that some things need no defense, then, I suggest, it belongs to the category of ideology. For it then shows, even if it does not say that they have them, the rights of the haves against the have-nots, and, by what it excludes, it projects a state of affairs in which the good life described really is an innocent, as opposed to an innocuous life....

Regarded in the value-neutral terms of descriptive sociology, the philosophers we have mentioned can be seen to write without exception from a perspective of choice, plenty, and leisure. The activities and adventures—dining adventures, theatrical adventures, even romantic adventures—which they mention or discuss are plainly bound to a economic context and a milieu that is established in the large or middle-sized cities of the Western industrial democracies. Now, it might be said that it does not matter if the Nagel-Wolf vision of the good life is determined by the culture in which we happen to live; it only

matters that other people at other times and in other places should have been allowed to have their particularist ideas of the good life as well. The world of the Thai peasant contains its sensory delights, its music, tastes, colors, and fictions. But the concern here is not that the conception of a good life is narrowly defined or restricted. It is rather that a defense of immanence offered by one who, objectively speaking, enjoys a situation of privilege, is itself an ideology, or, if it is not, nothing has been said to block the charge that it is.

Nagel was troubled by this question: Could a life that is not obviously exploitative and egotistical by the standards of the immediate community nevertheless be criticized from some more detached perspective? His answer, as I read it, is that it *could* be criticized, but that the incommensurability of subjective and objective points of view makes it impossible that this criticism could take the form of a slow, deliberate, willed comparison of one's mode of life with traditional philosophical conceptions of justice: rather, one would have to experience an inner revolution or revelation. The theological motif is further developed by Wolf, who concedes the existence of "saints" who reject the standards of the community. But she assumes the appropriateness of these standards and presents examples of pursuits that are not, in light of those standards, particularly contestable. If an author were to defend the excellence of driving large motorboats, collecting state-of-the-art electronics, and vacationing in resort condominiums, which, in our professional classes, are the primary objects of desire, rather than books and musical instruments, we would have been immediately aware that a certain "lifestyle" was being endorsed. But Wolf's version of the wonderful life is relatively noninvasive and nonaggrandizing. What is hidden, nevertheless, is the underlying excess, waste, and unfairness of the present system of production and distribution which make it possible to live a life of choice and plenty. How could there be a conflict between my playing the oboe and children surviving in drought-stricken Ethiopia when there is not even the slightest hint of a connection between the two? But might it not be the case that the apparent lack of any need for a defense of my oboe playing is a function only of the presentation, not a function of any distinction between public and private life which can be philosophically established?

The tendency in the new morality of private pursuits then is to make goodness more accessible, to relax the standards a person needs to meet to be good, so that a general innocuousness or minimal decency will suffice, so long as the person is achieving something worthwhile in his chosen areas of endeavor. But must we call people who excel at music, gardening, entertaining, the appreciation of literature, or at study, or writing *good*? It is often said or implied that Aristotle would have called them good. And Wolf says that the life she is representing as an ideal is Aristotelian and perhaps even Nietzschean. But it is possible to respond that Aristotle was not dealing with morality as such, and I would call on Nietzsche, who knew that the ancients were dealing with an ethos—an ethos of rank—that they were essentially articulating an idea about what it is to be a *noble* kind of person—to confirm this. Nietzsche's moral antinomianism and his call for a transvaluation of values bear in turn only a superficial relationship to the defense of the sort of life we are considering.

CONCLUSIONS

One comes away from the best contemporary moral philosophy with three strong impressions. First, one is struck by its desire to replace old-fashioned moral prescriptivism, with its unpleasant tendency to harangue the readership to little avail, with descriptive accounts of what we do care about, and how we in fact establish individual hierarchies of values. Second, one is struck by its perception that, not only is moral theory impoverished by failing to take contingency and partiality into account, but that the value of life is reduced when an effort is made to suppress or exclude them. Third, one is struck by the point that morality cannot, logically, do what it would like to do: draw a sphere around the whole of life and evaluate everything within that sphere in terms of its own requirements. For we have the option, always, simply to pay morality no mind. We may therefore expose ourselves to the condemnation of others; again, however, we have the option, always, to pay those judgments no mind.

The question that has to be faced is whether the resulting award of a philosophically protected status to life as it is lived by a percentage of the population in North America and Britain is not as or more objectionable than the faults ascribed to those impersonal theories of ethics that we are forced to recognize, following Strawson, as revisionary.

Revisionary ethics—ethics which is associated with the fervent wish that people would live differently than they do—is subject to attack on three fronts: on the grounds that the task of philosophy is not to present a utopian state of affairs and urge its realization but to produce an analysis of moral phenomena as they are actually experienced by us; on the grounds that the ideals it holds up are inhuman; and, finally, on the grounds that the binding character of the moral law of revisionary ethics lies itself in the realm of the imaginary. It is impossible not to feel the force of these criticisms, even when one comes as a nonspecialist to the field. Any honest person must recognize the existence of conflicts in herself, between impartial ideals of justice and the love of ease and luxury; between the desire for purity and integrity and the desire for experience and multiplicity. The world as I found it—as I stumbled into it—and its particular arrangements are not my fault. And though anyone may intone morality to us in the most solemn of accents, it is still up to us to reply that we do not care, or that we care about something else more. Thus, it is absurd to speak of an obligation on our part to be saints. It is even absurd to speak of an obligation to care about morality which philosophy can prove or reveal. But implicit in the practice of philosophy is the recognition of an obligation to criticize that which one is naturally inclined to believe and to do. This applies to the values of immanence as well as to the now more commonly targeted values of abstraction and impersonality.

The contemporary philosophical defense of the plurality of goods, immanence, and contingency contrasts with the historical tendency of moral philosophers to establish a distance between themselves and the values of their culture. The establishment of this distance should not be confused, however, with the establishment of a revisionary moral philosophy that is itself distanced from life and practice. The scrutiny of one's own life for adherence to pecuniary and other culturally determined canons of taste can become but need not be a manifestation of Veyne's neurotic scrupulousness which insists on a perfect obedience to impossible regulations. And the study of the relations between plenitude

and choice in an economically dominant society and hardship and confinement in others evinces no hint of an incommensurability between subjective and objective views, no hint of practices or desires so deeply entrenched in our way of life that it is impossible to imagine altering them. Rather, it is by painting a picture of a life in which no re-orientation will occur—unless by a magical act of conversion—because of the very fullness and excellence of that life, that one contributes to occluding the connections that bind the public to the private. Correspondingly, it is by letting the lives of people who do not shop, or travel, or enjoy professional entertainment, make their own impression on us that the perception of a gulf between the private and the public sphere is altered and the superstition that one's own good fortune is either morally deserved, or a highly improbable but lucky accident, undermined.

To the extent that our ordinary way of life does appear immune from criticism and is not perceived as the outcome of those forces which sustain, transmit, and defend privilege, it is, I have suggested, due to the desire that it be made to appear so. When it is suggested that no reconciliation between happiness and charitable practice can be found without a leap into the unknown, or that objective perception will result in the fragmentation of personal integrity, or the loss of one's humanity, or that philosophy, for metatheoretical reasons cannot speak to these issues at all, one can only wonder whether, under the impression that he is showing the hollowness of some cultural icons, the philosopher is not under the spell of some others.

THE CONTINUING DEBATE:
Do Moral Obligations Always Take Precedence?

What Is New

The demands of morality can grow at a healthy, and perhaps to some an alarming, rate. There has perhaps always been an obligation of aiding those in other parts of the world who are living in poverty, or victimized by natural disaster, or living under a repressive and brutal regime, or facing starvation from famine; but those demands were once at a distance, and a modest contribution to a decent charity could assuage our concern. But our much smaller world is one in which the horrific living conditions and eminent threat of early death are constantly before us. The suffering of the victims of an earthquake or famine or civil war is known to us within the hour, in graphic detail. Our obligations to suffering fellow humans seem more immediate and more substantial. Added to that is expanded concerns for other species as well as for ecosystems. Ironically, as the circle of moral concern expands, the tendency of many contemporary ethicists is toward more recognition of the moral importance of personal and family relationships. Of course that does not mean that the more global concerns must be ignored. For example, many who believe we should give greater emphasis to the special goods of relations among family and friends are also deeply committed to alleviating world poverty and stopping the mistreatment of other species. Nevertheless there is some sense of tension between the movements.

Michael Slote's "satisficing" version of consequentialism has become a major position among consequentialist theorists. While traditional utilitarian theories promote the *maximizing* of good benefits (if I could produce better overall benefits by donating my money to famine relief rather than enjoying a meal at a nice restaurant, then I am morally obligated to forgo the restaurant meal and make the donation), the *satisficing* version requires only that my acts produce benefits that are *satisfactory*, or *good enough*, without necessarily being the best of all possible results. While the moral demands of traditional utilitarianism may be quite severe, the demands of the satisficing version are much more moderate. Providing music lessons for my children may not result in the greatest possible balance of pleasure over suffering for everyone, but the results may be *sufficiently* beneficial to meet the requirements of satisficing consequentialism.

Where to Find More

Susan Wolf is well known for her provocative books and articles that cast old problems in a new and interesting light. Her *Freedom Within Reason* (NY: Oxford University Press, 1990) is a particularly interesting rationalist account of autonomy. Robert Merrihew Adams, "Saints," *The Journal of Philosophy*, volume (1984): 392–401, develops extensive criticisms of Wolf's "Moral Saints" view from a more religious perspective. Thomas Nagel's views can be found in *The View From Nowhere* (NY: Oxford University Press, 1986); see also his *The Last Word* (NY: Oxford University Press, 1997).

Edmund L. Pincoffs argues that virtue ethics can explain how the unrestricted seeking of moral betterment is desirable; see his *Quandaries and Virtues: Against Reductivism in Ethics* (Lawrence: University Press of Kansas, 1986), especially Chapter 6, "A Defense of Perfectionism." Peter Singer's early position can be found in "Famine, Affluence and Morality," *Philosophy and Public Affairs*, volume 1 (1972): 229–243. Singer modified his views somewhat in *The Expanding Circle: Ethics and Sociobiology* (NY: Oxford, 1983); for more recent essays by Singer—which make ethical demands for significant changes in our privileged way of life—see *Writings on an Ethical Life* (NY: HarperCollins, 2000).

Bernard Williams, in "Morality, the Peculiar Institution," states that: "Ethical life itself is important, but it can see that things other than itself are important"; p. 184 in *Ethics and the Limits of Philosophy* (Cambridge, MA: Harvard University Press, 1985). Robert B. Louden's argument that "as concerns morality, more is always better than less," can be found in *Morality and Moral Theory: A Reappraisal and Reaffirmation* (NY: Oxford University Press, 1992); see especially chapter 3, "Morality and Maximization." The satisficing version of utilitarianism is presented in Michael A. Slote, *Common-Sense Morality and Consequentialism* (London: Routledge and Kegan, 1985).

Issues raised in debates 5 and 6 are relevant to this debate.

DO WOMEN HAVE A DISTINCTIVE ETHICAL PERSPECTIVE?

WOMEN HAVE A DISTINCTIVE ETHICAL PERSPECTIVE

ADVOCATE: Annette Baier, Distinguished Service Professor of Philosophy at the University of Pittsburgh.

SOURCE: "What Do Women Want in a Moral Theory?" *Noûs*, volume 19 (March 1985): 53–63. Reprinted in Annette Baier, *Moral Prejudices: Essays on Ethics* (Cambridge, MA: Harvard University Press, 1994).

GENDER DOES NOT DISTINGUISH DIFFERENT MORAL PERSPECTIVES

ADVOCATE: Marilyn Friedman, Professor of Philosophy, Washington University in St. Louis; author of *What Are Friends For? Feminist Perspectives on Personal Relationships and Moral Theory* (Ithaca, NY: Cornell University Press, 1993).

SOURCE: "Beyond Caring: The De-Moralization of Gender," from M. Hanen and K. Nielsen, eds., *Science, Morality, and Feminist Theory* (Calgary: Canadian Journal of Philosophy, 1987).

Though the question of gender difference in moral outlook is an old one, the major stimulus for the contemporary debate is psychologist Carol Gilligan's *In a Different Voice*. Gilligan's work is a response to the moral development research of Lawrence Kohlberg, who tracked a number of subjects from childhood well into their adult lives and charted their stages of moral development: from early preconventional stages (obey the rules to avoid punishment), through the conventional level (conform to the social rules and maintain good relationships), and finally into the post-conventional principled level, involving loyalty to the rules of the social contract or (the highest level of all) recognition of universal ethical principles grasped through rational deliberation. The highest level postulated by Kohlberg was a distinctively Kantian ethics, guided by purely rational principles independent of feelings or personal relations. In Kohlberg's longitudinal study, a number of men reached the post-conventional level, and some even achieved the postconventional principled level; but significantly fewer women achieved the level of postconventional moral development, and many of those later regressed to the conventional level. While Kohlberg sought an explanation for why women generally achieved less moral development than men, Carol Gilligan's work proposed a major shift in our understanding of moral development itself. For Gilligan, women's moral development was not inferior, but simply *different*, different in ways that emphasized moral goods and benefits that Kohlberg and most moral philosophy—especially the Kantian ethics that Kohlberg assumed in his research—had sorely neglected: the goods associated with personal relationships and affection. In short, Gilligan represented the moral perspective more frequently held by women as different, but *not* inferior: a prominent theme for many contemporary advocates of care ethics.

Whatever one concludes about the existence of a distinctive moral perspective enjoyed more often—but neither universally nor exclusively—by women, it is clear that there is no "women's moral viewpoint" shared by all members of the gender. Considering only the writings in this volume, the range of views represented by Jean Hampton, Virginia Held, Marilyn Friedman, Annette Baier, Rosalind Hursthouse, Carol Rovane, Ruth Macklin, Susan Wolf, Claudia Card and Catherine Wilson reflect great diversity and considerable conflict.

In the debate that follows, Marilyn Friedman notes the common belief that women and men have distinctly different approaches to ethics, with women focusing more on care and personal relationships while men emphasize impersonal justice and rights. Friedman argues that this difference is only apparent, since in fact the two approaches to ethics are compatible, and in practice they become intermingled and indistinguishable. Annette Baier sees love and obligation as distinct, but believes that an account of "appropriate trust" might make good use of both.

POINTS TO PONDER

➤ Jean Grimshaw writes: "If ethical concerns and priorities arise from different forms of social life, then those which have emerged from a social system in which women have so often been subordinate to men must be suspect." *If* it is true that the distinctive features of care (feminist) ethics—such as its focus on sustaining particular relationships rather than judging by impersonal universal rules—developed out of an oppressive cultural system, does that cast doubt on the legitimacy of that ethical view?

➤ It is sometimes suggested that personal relationships suffer when they are governed by the impersonal principles of justice rather than by affection. Or alternatively, that when personal relationships require justice considerations, they have already suffered a decline: If I must be prompted by considerations of justice and obligation to do a kind act for my friend, then that friendship is not all it should be. How would Friedman respond to such a claim? Is it a challenge to her view?

➤ Friedman acknowledges the importance of the "care" perspective, but she characterizes it as primarily a distinction between a focus on *particular* persons as opposed to focusing on *general* or universal *principles*. Would that way of drawing the distinction be acceptable for Annette Baier?

➤ Friedman concludes that "we need nothing less than to 'de-moralize' the genders"; would Baier agree (either partially or wholly)?

➤ Baier recommends the concept of "appropriate trust" as a means of bringing together the elements of obligation and love. Is "appropriate trust" just another name for Friedman's representation of care and obligation as compatible, or is Baier's account a distinctly different model of the relation between care (or love) and obligation? Are the views of Friedman and Baier compatible, though they emphasize different issues; or is there some basic area of disagreement between them?

Women Have a Distinctive Ethical Perspective

ANNETTE BAIER

When I finished reading Carol Gilligan's *In a Different Voice*, I asked myself the obvious question for a philosopher reader: what differences should one expect in the moral philosophy done by women, supposing Gilligan's sample of women to be representative and supposing her analysis of their moral attitudes and moral development to be correct? Should one expect women to want to produce moral theories, and if so, what sort of moral theories? How will any moral theories they produce differ from those produced by men?

Obviously one does not have to make this an entirely a priori and hypothetical question. One can look and see what sort of contributions women have made to moral philosophy. Such a look confirms, I think, Gilligan's findings. What one finds is a bit different in tone and approach from the standard sort of the moral philosophy as done by men following in the footsteps of the great moral philosophers (all men).... I hear the voice Gilligan heard, made reflective and philosophical. What women want in moral philosophy is what they are providing. And what they are providing seems to me to confirm Gilligan's theses about women....

Although we find out what sort of moral philosophy women want by looking to see what they have provided, if we do that for moral theory, the answer we get seems to be 'none'. None of the contributions to moral philosophy by women really counts as a moral theory, nor is seen as such by its author....

The paradigm examples of moral theories—those that are called by their authors 'moral theories'—are distinguished not by the comprehensiveness of their internally coherent account but by the *sort* of coherence which is aimed at over a fairly broad area. Their method is not the mosaic method but the broad brushstroke method. Moral theories, as we know them, are, to change the art form, vaults rather than walls—they are not built by assembling painstakingly made brick after brick. In *this* sense of theory—a fairly tightly systematic account of a large area of morality, with a keystone supporting all the rest—women moral philosophers have not yet, to my knowledge, produced moral theories or claimed that they have....

What key concept or guiding motif might hold together the structure of a moral theory hypothetically produced by a reflective woman, Gilligan-style, who has taken up moral theorizing as a calling? What would be a suitable central question, principle, or concept to structure a moral theory which might accommodate those moral insights which women tend to have more readily than men, and to answer those moral questions which, it seems, worry women more than men? I hypothesized that the women's theory, expressive mainly of women's insights and concerns, would be an ethics of love, and this hypothesis seems to be Gilligan's too, since she has gone on from *In a Different Voice* to write about the limitations of Freud's understanding of love as women know it. But presumably women theorists will be like enough to men to want their moral theory to be acceptable to all, so acceptable both to reflective women and to reflective men. Like any good theory, it will need not to ignore the partial truth of previous theories. It must therefore accommodate both the insights men have more easily than women and those women have more easily than men. It should swallow up its predecessor theories.... So women theorists will need to connect their ethics of love with what has been the men theorists' preoccupation, namely, obligation.

The great and influential moral theorists have in the modern era taken *obligation* as the key and the problematic concept, and have asked what justifies treating a person as morally bound or obliged to do a particular thing. Since to be bound is to be unfree, by making obligation central one at the same time makes central the question of the justification of coercion, of forcing or trying to force someone to act in a particular way. The concept of obligation as justified limitation of freedom does just what one wants a good theoretical concept to do—to divide up the field (as one looks at different ways one's freedom may be limited, freedom in different spheres, different sorts and versions and levels of justification) and at the same time to hold the subfields together. There must in a theory be some generalization and some speciation or diversification, and a good rich key concept guides one both in recognizing the diversity and in recognizing the unity in it. The concept of obligation has served this function very well for the area of morality it covers, and so we have some fine theories about that area. But as Aristotelians and Christians, as well as women, know, there is a lot of morality *not* covered by that concept, a lot of very great importance even for the area where there are obligations.

This is fairly easy to see if we look at what lies behind the perceived obligation

to keep promises. Unless there is some good moral reason why someone should assume the responsibility of rearing a child to be *capable* of taking promises seriously, once she understands what a promise is, the obligation to obey promises will not effectively tie her, and any force applied to punish her when she breaks promises or makes fraudulent ones will be of questionable justice. Is there an *obligation* on someone to make the child into a morally competent promisor? If so, on whom? Who has failed in his or her obligations when, say, war orphans who grew up without parental love or any other love arrive at legal adulthood very willing to be untrue to their word? Who failed in what obligation in all those less extreme cases of attempted but unsuccessful moral education?... The liberal version of our basic moral obligations tends to be fairly silent on who has what obligations to new members of the moral community, and it would throw most theories of the justification of obligations into some confusion if the obligation to rear one's children lovingly were added to the list of obligations. Such evidence as we have about the conditions in which children do successfully 'learn' the morality of the community of which they are members suggests that we cannot substitute 'conscientiously' for 'lovingly' in this hypothetical extra needed obligation. But an obligation to love, in the strong sense needed, would be an embarrassment to the theorist, given most accepted versions of 'ought implies can'....

Reliance on a recognized obligation to turn oneself into a good parent or else to avoid becoming a parent would be a problematic solution. Good parents tend to be the children of good parents, so this obligation would collapse into the obligation to avoid parenthood unless one expected to be a good parent. That, given available methods of contraception, may itself convert into the obligation, should one expect not to be a good parent, to sexual abstinence, or sterilization, or resolute resort to abortion when contraception fails. The conditional obligation to abort, and in effect also the conditional obligation to sterilization, falls on the women. There may be conditions in which the rational moral choice is between obligatory sexual abstinence and obligatory sterilization, but obligatory abortion, such as women in China now face, seems to me a moral monster. . . .

No liberal moral theorist, as far as I know, is advocating obligatory abortion or obligatory sterilization when necessary to prevent the conception of children whose parents do not expect to love them. My point rather is that they escape this conclusion only by avoiding the issue of what is to ensure that new members of the moral community do get the loving care they need to become morally competent persons. Liberal moral theories assume that women either will provide loving maternal care, or will persuade their mates to provide loving paternal care, or when pregnant will decide for abortion, encouraged by their freedom-loving men. These theories, in other words, exploit the culturally encouraged maternal instinct and/or the culturally encouraged docility of women. The liberal system would receive a nasty spanner in its works should women use their freedom of choice as regards abortion to choose *not* to abort, and then leave their newborn children on their fathers' doorsteps. That would test liberal morality's ability to provide for its own survival.

At this point it may be objected that every moral theory must make some assumptions about the natural psychology of these on whom obligations are imposed. Why shouldn't the liberal theory count on a continuing sufficient supply of good loving mothers, as it counts on continuing self-interest and, perhaps, on a continuing supply of pugnacious men who are able and willing to become good soldiers, without turning any of these into moral *obligations?* Why waste moral resources recognizing as obligatory or as virtuous what one can count on getting without moral pressure? If, in the moral economy, one can get enough good mothers and good warriors 'for free', why not gladly exploit what nature and cultural history offer? I cannot answer this question fully here, but my argument does depend upon the assumption that a decent morality will *not* depend for its stability on forces to which it gives no moral recognition. Its account books should be open to scrutiny, and there should be no unpaid debts, no loans with no prospect of repayment. I also assume that once we are clear about these matters and about the interdependencies involved, our principles of justice will not allow us to recognize either a special obligation on every woman to initiate the killing of the foetus she has conceived, should she and her mate be, or think they will be, deficient in parental love, or a special obligation on every young man to kill those his elders have labelled enemies of his country. Both such 'obligations' are prima facie suspect, and difficult to make consistent with any of the principles supposedly generating obligations in modern moral theories. I also assume that, on reflection, we will not want to recognize as *virtues* the character traits of women and men which lead them to supply such life and death services 'for free'. Neither maternal servitude, nor the resoluteness needed to kill off one's children to prevent their growing up unloved, nor the easy willingness to go out and kill when ordered to do so by authorities seems to me to be a character trait a decent morality will encourage by labelling it a virtue. But the liberals' morality must somehow encourage such traits if its stability depends on enough people showing them. There is, then, understandable motive for liberals' avoidance of the question of whether such qualities are or are not morally approved of, and of whether or not there is any obligation to act as one with such character traits would act.

It is symptomatic of the bad faith of liberal morality as understood by many of those who defend it that issues such as whether to fight or not to fight, to have or not to have an abortion, or to be or not to be an unpaid maternal drudge are left to individual conscience. Since there is no coherent guidance liberal morality can give on these issues, which clearly are *not* matters of moral indifference, liberal morality tells each of us, 'the choice is yours', hoping that enough will choose to be self-sacrificial life providers and self-sacrificial death dealers to suit the purposes of the rest....

Granted that the men's theories of obligation need supplementation, to have much chance of integrity and coherence, and that the women's hypothetical theories will want to cover obligation as well as love, then what concept brings them together? My tentative answer is—the concept of appropriate trust, oddly neglected in moral theory. This concept also nicely mediates between reason and feeling, those tired old candidates for moral authority, since to trust is neither quite to believe something about the trusted nor necessarily to feel any emotion towards them—but to have a belief-informed and action-influencing attitude. To make it plausible that the neglected concept of appropriate trust is a good one for the enlightened moral theorist to make central, I need to show, or begin to show, how it could include obligation, indeed shed light on obligations and their justification,

as well as include love, the other moral concerns of Gilligan's women, and many of the topics women moral philosophers have chosen to address, mosaic fashion. I would also need to show that it could connect all of these in a way which holds out promise both of synthesis and of comprehensive moral coverage. A moral theory which looked at the conditions for proper trust of all the various sorts we show, and at what sorts of reasons justify inviting such trust, giving it, and meeting it, would, I believe, not have to avoid turning its gaze on the conditions for the survival of the practices it endorses, so it could avoid that unpleasant choice many current liberal theories seem to have—between incoherence and bad faith. I do not pretend that we will easily agree once we raise the questions I think we should raise, but at least we may have a language adequate to the expression of both men's and women's moral viewpoints.

My trust in the concept of trust is based in part on my own attempts to restate and consider what is right and what wrong with men's theories, especially Hume's, which I consider the best of the lot. I have found myself reconstructing his account of the artifices of justice as an account of the progressive enlargement of a climate of trust, and have found that a helpful way to see it. It has some textual basis, but is nevertheless a reconstruction, and one I have found, immodestly, an improvement. So it is because I have tried the concept and explored its dimensions a bit—the variety of goods we may trust others not to take from us, the sort of security or insurance we have when we do, the sorts of defences or potential defences we lay down when we trust, the various conditions for reasonable trust of various types—that I am hopeful about its power as a theoretical, and not just an exegetical, tool. I also found myself needing to use it when I made a brief rash attempt at that women's topic, caring (invited in by a male philosopher, I should say). I am reasonably sure that trust does generalize some central moral features of the recognition of binding obligations and moral virtues and of loving, as well as of other important relations between persons, such as teacher-pupil, confider-confidante, worker to co-worker in the same cause, and professional to client. Indeed it is fairly obvious that love, the main moral phenomenon women want attended to, involves trust, so I anticipate little quarrel when I claim that, if we had a moral theory spelling out the conditions for appropriate trust and distrust, that would include a morality of love in all its variants—parental love, love of children for their parents, love of family members, love of friends, of lovers in the strict sense, of co-workers, of one's country and its figureheads, of exemplary heroines and heroes, of goddesses and gods.

Love and loyalty demand maximal trust of one sort, and maximal trustworthiness, and in investigating the conditions for maximal trust and maximal risk we must think about the ethics of love. More controversial may be my claim that the ethics of obligation will also be covered. I see it as covered because to recognize a set of obligations is to trust some group of persons to instil them, to demand that they be met, possibly to levy sanctions if they are not, and this is to trust persons with very significant coercive power over others. Less coercive but still significant power is possessed by those shaping our conception of the virtues and expecting us to display them, approving when we do, disapproving and perhaps shunning us when we do not. Such coercive and manipulative power over others requires justification, and is justified only if we have reason to trust those who have

it to use it properly and to use the discretion which is always given when trust is given in a way which serves the purpose of the whole system of moral control, and not merely self-serving or morally improper purposes. Since the question of the justification of coercion becomes, at least in part, the question of the wisdom of trusting the coercers to do their job properly, the morality of obligation, in as far as it reduces to the morality of coercion, is covered by the morality of proper trust. Other forms of trust may also be involved, but trusting enforcers with the use of force is the most problematic form of trust involved.

The coercers and manipulators are, to some extent, all of us, so to ask what our obligations are and what virtues we should exhibit is to ask what it is reasonable to trust us to demand, expect, and contrive to get from one another. It becomes, in part, a question of what powers we can in reason trust ourselves to exercise properly. But self-trust is a dubious or limit case of trust, so I prefer to postpone the examination of the concept of proper self-trust at least until proper trust of others is more clearly understood. Nor do we distort matters too much if we concentrate on those cases where moral sanctions and moral pressure and moral manipulation are not self-applied but applied to others, particularly by older persons to younger persons. Most moral pressuring that has any effect goes on in childhood and early youth. Moral sanctions may continue to be applied, formally and informally, to adults, but unless the criminal courts apply them it is easy enough for adults to ignore them, to brush them aside. It is not difficult to become a sensible knave, and to harden one's heart so that one is insensible to the moral condemnation of one's victims and those who sympathize with them. Only if the pressures applied in the morally formative stage have given one a heart that rebels against the thought of such ruthless independence of what others think will one see any reason *not* to ignore moral condemnation, not to treat it as mere powerless words and breath. Condemning sensible knaves is as much a waste of breath as arguing with them—all we can sensibly do is to try to protect children against their influence, and ourselves against their knavery. Adding to the criminal law will not be the way to do the latter, since such moves will merely challenge sensible knaves to find new knavish exceptions and loopholes, not protect us from sensible knavery. Sensible knaves are precisely those who exploit us without breaking the law. So the whole question of when moral pressure of various sorts, formative, reformative, and punitive, ought to be brought to bear by whom is subsumed under the question of whom to trust when and with what, and for what good reasons.

In concentrating on obligations, rather than virtues, modern moral theorists have chosen to look at the cases where more trust is placed in enforcers of obligations than is placed in ordinary moral agents, the bearers of the obligations. In taking, as contractarians do, contractual obligations as the model of obligations, they concentrate on a case where the very minimal trust is put in the obligated person, and considerable punitive power entrusted to the one to whom the obligation is owed (I assume here that Hume is right in saying that when we promise or contract, we formally subject ourselves to the penalty, in case of failure, of never being trusted as a promisor again). This is an interesting case of the allocation of trust of various sorts, but it surely distorts our moral vision to suppose that *all* obligations, let alone all morally pressured expectations we impose on others, conform to that abnormally

coercive model. It takes very special conditions for it to be safe to trust persons to inflict penalties on other persons, conditions in which either we can trust the penalizers to have the virtues necessary to penalize wisely and fairly, or else we can rely on effective threats to keep unvirtuous penalizers from abusing their power—that is to say, rely on others to coerce the first coercers into proper behaviour. But that reliance too will either be trust or will have to rely on threats from coercers of the coercers of coercers, and so on. Morality on this model becomes a nasty, if intellectually intriguing, game of mutual mutually corrective threats. The central question of who should deprive whom of what freedom soon becomes the question of whose anger should be dreaded by whom (the theory of obligation), supplemented perhaps by an afterthought on whose favour should be courted by whom (the theory of the virtues).

Undoubtedly some important part of morality does depend in part on a system of threats and bribes, at least for its survival in difficult conditions when normal goodwill and normally virtuous dispositions may be insufficient to motivate the conduct required for the preservation and justice of the moral network of relationships. But equally undoubtedly life will be nasty, emotionally poor, and worse than brutish (even if longer), if that is all morality is, or even if that coercive structure of morality is regarded as the backbone, rather than as an available crutch, should the main support fail. For the main support has to come from those we entrust with the job of rearing and training persons so that they can be trusted in various ways, some trusted with extraordinary coercive powers, some with public decision-making powers, all trusted as parties to promise, most trusted by some who love them and by one or more willing to become co-parents with them, most trusted by dependent children, dependent elderly relatives, sick friends, and so on. A very complex network of a great variety of sorts of trust structures our moral relationships with our fellows, and if there is a *main* support to this network it is the trust we place in those who respond to the trust of new members of the moral community, namely, children, and prepare them for new forms of trust.

A theory which took as its central question 'Who should trust whom with what, and why?' would not have to forgo the intellectual fun and games previous theorists have had with the various paradoxes of morality—curbing freedom to increase freedom, curbing self-interest the better to satisfy self-interest, not aiming at happiness in order to become happier. For it is easy enough to get a paradox of trust to accompany or, if I am right, to generalize the paradoxes of freedom, self-interest, and hedonism. To trust is to make oneself or to let oneself be more vulnerable than one might have been to harm from others—to give them an opportunity to harm one, in the confidence that they will not take it, because they have no good reason to. Why would one take such a risk? For risk it always is, given the partial opaqueness to us of the reasoning and motivation of those we trust and with whom we cooperate. Our confidence may be, and quite often is, misplaced. That is what we risk when we trust. If the best reason to take such a risk is the expected gain in security which comes from a climate of trust, then in trusting we are always giving up security to get greater security, exposing our throats so that others become accustomed to not biting. A moral theory which made proper trust its central concern could have its own categorical imperative, could replace obedience to self-made laws and freely chosen restraint

on freedom with security-increasing sacrifice of security, distrust in the promoters of a climate of distrust, and so on.

Such reflexive use of one's central concept, negative or affirmative, is an intellectually satisfying activity which is bound to have appeal to those system lovers who want to construct moral theories, and it may help them design their theory in an intellectually pleasing manner. But we should beware of becoming hypnotized by our slogans or of sacrificing truth to intellectual elegance. Any theory of proper trust should not *prejudge* the question of when distrust is proper. We might find more objects of proper distrust than just the contributors to a climate of reasonable distrust, just as freedom should be restricted not just to increase human freedom but to protect human life from poisoners and other killers. I suspect, however, that all the objects of reasonable distrust are more reasonably seen as falling into the category of ones who contribute to a decrease in the scope of proper trust than can all who are reasonably coerced be seen as themselves guilty of wrongful coercion. Still, even if all proper trust turns out to be for such persons and on such matters as will increase the scope or stability of a climate of reasonable trust, and all proper distrust for such persons and on such matters as increase the scope of reasonable distrust, overreliance on such nice reflexive formulae can distract us from asking all the questions about trust which need to be asked if an adequate moral theory is to be constructed around that concept. These questions should include when to *respond* to trust with *un*trustworthiness, when and when not to invite trust, as well as when to give and refuse trust. We should not assume that promiscuous trustworthiness is any more a virtue than is undiscriminating distrust. It is appropriate trustworthiness, appropriate trustingness, appropriate encouragement to trust which will be virtues, as will be judicious untrustworthiness, selective refusal to trust, discriminating discouragement of trust.

Women are particularly well placed to appreciate these last virtues, since they have sometimes needed them to get into a position even to consider becoming moral theorizers. The long exploitation and domination of women by men depended on men's trust in women and women's trustworthiness to play their allotted role and so to perpetuate their own and their daughters' servitude. However keen women now are to end the lovelessness of modern moral philosophy, they are unlikely to lose sight of the cautious virtue of appropriate distrust or of the tough virtue of principled betrayal of the exploiters' trust.

Gilligan's girls and women saw morality as a matter of preserving valued ties to others, of preserving the conditions for that care and mutual care without which human life becomes bleak, lonely, and after a while, as the mature men in her study found, not self-affirming, however successful in achieving the egoistic goals which had been set. The boys and men saw morality as a matter of finding workable traffic rules for self-assertors, so that they might not needlessly frustrate one another and so that they could, should they so choose, cooperate in more positive ways to mutual advantage. Both for the women's sometimes unchosen and valued ties with others and for the men's mutual respect as sovereigns and subjects of the same minimal moral traffic rules (and for their more voluntary and more selective associations of profiteers), trust is important. Both men and women are concerned with cooperation, and the dimensions of trust-distrust structure the different cooperative relations each emphasize. The various considerations which arise when we try to defend an answer to any question about the appropriateness of a particular form of cooperation with its distinctive form of trust or distrust, that is, when we look into the terms of all sorts of cooperation, at the terms of trust in different cases of trust, at what are fair terms and what are trust-enhancing and trust-preserving terms, are suitably many and richly interconnected. A moral theory (or family of theories) that made trust its central problem could do better justice to men's and women's moral intuitions than do the going men's theories. Even if we don't easily agree on the answer to the question of who should trust whom with what, who should accept and who should meet various sorts of trust, and why, these questions might enable us better to reason morally together than we can when the central moral questions are reduced to those of whose favour one must court and whose anger one must dread....

Gender Does Not Distinguish Different Moral Perspectives

MARILYN FRIEDMAN

Carol Gilligan heard a "distinct moral language" in the voices of women who were subjects in her studies of moral reasoning. Though herself a developmental psychologist, Gilligan has put her mark on contemporary feminist moral philosophy by daring to claim the competence of this voice and the worth of its message. Her book, *In a Different Voice*, explored the concern with care and relationships which Gilligan discerned in the moral reasoning of women and contrasted it with the orientation toward justice and rights which she found to typify the moral reasoning of men.

According to Gilligan, the standard (or "male") moral voice articulated in moral psychology derives moral judgments about particular cases from abstract, universalized moral rules and principles which are substantively concerned with justice and rights. For justice reasoners: the major moral imperative enjoins respect for the rights of others; the concept of duty is limited to reciprocal noninterference; the motivating vision is one of the equal worth of self and other; and one important underlying presupposition is a highly individuated conception of persons.

By contrast, the other (or "female") moral voice which Gilligan heard in her studies eschews abstract rules and principles. This moral voice derives moral judgments from the contextual detail of situations grasped as specific and unique. The substantive concern for this moral voice is care and responsibility, particularly as these arise in the context of interpersonal relationships. Moral judgments,

for care reasoners, are tied to feelings of empathy and compassion; the major moral imperatives center around caring, not hurting others, and avoiding selfishness; and the motivating vision of this ethic is "that everyone will be responded to and included, that no one will be left alone or hurt."

While these two voices are not necessarily contradictory in all respects, they seem, at the very least, to be different in their orientation. Gilligan's writings about the differences have stimulated extensive feminist reconsideration of various ethical themes. In this paper, I use Gilligan's work as a springboard for extending certain of those themes in new directions....

THE GENDER DIFFERENCE CONTROVERSY

Gilligan has advanced at least two different positions about the care and the justice perspectives. One is that the care perspective is distinct from the moral perspective which is centered on justice and rights. Following Gilligan, I will call this the "different voice" hypothesis about moral reasoning. Gilligan's other hypothesis is that the care perspective is typically, or characteristically, a *woman's* moral voice, while the justice perspective is typically, or characteristically a *man's* moral voice. Let's call this the "gender difference" hypothesis about moral reasoning.

The truth of Gilligan's gender difference hypothesis has been questioned by a number of critics who cite what seems to be disconfirming empirical evidence. This evidence includes studies by the psychologist Norma Haan, who has discerned two distinct moral voices among her research subjects, but has found them to be utilized to approximately the same extent by both females and males.

In an attempt to dismiss the research-based objections to her gender difference hypothesis, Gilligan now asserts that her aim was not to disclose a statistical gender difference in moral reasoning, but rather simply to disclose and interpret the differences in the two perspectives. Psychologist John Broughton has argued that if the gender difference is not maintained, then Gilligan's whole explanatory framework is undermined. However, Broughton is wrong. The different voice hypothesis has a significance for moral psychology and moral philosophy which would survive the demise of the gender difference hypothesis. At least part of its significance lies in revealing the lopsided obsession of contemporary theories of morality, in both disciplines, with universal and impartial conceptions of justice and rights and the relative disregard of *particular*, inter-personal relationships based on partiality and affective ties....

But *what about* that supposed empirical disconfirmation of the gender difference hypothesis? Researchers who otherwise accept the disconfirming evidence have nevertheless noticed that many women readers of Gilligan's book find it to "resonate... thoroughly with their own experience." Gilligan notes that it was precisely one of her purposes to expose the gap between women's experience and the findings of psychological research, and, we may suppose, to critique the latter in light of the former.

These unsystematic, anecdotal observations that females and males do differ in ways examined by Gilligan's research should lead us either: (1) to question, and examine carefully, the methods of that empirical research which does not reveal such differences; or (2) to suspect that a gender difference exists but in some form which is not, strictly speaking, a matter of statistical differences in the moral reasoning of women and men. Gilligan has herself expressed the first of these alternatives. I would like to explore the second possibility.

Suppose that there were a gender difference of a sort, but one which was not a simple matter of differences among the form or substance of women's and men's moral reasonings. A plausible account might take this form. Among the white middle classes of such Western industrial societies as Canada and the United States, women and men are associated with different moral norms and values at the level of the stereotypes, symbols, and myths which contribute to the social construction of gender. One might say that morality is "gendered" and that the genders are "moralized." Our very conceptions of femininity and masculinity, female and male, incorporate norms about appropriate behavior, characteristic virtues, and typical vices.

Morality, I suggest, is fragmented into a "division of moral labor" along the lines of gender, the rationale for which is rooted in historic developments pertaining to family, state, and economy. The tasks of governing, regulating social order, and managing other "public" institutions have been monopolized by men as their privileged domain, and the tasks of sustaining privatized personal relationships have been imposed on, or left to, women. The genders have thus been conceived in terms of special and distinctive moral projects. Justice and rights have structured male moral norms, values, and virtues, while care and responsiveness have defined female moral norms, values, and virtues. The division of moral labor has had the dual function both of preparing us each for our respective socially defined domains and of rendering us incompetent to manage the affairs of the realm from which we have been excluded. That justice is symbolized in our culture by the figure of a woman is a remarkable irony; her blindfold hides more than the scales she holds.

To say that the genders are moralized is to say that specific moral ideals, values, virtues, and practices are culturally conceived as the special projects or domains of specific genders. These conceptions would determine which commitments and behaviors were to be considered normal, appropriate, and expected of each gender, which commitments and behaviors were to be considered remarkable or heroic, and which commitments and behaviors were to be considered deviant, improper, outrageous, and intolerable....

Social science provides ample literature to show that gender differences are alive and well at the level of popular perception. Both men and women, on average, still conceive women and men in a moralized fashion. For example, expectations and perceptions of women's greater empathy and altruism are expressed by both women and men. The gender stereotypes of women center around qualities which some authors call "communal." These include: a concern for the welfare of others; the predominance of caring and nurturant traits; and, to a lesser extent, interpersonal sensitivity, emotional expressiveness, and a gentle personal style....

By contrast, men are stereotyped according to what are referred to as "agentic" norms. These norms center primarily around assertive and controlling tendencies. The paradigmatic behaviors are self-assertion, including forceful dominance, and independence from other people. Also encompassed by these norms are patterns of self-confidence, personal efficacy, and a direct, adventurous personal style....

If I am right, then Gilligan has discerned the *symbolically* female moral voice, and has disentangled it from the *symbolically* male moral voice, The moralization of gender is more a matter of how we *think* we reason than of how we actually reason, more a matter of the moral concerns we *attribute* to women and men than of true statistical differences between women's and men's moral reasoning. Gilligan's findings resonate with the experiences of many people because those experiences are shaped, in part, by cultural myths and stereotypes of gender which even feminist theorizing may dispel. Thus, both women and men in our culture *expect* women and men to exhibit this moral dichotomy, and, on my hypothesis, it is this expectation which has shaped both Gilligan's observations and the plausibility which we attribute to them. Or, to put it somewhat differently, *whatever* moral matters men concern themselves with are categorized, estimably, as matters of "justice and rights," whereas the moral concerns of women are assigned to the devalued categories of "care and personal relationships."

It is important to ask why, if these beliefs are so vividly held, they might, nevertheless, still not have produced a reality in conformity with them. How could those critics who challenge Gilligan's gender hypothesis be right to suggest that women and men show no significant differences in moral reasoning, if women and men are culturally educated, trained, pressured, expected, and perceived to be so radically different?...

My admittedly *partial* answer to it depends upon showing that the care/justice dichotomy is rationally implausible and that the two concepts are conceptually compatible. This conceptual compatibility creates the empirical possibility that the two moral concerns will he intermingled in practice....

SURPASSING THE CARE/JUSTICE DICHOTOMY

I have suggested that if women and men do not show statistical differences in moral reasoning along the lines of a care/justice dichotomy, this should not be thought surprising since the concepts of care and justice are mutually compatible. People who treat each other justly can also care about each other. Conversely, personal relationships are arenas in which people have rights to certain forms of treatment, and in which fairness can be reflected in ongoing interpersonal mutuality. It is this latter insight—the relevance of justice to close personal relationships—which I will emphasize here.

Justice, at the most general level, is a matter of giving people their due, of treating them appropriately. Justice is relevant to personal relationships and to care precisely to the extent that considerations of justice itself determine appropriate ways to treat friends or intimates. Justice as it bears on relationships among friends or family, or on other close personal ties, might not involve duties which are universalizable, in the sense of being owed to all persons simply in virtue of shared moral personhood. But this does not entail the irrelevance of justice among friends or intimates....

One sort of role for justice in close relationships among people of comparable moral personhood may be discerned by considering that a personal relationship is a miniature social system, which provides valued mutual intimacy, support, and concern for those who are involved. The maintenance of a relationship requires effort by the participants. One intimate may bear a much greater burden for sus-

taining a relationship than the other participant(s) and may derive less support, concern, and so forth than she deserves for her efforts. Justice sets a constraint on such relationships by calling for an appropriate sharing, among the participants, of the benefits and burdens which constitute their relationship....

Justice is relevant to close personal relationships among comparable moral persons in a second way as well. The trust and intimacy which characterize special relationships create special vulnerabilities to harm. Commonly recognized harms, such as physical injury and sexual assault, become more feasible; and special relationships, in corrupt, abusive, or degenerate forms, make possible certain uncommon emotional harms not even possible in impersonal relationships. When someone is harmed in a personal relationship, she is owed a rectification of some sort, a righting of the wrong which has been done her. The notion of justice emerges, once again, as a relevant moral notion.

Thus, in a close relationship among persons of comparable moral personhood, care may degenerate into the injustices of exploitation, or oppression. Many such problems have been given wide public scrutiny recently as a result of feminist analysis of various aspects of family life and sexual relationships. Woman battering, acquaintance rape, and sexual harassment are but a few of the many recently publicized injustices of "personal" life. The notion of distributive or corrective injustice seems almost too mild to capture these indignities, involving, as they do, violation of bodily integrity and an assumption of the right to assault and injure. But to call these harms injustices is certainly not to rule out impassioned moral criticism in other terms as well.

The two requirements of justice which I have just discussed exemplify the standard distinction between distributive and corrective justice. They illustrate the role of justice in personal relationships regarded in abstraction from a social context. Personal relationships may also be regarded in the context of their various institutional settings, such as marriage and family. Here justice emerges again as a relevant ideal, its role being to define appropriate institutions to structure interactions among family members, other household cohabitants, and intimates in general. The family, for example is a miniature society, exhibiting all the major facets of large-scale social life: decision-making affecting the whole unit; executive action; judgments of guilt and innocence; reward and punishment; allocation of responsibilities and privileges, of burdens and benefits; and monumental influences on the life-chances of both its maturing and its matured members. Any of these features *alone* would invoke the relevance of justice; together, they make the case overwhelming.

Women's historically paradigmatic role of mothering has provided a multitude of insights which can be reconstructed as insights about the importance of justice in family relationships, especially those relationships involving remarkable disparities in maturity, capability, and power. In these familial relationships, one party grows into moral personhood over time, gradually acquiring the capacity to be a responsible moral agent. Considerations of justice pertain to the mothering of children in numerous ways. For one thing, there may be siblings to deal with, whose demands and conflicts create the context for parental arbitration and the need for a fair allotment of responsibilities and privileges. Then there are decisions to be made, involving the well-being of all persons in the family unit, whose immature members become increasingly capable over

time of participating in such administrative affairs. Of special importance in the practice of raising children are the duties to nurture and to promote growth and maturation. These duties may be seen as counterparts to the welfare rights viewed by many as a matter of social justice. Motherhood continually presents its practitioners with moral problems best seen in terms of a complex framework which integrates justice with care, even though the politico-legal discourse of justice has not shaped its domestic expression.

I have been discussing the relevance of justice to close personal relationships. A few words about my companion thesis— the relevance of care to the public domain—is also in order. In its more noble manifestation, care in the public realm would show itself, perhaps, in foreign aid, welfare programs, famine or disaster relief, or other social programs designed to relieve suffering and attend to human needs. If untempered by justice in the public domain, care degenerates precipitously. The infamous "boss" of Chicago's old-time Democratic machine, Mayor Richard J. Daley, was legendary for his nepotism and political partisanship; he cared extravagantly for his relatives, friends, and political cronies.

In recounting the moral reasoning of one of her research subjects, Gilligan once wrote that the "justice" perspective fails "to take into account the reality of relationships." What she meant is that the "justice" perspective emphasizes a self's various rights to noninterference by others. Gilligan worried that if this is all that a concern for justice involved, then such a perspective would disregard the moral value of positive interaction, connection, and commitment among persons.

However, Gilligan's interpretation of justice is far too limited. For one thing, it fails to recognize positive rights, such as welfare rights, which may be endorsed from a "justice" perspective. But beyond this minor point, a more important problem is Gilligan's failure to acknowledge the potential for *violence and harm* in human interrelationships and human community. The concept of justice, in general, arises out of relational conditions in which most human beings have the capacity, and many have the inclination, to treat each other badly.

Thus, notions of distributive justice are impelled by the realization that people who together comprise a social system may not share fairly in the benefits and burdens of their social cooperation. Conceptions of rectificatory or corrective, justice are founded on the concern that when harms are done, action should he taken either to restore those harmed as fully as possible to their previous state, or to prevent further similar harm, or both. And the specific rights which people are variously thought to have are just so many manifestations of our interest in identifying ways in which people deserve protection against harm by others. The complex reality of social life encompasses the human potential for helping, caring for, and nurturing others as *well as* the potential for harming, exploiting, and oppressing others. Thus, Gilligan is wrong to think that the justice perspective completely neglects "the reality of relationships." Rather, it arises from a more complex, and more realistic, estimate of the nature of human interrelationship.

In light of these reflections, it seems wise both to reconsider the seeming dichotomy of care and justice, and to question the moral adequacy of either orientation dissociated from the other. Our aim would be to advance "beyond caring," that is, beyond *mere* caring dissociated from a concern for justice. In addition, we would do well to progress beyond gender stereotypes which assign distinct and different moral roles to women and men. Our ultimate goal should be a nongendered, nondichotomized, moral framework in which all moral concerns could be expressed. We might, with intentional irony, call this project, "de-moralizing the genders."

COMMITMENTS TO PARTICULAR PERSONS

Even though care and justice do not define mutually exclusive moral frameworks, it is still too early to dispose of the "different voice hypothesis." I believe that there is something to be said for the thesis that there are different moral orientations, even if the concepts of care and justice do not capture the relevant differences and even if the differences do not correlate statistically with gender differences.

My suggestion is that one important distinction has to do with the nature and focus of what may be called "primary moral commitments." Let us begin with the observation that, from the so-called "care standpoint," responsiveness to other persons in their wholeness and their particularity is of singular importance. This idea, in turn, points toward a notion of moral commitment which takes *particular persons* as its primary focus. A form of moral commitment which contrasts with this is one which involves a focus on general and abstract rules, values, or principles. It is no mere coincidence, I believe, that Gilligan found the so-called "justice" perspective to feature an emphasis on *rules*.

In the second part of this paper, I argued that the concepts of justice and care are mutually compatible and, to at least some extent, mutually dependent. Based on my analysis, the "justice perspective" might be said to rest, at bottom, on the assumption that the best way to *care* for persons is to respect their rights, and to accord them their due, both in distribution of the burdens and benefits of social cooperation, and in the rectification of wrongs done. But to uphold these principles, it is not necessary to respond with emotion, feeling, passion, or compassion to other persons. Upholding justice does not require the full range of mutual responsiveness which is possible between persons.

By contrast, the so-called "ethic of care" stresses an ongoing responsiveness. This ethic is, after all, the stereotypic moral norm for women in the domestic role of sustaining a family in the face of the harsh realities of a competitive marketplace and an indifferent polis. The domestic realm has been idealized as the realm in which people, as specific individuals, were to have been nurtured, cherished, and succored. The "care" perspective discussed by Gilligan is a limited one; it is not really about care in all its complexity, for, as I have argued, that notion *includes* just treatment. But it is about the nature of relationships to particular persons grasped as such. The key issue is the sensitivity and responsiveness to another person's emotional states, individuating differences, specific uniqueness, and whole particularity. The "care" orientation focuses on whole persons and deemphasizes adherence to moral rules.

Thus, the important conception which I am extracting from the so-called "care" perspective is that of commitment to particular persons. What is the nature of this form of moral commitment? Commitment to a specific person, such as a lover, child, or friend, takes as its primary focus the needs, wants, attitudes, judgments, behavior, and overall way of being of that particular person. It is specific to that individual and is not generalizable to others. We show a commitment to someone whenever we attend to her needs, enjoy her successes, defer to her judgment, and find inspiration in her values and goals simply because they are *hers*. If it is *who she is*, and not her actions or traits subsumed under general rules, which matters as one's motivating guide, then one's responsiveness to her reflects a person-oriented, rather than a rule-based, moral commitment.

Thus, the different perspectives which Gilligan called "care" and "justice" do point toward substantive differences in human interrelationship and commitment. Both orientations take account of relationships in some way; both may legitimately incorporate a concern for justice and for care, and both aim to avoid harm to others and (at the highest stages) to the self. But from the standpoint of "care," self and other are conceptualized in their *particularity* rather than as instances for the application of generalized moral notions. This difference ramifies into what appears to be a major difference in the organization and focus of moral thought.

This analysis requires a subtle expansion. Like care and justice, commitments to particular persons and commitments to values, rules, and principles are not mutually exclusive within the entire panorama of one person's moral concerns. Doubtless, they are intermingled in most people's moral outlooks. Pat likes and admires Mary because of Mary's resilience in the face of tragedy, her intelligent courage, and her good-humored audacity. Pat thereby shows a commitment *in general* to resilience, courage, and good-humored audacity as traits of human personality.

However, in Mary, these traits coalesce in a unique manner: perhaps no one will stand by a friend in deep trouble quite so steadfastly as Mary; perhaps no one petitions the university president as effectively as Mary. The traits which Pat likes, in general, converge to make *Mary*, in Pat's eyes, an especially admirable human individual, a sort of moral exemplar. In virtue of Pat's loyalty to her, Mary may come to play a role in Pat's life which exceeds, in its weightiness, the sum total of the values which Pat sees in Mary's virtues, taken individually and in abstraction from any particular human personality.

Pat is someone with commitments both to moral abstractions and to particular persons. Pat is, in short, like most of us. When we reason morally, we can take up a stance which makes either of these forms of commitment the focal point of our attention. The choice of which stance to adopt at a given time is probably, like other moral alternatives, most poignant and difficult in situations of moral ambiguity or uncertainty when we don't know how to proceed. In such situations, one can turn *either* to the guidance of principled commitments to values, forms of conduct, or human virtues, *or* one can turn to the guidance which inheres in the example set by a trusted friend or associate—the example of how *she* interprets those same moral ambiguities, or how *she* resolves those same moral uncertainties.

Of course, the commitment to a particular person is evident in more situations than simply those of moral irresolution. But the experience of moral irresolution may make clearer the different sorts of moral commitment which structure our thinking. Following cherished values will lead one out of one's moral uncertainties in a very different way than following someone else's example.

Thus, the insight that each person needs some others in her life who recognize, respect, and cherish her particularity in its richness and wholeness is the distinctive motivating vision of the "care" perspective The sort of respect for persons which grows out of this vision is not the abstract respect which is owed to all persons in virtue of their common humanity, but a respect for individual worth, merit, need, or, even, idiosyncrasy. It is a form of respect which involves admiration and cherishing, when the distinctive qualities are valued intrinsically, and which, at the least, involves toleration when the distinctive qualities are not valued intrinsically.

Indeed, there is an apparent irony in the notion of personhood which underlies some philosophers' conceptions of the universalized moral duties owed to all persons. The rational nature which Kant, for example, takes to give each person dignity and to make each of absolute value and, therefore, irreplaceable, is no more than an abstract rational nature in virtue of which we are all alike. But if we are all alike in this respect, it is hard to understand why we would be irreplaceable. Our common rational nature would seem to make us indistinguishable and, therefore, mutually interchangeable. Specific identity would be a matter of indifference, so far as absolute value is concerned. Yet it would seem that only in *virtue* of our distinctive particularity could we each be truly irreplaceable.

Of course, our particularity does not *exclude* a common nature, conceptualized at a level of suitable generality. We still deserve equal respect in virtue of our common humanity. But we are also *more* than abstractly and equivalently human. It is this "more" to which we commit ourselves when we care for others in their particularity.

Thus, as I interpret it, there is at least one important difference in moral reasoning brought to our attention by Gilligan's "care" and "justice" frameworks. This difference hinges on the primary form of moral commitment which structures moral thought and the resulting nature of the response to other persons. For so-called "care" reasoners, recognition of, and commitment to, persons in their particularity is an overriding moral concern.

Unlike the concepts of justice and care, which admit of a mutual integration, it is less clear that these two distinct forms of moral commitment can jointly comprise the focus of one's moral attention, in any single case. Nor can we respond to all other persons equally well in either way. The only integration possible here may be to seek the more intimate, responsive, committed relationships with people who are known closely, or known in contexts in which differential needs are important and can be known with some reliability, and to settle for rule-based equal respect toward that vast number of others whom one cannot know in any particularity.

At any rate, to tie together the varied threads of this discussion, we may conclude that nothing intrinsic to gender demands a division of moral norms which assigns particularized, personalized commitments to women and universalized, rule-based commitments to men. We need nothing less than to "de-moralize" the genders, advance beyond the dissociation of justice from care, and enlarge the symbolic access of each gender to all available conceptual and social resources for the sustenance and enrichment of our collective moral life.

THE CONTINUING DEBATE:
Do Women Have a Distinctive Ethical Perspective?

What Is New

Debate continues over whether women bring a uniquely enriching and enlarging perspective to ethical understanding, as well as over the best model for representing the ethical perspective of care. Sandra Lee Bartky and Jean Grimshaw emphasize that some elements of women's experience as caregivers may involve negatives: Women are sometimes pushed into that role by being deprived of other opportunities, or because others refuse to share these important responsibilities. Friedman adds that some of these caring relations may occur in a patriarchal framework in which women's work is denigrated as subordinate and inferior, and she favors a friendship model of care rather than the traditional maternal or parenting model. In any case, the recognition that women have been—and often still are—socially and economically exploited continues to have an impact on the old but continuing debate over what (if anything) counts as the distinctive contribution of women to ethical theory. There is no doubt, however, that the recent emphasis among many ethicists (such as Michael Stocker, in debate 4) on particular relations of caring and friendship (as opposed to an exclusive focus on impersonal universal principles) has been stimulated by writers on care ethics.

Where to Find More

Annette Baier's work (in addition to Moral Prejudices) includes *A Progress of Sentiments: Reflections on Hume's Treatise* (Cambridge, MA: Harvard University Press, 1991) and *The Commons of the Mind* (Chicago: Open Court, 1997).

Marilyn Friedman has written *What Are Friends For? Feminist Perspectives on Personal Relationships and Moral Theory* (Ithaca, NY: Cornell University Press, 1993), as well as *Autonomy, Gender, Politics* (Oxford: Oxford University Press, 2003).

Lawrence Kohlberg's account of his research on moral development can be found in *The Philosophy of Moral Development: Moral Stages and the Idea of Justice* (NY: Harper and Row, 1981). A good brief description and critique of Kohlberg's work can be found in Laurence Thomas, "Morality and Psychological Development," in Peter Singer, ed., *A Companion to Ethics* (Oxford: Blackwell Publishers, 1991): 464–475.

Carol Gilligan, *In a Different Voice: Psychological Theory and Women's Development* (Cambridge, MA: Harvard University Press, 1982), had a powerful impact on the contemporary development of care ethics.

For more on Kohlberg and Gilligan, see Lawrence Kohlberg and Owen Flanagan, "Virtue, Sex, and Gender," *Ethics*, Volume 92, number 3 (April, 1982): 499–512; Lawrence Kohlberg, "A Reply to Owen Flanagan and some Comments on the Puka-Goodpaster Exchange," *Ethics*, Volume 92, number 3 (April, 1982): 513–528; Owen Flanagan and Kathryn Jackson, "Justice, Care, and Gender: The Kohlberg-Gilligan Debate Revisited," *Ethics*, Volume 97 (1987): 622–637; and Lawrence Blum, "Gilligan and Kohlberg: Implications for Moral Theory," *Ethics*, Volume 98, number 3 (April, 1988): 472–491.

Jean Grimshaw, "The Idea of a Female Ethic," in Peter Singer, ed., *A Companion to Ethics* (Oxford: Blackwell Publishers, 1991): 491–499, is a superb introduction to many of the issues surrounding this debate, and offers a strong critique of the view that women have a distinctly different approach to ethics. Sandra Lee Bartky, in her contribution to her edited volume, *Femininity and Domination* (NY: Routledge, 1990), offers an interesting analysis of caregiving in a larger (and sometimes quite negative) social context.

A brief survey of Alison M. Jaggar, ed., *Living With Contradictions: Controversies in Feminist Social Ethics* (Boulder, CO: Westview Press, 1994) is sufficient evidence of the wide variety and divergence of positions held even among those who identify themselves as taking a feminist approach to ethics.

Virginia Held's edited collection, *Justice and Care* (Boulder, CO: Westview Press, 1995), is an excellent collection of essays on the subject. A very good and wide-ranging anthology is Eva Feder Kittay and Diana T. Meyers, eds., *Women and Moral Theory* (Totowa, NJ: Rowman & Littlefield, 1987). Mary Jeanne Larrabee, *An Ethic of Care: Feminist and Interdisciplinary Perspectives* (NY: Routledge, 1993), contains key essays, particularly on the Kohlberg-Gilligan debate.

Helpful internet resources include the Gender and Ethical Theory section of Ethics Updates, at *http://ethics/acusd.edu/theories/Gender/index.html*, and the Feminist Ethics entry (by Rosemary Tong) in the *Stanford Encyclopedia of Philosophy*, at *http://plato.stanford.edu/entries/feminism-ethics*

Further readings are suggested in debate 5.

CAN VIRTUE THEORY OFFER MORAL DIRECTION?

VIRTUE ETHICS OFFERS EFFECTIVE MORAL GUIDANCE

ADVOCATE: Rosalind Hursthouse, Professor of Philosophy, The University of Auckland, NZ; author of *Ethics, Humans and Other Animals* (NY: Routledge, 2000)

SOURCE: *On Virtue Ethics* (NY: Oxford University Press, 1999)

VIRTUE ETHICS LEAVES LOOSE ENDS

ADVOCATE: David Copp, Professor of Philosophy, University of Florida, author of *Morality, Normativity, and Society* (NY: Oxford University Press, 1995); and David Sobel, Associate Professor of Philosophy, Bowling Green State University, author of numerous articles in ethics.

SOURCE: "Morality and Virtue: An Assessment of Some Recent Work in Virtue Ethics," *Ethics* Volume 114 (April 2004): 514–554

Virtue ethics has ancient roots, stretching back at least to ancient Greece, and perhaps even earlier in Chinese philosophy. Aristotle's *Nicomachean Ethics* is the classic source for virtue ethics, and it dominated ethical thought for many centuries. Thomas Aquinas, in the thirteenth century, attempted to join Christian thought with Aristotelian virtue ethics, adding such Christian virtues as faith, charity, and humility to Aristotle's account of the virtues. From the Enlightenment through the nineteenth century virtue theory was less prominent, as first Kantian and then utilitarian views shifted the emphasis from virtuous character to good acts. In recent years, however, virtue ethics has been revived as a major ethical theory.

Many date the revival of interest in virtue ethics to 1958, when Elizabeth Anscombe published her trenchant critique of contemporary views of moral obligation, claiming they were empty of content and detached from real human needs. Her view is echoed by Joel Kupperman (1988), who speaks of Kantians and utilitarians depicting the moral person as "an essentially faceless ethical agent who is equipped by theory to make moral choices that lack psychological connection with either the agent's past or future." Virtue ethicists shifted the emphasis to the development of virtuous persons rather than the performing of good acts, and added flesh to the rather abstract principles that governed earlier moral philosophy: What is the nature of a virtuous person, how is a virtuous character developed, what is the structure of a virtuous life, what is the role of the community and culture in the development of virtuous character?

Virtue ethics also prompts us to look harder at how an act fits into our larger lives. The Kantian perspective may be helpful if I am considering telling a lie: How would you like it if someone lied to you? Could you really approve of *everyone* telling lies? Utilitarian ethics also offers a useful perspective: Telling lies damages trust, undermines social reliability, and causes a great deal more harm than benefit. But virtue ethics offers a rich perspective: Do you really want to be the sort of person who cannot be trusted by your friends, who practices deceit and acts in an underhanded way? What you practice is what you become; practice telling lies, and you become a practiced liar. Is that a character you think worthwhile, a character you approve for yourself, a reliable path to genuine flourishing?

In the following article Rosalind Hursthouse grapples with a key question for virtue theory: How do we *identify* virtuous acts. It is tempting to say that a virtuous act is the sort of act performed by a virtuous person, but that doesn't take us very far. Hursthouse, following the Aristotelian tradition, characterizes virtue in relation to *eudaimonia*. Sometimes translated as "happiness," eudaimonia involves a rich conception of human well-being, encompassing the idea of a deeply satisfying life lived deliberately in accordance with one's highest nature. The question of what constitutes eudaimonia, and whether eudaimonia is the best guide to the virtues, are issues that continue to be debated among contemporary virtue ethicists.

POINTS TO PONDER

➤ Rosalind Hursthouse suggests that a *virtue* is a characteristic that helps human beings *flourish* or live well; and she acknowledges that the notion of "living well" involves value presuppositions. Does this involve her account of moral virtue in a fatal circularity?

➤ Is there only one set of virtues, or more than one? Obviously the Greek virtues that Aristotle emphasized are somewhat different from the traditional Christian virtues, and both are rather different from the virtues of the good guys in traditional Western movies. Could all those virtues ultimately be combined? If not, are there different virtue sets for different cultures? Or is there only one right and legitimate set of virtues, and any conflicting virtue set is simply wrong?

➤ David Copp and David Sobel note that Hursthouse's claim that the virtues promote human flourishing is focused on the flourishing of humans as individuals; but she gives no reason why the focus should not instead be on the flourishing of the species. What justification might Hursthouse offer for concentrating on the flourishing of the individual, rather than on the species?

➤ Is human rationality a distinctive natural characteristic of humans, or is rationality a special human attribute that sets humans apart from the influences of the natural world? Copp and Sobel suggest that Hursthouse tries to have it both ways; could Hursthouse answer that criticism? Why is it such a central issue for the ethical account Hursthouse is developing?

Virtue Ethics Offers Effective Moral Guidance

ROSALIND HURSTHOUSE

PREAMBLE

... Can we hope to achieve a justified conviction that certain views about which character traits are the virtues (and which not) are objectively correct? That is the problem with which I am concerned.

My answer to this question will be a (highly qualified) 'Yes' but... I follow McDowell in supposing that the validation must take place from within an acquired ethical outlook, not from some external 'neutral' point of view....

The general idea is that I take one of my beliefs—say, that courage is a virtue—and, holding the rest of my ethical outlook intact, put it up for question. Is it true? But where do I go from there? How do I set about trying to validate it? The neo-Aristotelian virtue ethics answer... is that...

> A virtue is a character trait a human being needs for *eudaimonia*, to flourish or live well.

I still stand by this claim, but now is the time to point out that it is much more complicated than is usually supposed... I now regard it as encapsulating something that I will dub... 'Plato's requirement on the virtues'. This, I shall say, is made up of three theses.

(1) The virtues benefit their possessor. (They enable her to flourish, to be, and live a life that is, *eudaimon*.)
(2) The virtues make their possessor a good human being. (Human beings need the virtues in order to live well, to flourish as human beings, to live a

characteristically good, *eudaimon*, human life.)
(3) The above two features of the virtues are interrelated.

By way of very crude illustration, consider two significantly different sorts of answers that a fairly honest philosopher might give to the self-addressed question 'What's good about the character trait of honesty?'

(i) It's so much easier than being dishonest; you don't have to keep a constant guard on your tongue and worry about the details of what you should say—mostly you just tell the truth. Lying is usually so pointless and silly. People know and you just look a fool, trying to pretend that you never make mistakes or are admirable when you're not. It's such an essential part of good relationships that there should be trust between you....

(ii) It plays such an important role in human life; it enables human beings to rely on each other, trust each other and form intimate relationships, learn from each other, do science, run various beneficial and/or worthwhile institutions efficiently. Think how much in human life hangs on the simple fact that you can ask a stranger the time or how to get somewhere in the reasonable expectation of getting an honest answer.

I hope it is clear that the significant difference between these two answers is that the first might well be construed as an answer to the question 'What is good, *for me*, about my being honest?' or even 'What do I like or enjoy about being honest? Why am I happy to be that way?' while the second might well be construed as an answer to 'Why does honesty make its possessor a good human being?' The first answer pertains to thesis (1), the second to thesis (2). And concerning thesis (a), I hope it is also clear that, despite their difference, the answers (i) and (ii) are interrelated....

And I hope it is also clear that (i), at least, is a collection of remarks that could come only from someone with a certain ethical outlook, one according to which the exercise of honesty... is partially constitutive of what the speaker thinks of as flourishing or living well....

OBJECTIONS TO THE VERY IDEA

The claim that the virtues benefit their possessor because they enable her to flourish, to be, and live a life that is *eudaimon*, is standardly taken as intended to provide a motivating reason, perhaps to most, perhaps to everyone, for being virtuous (or indeed, moral) in accordance with the standard list of the virtues. It is important for me to emphasize that that is not primarily how I intend it. I am thinking of it as a starting point in an enterprise of critical reflection on the standard list—on whether one's views about which character traits are the virtues are correct.

However, in order to fulfil this role, the claim must have at least a *prima facie* plausibility with respect to the standard list, so I need to defend it against those who, construing it as a claim about the standard list, think that it is obviously false.

The first essential step towards getting clear about what is at issue is to recognize that 'the' question 'Does being virtuous (honest, just, charitable, etc.) benefit the

one who is?' is ambiguous. It can mean 'Does doing what is virtuous, being virtuous on a particular occasion, always benefit the agent?' (Call this 'the particular question'.) Or it can mean 'Does possession and exercise of the virtues benefit the one who has them over all?' (Call this 'the general question'.) A plausible answer to one version of the question might well be an implausible answer to the other....

It should be immediately obvious that the answer to the particular question 'Does doing what is virtuous (what is, say, honest or courageous or charitable) on a particular occasion always benefit the agent, enabling her to flourish etc?' is 'No'. Here is an occasion where, say, if I speak out as I should, I am going to be shut in an asylum and subjected to enforced drugging; here is another where doing what is courageous maims me for life; here is another where if I do what is charitable I shall probably die. The answer to the particular question, on these occasions, just cannot be 'If you want to be happy, lead a successful, flourishing life, you should do what is honest or courageous or charitable *here*—you will find that it pays off'....

Let us concentrate on 'the general question' of whether the virtues (on the standard list) benefit their possessor, enabling her to flourish over all. Here too, many people think the answer must be 'No', for two reasons. One is the claim that virtue is not sufficient for happiness or *eudaimonia* and the second is the claim that it is not necessary. It is not necessary, since it is generally acknowledged that the wicked may flourish like the green bay tree. And it is not sufficient because of those nasty cases that came up in consideration of the particular question.... As soon as it is admitted that exercising virtue on a particular occasion may lead to my life's being cut short, or to its ruin, the claim that virtue is sufficient for *eudaimonia* is undercut.

The brisk response to the first claim is to deny that 'The virtues benefit their possessor, enabling her to flourish' was ever supposed to provide a guarantee or a sufficient condition.

Suppose my doctor said, 'You would benefit from a regimen in which you gave up smoking, took regular exercise, and moderated your drinking.' Her grounds are that that's the way to flourish physically, to be healthy, to live a long, healthy life.... She and I both know that doing as she says does not guarantee perfect health; nevertheless, if perfect health is what I want, the only thing to do is to follow her advice and hope that I shall not be unlucky.

Similarly, the claim is not that possession of the virtues guarantees that one will flourish. The claim is that they are the only reliable bet—even though, it is agreed, I might be unlucky and, precisely because of my virtue, wind up dying early or with my life marred or ruined....

The health analogy, with its claim that acquiring and exercising the virtues is the only reliable bet, seems to lay us open to the second objection. Why should we accept that 'the only thing to do' is to acquire and exercise the virtues, as if, despite not being a sufficient condition of happiness, virtue was necessary? Given the acknowledged threat of the possibility that one's life will be cut short or ruined, shouldn't we, if we have any sense, be looking for an alternative? And don't the wicked, flourishing like the green bay tree, offer one?

There is a brisk response to this objection too which, once again, exploits the medical analogy. Does my doctor's right answer to my question about how I should live claim that following the regimen she outlines is necessary for a long healthy life? No, because if it did, it would be readily falsified; the newspapers regularly describe the lives of people who have achieved remarkable longevity and are in as healthy a state as anyone of their age could possibly be expected to be, despite flouting at least some of the requirements she laid down.... To claim that the virtues, for the most part, benefit their possessor, enabling her to flourish, is not to claim that virtue is necessary for happiness. It is to claim that no 'regimen' will serve one better—no other candidate 'regimen' is remotely plausible.

As with the appeal to the possibility that my virtue may lead to my downfall, there is something odd about the way in which the appeal to the wicked who flourish operates in this debate. Given the medical analogy, the mere fact that some wicked people flourish—for example, some of the Nazis who ran concentration camps and then escaped to South America and lived (and perhaps, in a few cases are still living) the life of Riley, benefited materially by their past wickedness, and happily unwracked by any remorse—should be neither here nor there. Logically, their existence no more impugns the correctness of 'The virtues benefit their possessor' than the existence of the few centenarians who have regularly smoked and consumed remarkable quantities of alcohol impugns the correctness of my doctor's saying, 'A regimen of not smoking, moderate alcohol intake, regular exercise, etc. benefits those who follow it.' What is needed, to discredit the answer, is not just a few cases, but a clearly identifiable pattern. The objection should be not 'What about those few Nazis and murderous bank robbers in South America?' but 'What about this pattern that we can all perceive in life, the pattern according to which the evil regularly triumph and the good get done down?'...

DIFFERENT CONTEXTS

It is too readily assumed that a failure to convince the wicked or the moral sceptic that the virtues benefit their possessor (because possessing virtue is the only reliable way to lead a happy life) discredits the claim, showing it to be generally implausible and a non-starter. But once that assumption is made manifest, it does not look clearly true. Few of us (by which I mean myself and you, my readers) are likely to be steeped in vice or to be genuine moral sceptics. Thereby we believe many things we know we couldn't convince them of, but we do not reject those beliefs as implausible just because of that. We should look at what we think about the virtues benefiting their possessor in other contexts before abandoning it as a non-starter....

Good parents have their children's interests at heart. They want to do what is best or good for *them*, the individual children, to enable them to live well, be happy, make a success of their lives. But, having their children's interests at heart, it does not occur to most of them to bring them up to be entirely self-interested and immoral. On the contrary, they see the natural childish impulses to self-gratification and self-indulgence as impulses that need to be modified and redirected, and their natural impulses to love and generosity and fairness as impulses that need to be developed; they see the naturally self-centred perspective of children as something that has to be enlarged—for the child's own sake.

And thereby, good parents start inculcating the virtues—developing the character traits on the standard list—in their children from a very early age, in the belief, conscious or unconscious, that this is

indeed preparing them for their lives, laying the foundations that will enable them to live well....

Perhaps in philosophic or reflective mode they might profess sincere doubt as to whether acquiring and exercising the virtues is the best way to achieve a good life; perhaps they might even deny it. But, I would say, the way they bring up their children manifests their belief that it is so....

Suppose our lives were to change horribly; we fall under a vicious regime in which, it might be said, to be virtuous is not merely to run the risk of dying young or spending one's life in misery, but to court it. Under these circumstances, would we not have to admit that virtue is far from being the only reliable way to achieve *eudaimonia*? And would we not have to give our children, for their sakes, something very different from a moral education which began inculcating the virtues, to prepare them for the hard lives they were going to lead?

In neither case, I believe, is the answer a simple 'Yes.' In times of great evil, it can indeed cease to be true that those who have and exercise the virtues characteristically achieve *eudaimonia*, and thereby, virtue can indeed cease to be a reliable way to achieve it. So, to that extent, the answer to the first question is 'Yes'. But, even in such times, it is still not the case that there is some *other* reliable way. In evil times, life for most people is, or threatens to be, nasty, brutish, and short and *eudaimonia* is something that will be impossible until better times come. And in the hope that better times will come, and that their children, at least, will live to enjoy them, many parents, living under the most oppressive and dangerous regimes, have still tried to inculcate some version of virtue in their children. No doubt they have taught them versions tailored to the extreme circumstances in which they live; no doubt they have to lay great emphasis on prudence, to teach a caution about, and detachment from, others that would count as lacking trust and being callous in a better society. But teaching a tailored version is a far cry from abandoning the whole idea and bringing them up to hope for nothing better than survival at the expense of others....

Personally, our answer to the question 'Why should I be virtuous/moral?' may be 'I want to be—that's the sort of life I want to live, the sort that I think is a good and successful and rewarding one.'

Contemplating the lives of, say, those who are wealthy and powerful, and, apparently at least, perfectly happy, but who lie and cheat and ruthlessly sacrifice some others when it suits them, we may find that we do not regard them as enviable or desirable at all. The wealth and influence might be nice to have, but not at the cost of living like that. And contemplating our own lives, we may find many sources of dissatisfaction, but quite possibly none that we attribute to our possession of such virtues as we have. On the contrary, we may find ourselves inclined to attribute some of them to the imperfection of such possession. 'If only I could be less selfish and self-centred, more thankful for what I have, more concerned with the good of others and the good *in* them, how much happier I would be,' is not an uncommon thought....

NO NEUTRAL VIEWPOINT

I do not think that we have conceptions of *eudaimonia*, benefit, harm, disaster, etc. such that no sacrifice necessitated by virtue counts as a loss, nor do I think that this is because we are all imperfect in virtue. I think our conceptions of loss, harm, disaster, the conceptions we began to form in our childhood, though distinc-

tively different from those of the immoralist, overlap with his with respect to such things as death, physical injury, suffering, and helplessness. But one way in which we differ from him is that we do not think that the exercise of virtue characteristically brings these things in their train, or is more likely to do so than the exercise of egoism (except, as noted above, in evil times). We think that (for the most part, by and large), if we act well, things go well for us. When it does not, when *eudaimonia* is impossible to achieve or maintain, that's not 'what we should have expected' but tragically bad luck.

Our conceptions overlap with those of the immoralist in another respect too. That the life of virtue can be represented as enjoyable and satisfying is not solely a matter of a special employment of the terms 'enjoyable' and 'satisfying' that only the virtuous can understand. Although, if we are fairly virtuous, we and the immoralist do not enjoy, or take delight in, or find satisfying many of the same things, it is a fact, observable by the immoralist, that we really do enjoy ours. He may (if he bothers to think about it) find it strange or risible that our lives manifestly contain 'joy and warmth', and that we are manifestly 'living happily',... He may despise us for being content with, from his point of view, so little, but we do not need to tell him that we are enjoying ourselves in some arcane sense that he does not grasp—he can see and hear that we are, in a sense he grasps perfectly well. (I need a shorthand description for the indications of enjoyment—that things are done with zest and enthusiasm, anticipated and recalled in certain tones of voice with certain facial expressions, and in a certain vocabulary, and so on—so I shall call them 'the smile factor'....)

And this, once again, is an important factor in our bringing up of our children.

We can, and do, represent the life lived in accordance with the virtues to our children as (for the most part) enjoyable and satisfying, as containing the benefit and advantage of enjoyment and satisfaction. True, we have to 'train them from infancy to feel joy and grief at the right things', amending, developing, complicating, and enriching their desires, but we should find striking the fact that the upshot of such training can *be* the enjoyment of virtuous activity. We can represent giving pleasure to others, helping, co-operative activity, companionship, harmony rather than strife, truth-telling, even the conquering of (some) fear and the endurance of (some) pain and discomfort, to our children as enjoyable in themselves, as well as being good or praiseworthy or having to be done, in the full confidence that they will indeed come to find them enjoyable, as we have....

NATURALISM

[Next] I turn to... the thesis that the virtues make their possessor good *qua* human being.... The aim is to show that the thesis can get off the ground as a criterion for a particular character trait's being a virtue. Virtue ethics, or at least any form of it that takes its inspiration from Aristotle, is usually taken to be a form of ethical naturalism—broadly, the enterprise of basing ethics in some way on considerations of human nature, on what is involved in being good *qua* human being....

EVALUATING PLANTS
AND ANIMALS

Living things can be chosen and evaluated according to all sorts of criteria. We may evaluate them as potential food, as entries in competitive shows, even as 'decorative object for *my* windowsill given *my* preferences', and each noun or noun phrase brings its own criteria of goodness with it.

In the context of naturalism we focus on evaluations of individual living things as or *qua* specimens of their natural kind, as some well-informed gardeners do with respect to plants and ethologists do with respect to animals.

An individual plant is a good (or bad/poor) specimen of its species (or sub-species), a good rose or nettle, according as (i) its parts and (ii) its operations (including reactions under this heading where relevant) are good or not. By a plant's parts, I mean such things as its leaves, roots, petals; by its operations such things as growing, taking in water, developing buds, dying back, setting seed; by its reactions, such things as sunflowers and pansies turning towards the sun, and some plants' leaves drooping and curling inwards as a moisture-conserving measure.

An individual plant's parts and operations are evaluated as good in the light of two ends; they are good according to whether they are contributing, in the way characteristic of such a member of such a species, to (1) individual survival through the characteristic life span of such a member of such a species and (2) continuance of the species....

So, in the evaluation of individual plants, we find that we evaluate *two* aspects—parts and operations—in relation to *two* ends. A good *x* is one that is well fitted or endowed with respect to its parts and operations; whether it is thus well fitted or endowed is determined by whether its parts and operations serve its individual survival and the continuance of its species well, in the way characteristic of *x*s.

What happens when we, as we say, 'ascend the ladder of nature' to animals? We continue to evaluate individual animals as members of their species or sub-species; we continue to do so by evaluating the same two aspects in relation to the same two ends; but, somewhere along the ladder, two further aspects and two further ends become involved.

First, there is some indeterminate point at which we have to go beyond talking about mere reacting (as pansies and sunflowers react to the sun) and start talking about acting or doing. Even fish and birds 'do' things in a way that no plant 'does' things. So, in evaluating animals which act, we consider not only whether they operate well but also whether they act well with respect to the two ends of individual survival and continuance of the species.

So, animals of a certain level of sophistication are evaluated as good or bad/defective specimens of their kind according to whether they act well, in the way characteristic of their species, as well as according to whether they have good parts and good operations....

So much for the third aspect—acting—on the basis of which we evaluate many animals. Now let us consider a third end, beyond individual survival and continuance of the species. Somewhere along the ladder of nature—once again, quite possibly somewhere indeterminate—we start ascribing pain, and somewhere—perhaps at the same point, perhaps not—pleasure. Animals that can feel pain and that are capable of pleasure or enjoyment are evaluated in relation to not only the first two ends, but a third one, namely characteristic freedom from pain and characteristic pleasure or enjoyment....

So there is our third end—characteristic freedom from pain and (where appropriate) characteristic pleasure or enjoyment. It brings to our attention a fourth aspect of animals which we evaluate in evaluating them as good or defective. Closely associated with the ascription of pain and pleasure to the more sophisticated animals is the ascription of a certain, at least minimal, psychology, of emotions and desires. Animals capable of such a psychology are

evaluated as good or defective not only with respect to the three other aspects but also with respect to some emotions and desires....

So now we have, for the more sophisticated animals, four aspects—(i) parts, (ii) operations/reactions, (iii) actions, and (iv) emotions/desires—and three ends with respect to which they are evaluated—(i) individual survival, (ii) the continuance of the species, and (iii) characteristic pleasure or enjoyment/characteristic freedom from pain. If we now move onto another rung, and consider, specifically, social animals, we find that a fourth end comes in, namely (iv) the good functioning of the social group....

What is 'the good functioning of the social group'? Or, in other words, what is it for such a group to function well? The function of such a group is to enable its members to live well (in the way characteristic of their species); that is, to foster their characteristic individual survival, their characteristic contribution to the continuance of the species and their characteristic freedom from pain and enjoyment of such things as it is characteristic of their species to enjoy. And all this involves its fostering the development of its members' characteristic capacities. That is what a social group should do. So if it is doing it well, it is functioning well....

So, summing up, a good social animal (of one of the more sophisticated species) is one that is well fitted or endowed with respect to (i) its parts, (ii) its operations, (iii) its actions, and (iv) its desires and emotions; whether it is thus well fitted or endowed is determined by whether these four aspects well serve (1) its individual survival, (2) the continuance of its species, (3) its characteristic freedom from pain and characteristic enjoyment, and (4) the good functioning of its social group—in the ways characteristic of the species....

The truth of such evaluations of living things does not depend in any way on my wants, interests, or values, nor indeed on 'ours'. They are, in the most straightforward sense of the term, 'objective'; indeed, given that botany, zoology, ethology, etc. are sciences, they are scientific....

The overall summing-up evaluation—that this *x* is a good specimen of its kind—identifies it as an *x* that is as ordinarily well fitted or endowed as an *x* can be to do or live well, to thrive or flourish (in a characteristically *x* way). What living things *do* is live; quite generally, a good living thing lives well—unless prevented by something outside itself....

EVALUATING OURSELVES

If there is any truth in ethical naturalism, our ethical evaluations of ourselves ought to exhibit at least a recognizably similar structure to what we find in the botanists' and ethologists' evaluations of other living things. More particularly, we would expect the structure of our ethical evaluations of ourselves to resemble that of a sophisticated social animal with some differences necessitated by our being not only social but also rational....

The preceding evaluations are all concerned with good *x*s as *healthy* specimens of their kind. And one very obvious way in which our ethical evaluations are a bit different is that we hive off overall evaluations that supervene on our evaluations of our physical aspects—our parts and operations, at least—into human biology and/or medicine. The evaluation of someone as a good, physically healthy, specimen of humanity is, for us (as it was not, perhaps, for the ancient Greeks) quite distinct from those evaluations we call 'ethical'. That granted, let us consider whether our ethical evaluations exhibit what remains of the structure when the merely physical has been thus hived off.

That would leave the aspects to be evaluated as reactions that were not merely physical, actions and emotions and desires, and our rationality makes for one obvious addition to this list.... If we were simply transferring our talk about the other social animals to us, we would be evaluating 'actions' only in the limited sense in which the other animals (and small children) act—'from inclination', not 'from reason'.... But it is quite certain that it is primarily our acting from reason, well or ill, rather than those occasional actions we do 'from inclination', that make us good or bad human beings in the ethical sense. So that would be a further aspect to be added....

Is it plausible in so far as it claims that we are ethically good (or bad) human beings according to whether we are well (or ill) endowed with respect to reactions that are not merely physical, our (occasional) actions from inclination, our emotions and desires, and our actions from reason? *Are* those, in short, our ethically relevant aspects? As a list that has emerged from a consideration of plants and animals and then had the merely physical hived off and actions from reason added on, it may look like rather a rag-bag. But viewed from another perspective it has a notable unity; it is a list of just those aspects of us that manifest our ethical character, for well or ill....

Is it not plausible to say that, for example, courage plays much the same sort of role in human life as its analogue does in that of, say, wolves? Good wolves defend themselves and their cubs and each other, and risk life and limb as the pack attacks the prey, thereby fostering their individual survival, the continuance of the species, and the particular way the members of the social group cooperate in order to secure food for the group and protect themselves from danger. Human beings who are good in so far as they are courageous defend themselves, and their young, and each other, and risk life and limb to defend and preserve worthwhile things in and about their group, thereby fostering their individual survival, the continuance of the species, their own and others' enjoyment of various good things, and the good functioning of the social group.... Other virtues which perhaps have no analogue amongst the other animals still serve some of the four ends (without being inimical to the others).Without honesty, generosity, and loyalty we would miss out on one of our greatest sources of characteristic enjoyment, namely loving relationships; without honesty we would be unable to cooperate or to acquire knowledge and pass it on to the next generation to build on. And it has long been a commonplace that justice and fidelity to promises enable us to function *as* a social, cooperating group....

WHAT DIFFERENCE DOES OUR RATIONALITY MAKE?

It is true of all other living things that (for the most part) if *x*s don't, then they can't.... It makes no sense to say that, for example, a male polar bear is a bad/defective polar bear because, far from defending its young, it has to be prevented by their mother from killing them. Nor is an exceptional male polar bear that hangs around its cubs offering food anything other than defective. There is no sense to be attached to saying that polar bears would be better fitted to flourish in a characteristically polar bear way, to live well, as polar bears, if the males were different, or indeed, if males and females banded together to hunt. Polar bears just *don't* act that way and thereby cannot... and that is all there is to it....

But in virtue of our rationality—our free will if you like—we are different.

Apart from obvious physical constraints and possible psychological constraints, there is no knowing what we *can* do from what we *do* do, because we can assess what we do do and at least try to change it.... Our concepts of 'a good human being' and 'living well, as a human being' are far from being completely constrained by what members and biologically specialized members of our species actually, or, at the moment, typically, do; we have room for the idea that we might be able to be and to live *better*....

This is a major part of the genuinely transforming effect the fact of our rationality has on the basic naturalistic structure.

But has it transformed the structure beyond recognition? I said that ethical naturalism looks to be doomed to failure *if* it depends on identifying what is characteristic of human beings as a species, in the way their pleasures and pains and ways of going on are characteristic of the other species. By and large we can't identify what is characteristic of human beings as a species in this way—there is too much variety. And even if we could, it looks as though we would not allow anything we identified to carry any normative weight if we thought it was something we could change. So is ethical naturalism, after all, a non-starter?

Not yet, for there is a standard claim to the effect that there *is* something characteristic of human beings, that we *do* have a characteristic way of going on, but not in the way that is true of the other animals. Their characteristic ways of going on are many and have to be described in detailed terms, specifically related to such things as the acquisition of nourishment, mating, feeding the young, hunting, selecting leaders, etc., and are discovered by observation. Our way of going on is just one, which remains the same across all areas of our life. Our characteristic way of going on, which distinguishes us from all the other species of animals, is a rational way. A 'rational way' is any way that we can rightly see as good, as something we have reason to do. Correspondingly, our characteristic enjoyments are any enjoyments we can rightly see as good, as something we in fact enjoy *and* that reason can rightly endorse.

Now as 'a characteristic way' for members of a species to go on, this is manifestly very different from all the others, and not just in virtue of being general rather than particularized.... To maintain, as I am recklessly doing, that 'our characteristic way of going on' is to do what we can rightly see we have reason to do, is to give up with a vengeance any idea that most human beings do what it is 'characteristic' of human beings to do. The notion is avowedly normative, and is clearly going to yield judgements to the effect that many human beings are *not* going on 'in the way characteristic of the species' and are thereby defective human beings.

But isn't this exactly what we should expect a plausible ethical naturalism to yield? Does anyone think that most human beings are good human beings? Does anyone think that, regarding ourselves as a collection of social groups or as one global one, we are flourishing, living well, as human beings? Surely not. We know that, ethically, many of us are rather poor ethical specimens, and when 'we'—human beings living in the kind of circumstances that enable us to write and read this sort of book—think about how life is for the majority of other human beings, 'we' know that our ('human beings') aspirations to live well even as healthy animals, let alone as human beings, are still, in general, but unrealized hopes....

But, it may be objected, if we introduce a normative notion of 'a characteristic way

of going on', how have we preserved any vestige of naturalism? Well, we have preserved the structure; it is still the case that human beings are ethically good in so far as their ethically relevant aspects foster the four ends appropriate to a social animal, in the way characteristic of the species. And the structure—the appeal to just those four ends—really does constrain, substantially, what I can reasonably maintain is a virtue in human beings. I cannot just proceed from some premises about what it is reasonable or rational to do to some conclusion that it is rational to act in such-and-such a way, and hence that a good human being is one who acts that way. I have to consider whether the corresponding character trait (if such a thing could be imagined) would foster or be inimical to those four ends.

Consider, by way of illustration, the claim that completely impersonal benevolence, conceived of as, perhaps, Peter Singer would conceive of it, is a virtue. This would be a benevolence that knows no species-boundaries and recognizes no special bonds of family or friendship. To someone who is convinced that we have no reason to take any account of animal suffering, that animals are just here for us to use,... this is bound to seem an utterly implausible claim. To someone whose ethical outlook includes the view that charity and compassion extend to animals, and are virtues,... the claim is not immediately implausible. But could it be maintained, within the terms laid down by the naturalistic structure?

To consider this question fairly we would have to take seriously the point that the impersonal benevolence is being considered as a *virtue*.... But, thinking of benevolence as a character trait, we do have to think of its possessor as someone who does not think of 'That's a fellow human being' or 'She's my child/parent/

friend/partner' as an X reason for seeking another's good; we have to think of her as someone whose emotions, being in harmony with her reason, do not particularly engage with her fellow human beings or her own children or parents, as someone who does not have close emotion-involving attachments to other individual human beings that would make it difficult for her to act from this putative virtue.

Such a character trait might well not be inimical to individual survival or enjoyment (of a 'characteristic', rationally informed sort); vegetarianism certainly is not, and the possibility that human beings could, by and large, live out their natural life span, by and large in harmony with the other animals, is perhaps something we could hope for.... But it is when we consider the other two ends, the continuance of the species and the good functioning of the social group, that the insistence that the benevolence be impersonal in the way Singer would require both comes into play and into question.

Could impersonal benevolence, as a character trait of human beings, foster these two ends?... It rather looks as though the species and familial bonding that are part of our biological, animal nature, and make us 'partial' to our own species and children, play an essential role in sustaining these two ends.... With respect to the continuance of the species and the good functioning of the social group, our natural tendency to bond to other human beings and our children seems to be serving us rather well. The onus is on those who recommend impersonal benevolence as a virtue to provide at least a speculation about how a species of rational animals who had brought themselves to care naught for their own children or each other's company might still be a species of *social* animals who, moreover, nurtured their young—and, indeed, went to the trouble of giving them a moral education and bringing them up to be impersonally benevolent in their turn.

So despite relying on a normative notion of 'our characteristic way of going on', ethical naturalism does not cease to be naturalism; the four ends appropriate to us just in virtue of our being social animals really do constrain what will pass reflective scrutiny as a candidate virtue.

Virtue Ethics Leaves Loose Ends

DAVID COPP AND DAVID SOBEL

THE KIND OF STATE THAT A VIRTUE IS

It is widely agreed that a virtue is a trait of character.... Rosalind Hursthouse has attempted to articulate in detail what such a trait would consist in. The key point, in her view, seems to be that a virtue is not merely a disposition to act in certain characteristic ways. To be sure, a virtue does lead one to act in characteristic ways, but beyond this, it leads one to act in such ways for characteristic reasons and in a characteristic manner, to have certain characteristic attitudes and emotions, to be acute in detecting cases in which the virtue is at issue, and so on. Honesty, generosity, and benevolence are examples. So, for example, a person with the character trait of being honest tends to be honest for the right reasons, and scrupulously; she tends to deplore dishonesty, and, perhaps, to be "delighted when honesty triumphs"; she sees when honesty is an issue and what it requires. This is Hursthouse's characterization of a virtuous trait of character...

It is crucial, and constitutive of virtue, that a person with a virtue reasons in relevant ways and takes characteristic kinds of considerations to be reasons for acting appropriately.... The important point is that Hursthouse see[s] the virtues as shaping the virtuous person's practical reasoning in characteristic ways, and not simply as shaping her actions or attitudes....

Rosalind Hursthouse's approach represents a marriage between an attempt to ground virtue in a notion of eudaimonia and an attempt to ground virtue in a notion of the human good....

THE VIRTUES AND A FLOURISHING LIFE

Hursthouse's program rests on the thesis that "a virtue is a character trait a human being needs for eudaimonia, to flourish or live well." She says that this thesis, which she calls "Plato's requirement on the virtues," is the key to "the rational validation of beliefs about which character traits are the virtues."... Hursthouse appears to be saying that, in her view, the virtues are whatever character traits a human being needs for eudaimonia. For her, it is not merely that character traits that are independently established to be virtues also turn out to have the property of being needed for eudaimonia, so that we can use the property as a (perhaps fallible) sign of whether a trait of character is a virtue. Rather, her view seems to be that Plato's requirement on the virtues identifies the virtues with states of character that have the property of being needed for eudaimonia. Her view appears to be that a character trait is constituted as a virtue by having this property.

For Hursthouse, when Plato's requirement on the virtues is fully spelled out, it is actually the conjunction of three theses: "(1) the virtues benefit their possessor. (They enable her to flourish, to be, and live a life that is, *eudaimon*.) [And] (2) the virtues make their possessor a good human being. (Human beings need the virtues in order to live well to flourish *as* human beings, to live a characteristically good, *eudaimon*, human life. [And] (3) the above two features of the virtues are interrelated." Hursthouse claims that, "not independently, but in combination, [these theses] provide us with the framework within which we can set about trying to validate our beliefs about which character traits are the virtues."

Hursthouse's three "Platonic theses" do not carry their interpretation on their faces. Consider the first such thesis, that the virtues benefit their possessor or enable her to flourish or to live a life that is eudaimon. One issue here is that Hursthouse does not offer an explicit definition of the key concept of eudaimonia. She suggests that it can be translated as "happiness" or "flourishing," but she admits that each translation has its drawbacks. She proposes that the notion in question is close to the "notion of 'true (or real) happiness,' or 'the sort of happiness worth having.'" It is the sort of happiness we would want for our children for their own sakes. A second issue is that Hursthouse seems to deny that the virtues are either necessary or sufficient for eudaimonia. She offers examples in which "doing what is courageous maims me for life" as counterexamples to the sufficiency claim, and the case of Nazis who escaped to South America with loot from their wicked endeavors and absent a guilty conscience as at least putative counter-examples to the necessity claim.

Hursthouse's view seems to be that being virtuous is the most reliable path to flourishing, and she seems to think there is no other reliable path. No other strategy for living well is, she claims, as likely to succeed. Just as the doctor authoritatively recommends not smoking despite this being neither necessary nor sufficient for health, so virtue is claimed to be the best plan for flourishing in an uncertain world. Thus Hursthouse claims, in effect, that although some people might think that their children would be better off if they were raised to be less than fully virtuous,

no one would be justified in believing this to be true of their child. One's child's being benefited by her lack of virtue is like one's lottery number winning in a fair lottery. It is unlikely and impossible to predict with justification.

Hursthouse hopes to make this claim seem more plausible by arguing that, however skeptical we may be of such claims in theory, in practice we live as if we agreed with her, for, she claims, we try to raise our children to be virtuous. Now of course there are issues about who are the "we" in question here. Such issues will return. But for now let us grant that there is something correct about the claim that good parents aim to make their children virtuous. A parent might have many reasons for doing this. To take examples that Hursthouse mentions, perhaps virtuous children are less of a bother to the parent or perhaps virtuous parents bring up their children to be virtuous because it is good for the group that children be so raised.... However, Hursthouse rejects such explanations and insists that good parents aim to make their children virtuous for the intrinsic benefit of the children.

Surely it is correct, for example, that our children need friends if they are to flourish, and if they were utterly without virtues such as trustworthiness, cooperativeness, and friendliness they would be unlikely to fare well in attracting real friends. Those who are not sincere, spontaneously affectionate, and respectful, at least toward an inner circle of confidants, are unlikely to be able to participate fully in the sorts of relationships that most of us find to be indispensable to our flourishing.

But presumably the question is not whether a life devoid of virtues is likely to be worse or less flourishing than a life not devoid of them (surely it is), but rather whether a fully virtuous life is predictably better than a life that is less than fully virtuous. After all, it could be true that a life devoid of virtue is likely to be worse than a life not devoid of virtue, yet also be the case that a life devoid of vice is similarly predictably worse than a life not so devoid. So, presumably, Hursthouse's claim, if it is to vindicate the virtues over the vices, must be the claim that a life of full virtue is the most reliable path to flourishing. And in discussing the aims of parents, she must mean to claim that good parents aim to raise their children to be fully virtuous. Perhaps she would respond that it is a mistake to focus on the idea of "full virtue." For perhaps she needs to show simply that a life tends to be better as it is more virtuous. If so, then her claim would be that good parents would want any child of theirs who is less than fully virtuous to become still more virtuous.

Now of course parental advice tends toward simplicity when children are young. But when they are a bit older, we would have thought that most parents seeking to advise their children recommend a mixed virtuousness. Surely to the promising college student considering taking time off from school to do social work in a desperately needy but dangerous place, the paradigm of the concerned parent would recommend a little less virtue and a little more selfishness.

Further, in rougher times, being fully virtuous might be more costly than it seems here today. Imagine a time and place in which a person who goes along with a vicious aspect of society, say slavery, has full opportunities for a long life of privilege, enjoyment, love, and achievement, whereas speaking up against the viciousness in society promises hostility from the powers that be and worse. Hursthouse seems to consider such a case when she writes that "in evil times, life for most people is, or threatens to be, nasty, brutish, and short and eudaimonia is

something that will be impossible until better times." Hursthouse allows that in such circumstances good parents will try to raise their children to be more prudent, detached, and less trusting than they would in a better society. Hursthouse seems to concede that in some such cases even good parents do not raise their children to be fully virtuous. But she seems to think it sufficient to maintain her thesis if she can show that flourishing is impossible in such circumstances and that, even in such cases, good parents would not raise children to be completely lacking in virtue. Again, however, it is hard to see how this thought could vindicate Hursthouse's thesis. For even if flourishing is impossible in such circumstances, one can live a better or a worse life, and the question can therefore arise whether virtue is the best route to a better life. Unfortunately, it is not obvious that it is. The key cases are those in which a privileged person in a vicious society goes along with the viciousness and has opportunities she would not otherwise have for a long life of "enjoyment and satisfaction," lived with "zest and enthusiasm," as indicated by what Hursthouse calls the "smile factor." To respond that such a person is not flourishing or enjoying a life of eudaimonia seems beside the point if the person's life is clearly better than it would otherwise be.

Hursthouse's best reply to this objection, it seems to us, is to point out that there can likewise be circumstances in which nonsmoking is not a good strategy for one who aims to be healthy. Imagine a time and place in which not to smoke would be viewed as counterrevolutionary and unpatriotic and would create a risk of imprisonment or worse. In such a society, we might say, smoking is good for your health, and good parents might encourage their children to take up smoking, so as to blend into the social woodwork.

But this is no argument against the proposition, understood as a generalization, that nonsmoking is of benefit to each person. It is a familiar point that generalizations can be true as generalizations even if the corresponding universally quantified statement is false. There is indeed a law-like connection between smoking and poor health yet there can still be circumstances in which smoking is better for one's health than nonsmoking. It would be worthwhile to attempt to make the idea of a law-like generalization more precise, but for our purposes, we can take it as a given. And so we take Hursthouse's first Platonic thesis to be a generalization; just in the way that it is a law-like generalization, and a true one, that nonsmoking benefits the nonsmoker, so, arguably, it is a true law-like generalization that (some) virtue is necessary for flourishing. As she says, her view is that "for the most part, by and large," the virtues benefit their possessor.

But there are two problems. First, on this reading, Hursthouse's view does not seem to square with much of what she says. For in some passages, she seems to hold that aiming for full virtue is a wise plan for anyone in attaining a flourishing life. Yet one obviously could admit that it is true as a generalization that the virtues tend to benefit their possessor while denying that a life of full virtue is the best strategy for everyone in every circumstance. So long as one can accurately predict in which cases the generalization does not hold, one interested in flourishing should presumably not aim at full virtue in such situations, and good parents should not aim to raise their children to be fully virtuous in such situations. And it does seem to us, as we argued above, that there are kinds of situations where, predictably, be-

ing less than fully virtuous is the best route to flourishing, or at least, to living the best life for oneself.

Second, this reading is in tension with Hursthouse's treatment of Plato's requirement on the virtues as a thesis about what constitutes a character trait as a virtue. Her view, as we said, seems to be that character traits are constituted as virtues by having the property of being needed for eudaimonia. Given this, she clearly cannot defend the Platonic thesis as a generalization about states of character that are independently taken to be virtues. We can independently identify people who are nonsmokers, so we can support the generalization that nonsmoking is good for one's health by studying the health of nonsmokers. Nonsmoking obviously is not constituted as such by the truth of this generalization. But in Hursthouse's approach, we are not supposed to be able to identify those who are virtuous independently of the Platonic theses. The virtues are taken to be those character traits, whichever they are, the possession of which benefits (or tends to benefit) their possessors—and makes (or tends to make) them good human beings. On this view, the generalization that the virtues tend to benefit their possessors would then be a necessary truth. If we are correct, however, there are familiar kinds of situations where being less than fully virtuous is the best route to flourishing. If Hursthouse agrees with us about this, it appears she must maintain that such situations necessarily are sufficiently rare or bizarre that it remains a necessarily true law-like generalization that the virtues tend to benefit their possessors. We find this implausible....

Hursthouse has given us no reason to think that traits of character that would ordinarily be considered as vices, or at least as not being virtues, are not equally plausible candidates for states that benefit their possessors. Perhaps it is true, despite our objections, that, "for the most part, by and large," being honest and generous and kind and caring benefits a person. But for all we have seen, it might also be true that, "for the most part, by and large," being selfish, detached, and cautious benefits a person. If so, then Hursthouse's argument is on its way to implying that the latter traits of character are virtues. Perhaps there are different kinds of character, each incompatible with the other, each of which is such that, "for the most part, by and large," having it benefits its possessor. If so, then Hursthouse's argument is on its way to implying that virtue is multifarious and disunified. Or perhaps it is not the case that there are any traits of character such that, "for the most part, by and large," their possession benefits their possessor. Maybe the circumstances of human life are too variable for any such generalization to be acceptable.

At this point Hursthouse might respond that virtue is at least partly constitutive of a flourishing life and that, moreover, virtue is necessary for even a minimally good life. In this way, as other virtue ethicists have done, she could resort to a moralized conception of flourishing. And she could use this conception to explain why the privileged but corrupted people in our earlier example of the vicious society really do not live flourishing lives and do not even have minimally good lives....

But one of the advantages of Hursthouse's proposal, as we have been understanding it, is that it does not depend on a moralized conception of flourishing. She admits, for instance, that sacrifices required by virtue can count as losses in eudaimonia. She says at one point that the issue, at least in part, is whether a life of virtue is "enjoyable and satisfying," with the terms "enjoyable" and "satisfying" be-

ing understood in an ordinary way, such that the presence of what she calls the "smile factor" is an indication of enjoyment. And she suggests that a life does not count as virtuous unless it includes an element of enjoyment as evidenced by the smile factor. Perhaps, however, she only meant to allow that virtue is not sufficient for a flourishing life, even though it is necessary, for the smile factor is also necessary. And virtue might not be sufficient for flourishing even if combined with the smile factor, for, in the vicious society of our example, virtuous people who exhibit the smile factor nevertheless might face a horrible end. As Hursthouse remarks, it might not be possible to flourish in evil times. Because of this, as the example shows, there could be circumstances in which it is not true that the more virtuous one is, the better one's prospects for flourishing.

Nevertheless, Hursthouse does appear to propose what one might call a partially moralized conception of flourishing. She holds that "as things are," morality cannot be justified "from the outside," on the basis of "facts recognizable by the virtuous and the vicious alike," presumably including facts about flourishing. Yet she holds that things could have been otherwise. It is a shame that we lack the space to consider this part of her view in adequate detail. We think, however, that the examples we have discussed show that it is not necessarily true, not even as a generalization, that being more virtuous tends to increase one's chances of flourishing. And if this is right, then Hursthouse's first Platonic thesis is not a good way to characterize the virtues. To be sure, if Hursthouse were to adopt a fully moralized conception of flourishing, she could maintain that since virtue is necessary for flourishing, a successful strategy for a flourishing life must take virtue on board. But this would be neither surprising nor interesting given a moralized conception of flourishing according to which virtue is necessary for flourishing. Moreover, if flourishing is understood in this sense, it is important to explain why we (who are perhaps not yet fully virtuous) should be especially interested in this kind of flourishing.

ARISTOTELIAN NATURALISM

Hursthouse's second Platonic thesis is that the virtues make their possessor a good human being. In spelling out what this might mean, Hursthouse aims to vindicate an "ethical naturalism [that] hopes to validate beliefs about which character traits are virtues by appeal to human nature." This ethical naturalism about humans is part of a larger story about virtue and defect in living things generally, with the story concerning virtue in humans comprising a special case of the broader story....

Hursthouse sums up what we learn from thinking of how we, or at any rate animal specialists, evaluate sophisticated (nonhuman) animals: We evaluate their parts, operations/reactions, actions, and emotions/desires. And we evaluate these aspects of them with respect to how they contribute to three ends: (1) the individual's survival, (2) the continuance of the species, and (3) the individual's characteristic pleasure or enjoyment/characteristic freedom from pain. When we consider "social animals," such as wolves, which hunt in packs, we add an additional end, (4) the good functioning of the social group. That is, the goodness or defectiveness of a social animal will be a function of how well those mentioned aspects of it serve the first three goals in the social group generally.

The underlying aim of... Hursthouse... is to apply the lessons learned in understanding goodness... in the plant and animal world to goodness in humans. Their central project is to show that there is a common structure to the "evaluations of individual living things as or qua specimens of their natural kinds." Both Hursthouse and Foot stress that the differences between sophisticated animals and humans will make for important disanalogies between the evaluation of humans and the evaluation of other animals. Yet we have reservations about the project that arise independently of worries about the extension of the model to the case of humans.

First, it seems to us that there might be several competing standards for evaluating the natural goodness of members of a given kind of living thing, even taking into consideration that we seek a standard for evaluating them as members of that kind rather than in terms of how well they serve the interests of some other living thing. The key question then is why Hursthouse thinks that her list of the goals and criteria of natural evaluation has a privileged status.

Hursthouse suggests that her account of natural evaluation has a scientific status. Perhaps she thinks that her list of goals and criteria of natural evaluation could be gleaned from the standards of evaluation used in the biological study of animals—by contrast with, for example, the standards used in agricultural science where the goal is to produce tender meat for humans. There are different ways of approaching the scientific study of animal kinds, however, and we think there can be correspondingly different conceptions of what makes an animal a good instance of its kind.

Evolutionary biologists, for example, have a solid claim to be trying to understand good functioning in animals in a scientific way. Yet the criteria of natural evaluation that an evolutionary biologist would recommend would differ significantly from Hursthouse's. Indeed, evolutionary biologists are likely to resist all of the items on Hursthouse's list on the ground that none of them is directly relevant to the good functioning of an animal. They are likely to say that the animal functions well when it does what maximizes its expected genetic contribution to future generations (or perhaps, what would have done so in the organism's traditional environment). And this might be, and often is, best served not by preserving the individual animal or by doing well at promoting the survival of the entire species but, rather, by caring for individuals that are especially closely related biologically to the animal.

A descriptive biologist working on the natural history of a species might use yet a different set of criteria for evaluating members of the species. She might be centrally interested in criteria that would be met by a paradigm member of the species as it is found in the environment that is at the heart of its historical range. Parrots in their historical habitat might have different standard characteristics in certain respects from parrots that have escaped into new habitats and survived there, for example, and our biologist might be interested in the former characteristics and treat them as virtues in Hursthouse's sense. Yet it might be that parrots with these characteristics do not thrive in the new habitats. Such a biologist would not then be evaluating aspects of parrots in the new habitats with respect to how well they contribute to the goals specified by Hursthouse, but with respect to how characteristic they are of parrots in historical habitats....

Thus it seems to us that Hursthouse cannot plausibly claim that her list is simply the list that any scientific investigation into animals would generate so long as it aimed to evaluate animals as members of their species rather than on the basis of

how well they serve human (or 'other species') wants or interests. It is therefore unclear where the authority of Hursthouse's list is supposed to come from. Hursthouse seems to think that the main problem is to show how to extend what we have learned in the case of animals to the case of humans. But we think this is misleading and that the case of animals is more controversial than she thinks. Because of this we think that the story she tells about other species does not provide significant momentum for the story that she wants to tell concerning humans. If the story is to be defensible it will have to explain better how the normative evaluations of nonhuman animals that Hursthouse makes can be vindicated as uniquely authoritative.

Second,... it will have to be better explained why, even if we look for the normative in the natural, we should look especially to the evaluation of the individual as a member of the species, as Hursthouse recommends, rather than as the bearer of a specific genotype, as a member of the local herd or a local population, or as a member of a genus. We are frequently told that the sort of evaluation being looked for is "intrinsic" goodness, not usefulness for something else. But this narrowing of concern does not lead uniquely toward species membership. The fundamental point is that Hursthouse and Foot need to explain why the evaluation of an individual as a member of a species is uniquely well suited to model the ethical evaluation of persons....

In short, we are disputing the idea that Foot's and Hursthouse's claims about how properly to evaluate animals can be vindicated by a morally neutral investigation of animal nature, an investigation that is not guided by a prior understanding of the moral evaluation of humans. Even if this worry is correct, Foot and Hursthouse might still be thought to escape unscathed. For they might concede that their investigation is guided by an understanding of the moral evaluation of humans, but claim that what results from the investigation is the discovery of an analogy between the moral evaluation of humans and a particular kind of naturalistic evaluation of animals, an analogy that in turn helps us to understand the nature of moral evaluation. But if so, then the existence of the analogy can carry no argumentative weight if Foot's and Hursthouse's understanding of the moral evaluation of humans is disputed. For there are other "natural" ways of evaluating animals, and these might point to a competing analogy that would have us evaluate humans differently. Hence, although it might be true that Foot's and Hursthouse's grand analogy helps to illuminate their understanding of the moral evaluation of humans, it does not support their understanding against alternatives....

One thing that changes, Foot and Hursthouse tell us, when we move from evaluating plants and animals to evaluating humans qua human is that we focus on evaluating the will or practical reason of the human rather than an assessment of all aspects of the human.... Whether or not this is what we always mean when we evaluate someone as an excellent example of the kind human, a move of this sort is clearly needed if we are to avoid treating physical defects as having the same kind of moral significance as rational defects. As Hursthouse and Foot conceive of matters, then, "good human" will be an evaluation of a human's practical reason and will be the same sort of evaluation we make of the peacock's display or the roots of an oak....

Hursthouse allows that the fact that we are rational and other animals are not creates a "huge gap" between them and us. So great, in fact, that although "nature determines how they should be,... the idea that nature could be normative with respect to us, that it could determine how we should be, is one we will no longer accept." She says that, unlike the other animals, humans live such diverse lives and have the capability to live in so many ways that we cannot determine what we ought to do from what humans characteristically do. Indeed, the only characteristic human way of going on, Hursthouse claims, is "a rational way. A 'rational way' is any way that we can rightly see as good, as something we have reason to do. Correspondingly, our characteristic enjoyments are any enjoyments we can rightly see as good, as something we in fact enjoy *and* that reason can rightly endorse." The emphasis here is on the word "rightly." Hursthouse tells us that this notion of a rational way is normative and not tied to any statistical notion of human tendency. Indeed she tells us that it might well be that very few humans are going on in the way that is characteristic of them in her sense, that is, in a rational way.

Thus, whereas a deer ought to be swift because this is how deer escape predators, we ought to do that which we can rightly see ourselves as having reason to do. This bit of advice might seem both to be less than helpful and to make little real use of the Footian naturalism that, we were promised, would be applied to humans.

Let us consider the latter worry first. Hursthouse claims that the Footian naturalism is still in place because "we have preserved the structure; it is still the case that human beings are ethically good in so far as their ethically relevant aspects foster the four ends appropriate to a social animal in the way characteristic of the species. And the structure—the appeal to those four ends—really does constrain, substantially, what I can reasonably maintain is a virtue in human beings." As an illustration Hursthouse wonders whether a benevolence that knows no species-boundaries, a benevolence for members of all species alike of the sort that Peter Singer recommends, could be a virtue. She hesitantly claims it could not be, because such benevolence seems unlikely to be able to serve the ends of continuance of the species and good functioning of the social group, at least it seems unlikely to be able to serve these ends as well as do current norms of benevolence. Her general point is that what counts as a virtue is still determined by what serves those four ends and this is a real constraint on the view and a real tie with Footian naturalism. But this is difficult to understand. The list of four ends that Hursthouse recommends we use to evaluate plants and animals was developed precisely by generalizing about how, according to Hursthouse, we evaluate the kind of creatures for whom it is the case that nature determines how they ought to be. How can Hursthouse reject the thought that nature determines how humans should be yet think that the same considerations that grounded the four ends in plants and animals also ground the normative status of the four ends for humans? She gives no new arguments to support such a status for the four ends in the case of humans.

Suppose, for example, she is correct that the sort of universal benevolence that Singer recommends would not foster the four ends. It seems that Hursthouse faces a dilemma. For either it follows from this, given the Footian naturalism and the argument from the four ends, that we have no good moral reason to adopt Singer's universal benevolence, or it does not follow. If she concedes that it does not follow, then despite the Footian naturalism and the argument from the four ends, it

seems she must concede that Singer's universal benevolence might well be ethically good. But she cannot accept this result without giving up Footian naturalism. Hence, it seems, she must claim that it follows from Footian naturalism and the argument from the four ends that we have no good moral reason to adopt Singer's universal benevolence. But in that case she seems committed to the idea she earlier rejected, "the idea that nature could be normative with respect to us, that it could determine how we should be." The dilemma is, in short, that she must either reject Footian naturalism or accept that nature can be normative with respect to us. If she rejects the idea that nature can be normative with respect to us, as she does, and if she concedes that, for humans, the normatively appropriate way of going on is to act in ways that we can rightly see ourselves as having reason to act, as she does, she must give up the Footian naturalism. One can see the tension easily by comparing Hursthouse's rejection of the idea that nature is normative for humans with her claim that her "ethical naturalism hopes to validate beliefs about which character traits are virtues by appeal to human nature."

Let us now return to the worry about the emptiness of Hursthouse's view that the normatively appropriate way of going on is to act in ways that we can rightly see ourselves as having reason to act. Hursthouse does try to show how the constraint of the four ends could help restrict the content of the view. But, as we just saw, it is difficult to see as plausible a view that tells us to do what we have reason to do provided that doing so furthers the four ends. Perhaps we will be told that a proper account of reasons restricts them from the start so that there is never a good reason to do otherwise than to further the four ends. But this account is not found in

Hursthouse, and we see no argument in Hursthouse that would incline us to be optimistic for such an account. Indeed, she explicitly rejects the one argumentative strategy we find in her writing that might have helped here—namely, the thought that in the ethical evaluation of humans we look for the normative in the natural in much the same way as we do with plants and animals. But without an account of why it is that good reasons are restricted in line with the four ends, Hursthouse seems to be left with the view that human beings ought to do what they can rightly see themselves as having reason to do. And this is not a theory. It leaves us looking for convincing accounts of what we have reason to do.

Hursthouse says that, on her view, "we evaluate ourselves as a natural kind, a species which is part of the natural biological order of things, not as creatures with an immortal soul or 'beings' who are persons or rational agents." But as we saw earlier in the case of animals, there are concerns about how to justify the special focus on the species.... We are human, but we-those to whom Hursthouse is addressing her argument-are also rational agents, sentient beings, philosophers, and mammals. Why should the species level description be thought to have priority in determining what our goodness consists in? We do not find an answer in Hursthouse....

THE CONTINUING DEBATE:
Can Virtue Theory Offer Moral Direction?

What Is New

Over the past fifty years, virtue ethics has reemerged to join Kantian ethics and consequentialism as one of the major approaches to ethical theory. There are now many different and distinctive approaches to virtue ethics, and debates flourish among virtue theorists as well as between virtue theorists and their critics. One particularly interesting approach to virtue ethics is Michael Slote's, which emphasizes the virtue of caring and uses it to develop a comprehensive "agent-based" account of virtue ethics that is quite different from the Aristotelian tradition.

Feminist (care) ethics, especially in the work of Annette Baier and Lawrence Blum, might be considered a distinctive development of the virtue ethics movement; see debate 5, and also debate 7.

Virtue ethics has long played a prominent role in medical ethics. An important way of approaching many medical ethics issues is through asking "what would a virtuous physician (or more broadly, a virtuous medical caregiver) do in these circumstances?" Recently it is becoming more prominent in other areas of applied ethics, particularly in consideration of professional roles. Rather than asking whether I think it right or obligatory to be a whistleblower, or calculating the utilitarian costs, I might ask whether I wish to be the sort of person who would acquiesce in corporate wrongdoing that costs small investors their life savings and dedicated employees their pensions.

Virtue ethics has of course drawn criticism from both Kantians and consequentialists, but one particularly interesting challenge stems from recent work in "situationist" social psychology that calls into question the very character traits that are fundamental to virtue ethics. For more on that issue, see debate 9.

Where to Find More

Aristotle's *Nicomachean Ethics* is widely available in printed versions as well as online. It is still the subject of extensive debate and commentary, both in philosophy and theology (so important is Aristotle to Catholic theology that he is often simply referred to as "the philosopher"), and remains the starting point for discussions of virtue ethics.

Elizabeth Anscombe, "Modern Moral Philosophy," *Philosophy*, Volume 33: 1–19, was very important in reviving contemporary interest in virtue theory. Alasdair MacIntyre's *After Virtue* (South Bend, IN: University of Notre Dame Press, 1981) is an influential and widely read book on virtue ethics, and it makes very interesting claims concerning the necessity of a supportive culture for a successful virtue tradition; see also MacIntyre's more recent *Dependent Rational Animals: Why Human Beings Need the Virtues* (Chicago: Open Court, 1999). Edmund Pincoffs is another important contemporary virtue theorist; see his *Quandaries and Virtues* (Lawrence, KS: University of Kansas Press, 1986).

Joel Kupperman is an excellent writer in the virtue ethics tradition; see his "Character and Ethical Theory," *Midwest Studies in Philosophy*, Volume 13 (1988): 115–125; and *Character* (NY: Oxford University Press, 1991).

There are several recent important books on virtue ethics (including Rosalind Hursthouse, *On Virtue Ethics*). Michael Slote, *Morals from Motives* (Oxford: Oxford University Press, 2001), emphasizes the virtue of caring. Philippa Foot, *Natural Goodness* (Oxford: Clarendon Press, 2001) is the work of an ethicist who has been particularly influential in the development of virtue ethics; see also her *Virtues and Vices* (Oxford: Blackwell, 1978).

Three Methods of Ethics: A Debate, by Marcia W. Baron, Philip Pettit, and Michael Slote (NY: Oxford University Press, 1993) is a focused and fascinating exchange among outstanding advocates of Kantian, consequentialist, and virtue approaches to ethics.

Among the outstanding anthologies on virtue ethics are Roger Crisp and Michael Slote, *Virtue Ethics* (Oxford: Oxford University Press, 1997); Daniel Statman, *Virtue Ethics* (Washington, DC: Georgetown University Press, 1997); and Stephen Darwall, *Virtue Ethics* (Oxford: Blackwell, 2003). See also R. Kruschwitz and R. Roberts, *The Virtues: Contemporary Essays on Moral Character* (Belmont, CA: Wadsworth, 1987), which contains an extensive bibliography.

There are several excellent online discussions of virtue ethics. See Virtue Ethics in the online Stanford Encyclopedia of Philosophy, at *http://plato.stanford.edu/entries/ethics-virtue*; also, virtue ethics in *The Internet Encyclopedia of Philosophy*, at *http://www.iep.utm.edu/v/virtue.htm*; and Aristotle and Virtue Ethics at Lawrence Hinman's Ethics Updates, at *http://ethics.acusd.edu/theories/Aristotle/index.html*.

DOES CONTEMPORARY PSYCHOLOGICAL RESEARCH THREATEN VIRTUE THEORY?

VIRTUE THEORY IS UNDERCUT BY CONTEMPORARY PSYCHOLOGICAL RESEARCH

ADVOCATE: Gilbert Harman, Stewart Professor of Philosophy at Princeton University; author of *The Nature of Morality* (NY: Oxford University Press, 1977), *Reasoning, Meaning, and Mind* (Oxford: Oxford University Press, 1999), and *Explaining Value and Other Essays in Moral Philosophy* (Oxford: Oxford University Press, 2000).

SOURCE: "Moral Philosophy Meets Social Psychology: Virtue Ethics and the Fundamental Attribution Error," *Proceedings of the Aristotelian Society*, volume 99 (1999): 315–332

VIRTUE THEORY IS NOT DAMAGED BY CONTEMPORARY PSYCHOLOGICAL RESEARCH

ADVOCATE: James Montmarquet, Professor of Philosophy at Tennessee State University; author of *Epistemic Virtue and Doxastic Responsibility* (Lanham, MD: Rowman and Littlefield, 1993).

SOURCE: "Moral Character and Social Science Research," *Philosophy*, Volume 78 (2003): 355–368

A substantial body of psychological research has developed in recent decades supporting a "situationist" interpretation of human behavior. According to *situationism*, our behavior is more powerfully influenced by our specific situations or circumstances than by our permanent character traits—much more than our "common sense" or "folk psychology" beliefs would allow. For example, whether I stop to help or pass by someone in distress depends less on my generous or selfish character than on my immediate circumstances (such as whether I am in a hurry, or have recently had good fortune, or am experiencing a pleasant aroma). Obviously if my virtuous or vicious acts are determined by my immediate environment rather than my deeply formed character, then the plausibility of virtue ethics is severely challenged: My virtuous character becomes at best a pleasant but ineffectual adornment. Gilbert Harman maintains that our best empirical studies indicate that character traits–as thought of by virtue ethics and folk psychology—do not exist; *and* that our ethical perspective will be significantly improved when we recognize that fact.

Virtue theorists facing the challenge of situationist psychology have two basic lines of defense. First, they can challenge the studies that support situationism, arguing that they are badly designed, that they fail to support the broad situationist claims, or that other empirical studies offer contradictory evidence. Or second, they can admit the legitimacy of the studies, but attempt to find some remaining space for the influence of virtuous character. James Montmarquet, in his response to Harman, combines elements of both those responses. In particular, he attempts to carve out an area for virtue in the shaping of long-term life projects. (There is a third more general response: Nothing in psychology can have any serious implications for ethics, because of the special nature of ethics. That more general line of argument is discussed in debate 10.)

Though situationism has obvious implications for virtue ethics, the implications may be much broader. Rachana Kametekar claims that "if situationism is true, then the answer to the practical question 'what can I do to take charge of my situation?' is 'nothing'—the features of situations that determine behavior are so subtle and surprising that no ordinary rational strategies could enable us to be masters of our situations. But such pessimism is premature, and if it were ever to become warranted, then it is not only virtue ethics and the notion of character that we would have to jettison, but the power of practical reasoning." Whatever the ultimate implications of situationist psychology, it is clear that many people find it a very disturbing prospect.

POINTS TO PONDER

➤ In the quotation above, Kametekar claims that if situationism is true, then "it is not only virtue ethics and the notion of character that we would have to jettison, but the power of practical reasoning". Would that actually follow?

➤ Our common sense "folk psychology" tells us that character is a major determinant of individual behavior (contrary to the findings of situationist research). Is there any reason to believe that our folk psychology is more reliable than our folk astronomy, which tells us that the Earth is stationary and the Sun, planets, and stars revolve around us? Or more reliable than our folk biology, that insists on the fixity and permanence of species? Or than our folk physics, that denies any spaces among the atoms making up my solid oak table?

➤ If Harman's claims and the legitimacy of situationist psychology were widely accepted, what effect would that have on our legal system?

➤ Could any possible experiment convince you that our belief in such character traits as honesty and generosity is based on illusion, and that such character traits have no real existence? *If not*, what would that show about the nature of such character trait beliefs? If no observational experiment could refute them, does that show they are not actually based on our observations and experiences at all? If *not* based on observation and experience, then where do such beliefs come from?

➤ Almost everyone who hears of Milgram's famous experiment (described in Harman's article) believes that he or she would not administer severe shock; yet almost all of the research subjects consented to administer severe shocks. What is the implication of that large difference?

Virtue Theory is Undercut by Contemporary Psychological Research

Gilbert Harman

Folk physics and folk morality. Ordinary untrained physical intuitions are often in error. For example, ordinary people expect that something dropped from a moving vehicle or airplane will fall straight down to the point on earth directly underneath the place from which it was released. In fact, the dropped object will fall in a parabolic arc in the direction of the movement of the vehicle or airplane from which it was dropped. This means, among other things, that bombardiers need to be trained to go against their own physical intuitions. There are many similar examples.

Considering the inadequacies of ordinary physical intuitions, it is natural to wonder whether ordinary moral intuitions might be similarly inadequate. And, while many moral philosophers seem to put great confidence at least in their own moral intuitions, others argue for revisions. Consequentialism may be put forward not as an attempt to capture intuitive folk morality but rather as a critique of ordinary intuitions. Similarly, moral relativism might be defended as the truth about morality, whether or not moral relativism accords with everyone's intuitions.

On this occasion I discuss a different kind of rejection of folk morality, one that derives from contemporary social psychology. It seems that ordinary attributions of character traits to people are often deeply misguided and it may even be the case that there is no such thing as character, no ordinary character traits of the sort people think there are, none of the usual moral virtues and vices.

In attempting to characterise and explain the movements of a body, folk physics places too much emphasis on assumed internal characteristics of the body, ignoring external forces. Similarly, in trying to characterise and explain a distinctive action, ordinary thinking tends to hypothesise a corresponding distinctive characteristic of the agent and tends to overlook the relevant details of the agent's perceived situation. Because of this tendency, folk social psychology and more specifically folk morality are subject to what Ross calls 'the fundamental attribution error'.

Empirical studies designed to test whether people behave differently in ways that might reflect their having different character traits have failed to find relevant differences. It is true that studies of this sort are very difficult to carry out and there have been very few such studies. Nevertheless, the existing studies have had negative results. Since it is possible to explain our ordinary belief in character traits as deriving from certain illusions, we must conclude that there is no empirical basis for the existence of character traits.

Character. Character traits must be distinguished from psychological disorders like schizophrenia, mania, and depression, and from innate aspects of temperament such as shyness or being basically a happy or sad person. Character traits include virtues and vices like courage, cowardice, honesty, dishonesty, benevolence, malevolence, friendliness, unfriendliness, as well as certain other traits like friendliness or talkativeness.

Aristotle describes the ordinary conception of such character traits. They are relatively long-term stable disposition to act in distinctive ways. An honest person is disposed to act honestly. A kind person is disposed to act kindly...

In ordinary conceptions of character traits and virtues, people differ in their possession of such traits and virtues.... Different ways in which people behave on different occasions are sometimes due to their having such different character traits. Finding a wallet on the sidewalk, an honest person tries to locate the owner, whereas a dishonest person pockets the contents and throws the rest of the wallet away. How a stranger reacts to you depends whether the stranger is basically friendly or unfriendly.

We ordinarily suppose that a person's character traits help to explain at least some things that the person does. The honest person tries to return the wallet *because* he or she is honest. The person who pockets the contents of the wallet and throws the rest of the wallet away does so *because* he or she is dishonest.

The fact that two people regularly behave in different ways does not establish that they have different character traits. The differences may be due to their different situations rather than differences in their characters. To have different character traits, they must be disposed to act differently in the same circumstances (as they perceive those circumstances)....

Virtue Ethics. Some theorists suppose that proper moral development requires moral instruction in virtue. In this view, moral instruction involves teaching relevant habits of action, perhaps habits of desire, in some cases also relevant skills. If a learner's dispositions fall more toward one of the extremes in one or another relevant range of behaviour, moral educators should encourage the learner to aim more towards the opposite extreme until the right balance is achieved. It is occasionally remarked that one thing wrong with contemporary American society is that too little attention is being paid to this sort of character development.

Some philosophers argue, further, that morality or perhaps the ordinary conception of morality is best analyzed by beginning with a conception of virtue and character and then explaining other aspects of morality in terms of that. In this view, we determine what a person *ought morally* to do in a particular situation by considering what a person of good character would do in that situation. An act is *morally right* to the extent that it is the result of the agent's good character and *morally wrong* to the extent that it is the result of the agent's bad character. Perhaps we can also say that a situation or state of affairs is morally good to the extent that it would be favoured by a good person.

Some versions of virtue ethics connect virtues with human flourishing. In one version, a virtue is a character trait that contributes to the flourishing of the agent. In another version, the virtues are character traits that contribute to the flourishing of people in general. In either version, it is not easy to provide a noncircular account of human flourishing that leaves the resulting view sounding plausible.

The details of how virtue ethics might be developed are interesting, but I do not want to get into them on this occasion. For present purposes, the main point is that this sort of virtue ethics presupposes that there are character traits of the relevant sort, that people differ in what character traits they have, and these traits help to explain differences in the way people behave.

Social Psychology. Philosophers have begun to notice that recent social psychology challenges ordinary and philosophical views about character traits....

Let me begin my own account by emphasising that the empirical results of contemporary social psychology can seem extremely counter-intuitive on first acquaintance....

Flanagan, who is a philosophical pioneer in discussing the relevant social-psychological literature, does not seem to me fully to appreciate its radical import. He mentions what he calls the 'extreme view', according to which 'Good behaviour is not the result of good character. It is the result of a certain kind of dominating environment. Take away the powerful external props, and what seems to be a consistently good character will evaporate into thin air'. He continues, 'Almost no one holds such an extreme view'. However, contrary to this remark of Flanagan's, the 'extreme view' is in fact widespread among social psychologists.

Nisbett and Ross report that '[t]he experience of serious graduate students, who, over the course of four or five years, are immersed in the problems and the orientation of the field [of social psychology],... is an intellectually wrenching one. Their most basic assumptions about the nature and the causes of human behaviour... are challenged'.

At one point, Nisbett and Ross 'seriously entertained the hypothesis that most of [the] seeming order [in ordinary human behaviour] was a kind of cognitive illusion. We believed that human beings are adept at seeing things as they believe them to be, at explaining away contradictions and, in particular, at perceiving people as more consistent than they really are'. Nisbett and Ross now think that there are at least regularities in human behaviour and that lay personality may work in the sense of enabling people to manage in ordinary life, just as lay physics works for many ordinary situations. 'That is, people often make correct predictions on the basis of erroneous beliefs and defective prediction strategies'.

[I]n everyday experience the characteristics of actors and those of the situations they face are typically confounded—in ways that contribute to precisely the consistency that we perceive and count on in our social dealings. People often choose the situations to which they are exposed; and people often are chosen for situations on the basis of their manifest or presumed abilities and dispositions. Thus, clerics and criminals rarely face an identical or equivalent set of situational challenges. Rather they place themselves, and are placed by others, in situations that differ precisely in ways that induce clergy to look, act, feel, and think rather consistently like clergy and that induce criminals to look, act, feel, and think like criminals.

In addition, 'individuals may behave in consistent ways that distinguish them from their peers not because of their enduring predispositions to be friendly, dependent, aggressive, or the like, but rather because they are pursuing consistent goals using consistent strategies, in the light of consistent ways of interpreting their social world'. And 'people sometimes feel *obliged*, even committed to act consistently. This may be because of their social roles, because of the real-world incentives' etc.

Two Experiments. Social psychologists have shown many different ways in which ordinary observers wrongly infer that actions are due to distinctive character traits of an agent rather than relevant aspects of the situation. Here I briefly review two well known experiments, one by Millgram and one by Darley and Batson.

1 Obedience to Authority

Millgram describes an experiment in which a subject was given the task of administering an increasingly intense electric shock to a second person, the 'learner', whenever the learner gave the wrong answer. (Subjects were also told to treat a failure to answer as a wrong answer.) The shocks started at 15 volts and increased in 15 volt intervals to the highest level of 450 volts. The device used had labels at various points indicating 'Slight Shock', 'Moderate Shock', 'Strong Shock', 'Very Strong Shock', 'Intense Shock', 'Extreme Intensity Shock', 'Danger: Severe Shock', and 'XXX'. At the 300 volt level the learner pounded loudly on the wall of the room but did not answer the question. This is repeated at the 315 volt level. At higher levels there was no further response from the learner.

Whenever the subject asked the experimenter for advice or the subject said he did not want to continue, the experimenter had a list of four things to say, which would be said only if needed and only in sequence: (1) 'Please continue' or 'Please go on'. (2) 'The experiment requires that you continue'. (3) 'It is absolutely essential that you continue', and (4) 'You have no other choice, you *must* go on'. If the subject persisted in asking to stop after being told these four things, he or she would then be excused.

The experiment was designed to test how far subjects would go in administering shock under these conditions. The experimenters had expected that few subjects would go beyond the designation 'Very Strong Shock' (150 volts). But in fact, of the 40 subjects in one (typical)

early experiment, *all* went past that point. Five stopped at the 300 volt level right before the label 'Extremely Intense Shock' and the point at which the learner pounded on the wall. Four more stopped at the next stage, 315 volts, when the learner pounded the wall again. Two stopped at 330 volts, when the learner made no response at all. One stopped at 345 volts and another at 360 volts. The 26 remaining subjects, 65 per cent of the total, continued on to 450 volts. In other words, most of the 40 subjects went all the way to give the maximum shock.

To repeat an important point, the experimenters (and others whom they questioned both before and after) did not at all expect this sort of result. They expected almost everyone to stop well before 300 volts, by 150 volts. In addition, people who have had the experiment described to them in detail, tend to be quite confident that, if they had participated in the original experiment, they would have stopped administering shocks at or before that relatively early point (150 volts), much earlier than anyone did in the actual experiment.

Now consider any one of the subjects who went all the way to 450 volts, past the label 'Danger: Severe Shock' and well past the point at which the learner had stopped responding in any way. It is hard not to think there is something terribly wrong with the subject. It is extremely tempting to attribute the subject's performance to a character defect in the subject rather than to details of the situation.

But can we really attribute a 2 to 1 majority response to a character defect? And what about the fact that *all* subjects were willing to go at least to the 300 volt level? Does *everyone* have this character defect? Is that really the right way to explain Millgram's results?

A different kind of explanation invokes relevant features of the situation. First, there is 'the step-wise character of the shift from relatively unobjectionable behaviour to complicity in a pointless, cruel, and dangerous ordeal', making it difficult to find a rationale to stop at one point rather than another. Second, 'the difficulty in moving from the intention to discontinue to the actual termination of their participation', given the experimenter's refusal to accept a simple announcement that the subject is quitting—'The experiment requires that you continue'. Third, as the experiment went on, 'the events that unfolded did not "make sense" or "add up".... The subjects' task was that of administering severe electric shocks to a learner who was no longer attempting to learn anything.... [T]here was simply no way for [subjects] to arrive at a stable "definition of the situation".'

The fundamental attribution error in this case consists in 'how readily the observer makes erroneous inferences about the actor's destructive obedience (or foolish conformity) by taking the behaviour at face value and presuming that extreme personal dispositions are at fault.'

2 Good Samaritans

The second experiment that I will mention derives from the parable of the Good Samaritan, which goes like this.

'And who is my neighbour?' Jesus replied. 'A man was going down from Jerusalem to Jericho, and he fell among robbers, who stripped him and beat him, and departed, leaving him half dead.' Now by chance a priest was going down the road; and when he saw him he passed by on the other side. So likewise a Levite, when he came to the place and saw him, passed by on the other side. [Levites were important participants in temple ceremonies.] But a Samaritan [a religious outcast], as he journeyed, came to where he was; and when he saw him, he had compassion and went to him and bound his wounds, pouring on oil and wine; then he set him on his own beast and brought him to an inn, and took care of him. And the next day he took out two dennarii and gave them to the innkeeper, saying, 'Take care of him; and whatever more you spend, I will repay you when I come back.' Which of these three, do you think, proved neighbour to him who fell among the robbers? He said, 'The one who showed mercy on him.' And Jesus said to him, 'Go and do likewise.' (Luke 10: 29–37, Revised Standard Version.)

Darley and Batson observe that people can envision various differences between the priest and Levite on the one hand and the Samaritan on the other hand. The priest and Levite might have well have had their minds on religious matters, whereas the Samaritan probably did not. The priest and Levite were probably hurrying along to various appointments, whereas the Samaritan was probably less in a hurry. The parable also suggests that there is a difference in type of religiosity or morality. The priest and Levite in Jesus's parable act virtuously in order to please God, where the Samaritan responds more directly to the needs of another person.

The standard interpretation of the parable focuses on the third of these variables, the type of religious or moral character of the agent.

Darley and Batson designed an experiment aimed at uncovering which of these differences might be most relevant to explaining the differences in behaviour. Subjects in this experiment were students at Princeton Theological Seminary. As each subject arrived, he was informed that he was to give a talk that would be recorded in another building. Along the way to the place for the talk, the subject encountered a 'victim' slumped in a doorway. The question was under what conditions would a subject stop to help the victim.

Half of the subjects were assigned to talk on the Good Samaritan Parable: the others were assigned a different topic. Some of the subjects were told they were late and should hurry; some were told they had just enough time to get to the recording room; and some were told they would arrive early. Judging by their responses to a questionnaire, they had different religious and moral orientations.

The only one of these variables that made a difference was how much of a hurry the subjects were in. 63 per cent of subjects that were in no hurry stopped to help, 45 per cent of those in a moderate hurry stopped, and 10 per cent of those that were in a great hurry stopped. It made no difference whether the students were assigned to talk on the Good Samaritan Parable, nor did it matter what their religious outlook was.

Standard interpretations of the Good Samaritan Parable commit the fundamental attribution error of overlooking the situational factors, in this case overlooking how much of a hurry the various agents might be in.

Direct Empirical Challenges to Character Traits.

... People take themselves to have lots of evidence that agents differ in character traits. Yet empirical studies have not found any objective basis for this confidence. Summarising a number of studies,

Ross and Nisbett report that the 'average correlation between different behavioural measures designed to tap the same personality trait (for examples, impulsivity, honesty, dependency, or the like) was typically in the range between 0.10 and 0.20, and often was even lower'. These are very low correlations, below the level which people can detect. Using such correlations to make predictions yields hardly any improvement over guessing. Even if predictions are limited to people one takes to be quite high on a particular trait, the correlations are still very low.

Ross and Nisbett observe that people have some appreciation of the role of situation in the way they understand such stories as *The Prince and the Pauper* or the movie *Trading Places*. But for the most part, people are quick to infer from specific actions to character traits.

It is true that there are better correlations for very specific situations. 'Hartshorne and May found that the tendency to copy from an answer key on a general information test on one occasion was correlated 0.79 with copying from an answer key on a similar test six months later. Newcomb found that talkativeness at lunch was a highly stable attribute; it just was not very highly correlated with talkativeness on other occasions....'

Surprisingly, Flanagan argues that this shows there really are character traits, 'albeit not traits of unrestricted globality or totally context-independent ones'. I guess he means such character traits as 'being disposed to copy from an answer key on a certain sort of test' and 'being talkative at lunch'. But, first, no reason has been given for thinking that these specific narrow regularities in behaviour reflect dispositions or habits rather than, for example, skills or strategies that have worked in the past. Second, and more importantly for our purposes, ordinary thinking about personality and character attributes is concerned with more global traits like honesty and talkativeness.

Flanagan concludes: 'Yes, there are character traits. The language of character traits picks out psychologically real phenomena.' But I do not see that he has cited any empirical evidence for this claim....

Summary. We very confidently attribute character traits to other people in order to explain their behaviour. But our attributions tend to be wildly incorrect and, in fact, there is no evidence that people differ in character traits. They differ in their situations and in their perceptions of their situations. They differ in their goals, strategies, neuroses, optimism, etc. But character traits do not explain what differences there are.

Our ordinary views about character traits can be explained without supposing that there are such traits. In trying to explain why someone has acted in a certain way, we concentrate on the figure and ignore the ground. We look at the agent and ignore the situation. We are naive in our understanding of the way others view a given situation. We suffer from a confirmation bias that leads us to ignore evidence against our attributions of character.

It is very hard to do studies that might indicate whether or not people differ in character traits, but the few studies that have been done do not support this idea. We must conclude that, despite appearances, there is no empirical support for the existence of character traits.

Furthermore, it is clear that ordinary thinking about character traits has deplorable results, leading to massive misunderstanding of other people, promoting unnecessary hostility between individuals and groups, distorting discussions of law and public policy, and preventing the implementation of situational changes that could have useful results.

Virtue Theory is not Damaged by Psychological Research

JAMES MONTMARQUET

I

Part of 'common sense morality,' I think we can allow, is that there is such a thing as moral character—meaning, roughly, some disposition to make and act on appropriate moral judgments; the idea, further, would be that some persons have this disposition to a greater extent than others—and these are in general 'morally better people' than these others. Now, an important school of thought in recent moral theory—best represented in the work of Gilbert Harman and John Doris—has attempted to cast doubt on the very existence of moral character in what they claim to be its common sense or 'folk' signification. This 'folk concept,' according to these theorists, does not stand up to rigorous empirical test: the claim is that social science research has shown, or certainly has tended to show, that human behaviour is better explained in terms of the 'situation' one is in, rather than in terms of one's moral character—in anything like the above sense.

What is this research? Here I will merely take note of the two experiments figuring most prominently in Harman's and Doris's arguments. In Stanley Milgram's well-known research concerning 'obedience to authority,' individuals were induced to perform acts of what would have been great cruelty, subject to such situational variables as the white laboratory jackets of the authorizing (pseudo-physicians). Although the extent of their seeming indifference to the sufferings of their 'victims' varied somewhat, virtually all were willing to inflict considerable pain under the circumstances of the experiment. In a somewhat similar experiment, Darley and Batson showed that 'Good Samaritan behaviour' was apparently sensitive to one main variable, how *late* one was for one's assigned appointment—and not such factors as one's moral or religious views, or even whether one had recently been studying this Biblical parable.

We may now state the Harman-Doris argument. It begins with a specification of what character traits are:

1. Character traits are 'broad based dispositions that help to explain what they are dispositions to do.' These dispositions are supposed to manifest themselves not just in isolated, particular situations, but across a significant variety of ones.

Harman's and Doris's take, then, on the relevant research findings might be fairly expressed in these terms:

2. Empirical research indicates that situations (situational variables) are salient in explaining behaviour, not character traits in the sense of the immediately preceding.

Insofar, then, as character traits play no evident role in explaining behaviour (and insofar as for such things, 'to be is to explain behaviour') we are led to the conclusion that:

3. Character traits do not exist (are a myth of folk morality).

II

This is a provocative, not to say, maddening, view. I pay my bills quite conscientiously the first of each month. My wealthier neighbor falls further and further into debt, as he lavishes money on a number of mistresses. To be sure, if I had allowed myself to fall into precisely his 'situation', I might exhibit some greater similarity to his behaviour (if only out of despair). All the same, part of what difference of character explains, or should explain, is why I do not, or have not as yet, allowed myself to fall into anything like this situation.

But I am getting ahead of myself, for there is much preliminary work to be done—before launching any such broadside attack....

III

... I now propose to explore, this question of the extensiveness (or 'cross-situational' nature) of moral character. In particular, I want to begin by exploring the relation between:

(1) displaying good moral character in a given situation, and

(2) displaying good character in *other*, significantly different types of situation.

Certainly, there are occasions, situations in which persons do act well, and are thought to exhibit 'good moral character'. Now one thing seems evident concerning these: namely, how virtuously one has acted in a given situation depends only on one's act and motivation *in that situation* and not, as such, on how one would have acted in other situations—or how one would have acted in this or other situations in the past. If John has exhibited great truthfulness in S (he told the truth much to his own personal disadvantage), the fact that he would not tell the truth in some quite different situation S' does not detract from the virtue of his act in S.

In Kantian (deontological) and in utilitarian terms, this contrast is clear enough.

So, for Kant, to act from a sense of duty will be to exhibit good moral character in a given situation, regardless of whether one acts, or tends to act, equally well in other situations, or even in that same situation if and when it recurs. Notice, too, even a sophisticated Aristotelian can—indeed must—accommodate this consideration, basically by distinguishing the moral value of an agent and the moral value of a given *act* of his. Thus an Aristotelian will hold that John would be a better person (agent) if he exhibited honesty across a greater variety of situations, but will also need to hold that the honesty he exhibits in this case is nonetheless, as an individual display, no worse for his tendencies in other cases.

In fact, if Aristotle did not maintain something like this, it is hard to see how he could offer the explanation he does of character change and development. For if the evaluation of each act depended on a *full* description of one's tendencies, a good act of a bad person would have so little value that it could hardly explain any resulting improvement in his character. Notice, then, to hold that the character one exhibits in any given situation must be assessed mainly in terms of what has been one's character to date will yield some very strange consequences. Sydney Carton's 'far, far better thing than I have ever done' would exhibit morally worse character than the *bad* act (say, a selfish lie) of a generally good person. If so, it is most unclear how this act can significantly contribute, as it has, to Carton's becoming a *good* person, at the end of his life. In short, no coherent theory of moral improvement, or of the virtuous quality of the individual act, can allow that its moral value, or the moral qualities it exhibits, are to be weighed down by the individual's past level of performance—or even their present tendencies in other types of situation.

Two further points, though, by way of clarification. Of course, how one would act in other situations is often a key to discovering what one's actual motivation *was* in a given case. If John only tells the truth to members of his fraternity, presumably this says something about his underlying motivation: he tells the truth because he is speaking to a fellow fraternity member and not for any better reasons than that. Still, this is quite compatible with our earlier claim: how well one acts (including a full characterization of one's motivation) in a given case depends only on factors pertaining to that case. Second, any disposition will have *some* implications for other situations—actual or possible. If John has acted well in S, arguably, this will imply—what some would take to be a tautology—that he would act well in any 'relevantly similar' situation. This, however, is hardly to make his acting well in a given situation depend in some more general way on how he would act in *other* types of situations. (Compare if x dissolves under condition C, it will dissolve under most any instantiation of C; but whether it will dissolve under other conditions is left open.)

Here, finally, a mechanical analogy may not be out of place. How well a given product works in a given situation, or type of situation, does not depend on how well it would work in other types. If a given vest stopped an ordinary bullet, one would be pleased at its performance. The fact that it would not have stopped an armor piercing bullet does not detract from its performance here—merely from its overall utility. Now, to be sure, if these good results had been merely *fortuitous*, that would count against that performance—say, it had stopped the bullet by deflecting it slightly so that it lodged in one's pocket watch. But, of course, that is not a case of good performance at all, only good

luck. (This is the analogue not of a good act in a given situation, but a badly intended one with fortuitous consequences.)

Now, the importance of the foregoing for the issues raised by Harman and Doris is as follows. Their claims concerning the 'nonexistence' of moral character, as we have seen, are pitched at the level of whether individuals exhibit significant consistencies of character across differences of situation. But this, while interesting, is really incidental to the more fundamental question of whether character, and character differences, exist *within* situations. Even if no cross-situational links obtain, it remains an open question whether, on a given occasion, a given individual exhibited a tendency to honesty, kindness, or some other good quality. It even remains an open question—what will concern us next—whether such an exhibition might distinguish certain agents from the 'norm' for that situation. For surely the question of whether cross-situationally exceptional behaviour exists is separate from the question of whether certain individuals may be exceptional in a given situation. In fact, given that dispositions (moral or otherwise) are typically of unequal strengths, it may be *expected* that some will rank near the top and some near the bottom in terms of such strength.

One last point in this regard. It may be objected: 'if *situational* variables are salient, issues of character are thereby excluded.' The error here is to confuse two quite different ways in which 'situation' might be important. A situation might 'trigger' a given genuinely moral response, without our having to conceive of that response as merely situational. Hearing a speech or sermon might occasion a genuine act of generosity—not a mere act of 'obedience to the speaker's message'. By contrast, one's behaviour in a given situation might genuinely be *motivated* by situational variables—the earlier case of honesty merely to fraternity members.

IV

Still, we are not out of the woods yet—by no means. For the real problem for moral character raised by this research quite remains—and has nothing to do, per se, with Harman's or Doris's characterization of moral character as extensive or cross-situational. It has to do, more simply, with whether in any given case, character *does* make a difference. If Mary and Bob are in the same situation, the question of whether differences of character can affect their behaviour in that situation does *not* concern, certainly, how they would act in other situations but in this one. The problem, then, raised by such cases as the Milgram and the Darley-Batson one concerns precisely that issue: whether, or the extent to which, persons in the same situation *do* act differently. Certainly, these experiments suggest that the differences between what we should expect of 'good' and of morally average or even subpar individuals in any given situation is not as great as we would have expected. I note in passing here that this reconfiguration is not purely negative. For even if the experimental situations have had the tendency to level downward our perception of how the virtuous would act, the reverse could also be true for other situations. One can easily imagine an experiment which indicated that convicted murderers shared many of the same moral sensibilities as 'normal' moral agents.

Does, then, moral character 'make a difference'—and, if so, how? I want to approach this in two ways. First, in a more limited way, in terms of how even the Milgram experiment reveals differences of character in terms of how different agents require different *incentives* to exhibit the same behaviour; second, in terms of the limited relevance of any such 'experiments' to the exhibition of character in *ordinary life*.

There is a saying—of folk morality no less—that 'every man has his price'. Roughly speaking, this means that given a sufficient incentive to vice, everyone (or certainly most anyone) would yield. Of course, this does not mean, and cannot mean, that every man has exactly the *same* price—in the sense that given exactly the same incentives, or even the same perceived incentive, everyone will act in the same way. Many of us have been amused by Russell's jest concerning a woman's chastity: once it is established that she would sleep with him for *some* amount of money, however great, all further discussion is but 'haggling over the price'. In fact, though, whether she would require ten cents or ten million dollars to sleep with him does say *something* about her character. And the same logic, notice, applies to Milgram type cases. Evidently, different individuals would, and did, require different degrees of urging (of incentive) to carry out their orders. While it is striking that virtually all participants eventually went along, this should not blind us to individual differences, for they are liable to reveal character differences which would come out under other, less artfully constrained circumstances. Again, not everyone has the same price—financially or morally.

This point, let us observe, has implications for the legal issue of entrapment (cases in which someone commits a crime upon being induced to by the authorities, e.g., in government 'sting cases'). In U.S. law, this has been seen in terms of whether the defendant already had some character 'predisposition' to commit the crime in question, or whether the inducement had come entirely or mainly from the authorities. But this should be seen as a kind of false dichotomy. For if the authorities have arranged the situation and its incentives sufficiently well, I would be in Harman's camp: it is grossly unfair to say that his conduct indicates bad character, even if he had some previous history of such vices; for perfectly honest citizens might be similarly enticed—in which case, what becomes of the claim that 'bad character' is really at fault or displayed here? Rather, the question should be whether the inducement in question was significantly less than what the 'average man' would require to commit such an offence. For if it was, and only if it was, can we begin to conclude that the fault lay in the defendant's character and not in the situation.

One's character as revealed in any given situation, then, is a function not just of one's act (including its motivation) and that situation broadly construed, but of what incentives to act contrary to the trait in question have been present. Individuals requiring different incentives to vice in what is otherwise 'the same situation', must be construed as having, to that extent, different moral characters. If, then, a given situation tends to provoke the same reaction from most anyone, this will be significant in demonstrating the nonexistence of character—or, more correctly, the failure of character to play any potential role in explaining differences of behaviour in this situation—only after we have explored the role of differences of incentive. If, as in the Darley-Batson experiment, one's being late is a critical variable, character differences may still be revealed most obviously in terms of how late one must be to provoke a 'not very good Samaritan' reaction.

V

I turn to my final and, I think, ultimately most telling point of discussion—which concerns character differences not as ex-

hibited in a given situation, but as they manifest themselves over the normal course of a *life*. To begin, then, consider how different human life would be if it were lived mainly as a succession of Milgram-type psychological experiments. I make this observation to highlight the difference between life, and character, in their normal and natural—as opposed to any such highly artificial—setting.

Perhaps the major difference in this regard concerns the role of character in determining not just what situations we find ourselves in, but in affecting in multiple ways how we orient ourselves in that situation. Recall here my earlier point concerning the unlikelihood that a basically thrifty, conscientious type would even allow himself to get into the situation of having massive, voluntarily acquired debts. In this way, even slight differences in character magnify themselves by feeding into situational differences: a person of type X tends to put himself in situations likely to produce X behaviour. To take a particularly salient example: basically honest people tend to keep themselves out of situations in which lies are required.

The issue of 'orientation' is important here as well. A generous person's generosity will most likely be revealed not in a series of isolated, unconnected acts of spontaneous generosity, but in 'projects'— longer termed enterprises in which generosity enters in on a number of different levels, ranging from over all planning to execution. Outside of these projects, the generous person may be no more so than the average person. Hence, insofar as psychological experiments catch one 'outside' of his normal projects, persistent character traits are less likely to reveal themselves here than in other situations. Some of Milgram's subjects may have exhibited well above average compassion in their regular projects—yet in a situation in which they have not oriented themselves with respect to generosity, they may well display no more of this quality than the average.

This is related, then, to the first of Sreenivasan's criteria: whether the subject sees the situation as calling for the character trait in question. While I disagree that virtue is strictly relative to this perception (again, there are many cases in which one claiming to have a certain virtue does not but *should* see a given quality as called for)—it remains true that an exclusive reliance on experimental situations abstracted from one's normal projects and the kind of orientation they involve, is not a very good way of estimating character.

Still a further difference would be that psychological experiments *end*. In normal life, differences of character often manifest themselves in one's follow up behaviour. Think of all the different ways in which Milgram's subjects might react upon being told what was actually going on—do these not manifest differences of character?

In short, part of the common sense, Aristotelian framework in which character plays a distinctive role has to do with the distinctive, *continuing* features of human life; features which are singularly ill-adapted to psychological experiments of the Milgram sort. These experiments, I concede, do tell us something, but not nearly as much, I think, as Harman and Doris make out. Insofar as one's life is an integrated, somewhat coherent series of active, relatively autonomous attempts to achieve our various ends (ends partly determined and partly constrained by character), the role of character in human life is not well measured in situations in which we are basically passive creatures, whose larger plans and purposes are 'on hold', as we respond to a situation of someone's else's construction.

Here, however, the following objection may suggest itself. 'The previous direction of your treatment of moral character had a highly 'particularist' or, one could even say, 'situationalist' bent to it. Character existed, and needed to be assessed, in situation. Now, though, you stress the 'cross situational' nature of character, its role tying our responses together, and achieving practical and moral coherence, across differences of situation. But does this not contradict, or stand certainly in very great tension with respect to, your earlier taken position?'

There is no contradiction, nor really a 'tension' here. Take, for instance, our parent claim that how well one acts in a given situation does not depend on how well one would have acted in some different type of situation. This is eminently consistent with such points as that character helps to determine what situations one is liable to be in. For what the first point implies is simply that our assessments of such 'situational selections' should be assessed, in terms of their quality of character, independently of how one would act in other situations. So, for instance, if it lies in my character to avoid situations in which I might be unable to pay my bills, this means that I will typically take, or avoid, certain acts. Insofar as I accomplish, my character may be positively evaluated for such accomplishments—in the situations in which they are carried out. Again, though, whether I would act similarly in other situations, while it says much about me as an agent, is not strictly relevant to how well I acted in that situation.

The difference here might be put as follows. The particularist strain in what I have to say is ethical and even ontological. Character exists, or manifests itself, in situations and must be assessed accordingly.

But the larger *goals* or purposes of one's situational activity are typically not comprehensible solely by reference to that situation, but extend into the future and back into the past. To revert to our earlier mechanical analogy, how well something is working needs to be assessed in terms of the particular situation in which it is functioning; but that is not to say that its larger purpose is comprehensible solely, or mainly, in terms of that situation. The larger purpose of bullet proof vests is not merely to stop bullets but to save lives.

VI

Summarizing, then, the fundamental flaw, as I see it, in the view of such critics of 'folk psychology' as Harman and the psychologists, Nisbett and Ross is this. They infer from the absence of confirming experimental evidence that the folk psychological notion is false. But why not infer that experiments are simply a poor way of revealing character? Evidently, their view is that experiments, being 'scientific', must have a greater initial credence than our common, unscientific views in this regard. Harman claims that relying on folk psychology is like relying on 'folk physics'. But this is a strained analogy—given the marked success of scientific physics, the marked lack of success of folk physics, the uncertain state of social scientific knowledge, and the quite sophisticated state of our knowledge within what Wilfrid Sellars called the 'manifest image'. Aristotle's and Tolstoy's systems of nature may have been bypassed by the progress of physics, but has contemporary social science rendered their understanding of human behaviour similarly 'obsolete'?

THE CONTINUING DEBATE:
Does Contemporary Psychological Research Threaten Virtue Theory?

What Is New

The psychological research on situationism continues, and there is significant disagreement among psychologists on its current findings. For more recent research and thought on the Milgram experiment, see T. Blass, editor, *Obedience to Authority: Current Perspectives on the Milgram Paradigm* (Mahwah, NJ: Erlbaum, 2000). Among those psychologists interested in defending character traits (and especially the importance of positive character traits) are Christopher Peterson and Martin E. P. Seligman, in *Character Strengths and Virtues: A Handbook and Classification* (Washington, DC: American Psychological Association, 2004); their book contains a very extensive bibliography. Other recent psychological work that looks favorably on character traits includes A. Colby, J. B. James and D. Hart (eds.), *Competence and Character Through Life* (Chicago: University of Chicago Press, 1998); and N. Emler, "Moral Character," in V. J. Derlega and B. A. Winstead (eds.), *Personality: Contemporary Theory and Research*, 2nd edition (Chicago: Nelson-Hall, 1999).

Where to Find More

The major social psychology research, which is the source of this controversy, includes S. Milgram, "Behavioral Study of Obedience," *Journal of Abnormal and Social Psychology*, volume 67 (1963); J. M. Darley and C. D. Batson, "'From Jerusalem to Jericho': A Study of Situational and Dispositional Variables in Helping Behavior," *Journal of Personality and Social Psychology*, volume 27 (1973); A. Isen and P. Levin, "Effect of Feeling Good on Helping: Cookies and Kindness," *Journal of Personality and Social Psychology*, volume 21 (1972); G. Blevins and T. Murphy, "Feeling Good and Helping: Further Phone Booth Findings," *Psychological Reports*, volume 34 (1974); R. Baron and M. Bronfen, "A Whiff of Reality: Empirical Evidence Concerning the Effects of Pleasant Fragrances on Work-Related Behavior," *Journal of Applied Social Psychology*, Volume 24 (1994); R. Nisbet and L. Ross, *The Person and the Situation: Perspectives of Social Psychology* (NY: McGraw-Hill, 1991). An early review of situationist research is available in G. Allport, "Traits Revisited," *American Psychologist*, volume 21 (1966).

John M. Doris, *Lack of Character: Personality and Moral Behavior* (Cambridge: Cambridge University Press, 2002), is an excellent and very readable book that offers a clear review of the relevant psychological research, as well as a provocative and well-argued position on the importance of the research for ethics and our understanding of moral behavior.

Nafsika Athanassoulis, in "A Response to Harman: Virtue Ethics and Character Traits," *Proceedings of the Aristotelian Society*, volume 100 (2000), offers an alternative explanation of the psychological research cited by Harman. Harman responds to Athanassoulis in "The Nonexistence of Character Traits," *Proceedings of the Aristotelian Society*, volume 100 (2000).

There have been a variety of virtue ethics responses to the situationist challenge. Gopal Sreenivasan, "Errors About Errors: Virtue Theory and Trait Attribution,"

Mind, Volume 111 (January 2002), offers an extensive attack on the legitimacy of the experiments supporting situationist psychology. Rachana Kamtekar, "Situationism and Virtue Ethics on the Content of our Character," *Ethics,* volume 114 (April 2004), argues that even if the situationist research is true, that does not undercut the importance of virtue ethics; rather, the intelligent virtue ethics response is "to identify the factors in one's environment that support the behavior one wants and then to see to the preservation of those factors." Christian Miller, "Social Psychology and Virtue Ethics," *The Journal of Ethics,* volume 7 (2003), claims that while the relevant social psychology experiments may show that virtue traits are not fully functional for most people, that is consistent with at least the moderate or weak possession of important virtue traits; and even if very few people are strongly or even moderately virtuous, that is not a refutation of virtue theory. Maria Merritt, "Virtue Ethics and Situationist Personality Psychology," *Ethical Theory and Moral Practice,* Volume 3 (2000), agrees that psychological research undercuts the Aristotelian virtue tradition, but argues that it does not threaten a different and more plausible account of virtue ethics.

IS MORAL PSYCHOLOGY RELEVANT 10
TO MORAL PHILOSOPHY?

MORAL PSYCHOLOGY REQUIRES CHANGES IN MORAL PHILOSOPHY

ADVOCATE: Mark L. Johnson, Knight Professor of Liberal Arts and Sciences, Department of Philosophy, University of Oregon; author (with George Lakoff) of *Philosophy in the Flesh: The Embodied Mind and its Challenge to Western Thought* (NY: Basic Books, 1999), and *Moral Imagination: Implications of Cognitive Science for Ethics* (Chicago: University of Chicago Press, 1993)

SOURCE: "How Moral Psychology Changes Moral Theory," from Larry May, Marilyn Friedman, and Andy Clark, eds., *Mind and Morals: Essays on Ethics and Cognitive Science* (Cambridge, MA: MIT Press, 1996): 45–68

MORAL PSYCHOLOGY HAS LITTLE EFFECT ON MORAL PHILOSOPHY

ADVOCATE: Virginia Held, Distinguished Professor of Philosophy at the City University Graduate Center of the City University of New York, and a well-known ethicist whose books include *Feminist Morality: Transforming Culture, Society, and Politics* (Chicago: University of Chicago Press, 1993); and *Rights and Goods: Justifying Social Action* (NY: The Free Press, 1984).

SOURCE: "Whose Agenda? Ethics Versus Cognitive Science," from Larry May, Marilyn Friedman, and Andy Clark, eds., *Mind and Morals: Essays on Ethics and Cognitive Science* (Cambridge, MA: MIT Press, 1996): 69–87.

What is the significance of empirical psychological studies for ethics? This contemporary controversy has a very long history. Plato believed that eternal truths and highest values could only be recognized by transcending our ignoble physical nature and exercising our pure reason: Our unworthy human nature must be constrained by our godlike powers of reason. While Aristotle also praised the special rational powers of humans, he denied that our natures were hopelessly corrupt: With the right training and cultural support, human nature could become well-adapted to the practice of virtue. As the Christian tradition developed over the centuries, the split between evil human nature and Godly righteousness became profound. John Calvin and Martin Luther regarded humans as hopelessly vicious and depraved, with no resources for reforming ourselves; redemption is possible only by God's miraculous grace, bestowed by God's election and having nothing to do with human effort or choice. In modern philosophy, the contrast remains: Hume maintained that human sentiments and affections are the essential foundation for ethics, while Kant insisted that only through the power of pure law-giving reason—rising above all feelings or inclinations—can we act ethically. For Kant—as for Plato and Luther—empirical psychological studies might reveal a great deal about human inclinations, but nothing whatsoever with any relevance for ethics; while for others (such as Aristotle and

191

10 Hume), psychological studies might reveal very important facts about our ethical natures.

This controversy arises in many contexts. In the previous debate, the issue concerned psychological research and virtue ethics. A few years ago similar issues were raised when the distinguished biologist E. O. Wilson (and others) presented their research on sociobiology, with some claiming that research in sociobiology has profound implications for ethics. Indeed, Wilson stated that "the time has come for ethics to be removed temporarily from the hands of the philosophers and biologicized." Thomas Nagel—who favors a version of Kantian ethics—dismissed sociobiological claims concerning ethics, insisting that ethics "is pursued by methods that are continually being developed in response to the problems that arise within it. Obviously the creatures who engage in this activity are organisms about whom we can learn a great deal from biology.... But it would be as foolish to seek a biological explanation of ethics as it would be to seek such an explanation of the development of physics."

The current controversy, represented by Mark Johnson and Virginia Held, raises an issue of basic priority. While Johnson is impressed by the results of cognitive science, and counsels ethicists to shape their theories in accordance with its findings, Held believes that ethicists are justified in giving precedence to the requirements of ethics: "Those of us interested in ethics should insist... on pursuing our agenda: finding a conception of mind compatible with what we understand and have good reason to believe about moral experience. If this conception of mind is incompatible with cognitive science, so much the worse for cognitive science." Thus there are two key questions in this debate: Does cognitive science conflict with our understanding of morality? And if it does, which should give way?

POINTS TO PONDER

➤ Owen Flanagan, a philosopher who embraces cognitive science, proposed the following principle to guide the work of moral philosophers: "Make sure when constructing a moral theory or projecting a moral ideal that the character, decision processing, and behavior prescribed are possible, or are perceived to be possible, for creatures like us." Suppose someone responds that such a position illegitimately forecloses the possibility that humans are profoundly corrupt and generally *not* capable of acting morally. (One might believe that to be a genuine possibility even if one supposes that humans are in fact capable of moral behavior.) Is that a legitimate objection? How would Flanagan reply?

➤ Mark Johnson insists that one implication of cognitive science research is that "morality must remain experimental." What would that involve?

➤ Johnson states that "Morality is not a set of absolute, universal rules but an ongoing experimental process." He also states, however, "At the heart of moral reasoning is our capacity to frame and to realize more comprehensive and inclusive ends that make it possible for us to live well together with others." Does that assume inclusiveness and cooperation as universal rules? That is, are those two statements in conflict?

➤ Held claims that "the aims of feminist moral theory and of cognitive science are very different and sometimes at odds." Would Claudia Card (debate 5) agree? Would Annette Baier, or Marilyn Friedman (debate 7)?

Moral Psychology Requires Changes to Moral Philosophy

MARK L. JOHNSON

THE MORAL PHILOSOPHY VERSUS MORAL PSYCHOLOGY SPLIT

A great many philosophers think that moral philosophy does not have to pay much attention to moral psychology. They think either that moral psychology is mostly irrelevant to moral theory, or they believe that rational self-reflection alone can generate an adequate set of psychological assumptions without relying on any empirical studies from moral psychology. Moral purists of this sort labor under the illusion that there exists a large gulf separating moral theory from moral psychology. They regard "pure" moral philosophy as being concerned only with how we ought to reason and act and with justifying the fundamental principles of morality. They then contrast this sharply with moral psychology, which they allege to be a merely empirical discipline describing the contingent facts about how people actually are motivated, how they understand things, and the factors that affect their moral reasoning. Armed with this grand distinction between moral theory and moral psychology, along with its attendant assumptions of an is-ought split and a fact-value dichotomy, defenders of a very narrow conception of moral philosophy pretend to dismiss the complex, messy concerns of moral psychology, which are regarded as being irrelevant, or at least tangential, to the tasks of moral theory.

Those who want to deny the relevance of moral psychology to moral theory typically try to make their case by assuming an extremely narrow and trivial conception of moral psychology as being concerned only with the psychological conditions that affect concrete deliberations and decisions within specific situations. Knowing why this or that individual or group reasoned and acted in a certain way, for instance, certainly does not tell whether they acted in a morally praiseworthy manner. Knowing why so many people were attracted to the values and social institutions of nazism does not indeed tell whether those values and institutions were good or bad. Consequently, this trivialized conception of moral psychology can make it seem as though psychology has no important relation to moral theory.

Moral psychology, however, is not psychology in this narrow sense. Rather, moral psychology should be understood broadly as what I will call the psychology of human moral understanding, which includes empirical inquiry into the conceptual systems that underlie moral reasoning. The psychology of moral understanding can give us profound insights into the origin, nature, and structure of our basic moral concepts and into the ways we reason with those concepts. There is no direct deductive link between such knowledge of our moral concepts and specific moral rules (such as rules telling us why nazism is immoral), and that is why moral psychology is not going to give an exhaustive set of prescriptions for moral living. However, moral psychology will tell what is involved in making moral judgments, and it will thereby cultivate in us a certain wisdom that comes from knowing about the nature and limits of human understanding—a wisdom that will help us live morally insightful and sensitive lives....

Many philosophers cling tenaciously to the moral philosophy versus moral psychology split because they think that this is the only way to preserve a governance theory of morality and, with it, the idea that moral philosophy can give us moral guidance. They fear that wading into moral psychology can only teach us how and why people do what they do, but without telling us definitively what people ought to be doing.

I am going to argue that the central purpose of moral theory should be the enrichment and cultivation of moral understanding and that moral psychology is essential to the development of our moral understanding. Moral psychology therefore lies at the heart of any adequate moral theory. There will be moral guidance from moral theory so construed, but only of the sort that comes from moral insight into complex situations and personalities, rather than the sort that comes from applications of moral rules. This is all the guidance we can have, all that we have ever had, and all that we need.

WHY DO WE NEED TO INCORPORATE MORAL PSYCHOLOGY?

The answer to the question of why moral theory needs a robust moral psychology is this: our morality is a human morality, and it must thus be a morality directed to our human concerns, realizable by human creatures like ourselves, and applicable to the kinds of problematic situations we encounter in our lives. This means that we cannot do good moral theory without knowing a tremendous amount about human motivation, the nature of the self, the nature of human concepts, how our reason works, how we are socially consti-

tuted, and a host of other facts about who we are and how the mind operates. Moreover, we cannot know how best to act unless we know something about the details of mental activity, such as how concepts are formed, what their structure is, what constrains our inferences, what limits there are on how we understand a given situation, how we frame moral problems, and so forth. Without knowledge of this sort, we are condemned to either a fool's or a tyrant's morality. We will be fools insofar as we make stupid mistakes because we lack knowledge of the mind, motivation, meaning, communication, and so forth. Or we will suffer the tyrannical morality of absolute standards that we impose on ourselves and others, without any attention to whether people could actually live up to such standards, apply them to real situations, and improve life by means of them....

I will argue that the exclusion from moral philosophy of a robust moral psychology stands directly in the way of genuine moral understanding and insight. Once we challenge this foundational dichotomy, it becomes necessary to reevaluate the nature and purpose of moral philosophy. The bottom line is that moral philosophy should be a theory of moral understanding, which necessarily incorporates the empirical results coming from studies in moral psychology and the cognitive sciences....

It is obviously impossible to survey the full range of relevant empirical results from the cognitive sciences that bear directly on moral theory. I propose to consider just one small part of the new discoveries we are making in second-generation cognitive science that change our view of what moral theory is. In particular, I call attention to the metaphoric nature of our most basic moral concepts and then ask whether this fact requires us to reassess both our understanding of moral experience and our conception of moral theory.

THE METAPHORIC NATURE OF MORAL UNDERSTANDING

In the past several years, one of the most robust and potentially revolutionary findings about the mind has been the discovery that the human conceptual system is fundamentally and irreducibly metaphoric. A large and rapidly growing number of studies have shown that our basic concepts in virtually every aspect of human experience are defined by systems of metaphors. A conceptual metaphor is a mapping of conceptual structure from a source domain, which is typically some aspect of our concrete bodily experience, onto a more abstract or less highly articulated target domain. It is crucial to keep in mind that conceptual metaphors are conceptual. They are structures in our conceptual system, not merely propositions or linguistic entities. They involve conceptual structure, the basis for the inferences we draw from the metaphor. The content and logic of the source domain thus determines our understanding of the target domain. In other words, the reasoning we do about the target domain is based on the embodied corporeal logic of the source domain. In this way, our systematic conceptual metaphors do not merely highlight preexisting structures in two different domains; rather, the structure and knowledge pertaining to the source domain partly construct our knowledge in the target domain.

As an example of the value and importance of moral psychology for moral theory, I focus on some recent work on the metaphorical nature of our basic moral concepts. We are just beginning to examine the complex web of systematic metaphors by means of which we define our values, ends, actions, principles, and every other aspect of our moral experience. Moreover, because our moral concepts are defined by systems of metaphors, our moral reasoning is based on the logic of these metaphors.

An incident in Amy Tan's *The Joy Luck Club* provides a concrete example of what I mean by metaphors of morality. Ying-ying was a beautiful, refined young woman living a luxurious and carefree life with her wealthy family just before World War II. "When I was a young girl in Wushi," she remembers. "I was *lihai*. Wild and stubborn. I wore a smirk on my face. Too good to listen. I was small and pretty. I had tiny feet which made me very vain.... I often unravelled my hair and wore it loose." At sixteen she finds herself inexplicably attracted to an older man from another town. Within six months she is married and then realizes that she has actually come to love him.

No sooner is she married than she realizes that he is a womanizing drunkard. He abuses her emotionally, impregnates her, pursues a series of extramarital affairs, and eventually abandons her for an opera singer. This public infidelity humiliates, shames, and destroys her. He has taken her soul and left her a mere ghost:

> So I will tell Lena of my shame. That I was rich and pretty. I was too good for any one man. That I became abandoned goods. I will tell her that at eighteen the prettiness drained from my cheeks. That I thought of throwing myself in the lake like the other ladies of shame. And I will tell her of the baby I killed because I came to hate this man.
>
> I took this baby from my womb before it could be born. This was not a bad thing to do in China back then, to kill a baby before it is born.

But even then, I thought it was bad, because my body flowed with terrible revenge as the juices of this man's firstborn son poured from me.

How are we to understand the logic by which this tortured innocent comes to kill her baby? In her mind it is an act of revenge. But what is the logic of revenge? In brief, Ying-ying's husband has taken her most precious possession: her spirit, her *chi*, her honor. She has "lost face" and is in shame. Ying-ying exacts her revenge by taking the most precious possession she can from him: his firstborn son: "When the nurses asked what they should do with the lifeless baby, I hurled a newspaper at them and said to wrap it like a fish and throw it in the lake." She symbolically drowns the baby in the lake, just as the women of shame drown themselves in the lake.

The logic of this tragic action stems from what I have called elsewhere the MORAL ACCOUNTING metaphor, which is concerned primarily with what we owe to other people to increase their well-being and what they, in turn, owe to us. Basically, we understand our moral interactions metaphorically as a species of economic transaction, according to the following conceptual mapping (see box below).

This conceptual mapping provides an experiential basis for a large number of inferences that we draw in evaluating ethical conduct. We use our basic knowledge of the source domain (economic transactions) to make moral inferences about situations in the target domain of moral interactions. Consider, for example, our knowledge about wealth and how it generates inferences about morality via the WELL-BEING IS WEALTH metaphor. Wealth is something that one amasses by owning property (land, commodities) or its surrogate, money. Typically, wealth is a product of labor, which is to say that people earn it by their work, although it may come to them by other means, such as inheritance. Being wealthy usually makes it possible for people to have more of the things they want to have and to do more of the things they want to do. It allows them to satisfy their needs and desires, and it may enhance the quality of their existence. There is a limited amount of wealth available in the world, and it must be divided up among many people. Fair exchange gives each person what is due him or her.

The MORAL ACCOUNTING Metaphor

Commodity Transaction	*Moral Interaction*
Objects, commodities	Deeds (actions), states
Utility or value of objects	Moral worth of actions
Wealth	Well-being
Accumulation of goods	Increase in well-being
Causing increase in goods	Moral = causing increase in well-being
Causing decrease in goods	Immoral = causing decrease in well-being
Giving/taking money	Performing moral/immoral deeds
Account of transactions	Moral account
Balance of account	Moral balance of deeds
Debt	Moral debt = owing something good to another
Credit	Moral credit = others owe you something good
Fair exchange/payment	Justice

In the context of the MORAL AC-COUNTING metaphor, we thus come to understand moral well-being as wealth, according to the following mapping (see box below).

The WEALTH metaphor is one of the two or three most important conceptions of moral well-being that we have. It shows itself in the ways we think and talk about well-being—for example:

> She has had an undeservedly *rich* life.
> The cynics of the world lead *impoverished* lives.
> Doing disaster relief work has *enriched* Sarah's life immeasurably.
> Prince Charles *profited* from his relationship with Princess Di. He is certainly a better person now.
> I've had a *wealth* of happiness in my life.
> Nothing can compare to the *riches* of family, friends, and loved ones.

Within the MORAL ACCOUNTING metaphors the WELL-BEING IS WEALTH metaphor gives rise to definite inferences about our moral obligations. That is, we reason on the basis of the metaphor. Given the conceptual mapping from source to target domain and based on our knowledge of the source domain, we then develop a corresponding knowledge in the target domain and draw the appropriate inferences. Moral well-being comes to a person as a result of his or her own efforts and also as something given by the good actions of other people. Moral well-being is something that can accumulate and that can also diminish. The more well-being you have, the better off you are. Immoral action decreases well-being. Consequently, moral acts toward others (acts that increase their well-being) put them in moral debt to you and thereby give you moral credit; you deserve an equal amount of well-being in return for what you have given.

The MORAL ACCOUNTING metaphor thus gives rise to a pattern of reasoning about our duties, rights, and obligations. On the basis of this metaphor, we reason about what is fair, and our moral discourse reveals this underlying conceptual metaphor system. If you do something to diminish my well-being, then you incur a debt to me, morally speaking, since you are expected to "pay me back" for what you have taken. When you perform noble acts, you build up moral credit. Thus, we say such things as:

> In *return* for our kindness, she *gave us* nothing but grief.
> In judging him, *take into account* all the good things he has done.
> I'm holding you *accountable* for her suffering.
> When you compare his kindness with what he is accused of doing, it just *doesn't add up*.
> All her sacrifices for others surely *balance out* the bad things she did.

The WELL-BEING IS WEALTH *Metaphor*

Financial Domain	Moral Domain
Wealth	Well-being
Accumulation of goods	Increase in well-being
Profitable = causing increase in wealth	Moral = causing increase in well-being
Unprofitable = causing decrease in wealth	Immoral = causing decrease in well-being

His noble deeds *far outweigh* his sins.

Mary certainly *deserves credit* for her exemplary acts.

I *owe* you my life!

I couldn't possibly *repay* your kindness.

Milken *owes a great debt* to society for his evil doings.

You must *pay* for your selfishness.

Elsewhere I have shown how the MORAL ACCOUNTING metaphor gives rise to a set of at least five basic schemas that people use to evaluate the moral merit of various actions and to determine what is due them, as well as what they owe others. Sarah Taub has outlined schemas for reciprocation, retribution, revenge, restitution, and altruism by which we draw inferences from the MORAL ACCOUNTING metaphor in deciding who gets moral credit. Take, for example, the REVENGE schema. Let us say that you do something bad to me and thereby diminish my well-being. In this sense, you have taken something from me—some of my well-being—and, via MORAL ACCOUNTING, you now owe me something that will increase my well-being to compensate for what you have taken away. But you will not give me back the measure of well-being that you owe me. Therefore, I balance the moral well-being books by taking an equal measure of *your* well-being, thus diminishing your moral wealth. That is why we speak of taking revenge on someone; we are taking something good from the person. The REVENGE schema thus has the following structure:

The REVENGE Schema
Event: A gives (does) *something bad* to B.
Judgment: A owes *something good* to B.
Complication: A will not give *something good* to B.

Expectation: B should take *something good* from A.
Moral inferences: A has an obligation to give *something good* to B.
B has a right to receive *something good* from A.
Monetary inference: B exacts payment from A.

For example:

Revenge is "an eye for an eye."
Carry *took revenge* on her classmates.
"I'll *make you pay* for what you did!"
"I'll *take it out of your hide.*"
"He'll *get even* with you for this."
"Jane *owes you one* for that." (What she owes is something bad that diminishes your well-being.)

We are now in a position to see why Ying-ying does what she does. We can understand the logic of her reasoning that is based on the REVENGE schema for interpreting the MORAL ACCOUNTING metaphor. In addition to the formal structure of the MORAL ACCOUNTING metaphor, she uses two additional metaphors:

1. FACE (HONOR) IS A VALUABLE POSSESSION.
2. A CHILD IS A VALUABLE POSSESSION.

Ying-ying's husband has taken her spirit. She has lost face and is shamed. She takes away the spirit of his firstborn son. It is an empty revenge that leaves her a ghost floating through time:

I became like the ladies of the lake. I threw white clothes over the mirrors in my bedroom so I did not have to see my grief. I lost my strength, so I could not even lift my hands to place pins in my hair. And then I floated like a dead leaf on the water until I drifted out of my mother-in-law's house and back to my family home.

The REVENGE schema and the other schemas Taub has identified are all modes of expectation, evaluation, and inference that follow from the various ways in which the MORAL ACCOUNTING metaphor can be filled in by various conceptions of well-being and differing kinds of actions. They are constitutive of a large part of the moral reasoning we do when we are trying to decide what to expect from others and how we ought to treat them.

The *Joy Luck Club* example reveals importantly that there are at least two levels of conceptual metaphor operative in our moral judgments. The first ("higher") level consists of metaphors for our moral interactions generally, such as the MORAL ACCOUNTING metaphor, which sets the parameters of our judgments about what is due us and what we owe others. Metaphors at this level define our moral framework and fundamental moral concepts. But in order for our moral frameworks to be applied to concrete situations, we need a second level of metaphor for conceptualizing the situations. The REVENGE schema, for example, is empty without the metaphors of BABY AS VALUABLE POSSESSION and FACE AS VALUABLE POSSESSION that give content to the schema and make it applicable to Yingying's situation. In sum, our moral reasoning typically depends on which of several possible metaphors we use at these two basic levels: (1) adopting a particular metaphorically defined framework for our interactions and (2) filling that framework in with metaphors that connect it to the particular situation (such as whether we understand the BODY AS A VALUABLE POSSESSION). These two levels must fit together to give concrete moral inferences. It follows also that moral critique can be directed at either or both of these levels, since we can criticize both our general moral framework and the more specific metaphors we use to understand aspects of situations.

BASIC METAPHORS FOR MORALITY

MORAL ACCOUNTING is only one of several fundamental metaphors that define our moral understanding and reasoning at this first, higher level. So far, we have discovered a small number of other basic metaphor systems for various parts of our conception of morality.... This list is by no means complete....

MORAL ACCOUNTING. Our good deeds increase the moral well-being of others (via WELL-BEING IS WEALTH). They earn us moral *credit*. We *owe* others for the good things they have done for us. We should *repay* their kindness. Our evil deeds create a *debt* to other people and society in general.

Inference patterns. Wealth is a valuable commodity that can be amassed, earned, wasted, stolen, given away according to standards of fair exchange. Therefore, our moral interactions are regarded as modes of moral exchange in which well-being is amassed and lost and in which people build up moral credit and create moral debts through their actions.

MORALITY IS HEALTH/IMMORALITY IS SICKNESS. Health requires cleanliness, exercise, proper diet, and rest. When moral well-being is understood as health, it follows that all forms of moral sickness are bad. Bad deeds are *sick*. Moral *pollution* makes the soul sick. We must strive for *purity* by avoiding *dirty deeds*, moral *filth*, *corruption*, and *infection* from immoral people.

Inference patterns. Sick people spread disease, so we try to stay away from them and to maintain the cleanliness and bodily conditions that allow us to resist disease.

Therefore, if moral evil is a disease, we must quarantine those who are immoral (by censoring them and shunning their company), so that we are not exposed to their influence. We must keep ourselves clean, pure, and protected from moral infection....

BEING MORAL IS BEING IN THE NORMAL PLACE. According to a pervasive metaphor for human action, which I have named the EVENT STRUCTURE metaphor, actions are self-propelled motions along paths to destinations (goals). Certain ends (destinations) are moral *ends*. They are ends we have a duty to realize through our actions. The moral path is *straight and narrow*. Moral *deviance* is a *straying* from the true path. *Violating other people's boundaries* is immoral.

Inference patterns. Motion along a path gets you to your desired destination. In purposeful action, ends or goals are metaphoric destinations on these motion-paths. Moral "ends" are the metaphorical places we should strive to reach, and they are socially, religiously, and morally established. Being moral is going where you ought to go, along paths set up by society. Deviance is immoral because it takes you away from or out of the region you ought to be in, along with other people. Deviants can lead other people astray, and so they are perceived as a threat to the moral community....

It is vital to notice that basic moral terms like "ought" and "should" really have meaning and lead to moral inferences only through one or more of the above metaphors, along with the second-level metaphors by which we conceptualize actual situations. "Ought" means one thing and supports certain very specific moral inferences in the context of the MORAL ACCOUNTING metaphor, compared to the quite different set of inferences that it generates relative to the MORALITY IS HEALTH metaphor. According to the MORAL ACCOUNTING metaphor, for instance, "ought" is spelled out in terms of economic transactions of fair exchange, credit, and debt. MORALITY IS HEALTH, by contrast, establishes imperatives that direct us to fight moral sickness and promote certain states of moral flourishing within individuals and the community. "Ought" therefore gets its content and concrete applicability by means of its role in metaphorically defined moral frameworks....

METAPHOR AND MORAL REASONING

The most important epistemological and moral implication of the fact that our basic moral concepts are defined by metaphors is that we reason on the basis of these metaphors about how we ought to act and what kind of person we ought to be. The logic of the source domain, as it is mapped onto the target domain, constrains the inferences we make about the target domain of morality. We have seen this already in the way that the REVENGE schema leads to judgments and actions within the framework of the MORAL ACCOUNTING metaphor. The crucial point is that each metaphor has its own logic and generates epistemic entailments about the target domain (which is here some part of morality)....

These conceptual metaphors are not merely optional ways of talking about morality. There is nothing optional about them at all, and they are not merely matters of words. They are the means by which we define our moral concepts. Although we may not be limited to just one unique metaphor system for a particular concept (for example, we have both WELL-BEING IS WEALTH and WELL-BEING IS HEALTH), neither can we use just any metaphor especially since this is seldom a matter of conscious choice and the range of metaphors available is relatively small. Most important, the nature and structure of the source domain constrains the inferences we make about the aspect of morality that is the target domain. The metaphor, in other words, sets limits on our reasoning about how we ought to behave and how we ought to regard others. If, for instance, we understand moral well-being as WEALTH, we will act and reason quite differently than if we understood it as HEALTH. The logic of the WEALTH metaphor contains notions of fair exchange, quantification, and balance, while the logic of moral HEALTH emphasizes avoidance of immoral people, staying pure, fighting moral disease, and maintaining moral discipline.

HOW COGNITIVE SCIENCE CHANGES ETHICS

Having surveyed some of the basic metaphors that define our moral understanding, the nagging question arises, So what? "So what?" the moral apriorist will ask. "What difference could it possibly make to learn that people typically use metaphors to understand their experience? We want to know how they *ought* to reason, not how they tend to reason."

The answer to this question is clear and straightforward, and in offering an answer, I am suggesting in general how empirical studies in the cognitive sciences bear on morality and moral theory. The general answer is that our morality is a *human* morality, one that must work for people who understand, and think, and act as we do. Consequently, if moral theory is to be more than a meaningless exploration of utopian ideals, it must be grounded in human psychology.

The moral purist, in pursuit of the illusory ideal of a strict governance theory of morality, demands a nonexistent direct

connection between moral understanding and morally correct action. The only answer that a moral purist will allow is one that shows how learning about the metaphoric structure of morality, for instance, would lead, in a step-by-step fashion, directly to rules that would tell us how to act. But this is not possible in any but the most obvious, well-worn, unproblematic cases. Knowing the nature and entailments of the MORAL ACCOUNTING metaphor does not tell us whether MORAL ACCOUNTING is a good form of moral interaction in any particular situation. However, knowing all we can about the MORAL ACCOUNTING metaphor can help us make informed judgments about the probable consequences of acting on the basis of this particular metaphor....

The empirical study of our moral conceptual system reveals the metaphors that define our moral frameworks, and it can open our eyes to the limitations of this or that metaphor of morality. It can show us what our metaphors highlight and what they hide. It reveals the partial nature of any metaphorical conceptualization and of the reasoning we do based on each metaphor, and it shows us that we may need multiple conceptualizations to discern the full range of possibilities open to us in a given situation. Knowledge of this sort is knowledge that should influence our judgments and actions. It is knowledge that comes from what I earlier called the psychology of moral understanding, which I contrasted with trivialized moral psychology, that is, moral psychology with blinders. A rich psychology of moral understanding looks not merely at people's beliefs and motivations but especially at their deepest moral concepts and the reasoning that stems from them.

The absence of rules for deriving moral judgments from knowledge about metaphorical concepts is not something to be lamented. It is simply a fact about the complexity of human moral understanding, and it is an extremely important fact that has the following significant implications for ethics....

Moral Reasoning

If our basic moral concepts are metaphoric and if we use metaphors to frame the situations we are deliberating about, then our moral reasoning is primarily an exploration of the entailments of the metaphors we live by. For the most part, then, moral reasoning is not deductive, and it is not primarily a matter of applying universal moral principles or rules to concrete situations. I have shown why this model cannot work for the kinds of beings we are and for the kinds of situations we encounter. The reason is that the traditional deductive model has no place for metaphoric concepts, or for any concepts that do not have classical (that is, necessary and sufficient conditions) structure.

Partial Understanding

It follows from the imaginative nature of moral concepts and reasoning that no understanding is exhaustive or comprehensive. Human moral understanding is a complex cluster of metaphor systems, some of which are mutually inconsistent, and yet we manage to live with them and plot our lives by them.

Beyond Absolutism

Because our moral understanding is necessarily partial, morality is not a set of absolute, universal rules but an ongoing experimental process. We must continually be experimenting with new possibilities for action, new conceptions of human flourishing, and new forms of interaction that permit us to adjust to, and also to manage, the ever-changing conditions of

human existence. As long as we and our entire ecological situation are evolving, morality must remain experimental. Any attempt to codify this procedure into a final method or absolute principles is a recipe for moral rigidity and obtuseness.

Grounded Moral Theory

The partial, nonabsolute character of our moral understanding might make one think that morality is historically and culturally contingent in a radical way. It would then seem that there is no point in trying to construct a normative moral theory. This is a mistaken view. The most basic source domains for our metaphors for morality are grounded in the nature of our bodily experiences and tied to the kinds of experiences that make it possible for us to survive and flourish, first as infants and then as developing moral agents. Whether these basic source domains are universal is an open question that awaits further cross-cultural investigation. But if anything is universal, we have good reason to think that structures such as these will be. I believe that these experiential source domains provide general constraints on what can be a psychologically realistic morality, as well as an adequate moral theory. The general nature of such constraints suggests, as Owen Flanagan has argued at length, that there will always be a plurality of appropriate conceptions of human flourishing and a range of possible ways of realizing such conceptions of the good. Although these constraints do not underwrite a universal governance theory, they do limit the range of acceptable alternatives.

Moral Imagination

Moral deliberation is an imaginative enterprise in which we explore the possibilities for enhancing the quality of human existence in the face of current and anticipated conditions and problems. When we are trying to figure out the best thing to do in a given situation, we are tracing out the implications of various metaphors to see what they entail concerning how we should act. Projecting possible actions to determine their probable results, taking up the part of other people who may be affected, and reading with sensitivity the relevant dimensions of a particular situation are all forms of imaginative activity.

People who stress the imaginative and affective dimensions of human understanding are often mistakenly accused of being irrationalist and subjectivist. This serious misinterpretation is the result of a continued adherence to traditional rigid distinctions between such capacities as perception, imagination, feeling, and reason. Stressing the imaginative nature of our moral understanding in no way impugns the rationality of morality. I am arguing here for an enriched conception of human reason as fundamentally imaginative. My point is that moral reasoning is a much richer, more complex, and more flexible capacity than it has been conceived to be in traditional Enlightenment accounts of practical reason. Moral reasoning is reasoning, but it is a reasoning that is thoroughly imaginative in character.

WHAT SHOULD A THEORY OF MORALITY BE?

A theory of morality should be a theory of moral understanding. Its goal should be moral insight and the guidance and direction that come from a deep and rich understanding of oneself, other people, and the complexities of human existence. At the heart of moral reasoning is our capacity to frame and to realize more comprehensive and inclusive ends that make it possible for us to live well together with others. It involves an expansive form of imaginative reason that is flexible enough to manage our changing experience and to meet new contingencies intelligently. The key to moral intelligence is to grasp imaginatively the possibilities for action in a given situation and to discern which one is most likely to enhance meaning and well-being.

The idea of moral theory as providing governance through rules and principles is fundamentally mistaken. In fact, it is counterproductive to the extent that it overlooks the changing character of experience and does not allow us to see creatively new possibilities for action and response....

It should now be obvious why I think that the alleged split between moral theory and moral psychology is not just bogus but detrimental to a sound moral philosophy. The goal of moral psychology and moral philosophy alike should be understanding and liberation. Moral philosophy will give us the guidance that comes from moral understanding, critical intelligence, and the cultivation of moral imagination. It will not tell us what to do, but it will help us struggle to discern better from worse possibilities within a given situation. Moral philosophy cannot, and never did, give us an adequate theory of moral governance. Once we are liberated from this illusion, we can interpret Kant's dictum—always to think for yourself—as a call for a mature attitude of continual, well-informed, critical, and imaginative moral experimentation. And in our ongoing communal moral experimentation, good cognitive science, coupled with the cultivation of moral imagination, should lead the way.

Moral Psychology Has Little Effect on Moral Philosophy

Virginia Held

ETHICS AND SCIENCE

I will argue that cognitive science has rather little to offer ethics, and that what it has should be subordinate to rather than determinative of the agenda of moral philosophy. Moral philosophers often make clear at the outset that moral philosophy should not see the scientific or other explanation of behavior and moral belief, or the prediction and control that science has aimed at, as our primary concerns. Our primary concern is not explanation but recommendation. I start from this position: ethics is normative rather than descriptive.

In addition to ethics in its most general form, we need inquiries in all the more specific areas where ethical considerations should guide us. We need to be aware of the natural human tendencies and empirical realities that make moral recommendations feasible or not. We need to specify normative recommendations for particular types of cases, values that will be suitable for teaching and practicing, and so forth. So we ought to have inquiries we could call moral sociology, moral psychology, moral economics, moral political science, moral health sciences, and so on.

In these areas, the normative and the descriptive would intermingle. But it might be unwise to think of the sum of all of these—ethics plus moral social science, and so on—as "naturalized ethics." One reason is that it would misrepresent these fields. Another is that in the culture in which we live and work, the normative is constantly in danger of becoming swallowed by the empirical, not just in the social sciences themselves but even within philosophy. Areas such as moral economics, moral sociology, and so on do not even exist as "fields" in the academy, although, of course, moral assumptions are necessarily being smuggled into the social sciences unacknowledged much of the time. It is true that many political science departments may have one political theorist who may be interested in the moral norms of political theory. But how many economics departments have a comparable scholar engaged in inquiry about moral theory in the area of economics? To help us keep our inquiries in perspective, we might compare the number of academic appointments in ethics with the number in the empirical social sciences and psychology combined. The important task for moral philosophy in relation to these other areas seems to be to keep the distinctively normative alive and well.

Certainly moral philosophy should not ignore cognitive science. Moral philosophy needs to pay attention to findings in psychology, as to those in economics, sociology, anthropology, and so forth. It should, however, put no special premium on psychology. What ethics should not do is to lose sight of the distinctive and primarily normative and evaluative agenda for which it should continue to press.

Many of us are not arguing for a pure, rationalistic conception of normative ethics—the kind of theory disparaged by many of those enthusiastic about the contributions that cognitive science can make to ethics. We argue for a complex but meaningful and important extension of genuinely normative moral philosophy into many domains now restricted by their primarily empirical agenda. Moral philosophy needs to understand the empirical realities in all these areas, but it should set its own goals and recommend that in all these various fields we not only include a normative component along with everything else that is to be explained but that we give priority to our normative aims. The key is whether what is primarily being sought is causal explanation or moral guidance.

The search for causal explanation dominates in cognitive science and in moral psychology as usually pursued. It has led to various attempted takeovers even of moral philosophy itself. If those interested in moral psychology want it to be genuinely normative (as some do), then our positions are not far apart. But most of the interest in the normative shown by those engaged in the kind of moral psychology influenced by cognitive science is an interest in the explanatory role of moral beliefs, not the validity of moral claims.

If moral psychology is the psychology of making moral judgments and developing moral attitudes, it seeks causal explanations of how this is done. This leaves unaddressed the normative questions of whether the positions arrived at are morally justifiable. If, on the other hand, moral psychology deals with how we ought to cultivate the right kinds of moral attitudes and tendencies, to achieve the morally best outcomes, and to express the most morally admirable ways of living human lives, then it is a branch of moral philosophy. It is moral philosophy of a particular kind, making recommendations in a particular region, the region of psychological traits and responses and of

learning, as distinct, say, from the regions of organizing economic life or shaping political institutions. But it gives priority to a normative agenda....

Adherents of the view that cognitive science can greatly advance moral inquiry usually reject the fact-value distinction as a mistake. We can agree that the line between fact and value is neither sharp nor stable but still hold that there are important differences between clear cases of fact and clear cases of value. To know the caloric intake per day that a child needs to survive is different from deciding that we morally ought to provide these calories. Many of us think there are good reasons to assert such distinctions....

What some of us would like to see satisfactory explanations of is why so much of the dominant philosophy of the twentieth century in the United States and England has been so subservient to science. These explanations would be in terms of the sociology of knowledge and of psychological explanation. They would require an understanding of the politics of inquiry and the politics of education. They would ask why it is that so many philosophers have devoted themselves to fitting whatever they wanted to say about mental states and human experience and moral choice and evaluation into the framework of scientific description and explanation. These inquiries would ask why philosophy has so seldom resisted rather than accepted domination by the intellectual outlook of science. Thomas Nagel writes about how philosophy is currently "infected by a broader tendency of contemporary intellectual life: scientism. Scientism is actually a special form of idealism, for it puts one type of human understanding in charge of the universe and what can be said about it. At its most myopic it assumes that everything there is must be understandable by the employment of scientific theories like those we have developed to date". But, of course, the scientific outlook is just one of a long series of historical outlooks and is, in Nagel's view, "ripe for attack".

Ethical naturalism has lately been presented as a view hospitable to cognitive science, one that avoids such metaphysically peculiar entities as moral norms or normative properties. Ethical naturalism is seen as having what is taken as the great advantage of being consistent with science and metaphysical materialism. But as Jean Hampton usefully reminds us, such a view is hardly new; it has already had an eloquent exponent in Hobbes. She shows how even Hobbes "cannot keep normative standards of value and reasoning out of his theory" and argues that since contemporary naturalists employ objective normative standards for such matters as instrumental rationality and coherent, healthy preferences, they have no defensible grounds for dismissing objective moral norms....

MORAL EXPERIENCE

Suppose we start with the other fork of the Kantian antinomy between, on the one hand, the freedom we must assume to make sense of moral responsibility and explanation and prediction in terms of the causal laws of nature. Then we might hold that moral philosophy should make room, first of all, for moral experience and its mental states as these appear to the moral subject rather than to an observer of that subject.

Experience should most certainly not be limited to the empirical observation so much philosophy has seen it as equivalent to. Moral experience includes deliberation and choice and responsibility for action; it includes the adoption of moral attitudes, the making of moral judgments about our own and others' actions and their consequences and evaluation of the characters

and lives we and others have and aspire to. And it includes these as experienced subjectively.

Moral experience includes deciding what to do. It requires us to assume we can choose between alternatives in ways that should not be expected a priori to be subsumable under scientific explanations whether psychological, biological, ecological, or any other. I have a different view of moral experience than did Kant, but I share the view that moral experience requires assumptions that cannot be reconciled with causal explanation as so far understood and that this should not lead us to give up the distinction between recommendations that we can accept or reject and explanations of what it is that we do.

Moral experience finds us deliberating about which moral recommendations to make into our reasons for acting, and reflecting on whether, after acting, we consider what we have done to be justifiable. It finds us weighing the arguments for evaluating the actions of others one way or another, and evaluating the states of affairs we and others are in and can bring about. It finds us approving or disapproving of the traits and practices we and others develop and display.

My view of moral epistemology is in some respects rather like that of many ethical naturalists: I agree that the picture of convergence and progress in science as contrasted with continued disagreement and lack of progress in ethics is a distorted one. In the area of moral inquiry, there are what can be thought of as the equivalents of observation statements: they are the particular moral judgments whose acceptance allows us to "test" our moral principles, which principles can be taken as comparable to hypotheses. There is thus to some extent a parallel between moral and scientific inquiry. But in another way moral inquiry is fundamentally unlike sci- entific inquiry: the objective moral norms we can come to think of as valid are not about "natural" entities or events, and whereas with observation statements we are trying to report what the world causes us to observe, with moral judgments we are trying to choose how we will act in and upon the world.

We need a conception of mind that al- lows us to make sense of moral experience, moral choice, and moral evaluation. Cog- nitive science and conceptualizations consistent with it are highly influential in philosophy. Huge amounts of philosophy of mind are now devoted to the task of constructing conceptions of mind com- patible with cognitive science. But those of us interested in ethics should insist, I think, on pursuing our agenda: finding a conception of mind compatible with what we understand and have good reason to believe about moral experience. If this conception of mind is incompatible with cognitive science, so much the worse for cognitive science. It has only been so much the worse for ethics because we have let the agenda be set by those who have little, or only marginal, interest in ethics. I thus subscribe to Thomas Nagel's recom- mendation that when the subjective and objective standpoints "cannot be satisfac- torily integrated... the correct course is not to assign victory to either standpoint but to hold the opposition clearly in one's mind without suppressing either ele- ment"....

Some philosophers think that a natura- listic view will avoid certain characteristic distortions with which many other moral theories have presented moral life. An- nette Baier, for instance, discusses male concepts of the person that rest on denials that a person *qua* person need be born at all or need be a family member. Moral theories built on agreements that might be reached by purely rational beings, or on notions of rationally maximizing individ- ual preferences often assume such concep- tions of the person. Baier observes that it is "unlikely that women, who have tradi- tionally been allocated the care of the very dependent young and old persons will take persons as anything except interde- pendent persons." Women are not likely to forget that persons cannot come into existence any other way than by being born of women. But this issue, in my view, is independent of whether ethics should be naturalized.

Feminist reconceptualizations of the person are having a profound influence on feminist moral philosophy. The persons whom morality is for will need quite dif- ferent moralities from the currently still dominant ones, depending on what per- sons are understood to be. And these will be moralities for both supposedly public persons and supposedly private persons since they are, after all, the same persons.

This large and deep revision of moral concepts and theories has not needed much assistance from cognitive science. The latter can sometimes strengthen one suggestion or another, as when it offers ev- idence that self-interest is in fact not the only motive determining human behavior. But evidence for this has always been all around us in our moral experience, if we would be willing to see it. And women will often do well to trust our own experi- ence when it conflicts with the assertions of science, cognitive or other. The history of psychological and social scientific mis- interpretation of women's experience is a horror story not to be forgotten.

EMPATHY AND ETHICS

Alvin Goldman has provided a useful summary of work in cognitive science on various aspects of empathy and on the role of empathy in influencing moral behavior.

He notes that a satisfactory prescriptive theory should be "rooted in human nature" and thus that findings in cognitive science are relevant to normative moral theory. We can all agree that a normative moral theory should not ask the impossible of human beings and that findings in cognitive science can inform us of emotional tendencies and limitations that may be relevant to what we ask morality to recommend. But we should not exaggerate the contributions of cognitive science.

We can study the tendencies of human beings, especially some of them, toward aggression and violence. Ethics needs to recommend how to counter and limit such tendencies. We can study how stereotypes are formed and how prejudices develop; ethics should instruct us on what fairness and consideration require in opposition to such prejudices. Knowing what tendencies people have and how attitudes develop is useful knowledge surely, but it does not do the work of moral evaluation and recommendation.

A neural network model, for instance, may explain how children come to learn various moral attitudes and to make interconnected moral judgments. But it may be as useful for explaining how children learn to disparage weaker groups and to take advantage of their members as it is for explaining how admirable moral attitudes are learned. It does rather little to answer questions about what we ought to teach our children, though once we have decided what we ought to teach them, it may help us understand how to do so more effectively. Paul Churchland writes that on the basis of the neural network models of cognitive function now emerging, "knowledge acquisition is primarily a process of learning *how*: how to recognize a wide variety of complex situations and how to respond to them appropriately... moral knowledge does not automatically suffer by contrast with other forms of knowledge". But questions about which responses are appropriate and which are not are just those ethics must address, and before we can decide what moral "knowledge acquisition" should be promoted and what beliefs and attitudes should be discouraged, we need to evaluate alternative moral norms.

The facts of how human beings can and do feel empathy are certainly relevant to morality. But many of these facts have been as plain to those wishing to see them as the facts of how human beings can and do reason. Evidence of empathy and its role in benevolent action has been ubiquitous, but it has often not been noticed by moral philosophers or it has not been considered of importance for morality. Some of us find it extraordinary that only after cognitive science informs us that empathy exists, and can motivate people to act in ways that are not primarily a matter of satisfying their own individual interests, is this believed by many philosophers. We may wish to ask: what can be the explanation of this?

One factor helping to explain why the facts about empathy have not been noticed, or have not been deemed relevant to morality, has been the deep association between reason and men and between emotion and women, and the discounting of the experience of women. The moral experience of women offers a vast source of insights into the phenomena of empathy and how it may be excessive at times, as well as deficient in other cases. These insights have already greatly affected feminist moral theory, with no particular need to make use of cognitive science.

One can point to a long history of denying the evidence when the evidence was presented by the actions, motives, or experience of women. The whole realm of women's actions and experience within the family and in the household has been dismissed as not relevant to morality, as not even moral action but rather as behavior belonging to the realm of the biological. Women have been conceptualized as merely carrying out the dictates of their maternal natures rather than exercising moral judgment. Even those who hold that all action is determined but that we can think of some of it as relatively free if self-determined have not conceptualized women's mothering activities as offering examples of action that might be free in this sense. Rather, they too have usually seen it as instinctive behavior, not action guided by and relevant to the revising of moral principles. Feminist theorists point out the distortions in nearly all traditional and standard moral theories. Such theories give, in the construction of morality, unjustified privilege to the public domain where men have been predominant, and unreasonable disadvantage to the private domain to which women have largely been confined.

Cognitive science can confirm that action within the household, like much other action, is often determined by natural emotions. But cognitive science cannot make the case that there are moral choices to be made about what sorts of actions within the family and between friends are to be recommended as distinct from observed and explained, and that experience in this domain is highly relevant to moral theory. At the moment, it seems to be only feminist moral theorizing that is taking this moral experience of women seriously. And the aims of feminist moral theory and of cognitive science are very different and sometimes at odds.

Goldman usefully points out that empathy need not be merely particularistic, extending to those we are close to or who are like ourselves. Although there are certainly limits to our benevolence, we can feel empathy for persons quite distant from us, and there are "sympathy-based theories that are quite universalistic". But cognitive science can do little to guide us in deciding how universalistic our moral theories ought to be. Owen Flanagan is content to have them more local. Others find moral theories deficient unless they are universal. Cognitive science can suggest limits on what we deem reasonable to expect of persons, and it can certainly help us to teach and to gain compliance with the moral norms we deem best, but it cannot itself assist us with decisions about which moral norms to adopt and which moral theory is best. Within feminist moral theorizing, there is much disagreement, ample for healthy debate, including disagreement about how universalistic and how naturalistic ethics should be. My own view is, of course, not *the* view of feminist moral theory. But no moral theory can be acceptable from a feminist point of view unless it includes a strong moral commitment to gender equality and an end to gender dominance and unless it pays adequate attention to the experience of women. Some of these commitments, in my view, escape naturalistic description.

METAPHOR AND PHILOSOPHICAL THOUGHT

Many of us agree with Mark Johnson that our basic moral concepts are importantly metaphoric. But understanding this does not lessen our need to make moral choices between alternative metaphors. Consider some examples. For centuries, the concept of "human" has been based on images of a male human being, often a warrior, or on images reflecting other aspects of what men do when they exercise political power or create works of art or science or industry. Feminist critiques of prevailing conceptions of the human as "man" insist that the concept include images of "woman" and of "girl," and in reasonable ways rather than always as an "other".

We can see in the history of ethics and social and political philosophy overwhelming reliance on the metaphor of man in the public sphere contracting with other men to limit the means by which male heads of household pursue their own interests, in political life and in the marketplace. Once we become conscious of such dominant metaphors, through perceptive interpretations of them, we can decide to expand them or modify them or limit them or replace them. This has been a continual task of philosophy.

I have discussed in various places the concept of property and how Lockean images of the independent farmer or tradesman who can acquire what he needs if only he is not interfered with still permeate contemporary interpretations of property. These metaphors are woefully inadequate for the task of evaluating economic arrangements, especially in contemporary economic systems. I have also discussed how the image of the orator in the square who can speak if only not prevented still guides interpretations of freedom of expression and First Amendment decisions in the law, though this metaphor is grievously unsuited for dealing with contemporary cultures, such as our own, that are dominated by the realities of the media and where getting a hearing through the media bears very little resemblance to speaking out in the public square. And I have argued that the metaphors of economic exchange are not the right ones for dealing with many moral issues where they have been employed routinely. I am clearly highly sympathetic with efforts to clarify the metaphors used in moral thinking. However, once we have understood how deficient reigning metaphors often are, we need to choose alternatives that will be morally and descriptively better.

Some philosophers hold that the metaphor of the contract and its ways of thinking should be applied not only to a social contract underlying political institutions but to most or all human relationships and even to the whole of morality. Others argue, on the contrary, that contractual thinking is very unsuitable for thinking about large parts of morality and about much that matters in families and societies. The arguments between us on these issues cannot be settled by examining how people learn, how they come to think what they do, or how contractual norms and ways of thinking explain what people believe or do. The argument some of us are making is that contractual thinking is rampant in the society around us but that it should not be as pervasive as it is. In our view, this metaphor is not appropriate for a great deal of moral understanding. Cognitive science cannot recommend such choices among metaphors, though it may help us explain why the choices that have been made have been accepted, and other empirical studies will help explain why the choices made have so often been advantageous to some and disadvantageous to others.

Mark Johnson thinks we are just beginning to understand, by means of cognitive science, how the metaphors we use influence the ways we think about morality. This seems to me wildly to overstate the contributions of cognitive science. Philosophers and others frequently illuminate and examine the dominant metaphors of various outlooks and ways of thinking. One can think of such examples as C. B. Macpherson's "possessive individualism" in Hobbes and Locke, the use of Isaiah Berlin's hedgehog and fox images to distinguish the outlooks of continental and British philosophy, Nancy Hartsock's analysis of the metaphor of the barracks community in thinking about politics, and countless others. Carolyn Merchant suggests some implications of the metaphors by which the earth was conceptualized and thought and felt about. Before the sixteenth century, the earth had been seen as a generative and nurturing mother; there had been a reluctance to violate it, and commercial mining was thought morally problematic because of the way it cut into the earth. By the seventeenth century, sexual metaphors had become prevalent. The earth was thought of as a woman to be dominated by the new science, a female who should appropriately be mastered. Penetrating the earth through mining was no longer seen as a moral problem.

When persuasive, such interpretations of prevalent metaphors surely heighten our understanding; they need no support from cognitive science. We are all familiar with how illuminating it is to see the mechanical model at the heart of a great deal of philosophical and other thought and then to question its appropriateness. Or we recognize the metaphors of evolution and survival of the fittest at work, often for dubious purposes, in other bodies of thinking, and we have done this unaided by the lenses of cognitive science. Now, of course, we can see the metaphor of the computer and its programs, its hardware and its software, as pervasive in the philosophical and other thought affected by cognitive science. Some think that to use the metaphor of the computer and its programs for understanding moral experience is surely less than helpful. Thomas Nagel writes that "eventually... current attempts to understand the mind by analogy with man-made computers... will be recognized as a gigantic waste of time".

Mark Johnson seems to think that the logic of the metaphor used determines our reasoning in what is called the "target" area, in this case, the area of ethics. But

though it certainly colors it, we have to decide whether any given metaphor leads to good or poor reasoning in a given area, or to a better or worse interpretation of experience in it. When we decide the metaphor is unsuitable, we search for an alternative. Even if a metaphor gives rise to a certain way of thinking, this does not mean that the way of thinking in question can be evaluated on that basis. The distinction between how we happen to come to a position and what makes the position true or false or valid or invalid or a good or bad way of thinking about an issue is, of course, a distinction with a very long history. Many of us think there are good reasons to maintain it.

Cognitive science may suggest that in answering questions about how we come to think that we should keep our agreements, we answer questions about whether we should, and the same or the other moral judgments it looks at. But we can certainly disagree. It is the task of ethics to answer questions about what we ought to do and what has value. Knowledge about how we came to have the views we do can certainly be helpful, but it can never itself answer moral questions. We have to decide which metaphors are best for dealing with our values, our goals, our obligations. A quite different way of interpreting what is going on from the way Mark Johnson interprets it is to think that in ethics we start with various moral intuitions, judgments, and principles and use metaphors to try to express them.

Let me offer what will be something of a parody of the approach of cognitive science. Mark Johnson singles out various basic metaphors from what he sees as a physical domain and shows how, in his investigations, various types of moral discourse seem to be determined by them. Without the benefit of cognitive science, let me suggest two other basic metaphors from the ones he finds that can easily be seen in moral thinking and discussion.

The first is the SEXUAL/HUNGER metaphor. We have wants and desires, whose satisfaction is pleasurable; it is good to achieve the satisfaction of desire. What we ought to do is to maximize satisfaction. When we are sated, the pleasure decreases; the pleasure is most intense when our desire is greatest. Sometimes we desire the desire even more than the satisfaction. Pleasure is desired and desirable; pain is avoided and undesirable. It is good to minimize frustration, though we should not be misled by our short-term wants. We should consider what goals to pursue and that there are second-order desires as well as immediate ones.

To think of the SEXUAL/HUNGER metaphor that can be discerned in such discourse as coming from a basic physical domain and that this metaphor determines what can be said in the moral domain employing it may well be misleading. We often start with a mix of moral thoughts and feelings, attitudes and judgments. We try to express them using metaphoric language. It might be more accurate, at least sometimes, to say that the moral terms belong to a basic domain and the physical ones, used in the context of moral discourse, to what could be called, in this parody, a "vehicle" domain.

According to a second metaphor, the GROWTH metaphor, the normal person develops moral understanding. When moral growth is interfered with, the person may be morally stunted. Without an environment that facilitates moral growth the person may be morally deformed. Noxious conditions sometimes impede natural moral development. Morality enables persons to grow as human beings.

One could say of this way of speaking that in the basic, moral domain, growth is given a moral interpretation; in the "vehi-cle" domain it is given a biological one. Philosophers who have relied on the GROWTH metaphor have assumed rather than argued that growth is good. Now that we find it easy to question this in areas such as population growth and the effects of industrialization on the environment, it may be easier for us to see what is wrong with such a metaphor. But one could see it, as many did, long before the questioning of growth as good became popular.

One could go on, designating other "vehicle" domains and drawing word pictures of them. Of course, metaphors can be discerned in moral discourse without the aid of cognitive science and without suggesting we need a research program in "vehicle domains." Moral deliberation is an imaginative enterprise, we can agree. But there may be more in literature and art and in listening to others with experiences like and unlike our own to nourish this imaginative enterprise than in cognitive science, unless, to conclude our story, the latter becomes so fanciful a narrative that it is no longer recognizable as science.

MORAL PHILOSOPHY

John Dewey's ethics remain fundamentally unsatisfactory, in my view, because he thought moral theory was the sort of theory to which sciences like cognitive science could provide answers. He wrote as if moral problems simply present themselves and as if the tasks of morality are to find empirical solutions to such problems. Moral problems, however, do not simply present themselves. We decide to make certain empirical situations into moral problems, to interpret them as moral problems. Forty years ago, very few people saw the prevalent confinement of women to household roles as a moral problem, a matter of injustice. On the contrary, dissatisfaction with such confinement was interpreted as a personal problem of psychological adjustment. But because a few persons, later joined by others, made the normative as distinct from empirical judgment that it was unjust that opportunities outside the household were so widely closed to women, opportunities have gradually increased.

Many of us are not arguing for a morality of rules, either Kantian or utilitarian. These rule moralities can be interpreted as generalizations to the level of moral theory of the norms of law and public policy. Many feminists have criticized the excessively rationalistic moral theories that have been dominant in recent decades. We argue that we should seek a morality that adequately considers the activities, emotions, and values involved in caring and that takes these as seriously as moral theories have taken justice and reason and utility. But we may still think that moral philosophy should give priority to the normative over the empirical, to recommendation and evaluation over explanation and prediction.

Of course, if one supposes that the categories into which everything conceivable must fall are the "natural" and the "supernatural," it is easy to think that ethics belongs in the realm of the natural. I would think this also if I accepted this division, but to take it as presented seems highly misleading. The division between the natural and the supernatural may be one of the most unfortunate metaphors of all. There are other distinctions that may be far more useful, especially for ethics: the distinction between that which is specifically human and that which belongs to a natural world that would be much as it is with no humans in it, or the distinction between the subjective point of view of the conscious self and the objective point of view of the observer studying nature and the human beings in it and seeking explanations of its events. These distinctions require us to recognize realms that are not supernatural but are not natural either in the sense just suggested.

It is to these other domains of conscious human subject, constantly shaping and being shaped by the social relationships that are part of what he or she is, that normative recommendations are addressed. We do not address our moral recommendations to the nature studied by the natural sciences but to persons consciously choosing how to live our lives, change our surroundings, express our hopes, and continue or perhaps even improve the futures of human beings in nature.

THE CONTINUING DEBATE:
Is Moral Psychology Relevant to Moral Philosophy?

What Is New

Contemporary science swiftly generates new insights into the nature of ethics; or–depending on your perspective—new challenges to the structure of ethics. One of the most interesting and profound challenges comes from recent work in neuropsychology, which challenges our "folk psychology" common sense belief that our free choices to exert will power are the source of our voluntary acts—including our choices of virtuous or vicious acts. Daniel M. Wegner, drawing on a range of recent neuropsychological research (made possible by technological advances in brain scanning), argues that the causal power of our conscious willing is an illusion, and that the actual causal sequence is initiated prior to our awareness. The experience of "conscious willing" is an effect, rather than a cause: an effect that usefully informs us that the behavior in question comes from ourselves (though of course not from our "acts of will power") rather than being imposed upon us by external forces. That is, the experience of conscious willing, when I move my hand, tells me that the motion of my hand was initiated within me, and not by someone else forcing my hand to move. If Wegner's interpretation of the relevant neuropsychological research is correct, it has profound implications for ethics (perhaps particularly for ethical issues related to moral responsibility); however, one might also respond (along the lines pursued by Virginia Held) that our moral beliefs should take precedence over such neuropsychological theorizing, and reject such claims.

Where to Find More

E. O. Wilson presented his views concerning the relevance of sociobiology for ethics in *Sociobiology: The New Synthesis* (Cambridge, MA: Harvard University Press, 1975); see also his *On Human Nature* (Cambridge, MA: Harvard University Press, 1978). Thomas Nagel denied the relevance of biological research to ethics in "Ethics as an Autonomous Theoretical Subject," in Gunther S. Stent, *Morality as a Biological Phenomenon* (Berlin: Dahlem Konferenzen, 1978). For further elaboration of Nagel's view, see *The View From Nowhere* (NY: Oxford University Press, 1986). More recent work examining the significance of evolutionary biology for ethics can be found in Richmond Campbell and Bruce Hunter, *Moral Epistemology Naturalized* (Calgary, AL: University of Calgary Press, 2000). For additional material, see the suggested readings for Debate 11.

Owen Flanagan's influential early work in cognitive science and ethics can be found in *Varieties of Moral Personality* (Cambridge, MA: Harvard University Press, 1991). Flanagan, together with Amélie Oksenberg Rorty, edited a volume of essays that largely suggests a more congenial relation between ethics and psychology: *Identity, Character, and Morality: Essays in Moral Psychology* (Cambridge, MA.: The MIT Press, 1990). An excellent collection of readings on contemporary work in cognitive science is William Bechtel and George Graham, eds., *A Companion to Cognitive Science* (Malden, MA: Blackwell Publishers, 1998); see particularly the paper by Mark L. Johnson, "Ethics."

Daniel M. Wegner's position is presented clearly and powerfully in *The Illusion of Conscious Will* (Cambridge, MA: MIT Press, 2002); criticisms of his view can be found in Daniel C. Dennett, *Freedoom Evolves* (NY: Penguin Putnam, 2003). For more on neuropsychological research and its implications for ethics, see the excellent anthology edited by Benjamin Libet, Anthony Freeman, and Keith Sutherland, *The Volitional Brain: Towards a Neuroscience of Free Will* (Thorverton, Exeter: Imprint Academic, 1999). Another perspective—and detailed arguments for the importance of neuropsychological research on ethics—is offered by Antonio R. Damasio, a distinguished neuropsychologist who is also a very engaging writer; see *Descartes' Error: Emotion, Reason, and the Human Brain* (NY: G. P. Putnam's Sons, 1994); and *Looking for Spinoza: Joy, Sorrow, and the Feeling Brain* (Orlando, FL: Harcourt, 2003).

HOW DID MORAL
BEHAVIOR DEVELOP?

MORALITY DEVELOPED AS A MEANS OF CONTROLLING POWERFUL GROUP MEMBERS

ADVOCATE: Christopher Boehm, Professor of Anthropology and Director of the Jane Goodall Research Center, University of Southern California

SOURCE: "Conflict and the Evolution of Social Control," *Journal of Consciousness Studies*, volume 7, No. 1–2, 2000: 79–90.

MORALITY DEVELOPED TO PROTECT SYSTEMS OF COOPERATIVE EXCHANGE

ADVOCATE: Dennis Krebs, Department of Psychology at Simon Fraser University; his research is primarily on altruism and morality

SOURCE: "As Moral as We Need to Be," *Journal of Consciousness Studies*, volume 7, No. 1–2, 2000: 98–101.

Charles Darwin's account of evolution has had revolutionary impact on almost every area of thought and inquiry, and ethics is certainly no exception. One of the early developments inspired by Darwin's work was *Social Darwinism*, an ethical theory that became quite popular among wealthy U.S. industrialists and bankers in the early twentieth century. Social Darwinism claims that nature is red in tooth and claw, competition is fierce and pits individual against individual, pity and compassion are wrong because they preserve weaker elements that should be eliminated for the good of the species, and those who survive and prosper are the superior ones. Aside from being simplistic and shallow (and ignoring the fact that humans are profoundly social and socially dependent animals), it is a gross distortion of Darwin's theory of natural selection: Darwin explicitly rejected the notion that evolution proceeds in a purposeful direction toward better and better individuals; rather, survivors are those who fit best into a particular niche, defined by the environmental conditions at that time.

More recent consideration of the implications of Darwinism for ethics have been considerably more sophisticated, but remain very controversial. There are a number of philosophers who believe that evolutionary research can tell us nothing whatsoever about ethics, because ethics is an independent discipline with its own distinctive methodology. There are even some philosophers who argue that the evolutionary process is brutal and cruel (as George C. Williams puts it, "Mother Nature is a Wicked Old Witch") and ethics must be formulated in direct contrast to the process of evolution.

There are also philosophers, however, who believe that we can gain a much better understanding of ethics through examining the biological origins of our deep motives and inclinations. Sociobiologist E. O. Wilson expressed this view provocatively: "The time has come for ethics to be removed temporarily from the hands of the philosophers and biologicized." Others have suggested that studying the biological origins of our strong feelings may be useful even if we ultimately decide that some of those feelings (such as racism and sexism) are morally unworthy, and that we must find effective ways of holding them in check.

Christopher Boehm brings the resources of anthropological research to his study of the origins of morality, arguing that morality developed from the dispositions of group members—including chimpanzees and the common ancestor of chimpanzees and humans—to control the bullying and dominance behavior of powerful individuals. With the development of language, this process of controlling dominance and reducing conflict could emerge as a full moral system. Thus for Boehm, biological dispositions are fundamental to the development of morality, but social groups do the actual work. Dennis Krebs favors a more strictly biological explanation of moral origins, claiming that both the tendency to hierarchical dominance and the disposition toward egalitarianism can be accounted for through biological evolutionary explanations.

POINTS TO PONDER

➤ How would Virginia Held (debate 10) respond to this scientific examination of morality?

➤ In debate 2, Thomas Nagel agrees that sometimes we can give a plausible causal account of why we hold the personal ethical views we do hold. However, he insists that often that does *not* undermine our belief in the reasonableness and objectivity of holding those ethical beliefs. Suppose that you accept Boehm's account of the origins of morality as correct; would that make it unreasonable to hold that your moral beliefs are reasonable and right?

➤ If we accept Christopher Boehm's account of the origins of morality, would that support or contradict the claim that chimpanzees sometimes act morally?

➤ Boehm holds that "humans are innately disposed to despotism," and "humans are not just naturally egalitarian" (but *are* opposed to being dominated by others, and can avoid such domination by forming social groups that hold in check the natural despotic domination tendency of powerful individuals). Krebs maintains that *both* despotism and egalitarianism are natural or "innate" biologically given, evolved human tendencies. What is the best evidence for each of the opposing sides of that dispute?

➤ Dennis Krebs asserts that "we are evolved to behave morally, that is to say to cooperate, when it is in our genetic interests, but we also are evolved to behave immorally when it is not." If Krebs is correct, does social contract theory become a more plausible account of ethics? If Krebs could offer empirical verification of his claim, would that count as empirical verification of the social contract theory of ethics?

Morality Developed as a Means of Controlling Powerful Group Members

CHRISTOPHER BOEHM

MORALITY AS POLITICS

All humans live in moral communities of the type discussed by Durkheim, in which public opinion decisively shapes the behaviour of individuals. Shared values define specific rights and wrongs of behaviour, and the group decides which individuals are deviant and sanctions them accordingly. These are constants of human social life, and on this basis a moral community engages actively in social control....

Social control is about the power of deviants to harm or distress others, but it is also about the power of a vigilant, assertive group that is bent upon manipulating or eliminating its deviants. In even the smallest band or tribe, the price of deviance can be assassination: capital punishment is one of the sanctions used against those who become seriously out of line. This universal pattern of group vigilance is based on behavioural dispositions that are quite ancient, for in effect moral communities amount to political coalitions and power coalitions are found in many of the higher primates. In fact, they also are found in other social mammals, and coalitions sometimes grow very large as entire communities defend themselves against external predators, sometimes unite against neighbouring groups, and, rarely but significantly, sometimes turn against individuals in the same group.

There is far more to morality than a group's momentarily uniting against a deviant individual: morality involves common agreement as to which behaviours are unacceptable, and it also involves a group's overall conception of a satisfactory quality of social and political life. There also has to be a precise exchange of information among group members as they carefully track the behaviours of other individuals, and a capacity to manipulate deviants strategically in order to satisfy this pattern. Thus, some major further developments had to take place, and in their definitive form they probably arrived in the Late Palaeolithic, as modern humans emerged.

If we could hypothesize what other pre-adaptations existed, and how those developments evolved, we would be on the road to an evolutionary explanation of moral behaviour. A first task, however, is to determine what the overall social life of Late Palaeolithic foragers was like. Fortunately, there are some important shreds of direct archaeological evidence. Anatomically Modern Humans foraged as nomads as they hunted and gathered in smallish bands, and it seems likely that bands were composed of at least thirty persons and therefore were larger than nuclear families. There is no evidence of humans being sedentary 100,000 years ago, or even 25,000 years ago, so presumably their bands moved around within familiar home ranges. However, radical changes of climate led them periodically to undertake migrations that eventually led to major geographic radiations of this species. These people sometimes seem to have cared for the injured, and they sometimes buried their dead—an act also performed by Neanderthals. However, aside from group size there is little evidence that can be related directly to social control.

This very minimal social portrait fits with extant foragers who remain nomadic, and the similarities of band size, local migration pattern, and subsistence strategy at least provide an anchor for analysis-by-triangulation. We may now consider central behavioural tendencies of extant bands, and ask whether they might be projected back into the Late Palaeolithic. Such bands are highly variable in their social organization and subsistence pattern, but so long as they remain mobile—rather than sedentary—they are remarkably uniform in their social, moral, and political makeup. Band size fits nicely with the range suggested by Dunbar, while bands are composed of some related and some unrelated families. Families tend to move back and forth from band to band, but in spite of this the members of a band co-operate intensively, particularly in sharing their large-game meat. Bands invariably are moralistic, for they practice sanctioning according to established values that assist in identifying deviants. The lists of deviant behaviour are remarkably uniform from one continent to another, and these mobile bands are uniformly egalitarian with respect to relations among adult males. By this I mean that they suppress undue competition, and head off attempts of individuals to exert domination or control; as a result, they tolerate very little leadership. It is very likely that all of these features of extant bands pertain to the Late Palaeolithic.

There is another avenue for drawing some *general* inferences about that earlier epoch. Cladistic analysis enables us to compare the two *Pan* species with our own, and see which social and political features all three share. The assumption is that any feature shared by all three is likely

to have been present in the ancestor shared by *Homo* and *Pan*, who lived five million years ago by molecular reckoning. In the area of social and political behaviour, our beginning list of shared features is impressive. All three species forage for a living and live in territorially-oriented communities that are subject to internal fission and fusion. All three are prone to status rivalry and competition based on flexible innate dispositions to dominate and submit, and all three work in political coalitions that often are dyadic but can become triadic or larger. Therefore, all three experience conflict. All three also engage in deliberate conflict resolution. These basic socio-political factors pertain to the Mutual Ancestor of *Pan* and *Homo*, and to any intermediate lineage that connects directly with one of the three extant species....

Morality is based heavily on social pressure, punishment, and other kinds of direct social manipulation by which the hostilely aroused majority use their power over individuals in a band. To understand such use of power in nomadic bands, one must focus on the fact that extant hunter-gatherers are politically egalitarian, and that Late Palaeolithic bands surely assumed a similar political form. This means that members of Late Palaeolithic band communities formed broad coalitions of subordinates which severely limited the potential of any male (or female) to attain ascendancy over other adults in the band....

This suppression of dominance behaviour among family heads enabled the local group, as a large political coalition, to control the actions of all its members. These included individuals endowed with great physical strength or aggressiveness, those chosen to lead, those who produced strongly as hunters, and shamans connected with unusual supernatural powers.

It did so as a local moral community that held commonly established views about which behaviours were likely to threaten members individually, or spoil the group's quality of life. It was prepared to deal with antisocial deviants, and, as with extant foragers who make their livings as nomads, a major focus was on the proscription of bullying behaviour at the level of band politics....

Ultimately, the moral sanctioning I am speaking of would appear to stem heavily from individual self interest, for many types of socially-defined deviance (for example, rape, theft, deception, adultery, and murder) are predatory behaviours that directly threaten such interests. But I emphasize that social control cannot be reduced entirely to individual interests; indeed, collective interests appear to be very important in guiding both moral sanctioning and the management of conflict....

It also makes sense to view moral communities as groups of people who have common concerns that go well beyond such individual interests. Hunter-gatherers are concerned with the overall quality of socio-political life they share, and they realize that if the entire group works together, it can improve the quality of that life. In short, they have social ideals, and they are able to speak about what is good or bad for the group. In this context, they identify any serious dyadic conflict as the entire group's social problem, no matter who is involved individually, because life is disrupted for the entire group. Usually, they see this as a problem that must be resolved, or 'managed', collectively.

Both individualistic and collectivistic methodologies can be useful in explaining social control, and they may also be appropriate for considering how natural selection has helped to produce this type of behaviour....

When humans act as moral communities, in many respects they can be very astute as non-literate social engineers. In matters of deviance and social conflict, they understand intuitively both the immediate social and political dynamics of their own groups, and the ultimate effects of conflict. Often, as they all but unanimously manipulate individual behaviour in desired directions, they consciously understand the social strategies they engage in. Often the strategies are directed squarely at the deviant, who they try to control, reform, or eliminate from the group. But sometimes they seem to be more interested in dealing with the conflict in its own right: they focus just on resolving the dispute—rather than on addressing the individual deviance involved—and this type of behaviour cannot easily be reduced to individual interests alone....

CONFLICT AS A STIMULUS FOR MORAL BEHAVIOUR

All human groups experience competition and conflict, and one major type of within-group conflict is *political*, in the sense that humans are innately disposed to vie for power and position. This is something we share with many species.... This applies to humans after the Neolithic, for our larger Societies exhibit a social order that an ethologist would call despotic. There is substantial social competition with a limited number of positions at the top and leaders have either substantial legitimate authority or coercive force at their disposal However, an older type of human society is the politically-equalized group I have described above. Vehrencamp would designate this ethologically as an egalitarian society, for the expression of tendencies to dominance and submission is not pronounced. This is because individual rank is not a major factor in reproductive success, and because leaders are not very dominant.

Normally, in discussions of ethological despotism or egalitarianism, the characterizations are specific to a species. But it would appear that humans, with their noteworthy cultural flexibility, are all over the map. When people live in chiefdoms, primitive kingdoms, or nation states, political life can be ethologically defined as despotic. When they live in mobile bands, small tribes, or tribal confederations, their political life is ethologically egalitarian.... The fact that human groups reach both of these extremes, and land at various intermediate points as well, raises an important question. As a species, are we innately given to ethological egalitarianism, to ethological despotism, or to neither?

To resolve this question, we must consider the fact that innately egalitarian primates like squirrel monkeys lack any very strong genetic preparations to dominate or submit. In this they are very different from chickens, or chimpanzees. Because the original humans were egalitarian for scores of millennia, we must ask if our species might be innately egalitarian—but that under Post-Palaeolithic conditions we somehow managed to 'hierarchize' ourselves on a cultural basis. These important questions were raised by Knauft, and subsequently I made the case that humans can remain egalitarian only if they consciously suppress innate tendencies that otherwise would make for a pronounced social dominance hierarchy. In effect, it is necessary for a large power-coalition (the rank and file of a band) to dominate the group's would-be 'bullies' if egalitarianism is to prevail—otherwise, the group will become hierarchical with marked status differences and strong leadership.

On this basis, it can be argued that humans are innately disposed to despotism.... My point is that humans are not just naturally egalitarian: if we wish to keep social hierarchy at a low level, we must act as intentional groups that vigilantly curtail alpha-type behaviours. This curtailment is accomplished through the cultural agency of social sanctioning, so political egalitarianism is the product of morality.

In this connection, I think that as moral communities began to form, the first type of behaviour to be dubbed 'deviant' could have been alpha-male type behaviour. There were two good reasons to suppress such behaviour. One was based on innate political dispositions: in a despotic species given to strong status rivalry there is a natural propensity for adults to behave dominantly. This results in a dislike of being dominated oneself, and it makes for subordinate rebellion against superiors. If resentful subordinates manage to collectivize and institutionalize their rebellion, you have a human type of politically egalitarian society, in which there is a major tension between the group and its more rivalrous individuals. The other reason was economic. Anatomically Modern Humans obtained an important part of their diet from large-game hunting, and this provided a practical reason to outlaw alpha males. In prehistoric bands that depended significantly on meat, the need for equalized distribution of food was great. People needed to reduce variation in their intake of rarely or sporadically acquired high-quality foods, notably large-game meat, and as brains grew larger humans gained enough actuarial acumen to set up uncentralized systems for *equalized* food redistribution, and also other kinds of co-operative security nets. The basic idea was to average out risks of individuals and families by collectivizing the products of hunting, and outlawing alpha domination behaviour was critical to satisfying these aims.

This eliminated bullies who would seek a lion's share, and thereby disrupt such a delicately-equalized system of give and take.

Extant hunter-gatherers uniformly insist on egalitarianism—at least until they settle in one place. If they do sedentarize, either as hunters or horticulturists, they often continue to be suspicious of authority—and politically egalitarian. But as people lose their obsession with staying equalized, they develop a substantial degree of hierarchy that is consistent with what anthropologists describe as 'chiefdoms'. In terms of culture change, hierarchy can assert itself quickly because of the innate political dispositions discussed above, and because, as they govern larger groups, strong, responsible leaders (the good ones) provide obvious benefits to all. This is so even though they also gain personal economic privileges and social status never seen in bands or tribes.

For human prehistory, this raises an important question. How did an innately despotic species manage to become phenotypically egalitarian in the first place? I have suggested, already, that the moral community might have developed originally as a collective means of eliminating the political, social, and economic problems that go with alpha domination. However, an alternative hypothesis would be that the moral community first developed for some other reason, but was put to use in the service of political egalitarianism once the subordinates realized they had collective power sufficient to eliminate the alpha role. Either way, there developed a full-blown egalitarian moral community that was in firm command of its own social life.

Here, I shall be developing a more general hypothesis that helps to account for either of these possibilities. Today, typical behaviours that are reasonably well-

controlled by the egalitarian band would seem to be: bullying behaviours; cheating or shirking in the context of co-operative efforts; serious degrees of deception or theft; and 'sexual crimes' like adultery, incest, and rape. If we examine this list of negatively sanctioned actions, these also are the behaviours that account for many of the serious conflicts in bands. Assuming that moral sanctioning is intentional, and this seems indisputable, this means that humans are singling out competitive or predatory behaviours that are likely to cause conflict, and, by suppressing them, they are, in effect, damping conflicts pre-emptively. On this basis, a formal hypothesis is possible. Moral communities arose out of group efforts to reduce levels of internecine conflict, as well as to avoid undue competition, domination, and victimization....

By contrast, among chimpanzees and bonobos we have seen that routine competition over food (and mating) is patterned by a self-organizing despotic social system that is based upon a social dominance hierarchy: the dominant individual (or the dominant dyadic-coalition) usually wins, so conflict is moderate. By establishing and maintaining a politically egalitarian order, human foragers obviously have rid themselves of this type of hierarchical system. In freeing themselves from domination by powerful individuals, they have lost the functional benefits of a typical primate linear dominance hierarchy—notably, a self-organizing social hierarchy with an alpha individual in the control role. In the absence of any authoritative central leadership on the part of strong, responsible individuals, they handle their social problems as well as they can. They do so on a collective and *deliberate* basis, through social control, and their main problem seems to be homicide involving male sexual competition.

I am suggesting that egalitarian societies are 'intentional communities', societies whose members have a certain type of social order in mind. As individuals they have decided to give up on climbing to the alpha level, and have settled, instead, for personal autonomy without either dominance or submission. They must work together *collectively* to accomplish this, and this same type of intentionality is applied to other spheres. It sometimes becomes quite reflective, for hunter-gatherers seem always to emphasize social harmony in philosophizing about their own social life. This normative emphasis is something that anthropologists have noted about non-literate people in general, and it is aimed at improving the quality of social life. Foragers' standard lists of deviant behaviour are lists of behaviours that are likely to cause conflict within the group, and degrade the overall quality of social life—for everyone....

At stake is the band's ability to live together in a not too stressful way, and to co-operate in ways that may be critical to health and survival. Having set aside hierarchical living except for within the family, hunter-gatherers have used their very large brains *collectively*, to diagnose and actively treat a wide variety of social problems at the band level. The pre-emptive side of conflict resolution involves suppressing deviant behaviours that lead to conflict. This helps to account for the peaceful, cooperative side of band life. When foragers do see conflicts developing, they are quite good at heading them off—so long as they do not reach the homicidal level. It is this corporate, highly deliberate, and basically *pre-emptive* approach to the avoidance of conflict that distinguishes human moral communities from largely self-organizing communities of other highly social animals, which actively control conflicts only when they

become active. This will be discussed further.

IS AVERSIVENESS TO CONFLICT INNATE?

Egalitarian moral communities work in a variety of ways, using praise and persuasion as well as negative social pressure, ostracism, and coercion. But one reason that 'social pressure' works so well is that deviants know the community can take things further, by seriously distancing them socially or by ejecting them from the group, occasionally by administering beatings, and, apparently everywhere if rarely, by putting them to death. Thus, the negative side of social sanctioning is ultimately *political.*

The implications of political power are pervasive in social control. First, problems of deviance often involve relations of power and domination, and second, social control is based on the group's power over individuals who are abusing power or are acting in some other predatory or otherwise antisocial capacity. Because the standard proscription-list of aggressive, self-interested behaviours is also a list of behaviours that cause conflict within the group, one must ask if there might be some innate aversion to conflict that helps to 'motivate' sanctioning strategies. An alternative hypothesis would be that the active social force is provided by the intelligence of non-literate humans, as social engineers who have rationally discerned the costs of conflict and therefore have invented ways to manipulate their own social environments in an anticipatory fashion.

The obvious intentionality of social control suggests that the latter hypothesis holds, but are these two hypotheses contradictory? I believe that human nature may be shaping human intentions rather decisively in this case. A specific prehistoric hypothesis would be that Anatomically Modern Humans were innately aversive to social conflict in their immediate social environments, that is, within their bands, and that precursors for such an aversion should be identifiable in the ape ancestral to both of *Homo* and *Pan*.

To explore this important question, we must return to the type of cladistic analysis that was employed earlier. Humans living in bands consistently try to mediate conflicts between individuals, with varying success depending on the nature of the conflict. Non-human primates seem to manage aggression in a variety of ways, which involve reconciliation, consolation, and active intervention by third-parties. With chimpanzees, high-ranking individuals and particularly the alpha males act in a control role to stop fights, often before they escalate very far. Bonobos are generally less prone to agonism but they, too, intervene in conflicts. This means that our Mutual Ancestor was likely to have intervened in conflicts, but what was the motivation?

It is difficult to discuss motives for an animal species five million years ago, but it helps to have worked with the very rich long-term data set at the Gombe Stream Research Centre, which spans decades.... It might seem far-fetched to suggest that chimpanzees actually have the intention to pacify a conflict when they engage in an intervention, but when a highly intelligent animal utilizes a wide variety of tactics to accomplish the same strategic end, the manipulative behaviour would appear to be deliberate.

Tactics I observed at Gombe did vary widely. Usually, a male or female dominant chimpanzee would display at the (subordinate) adult protagonists and scatter them, or a male would charge right between them with the same effect. But I also have watched the Gombe alpha male

successively herding two females in opposite directions to stop a serious fight up in a tree, and once I saw a high-ranking male pry apart two adolescent males after his charging at them had no effect. (Also, at Gombe, a subordinate female was also seen once to remove a stone from a male's hand when he was about to display at another group member.) In all of these cases, the dispute was ameliorated. In captivity, the same variegated tactical patterns prevail, but the prying-apart and removal-of-object behaviours are common, rather than rare. The argument for intentionality is further supported by the fact that a dominant animal trying to control a fight often will sit down for a time between the protagonists after having separated them, rather than immediately returning to feeding, resting, mating, grooming, or whatever the prior activity may have been. The fact that he has just decisively intimidated them makes this an effective means of forestalling further conflict.

In sum, these behaviours add up to a strategy of deliberate pacification that is present in a variety of chimpanzee environments. But what are the *specific* motives involved? It makes sense that chimpanzees could be protecting kin or coalition partners from injury, but in that case one would expect them to intervene on a partisan basis, directing their effort at one protagonist rather than both, and for them to intervene only when fights involved kin or partners. What is distinctive, with most of the intervention strategies I have described, is that they appear to be *impartial*—rather than partial....

If protection is at issue motivationally, it is afforded to both parties—and I should point out that victims sometimes wound aggressors. With protection being provided randomly to other group members, these impartial interventions in adult disputes would appear to be 'altruistic' in the genetic sense of the word—whatever the immediate motives. Some degree of a chimpanzee version of empathy does seem possible, however, insofar as the control individual himself has experienced the stress of being attacked, or of getting into a bad fight.

Another innately-prepared motivation could be operating. It is possible that these controlling third parties are reacting to the intensely-agonistic behaviours of others as an environmental irritant, and simply wish to remove this perturbation as a selfish act. This explanation alone could account for interventions that are impartial and pacifying. One might also argue that interventions are simply a means of reinforcing one's high status. All of these motivations are possible, and there may be others, as well. But one thing is clear. *Pacifying interventions* surely are motivated differently from those that stem from a desire to assist a relative or well-bonded coalition partner in winning a contest. Indeed, such interventions are quite different tactically, for the bluff or attack is directed at just one individual, not both of them. Partisan interventions tend to escalate, rather than damp, the original conflict.

Because the conflict itself seems to be a major focus, I suggest that chimpanzees are innately aversive to conflict. If one compares the two *Pan* species, evidence for generalized conflict aversiveness is far more evident in the one that actually exhibits more conflict, *Pan troglodytes*. Although bonobos do interfere sometimes in conflicts to pacify them, with chimpanzees this is a regular and prominent pattern, both in the wild and in captivity.

Active power-intervention is not the only tool that these apes have for reducing the effects of conflict. De Waal's work with a variety of primates demonstrates that reconciliation behaviour can be prominent, and functionally important at the level of social life. With *Pan troglodytes* and *Pan paniscus*, reconciliation is often dyadic. But after altercations there are also instances in which third parties assist in the reconciliation process that calms down the protagonists and consoles the victims in particular. Humans, too, 'make up' after many of their within-group fights, and sometimes tribal people who feud intensively devise elaborate rituals that involve asking for and granting forgiveness....

Scholars tend to treat ethics, social control, and conflict management as separate spheres. However, I view them as being closely related. We have seen that one good reason to crack down on socially-defined deviants is that many are predators who potentially or directly threaten other group members as individual victims. This personal sense of being threatened motivates people to unite as a moral community. However, another reason is that deviants create disturbing conflicts that degrade the immediate quality of social life and impair group functions. Thus, even if one is not being singled out as a victim, one's social environment will be disturbed, and a useful web of co-operation that everyone profits from can be seriously disrupted. Both are good reasons to crack down on deviant behaviour preemptively, rather than permitting it to lead to active conflict. However, once a conflict becomes a threat to group welfare, and creates a high degree of social stress, it is significant that moral considerations may be set aside as the resolution of the conflict takes precedence over the dislike of the group for deviants. The conclusion for humans is that aversion to conflict has an innate basis, and that this helps to draw people together as moral communities that are interested in addressing social problems....

PRE-ADAPTATIONS FOR
MORAL BEHAVIOUR

Let us focus, now, on the entire range of
pre-adaptations for moral life. First, there
are the basics of group size and social
composition, and the adaptations to
physical and political environments with
which they evolved. This ancestral ape
lived in multifamily foraging communities that were subject to fusion and fission: this is a pattern clearly shared by
chimpanzees, bonobos, and human
hunter-gatherers. These groups were at
least moderately 'territorial', and they
may have approached a chimpanzee degree of territoriality, with patrolling by
large coalitions of males and lethal attacks
on individual neighbours. I suggest this
because humans also engage in perimeter
defence—but bonobos are not fully
studied in this respect. At present, we
know that the adult male bonobos sometimes behave as hostile large-coalitions
when two groups meet—but so far they
have not been seen to engage in lethal
behaviour.

All three species do unite against neighbouring groups, then, and it seems likely
that all three unite to mob predators that
threaten them and possibly to hunt larger
game. There also are solid data that docu-
ment small male or female coalitions in all
three species, so in ancestral communities
small coalitions of males or females surely
worked together in vying for political status within the group. In doing so, they
mitigated (but came far from neutralizing)
the social dominance hierarchy that saw
high-ranking individuals (male or female)
decisively dominating those of lower rank.
If we put together all the large and small
coalition behaviours of all three species, it
seems likely that the Mutual Ancestor at
least had the potential to form large coalitions *within* its communities, and to direct political force at individuals who
aroused the ire of the rest of the group.

What about morality as I have discussed it?....

Recently, de Waal has considered the
possibilities of proto-moral behaviour in
both apes and monkeys, and has made a
persuasive case for moral-like behaviours
in certain restricted areas. Some of his insights relate to sympathy that extends beyond the confines of parental nurturance
or kinship, a response well documented in
the wild by Goodall in her discussion of
chimpanzee altruism. But other insights
relate more directly to the raw materials of
morality—taken as social control of commonly disapproved antisocial behaviour
by a concerned local community.

Captive chimpanzee colonies are particularly interesting in this respect. Spatial
constriction and easy availability of food
provide advantages of power to the adult
females: they now have time to devote to
'politics' because their lives are no longer
devoted to largely solitary foraging, and in
captivity these females form much larger
coalitions than the males. In the sizeable
groups at Arnhem Zoo in Holland and at
Yerkes Regional Primate Research Centre
in Atlanta, captive female allies have been
able to control certain behaviours of males
who are individually dominant over them,
and do so in ways that are striking. They
usually manage to play 'kingmaker', and
they always seem to control which male
will be involved with peacemaking; that is,
if they fail to get their choice of alpha
male they may at least divest him of his
control role (that of peacemaker) and permit his rival to perform those valuable
services for them. The females do this on a
manipulative basis that appears to be intentional, and the process is similar to social control in that a large, well-unified,
rank-and-file political coalition is successfully manipulating key behaviours of in-

dividuals that are threatening to other individuals.

Such behaviour is routine in large captive groups, and it can lead to rare behaviours that become startlingly similar to human social control. At Yerkes, it is recorded that the alpha male was chasing a sexual rival with the intention to do him damage, and the females reacted by collectively issuing hostile waa-barks, directed at the alpha. As the intensity and unanimity of the calls built, this signalled an impending attack by all of them—and the alpha male desisted. It was the size and cohesiveness of the female coalition that made the difference in controlling his behaviour, for in the wild the strongly defiant individual waa-barks of a few disapproving females will be ignored by high-ranking males that are engaged in making attacks.

Large-coalition political behaviour is not unknown in the wild. At Gombe, males regularly form large coalitions to go on patrol or cope with predators, but when they compete for power within the group normally they operate dyadically, as pairs of close allies. However, after over thirty years of field observation the following male behaviour was observed at Gombe. The alpha male had been defeated in a fight with a rival, and then he tried to make a comeback. Uncharacteristically, the males of the group threatened him *collectively*, and forced him to leave the group. He remained socially peripheralized until he was willing to return in a submissive role. Similar episodes, involving smaller coalitions that nonetheless surpass the dyadic level, have been recorded at Mahale....

In these rare wild episodes and well-routinized captive ones, it would appear that among members of large coalitions there is some kind of consensus that develops—as to what kind of behaviour they are taking issue with, what their po-litical objectives are, and whether they are in a position to exert control. I do not believe I am engaging in a fantasy about 'intentions at work'. Chimpanzees have the waa vocalization that is closely associated with hostile defiance, and when they hear the waa-barks of others they can decide individually whether to join in. The overall pattern would appear to involve something like 'public opinion', and in its dynamics this political process can be likened to social control because the same macro-coalition that arrives at a consensus may decide to intervene physically....

With chimpanzees, the collective reactions by large male or female coalitions are, respectively, of great interest in terms of protomorality. But with humans an important difference is that both males *and* females unite into one very large, community-wide political coalition, which manipulates or eliminates deviants. It does so on the basis of explicitly shared opinions about what is deviant, this in the context of long-term social objectives that are formally articulated. Another difference is that humans are constantly engaged in a vigilant search for deviance: this is accomplished quite systematically, by gossiping, and even predatory behaviour that takes place one-on-one becomes known to the entire group. Another difference stems from the egalitarian nature of human bands. Ethologically speaking, with an egalitarian as opposed to a despotic social order, it is far easier for the human group to unite against its higher-ranking deviants because they already have been placed in a relatively weak political position. Chimpanzees, being despotic, put down their leaders only partially, or episodically, and they always have strong leaders. Humans, as egalitarians, are in a position to do so continuously, routinely, and decisively.

The formation of major coalitions that deliberately suppress unwanted individual behaviours is basic to human morality. Chimpanzees have the potential to form male or female coalitions on a large scale, and bonobo female coalitions at least rise above the dyadic level as females unite to hold their own politically against the more physically powerful males. This means that such a potential was likely to be present in the Mutual Ancestor of *Pan* and *Homo,* and that therefore a major political pre-adaptation was already in place when human communities moved toward practising social control as we know it today.

THE FULL BLOWN MORAL COMMUNITY

My best hypothesis is as follows. A signal and fundamental accomplishment of early moral communities was to define domination behaviours as morally deviant, and then to back this up with sanctioning by the entire group. Because dominance tendencies operating at the community level are strongly innate, they are difficult to control. A vigilant egalitarian response became universal in the Late Palaeolithic, and the result was an egalitarian political order, one in which the band's main political actors—possibly just the adult males—enjoyed an essential political parity. Parity applied when it came to personal autonomy in the band, and also in the making of group decisions. There were, of course, definite differences of prestige, rank, and status; but tendencies of individuals to carry such differences too far were held in check, and the definition of 'too far' was quite restrictive....

I have chosen the Late Palaeolithic as the epoch during which this type of egalitarian moral community was likely to have reached its full development. In theory, such development was possible before the advent of Anatomically Moderns. We have seen that important pre-adaptations were in place five million years ago: the capacity to form coalitions larger than dyadic ones; the individual preference to dominate with a concomitant dislike of being subordinated that leads to egalitarianism, and the tendency to actively control conflicts within the group. But there was another pre-adaptation that probably was critical to the appearance of the fully modern moral community. This was the development of rapid-fire, phonemically-based communication that was referential and involved displacement—displacement involves the planning of future activities, or the description of events that took place elsewhere. Abstract communication, mostly verbal, permitted the articulation and refinement of group values having to do with morality, and it also facilitated the kind of highly specific gossiping (with displacement) that is universal in human groups. Gossiping serves as a means of building social networks; but, perhaps more importantly, it also enables group members to arrive privately and safely at a negative consensus about dangerous deviants. Language also makes it possible for groups to conspire, and ambush even the most fearsome dominator to execute him. Language probably was important to the establishment of egalitarian political orders. It definitely was critical to the invention of moral communities as we know them.

Both language ability and the capacity to devise and enforce moral codes are good candidates for gradual evolution at the genetic level, with genetic evolution interacting with cultural patterns. The advent of full linguistic communication (as we know it) is thought to have arrived, at latest, with Anatomically Modern Humans something over 100,000 years ago, and it would be difficult to argue that such an acumen arrived more recently.

However, let us consider what was happening with communication five million years ago. It is clear that today chimpanzees and bonobos have many and subtle ways of communication even though apparently they have no meaningless building-blocks like phonemes, and even though their communication system does not facilitate displacement.

Thus, the Mutual Ancestor was likely to have had a rather strong communication capacity—but language as we know it was absent. So was the capacity to develop anything like a modern moral community, which not only names and discusses different types of deviance but is capable of discussing the immediate and longer-term social future of the group. One selection pressure that might have acted on language evolution in its later phases could have been human tendencies to form moral communities that were egalitarian. I have in mind the attempts of subordinates to control more aggressive group members. This can be a risky enterprise, but it is one by which the allied subordinates individually gain reproductive success at the expense of their political superiors. Effective communication is important to their work as a large political coalition, for this enables them to track individual behaviours that may be deviant, including predatory acts that are perpetrated away from the group. If necessary, it also enables them to chart a precise course of action before the deviant is confronted by the group—as with assassination of a dominator too powerful to control otherwise.

A final detailed summary is in order. As they began to form moral communities, the pre-adaptive ingredients available to prehistoric humans included the capacity to form very large coalitions within the group, an increasingly potent communication capacity, and, of course, a developed capacity to transmit cultural traditions over generations—something we share with *Pan*. In the Late Palaeolithic, a full-blown moral community took the following form. It was nomadic and smallish, it was composed of related and unrelated families, and it was politically egalitarian: while males may have dominated their female partners within the family, group life was equalized with respect to relations among the heads of households and with respect to making decisions as a group. People had a high degree of what I have called 'actuarial intelligence', which helped them to set up cooperative systems of sharing and to calculate the damage that uncontrolled conflict might do to the group. While active conflicts were 'managed' as much as possible, as with *Pan*, the group also was able to *anticipate* conflict on a long-range basis and to manipulate the behaviours that were likely to produce it. These were basics of moral life. In addition, these people surely were capable of moral philosophizing—just as more gifted non-literate egalitarian individuals are today. This enabled people to fine-tune their moral systems.

CONCLUSIONS

… Morality surely did not emerge on an all-at-once basis. As de Waal has shown, protomoral behaviours are identifiable in extant non-human primates. The stronger the case for protomorality, the better the support or the idea that the moral community arrived in stages, and not as a saltation that definitively set aside humans from all other species. With *Pan troglodytes* the best instances of protomoral behaviour are found with captive female chimpanzees. At two different sites, they live in large groups and form permanent large coalitions that routinely target and decisively manipulate *certain* bullying behaviours of males…. It is female chimpanzees, at Arnhem Zoo and Yerkes, who have advanced the furthest in collectively exploiting their political potential to *routinely* suppress and manipulate behaviours they do not approve of....

My conclusion is that morality is essentially a political phenomenon as well as a social one, and that this political aspect lends itself rather nicely to evolutionary analysis. There is more to morality than politics, of course, and there is far more to deviance and social control than an innate aversiveness to conflict within the group. But in concentrating on these political basics I have been able to single out features of extant moral behaviour that not only are universal among humans living in bands, but can be linked to the behavioural repertoires of the two *Pan* species. The more widespread a human behaviour is, the greater the probability that it is receiving help from human nature. The general conflict-management features I have worked with are universal not only among mobile hunter-gatherers, but among all humans wherever they live autonomously in local groups. They also are highly probable in the ancestral ape I have modelled by triangulation, which makes innate propensities to conflict resolution quite likely for humans.

We may never create a perfect approximation of how morality evolved, as an adaptively useful form of cultural problem-solving by which entire groups routinely shape their socio-political life on the basis of clearly designated goals. We may never know which behaviours were first defined, moralistically, as sins that the entire group must react to. But if we look to our ancestral precursor, five million years ago, in all probability there existed some limited 'social control' of certain individual group members by the rest of the group. This involved subordinate rebelliousness which led to manipulation of powerful individuals at the top of the hierarchy, but basically the groups remained ethologically despotic—with a prominent role for alpha individuals.

The hypothesis is that the first behaviour to be decisively outlawed and controlled by a human group may well have been the expression of dominance—dominance of the type that occurs all the time in chimpanzee and bonobo groups in the wild, and which occurs rather predictably in our own post-Neolithic societies whenever scale increases dramatically. I favour this theory for several reasons. For one thing, dominance and submission seem to be firmly established in our nature. For another, we, like other primates, prefer usually to dominate rather than to be dominated. Thus, we tend to become rebellious in a subordinate role. It is institutionalized subordinate rebellion that leads to an egalitarian polity, in which individuals agree implicitly to eschew domination so that they may remain autonomous and uncontrolled. And it is the same united rank and file who crack down on deviance in a wide variety of other forms....

We remain an ethologically despotic species, one in which competitive dispositions to dominance remain strong in spite of scores of millennia under egalitarianism, and our economic, social, sexual, and political rivalries make for a group life that is prone to conflict. Morality is the human invention that addresses such problems, and it is based very heavily upon ancestral dispositions. These were the raw materials, out of which moral communities were forged....

Morality Developed to Protect Systems of Cooperative Exchange

Dennis Krebs

The anthropologist Christopher Boehm theorizes that morality originated when coalitions of subordinate primates suppressed the innate despotic behaviour of dominant members of ancestral groups, which fostered social harmony and gave rise to egalitarian moral norms. Boehm focuses on the prohibitive side of morality, particularly the suppression of bullying and excessive selfishness, and the conflicts such behaviours cause within groups. The main question I address in this commentary is, how close can we get to dispositions to uphold the egalitarian moral norms that characterize contemporary societies by way of the mechanisms of biological evolution? To answer this question, I need to say a few words about the mechanisms of biological evolution and my conception of morality.

I have been persuaded by Dawkins, Trivers, Williams and other evolutionary biologists that the most appropriate units of natural selection are genes, which are propagated by individuals. Although group selection is a theoretical possibility, the conditions necessary for selection at the group level to outpace selection at the individual or genetic level are rarely met. With respect to criteria for moral behaviour, I invoke prescriptiveness and universalizability. Universalizability implies behaving in ways that uphold the rights and duties of everyone involved in a moral decision in an unbiased way. In this sense, morality tends to be egalitarian with respect to opportunity.

The, or at least a, central problem of morality arises because dispositions that

have evolved through natural selection are dispositions that helped our ancestors maximize their genetic gains, but, on most people's definition, behaving morally entails a willingness to foster the interests of others and to forgo opportunities to foster one's interests. Natural selection and sociality seem incompatible. How can individuals bent on maximizing their gains coexist? In Boehm's terms, shouldn't everyone be evolved to be as dominant and despotic as possible? It isn't possible for everyone to obtain more than his or her share, so isn't conflict inevitable? Faced with suppression by and exploitation from dominant members of groups, it makes evolutionary sense to form a coalition with other subordinates, which, as Boehm documents, is exactly what some primates do. But note that the upshot of such coalition formation entails, in the first instance, substituting a dominant gang for a dominant individual. Yes, the coalition curtails the selfishness of dominant individuals, and in this sense the coalition's behaviour may qualify as moral, but if the coalition then keeps the resources it obtains for itself, it undoes the moralizing effect of its behaviour. And what is to stop the more powerful individuals in the coalition from taking the lion's share of the resources?

How can we get from dominant coalitions to egalitarian groups? Boehm suggests primates may inherit an aversion to conflict and, by implication, an attraction to social harmony, and that this innate disposition may motivate them to take measures to curtail conflicts among members of their groups. This idea is helpful in the sense that it suggests a kind of payoff to those performing a policing function that does not entail, directly at least, a disproportionate share of resources. But innate dispositions evolve because they foster the inclusive fitness of the ancestors of those who inherit them. What genetic benefits might an aversion to conflict and the disposition to curtail it have reaped? Citing evidence that some conflict-reducing interventions in primates are impartial and not directly rewarded—that is to say they are directed at breaking up fights rather than helping allies or obtaining resources—Boehm suggests these interventions may stem from empathy, be motivated to reduce an 'environmental irritant', or constitute a means of 'reinforcing status'. To flesh out these suggestions, Boehm would have to explore the adaptive value of each of these dispositions and motives in ancestral environments. If the capacity for empathy has evolved why don't we see more evidence of empathic behaviours in primates? What genetic benefits accrued to ancestors who found conflicts irritating? Why would dominant individuals or coalitions reinforce their status by breaking up fights instead of in more self-interested ways? Even if there were good answers to these questions, we would still have a long way to go to get to community control of within-group conflict for the common interest.

Boehm asks the question, 'are we innately given to ethological egalitarianism, to ethological despotism, or to neither'? His answer is that we are innately despotic, 'and can remain egalitarian only if [we] consciously suppress innate tendencies that otherwise would make for a pronounced social dominance hierarchy'. 'If we wish to keep social hierarchy at a low level, we must act as intentional groups that vigilantly curtail alpha-type

behaviours. This curtailment is accomplished through the cultural agency of social sanctioning...'. Fair enough, but where do dispositions to consciously suppress innate tendencies come from? How did we acquire dispositions to form intentional groups? How did cultural sanctions originate? Have these processes somehow become uncoupled from biological evolution, as Dawkins has suggested? Perhaps, but whatever autonomy mental structures may have obtained, they all evolved biologically.

I feel unwilling to give up on biological routes to human morality. I'm not sure they can take us the distance, but I believe they can get us a little closer than Boehm implies. Turning to Boehm's question, my answer is that we are innately given to both egalitarianism and despotism. All of us inherit despotic and egalitarian dispositions, as well as the higher order strategy of activating the disposition that paid off best genetically for our ancestors in various environmental conditions. I believe this duality is reflected in the structure of our social relations, with individuals dominating when they are able to, submitting when they must, and curtailing dominance in others when it is in their interest. The onus, then, is on me to explain how dispositions to uphold egalitarianism could evolve biologically, which, in my way of thinking, entails explaining how such dispositions could have enhanced the inclusive fitness of our ancestors.

I begin with the adaptive benefits of coalition-formation. By the same token as a coalition of two is usually more powerful than the most dominant individual in a group, a coalition of three is usually more powerful than a coalition of two, and so on. So, I hypothesize, there was an adaptive advantage among our ancestors of forming increasingly large coalitions. Individuals form coalitions when they share interests and need one another to advance their interests, the reason why individuals band together in groups is because they benefit from group living. Mutual defence against predators and large game hunting are important examples. Inasmuch as all members of a group benefit from the presence of the other members of the group, it is in their interest to preserve the group. So too with coalitions. The underlying principle is this: inasmuch as the probability of me propagating my genes is increased when I form a cooperative relationship with you, dispositions to form such relationships should evolve. Chimpanzees form relatively small groups when they go out on patrol and engage in mutual defence. Humans form much larger groups. Biologists such as Alexander have suggested that dispositions to form large cooperative groups were selected in the human species because large cooperative groups were necessary to combat other large cooperative groups of hominids, giving rise to a kind of arms race.

Given a group whose existence is threatened by hostile environmental forces such as other groups, it is in the genetic interest of every member of the group to cooperate enough to preserve the group on which he or she is dependent. This is not group selection in its usual form because it does not necessarily involve dispositions to sacrifice one's own interests for the sake of one's group. It involves mutuality and indirect reciprocity, with members working together and helping one another in order to advance their individual genetic interests. On this line of thought, the optimal size of a group would be defined as the smallest number necessary to optimize benefits. Environmental factors such as threats from outgroups create the conditions necessary for the formation of cooperative in-groups. It makes sense in these terms for members of

groups to invest energy in fostering the welfare of their fellows and cultivating enough harmony for the group to perform its function optimally, so each of them can reap the benefits.

I believe the benefits of cooperation contain the key that will unlock the door to an explanation of the evolution of morality. As demonstrated in game theory research, in certain conditions every single member of a group can obtain more for himself or herself by cooperating than by behaving selfishly. Particularly important is the mechanism of indirect reciprocity—helping one member of a group in return for help from another member of the group—, which Alexander believes has mediated the evolution of human morality. As demonstrated recently by game theorists, indirect reciprocity is a winning strategy in groups able to identify and discriminate against cheaters. Cooperation captures the essence of most people's conceptions of morality. If everyone cooperated, there would be no conflict within groups and everyone would come out ahead—the egalitarian moral ideal.

But there are at least four catches to this good-news principle. First, conditions must be conducive to cooperation, which means that individuals must be able to obtain more for themselves by cooperating than by not cooperating. Dominance hierarchies are not conducive to egalitarian cooperation because it is not in the interest of dominant individuals to give subordinates an equal share when they, the more dominant, are able to obtain more for themselves. I agree with Boehm that constraining the selfishness of dominant members of groups is an important aspect of morality.

Second, cooperative systems must contain antidotes to cheating, which may come in the despotic forms described by Boehm and other forms aimed at maximizing one's gains at the expense of others and exploiting systems of cooperation. One of the greatest evolutionary ironies is that although unabated cheating eventually produces a social system in which everyone gets less than he or she would by cooperating (because there are no cooperators left to exploit), cheating will evolve if it pays off better than cooperation on an individual basis. For moral systems based in indirect reciprocity to evolve, individuals must acquire the ability to identify cheaters and the wherewithal to discriminate against them. This, I believe, is why individuals value their reputations, experience moral indignation, possess a sense of justice, and are disposed to gossip about those they believe are not doing their share.

Third, people should be evolved to form cooperative coalitions with the smallest number of others necessary to maximize their individual benefits, and to compete against other coalitions when it is to their benefit, thereby confining their morality to relations with members of their in-groups. Finally, people should be evolved to show nepotistic biases favouring kin because, in assisting relatives, peo-

ple are, in effect, assisting replicas of their genes carried by their relatives.

I believe that the logic of evolution outlines a picture that captures well the human condition. We are evolved to behave morally, that is to say to cooperate, when it is in our genetic interests, but we also are evolved to behave immorally when it is not. We are evolved to cooperate with in-group members when we need them to advance our interests—or more exactly in circumstances in which they advanced the interests of our ancestors—and also to fudge, when we are able to, in favour of ourselves and our relatives. We are motivated to preach and impose morality—to exhort and force others to do their duties—and to punish transgressions, but we also are tempted to cheat when we believe we can get away with it. We are evolved to uphold egalitarianism because it is in our interest to curtail the dominance of others. However, we also are evolved to behave dominantly when it pays off for us and for our kin. Our social systems rest on a tenuous and dynamic equilibrium in which everyone holds everyone else in check. We are moral, but only as moral as we need to be.

THE CONTINUING DEBATE:
How Did Moral Behavior Develop?

What Is New

Humans traditionally have been thought to enjoy a monopoly on morality, but that tradition is under challenge. Primate ethologist Frans De Waal writes of a chimpanzee matriarch as a positive moral agent, who grieves the moral wrongness of another chimpanzee's act of murder against a community member; and Roger Fouts describes a selflessly courageous chimpanzee as a moral hero. Perhaps we can "explain away" such examples of nonhuman moral behavior so that they do not count as *real* moral acts; but if we observed a human performing the same act that was observed in the chimpanzees, we would not hesitate to classify the act as moral or immoral. As Frans de Waal states in *Good Natured*:

> A chimpanzee stroking and patting a victim of attack or sharing her food with a hungry companion shows attitudes that are hard to distinguish from those of a person picking up a crying child, or doing volunteer work in a soup kitchen. To classify the chimpanzee's behavior as based on instinct and the person's behavior as proof of moral decency is misleading, and probably incorrect. First of all, it is uneconomic in that it assumes different processes for similar behavior in two closely related species.

Where to Find More

Darwin's own ideas concerning the development of ethics can be found in *The Origin of Species* and particularly *The Descent of Man*, both available in many editions.

Mary Midgley provides a history and critique of social Darwinism in *Evolution as Religion: Strange Hopes and Stranger Fears* (London: Methuen, 1985), as well as an interesting brief examination of the origin of ethics in "The Origin of Ethics," in Peter Singer, ed., *A Companion to Ethics* (Oxford: Blackwell Publishers, 1991); the Singer volume also includes an excellent article by Michael Ruse, "The Significance of Evolution".

E. O. Wilson's account of sociobiology can be found in *Sociobiology: The New Synthesis* (Cambridge, MA: Harvard University Press, 1975); and *On Human Nature* (Cambridge, MA: Harvard University Press, 1978). More recent work by Wilson includes *Consilience* (NY: Alfred A. Knopf, 1998) and the beautifully written *Biophilia* (Cambridge, MA: Harvard University Press, 1984). Among the many anthologies exploring and debating sociobiology, a good example is Arthur L. Caplan, ed., *The Sociobiology Debate* (NY: Harper & Row, 1978).

Richard Dawkins writes interesting, thoughtful and controversial essays on the broad implications of Darwinism; see his *A Devil's Chaplain: Reflections on Hope, Lies, Science and Love* (Boston: Houghton Mifflin, 2003).

A number of books explore the implications of Darwinian evolution for ethics, including Peter Singer, *The Expanding Circle* (NY: Farrar, Straus & Giroux, 1981); Jeffrie G. Murphy, *Evolution, Morality, and the Meaning of Life* (Totowa, NJ: Rowman and Littlefield, 1982); Michael Ruse, *Taking Darwin Seriously* (Oxford: Basil Blackwell, 1986); James Rachels, *Created From Animals: The Moral Implications of*

Darwinism (Oxford: Oxford University Press, 1990); Eliot Sober and David S. Wilson, *Unto Others: The Evolution and Psychology of Unselfish Behavior* (Cambridge, MA: Harvard University Press, 1998); and Bruce N. Waller, *The Natural Selection of Autonomy* (Albany: State University of New York Press, 1998). Good anthologies on the subject include *Evolutionary Ethics*, Matthew H. Nitecki and Doris V. Nitecki, eds. (Albany: State University of New York Press, 1993); *Issues in Evolutionary Ethics*, edited by Paul Thompson (Albany: State University of New York Press, 1995); and *Evolutionary Origins of Morality*, edited by Leonard D. Katz (Thorverton, Exeter: Imprint Academic, 2000).

Frans de Waal has written a number of fascinating books that explore in detail the behavior of other primate species, including the possibility of moral acts by non-human primates; see especially his *Chimpanzee Politics* (London: Jonathan Cape, 1982); *Peacemaking Among Primates* (Cambridge, MA: Harvard University Press, 1989); and *Good Natured: The Origins of Right and Wrong in Humans and Other Animals* (Cambridge, MA: Harvard University Press, 1996). Roger Fouts, *Next of Kin: What Chimpanzees Have Taught Me About Who We Are* (NY: William Morrow, 1997) describes research on language capacities in chimpanzees as well as the widespread mistreatment of chimpanzees in some contemporary research facilities.

See Debate 10, including the suggested further readings, for more on the question of whether any empirical study is fundamentally important for the study of ethics.

PRAGMATISM AND THE DISPUTE OVER VALUE OBJECTIVITY

THERE ARE NO TRUTHS ABOUT VALUES

ADVOCATE: Richard Rorty, currently Professor of Comparative Literature at Stanford University; formerly Stuart Professor of Philosophy at Princeton and Professor of Humanities at the University of Virginia.

SOURCE: "Relativism: Finding and Making," from *Debating the State of Philosophy: Habermas, Rorty and Kolokowski,* Jozef Niznik and John T. Sanders, eds. (Westport, CT: Praeger, 1996).

THERE ARE TRUTHS ABOUT VALUES

ADVOCATE: Hilary Putnam, Cogan University Professor Emeritus in Philosophy, Harvard University; among his many important books are *The Many Faces of Realism* (LaSalle, IL: Open Court, 1987); *Realism with a Human Face* (Cambridge, MA: Harvard University Press, 1990); and *Renewing Philosophy* (Cambridge, MA: Harvard University Press, 1992).

SOURCE: "Are Values Made or Discovered?" in *The Collapse of the Fact-Value Dichotomy and Other Essays* (Cambridge, MA: Harvard University Press, 2002): 96–110.

Pragmatism emphasizes experimental processes and evolving ideas, and rejects final fixed truth. Pragmatists do seek truth, but that does not imply that they find truth located out there in the world, ready-made (the way a treasure hunter might discover a buried chest filled with gold coins, just waiting to be hauled up). For pragmatists, a true belief or theory (whether of physics or ethics) is not a belief that mirrors or matches or copies the "true structure of the world-as-it-is, independently of us"; rather, "true" ideas are those that provide useful guides, ideas that lead us well, ideas that prove their worth in prompting better ways of thinking and living and exploring. Pragmatists maintain that truth is not a fixed external standard, but they do not argue that truth is whatever we wish it to be. Cherished ideas and beliefs can turn out to lead us badly, may prove unhelpful or even harmful: What we hoped and believed would be a useful and productive idea or theory may prove a failure. The pragmatist insists that ideas and theories must be constantly tested for their usefulness. Just as a species may prove very successful in a particular setting at a specific time, so also our theories and ideas may be very effective at one stage and prove unfit in later contexts. For pragmatists, true ideas are useful guides for human animals, not final destinations for demi-gods on a quest for absolute truth.

Many people are disturbed by the pragmatist interpretation of truth and of scientific inquiry; it is especially disturbing to those whose image of science is of "reading the mind of God" and discovering fixed and final truths that will never be refuted or replaced. But when pragmatism is applied to ethics, the reactions are often even more negative. The rejection of fixed and eternal moral standards, in favor of experimental and impermanent ethical guides judged in terms of human usefulness, seems to many to be a rejection of ethics itself.

While pragmatists generally reject belief in final immutable ethical truths, some pragmatists push that rejection further than others. That is the source of a longstanding conflict between two leading contemporary pragmatists, Hilary Putnam and Richard Rorty. Rorty considers "objective reality" an empty notion: It makes no sense to speak of a reality that is objectively true and that stands independent of us, because we could never get outside ourselves and our values and experiences to examine what is "objectively there" independent of us. Putnam argues that Rorty sets up a false dilemma between perfect knowledge of things as they are in themselves and no real objective knowledge whatsoever. Putnam sees another alternative: we do have objective knowledge of the world outside ourselves, but such objective knowledge is not knowledge of things in themselves; rather, it is the well-confirmed scientific and common sense knowledge we have of our world. It may not be absolute and immutable knowledge, but that exalted standard can be rejected without rejecting all objective knowledge. Indeed, Putnam goes so far as to suggest that Rorty's skepticism about "objective reality" is just "the flip side of the craving for an unintelligible kind of certainty". Putnam also criticizes other pragmatists who reject objective morality, claiming that they are still in the grip of a fact/value distinction that is inconsistent with the pragmatist perspective. In short, Putnam argues that his critics—who accuse him of belief in an objective reality of true facts, including value facts, that is inconsistent with pragmatism—are themselves beguiled by absolutist assumptions.

POINTS TO PONDER

➤ What would you *count* as objectively validating an ethical system or a principle of ethics? How does that compare with the pragmatist account of validation of ethics?

➤ Richard Rorty's critics call him a relativist; Rorty disputes that description of his view, calling himself instead a pragmatist or antifoundationalist. *Is* Rorty a relativist?

➤ Putnam and Rorty agree in rejecting traditional metaphysical notions of "things-in-themselves"; both find them empty, meaningless. But Rorty draws the further conclusion that we are better off without any notion of "objective truth," while Putnam rejects that claim. How do they draw such different conclusions from a similar starting point?

➤ Hilary Putnam and Richard Rorty are both pragmatists, and both reject notions of absolute truth, and each believes that his own version of pragmatism is more consistent with that rejection. Given the pragmatic methodology that Rorty and Putnam *share*, is there any way they could settle this debate?

There Are No Truths About Values

RICHARD RORTY

... Philosophers are called 'relativists' when they do not accept the Greek distinction between the way things are in themselves and the relations which they have to other things, and in particular to human needs and interests.

Philosophers who, like myself, eschew this distinction must abandon the traditional philosophical project of finding something stable which will serve as a criterion for judging the transitory products of our transitory needs and interests. This means, for example, that we cannot employ the Kantian distinction between morality and prudence. We have to give up on the idea that there are unconditional, transcultural moral obligations, obligations rooted in an unchanging, ahistorical human nature....

The philosopher whom I most admire, and of whom I should most like to think of myself as a disciple, is John Dewey. Dewey was one of the founders of American pragmatism. He was a thinker who spent 60 years trying to get us out from under the thrall of Plato and Kant. Dewey was often denounced as a relativist, and so am I. But of course we pragmatists never call *ourselves* relativists. Usually, we define ourselves in negative terms. We call ourselves 'anti-Platonists' or 'antimetaphysicians' or 'antifoundationalists'. Equally, our opponents almost never call themselves 'Platonists' or 'metaphysicians' or 'foundationalists'. They usually call themselves defenders of common sense, or of reason.

Predictably, each side in this quarrel tries to define the terms of the quarrel in a way favourable to itself. Nobody wants to be called a Platonist, just as nobody wants to be called a relativist or an irrationalist. We so-called 'relativists' refuse, predictably, to admit that we are enemies of reason and common sense. We say that we are only criticizing some antiquated, specifically philosophical, dogmas. But, of course, what we call dogmas are exactly what our opponents call common sense. Adherence to these dogmas is what they call being rational. So discussion between us and our opponents tends to get bogged down in, for example, the question of whether the slogan 'truth is correspondence to the intrinsic nature of reality' expresses common sense, or is just a bit of outdated Platonist jargon.

In other words, one of the things we disagree about is whether this slogan embodies an obvious truth which philosophy must respect and protect, or instead simply puts forward one philosophical view among others. Our opponents say that the correspondence theory of truth is so obvious, so self-evident, that it is merely perverse to question it. We say that this theory is barely intelligible, and of no particular importance—that it is not so much a theory as a slogan which we have been mindlessly chanting for centuries. We pragmatists think that we might stop chanting it without any harmful consequences.

One way to describe this impasse is to say that we so-called 'relativists' claim that many of the things which common sense thinks are found or discovered are really made or invented. Scientific and moral truths, for example, are described by our opponents as 'objective', meaning that they are in some sense out there waiting to be recognized by us human beings.... They think of us as saying that what was previously thought to be objective has turned out to be merely subjective....

Our opponents like to suggest that to abandon that vocabulary is to abandon rationality—that to be rational consists precisely in respecting the distinctions between the absolute and the relative, the found and the made, object and subject, nature and convention, reality and appearance. We pragmatists reply that if that were what rationality was, then no doubt we are, indeed, irrationalists. But of course we go on to add that being an irrationalist in *that* sense is not to be incapable of argument. We irrationalists do not foam at the mouth and behave like animals. We simply refuse to talk in a certain way, the Platonic way. The views we hope to persuade people to accept cannot be stated in Platonic terminology. So our efforts at persuasion must take the form of gradual inculcation of new ways of speaking, rather than of straightforward argument within old ways of speaking.

To sum up what I have said so far: We pragmatists shrug off charges that we are 'relativists' or 'irrationalists' by saying that these charges presuppose precisely the distinctions we reject. If we have to describe ourselves, perhaps it would be best for us to call ourselves anti-dualists. This does not, of course, mean that we are against what Derrida calls 'binary oppositions': dividing the world up into the good Xs and the bad non-Xs will always be an indispensable tool of inquiry. But we are against a certain *specific* set of distinctions, the Platonic distinctions. We have to admit that these distinctions have become part of Western common sense, but we do not regard this as a sufficient argument for retaining them....

So far I have been sketching the pragmatists' attitude towards their opponents, and the difficulties they encounter in avoiding the use of terms whose use would beg the question at issue between them and their opponents. Now I should like to describe in somewhat more detail how human inquiry looks from a pragmatist point of view—how it looks once one stops describing it as an attempt to correspond to the intrinsic nature of reality, and starts describing it as an attempt to serve transitory purposes and solve transitory problems.

Pragmatists hope to break with the picture which, in Wittgenstein's words, 'holds us captive'—the Cartesian-Lockean picture of a mind seeking to get in touch with a reality outside itself. So they start with a Darwinian account of human beings as animals doing their best to cope with the environment—doing their best to develop tools which will enable them to enjoy more pleasure and less pain. Words are among the tools which these clever animals have developed.

There is no way in which tools can take one out of touch with reality. No matter whether the tool is a hammer or a gun or a belief or a statement, tool-using is part of the interaction of the organism with its environment. To see the employment of words as the use of tools to deal with the environment, rather than as an attempt to represent the intrinsic nature of that environment, is to repudiate the question of whether human minds are in touch with reality—the question asked by the epistemological sceptic. No organism, human or non-human, is ever more or less in touch with reality than any other organism. The very idea of 'being out of touch with reality' presupposes the un-Darwinian, Cartesian picture of a mind which somehow swings free of the causal forces exerted on the body. The Cartesian mind is an entity whose relations with the rest of the universe are representational rather than causal. So to rid our thinking of the vestiges of Cartesianism, to become fully Darwinian in our thinking, we need to stop thinking of words as representations and to start thinking of them as nodes in the causal network which binds the organism together with its environment.

Seeing language and inquiry in this biologistic way... permits us to discard the picture of the human mind as an interior space within which the human person is located. As the American philosopher of mind Daniel Dennett has argued, it is only this picture of a Cartesian Theatre which makes one think that there is a big philosophical or scientific problem about the nature of the origin of consciousness. We should substitute a picture of an adult human organism as one whose behaviour is so complex that it can be predicted only by attributing intentional states—beliefs and desires—to the organism. On this account, beliefs and desires are not prelinguistic modes of consciousness, which may or may not be expressible in language. Nor are they names of immaterial events. Rather, they are what in philosophical jargon are called 'sentential attitudes'—that is to say, dispositions on the part of organisms, or of computers, to assert or deny certain sentences. To attribute beliefs and desires to non-users of language (such as dogs, infants and thermostats) is, for us pragmatists, to speak metaphorically.

Pragmatists complement this biologistic approach with Charles Sanders Peirce's definition of a belief as a habit of action. On this definition, to ascribe a belief to someone is simply to say that he or she will tend to behave as I behave when I am willing affirm the truth of a certain sentence. We ascribe beliefs to things which use, or can be imagined to use, sentences, but not to rocks and plants. This is not because the former have a special organ or capacity—consciousness—which the latter lack, but simply because the habits of action of rocks and plants are sufficiently familiar and simple that their behaviour can be predicted without ascribing sentential attitudes to them.

On this view, when we utter such sentences as 'I am hungry' we are not making external what was previously internal, but are simply helping those around to us to predict our future actions. Such sentences are not used to report events going on within the Cartesian Theatre which is a person's consciousness. They are simply tools for coordinating our behaviour with those of others. This is not to say that one can 'reduce' mental states such as beliefs and desires to physiological or behavioural states. It is merely to say that there is no point in asking whether a belief represents reality, either mental reality or physical reality, accurately. That is, for pragmatists, not only a bad question, but the root of much wasted philosophical energy.

The right question to ask is, 'For what purposes would it be useful to hold that belief?' This is like the question, 'For what purposes would it be useful to load this program into my computer?' On the Putnamesque view I am suggesting, a person's body is analogous to the computer's hardware, and his or her beliefs and desires are analogous to the software. Nobody knows or cares whether a given piece of computer software represents reality accurately. What we care about is whether it is the software which will most efficiently accomplish a certain task. Analogously, pragmatists think that the question to ask about our beliefs is not whether they are about reality or merely about appearance, but simply whether they are the best habits of action for gratifying our desires.

On this view, to say that a belief is, as far as we know, true, is to say that no alternative belief is, as far as we know, a better habit of acting. When we say that our ancestors believed, falsely, that the sun went around the earth, and that we believe, truly, that the earth goes round the sun, we are saying that we have a better tool than our ancestors did. Our ancestors might rejoin that their tool enabled them to believe in the literal truth of the Christian Scriptures, whereas ours does not. Our reply has to be, I think, that the benefits of modern astronomy and of space travel outweigh the advantages of Christian fundamentalism. The argument between us and our medieval ancestors should not be about which of us has got the universe right. It should be about the point of holding views about the motion of heavenly bodies, the ends to be achieved by the use of certain tools. Confirming the truth of Scripture is one such aim, space travel is another.

Another way of making this last point is to say that we pragmatists cannot make sense of the idea that we should pursue truth for its own sake. We cannot regard truth as a goal of inquiry. The purpose of inquiry is to achieve agreement among human beings about what to do, to bring about consensus on the ends to be achieved and the means to be used to achieve those ends. Inquiry that does not achieve coordination of behaviour is not inquiry but simply wordplay. To argue for a certain theory about the microstructure of material bodies, or about the proper balance of powers between branches of government, is to argue about what we should do: how we should use the tools at our disposal in order to make technological, or political, progress. So, for prag-

matists there is no sharp break between natural science and social science, nor between social science and politics, nor between politics, philosophy and literature. All areas of culture are parts of the same endeavour to make life better. There is no deep split between theory and practice, because on a pragmatist view all so-called 'theory' which is not wordplay is always already practice.

To treat beliefs not as representations but as habits of action, and words not as representations but as tools, is to make it pointless to ask, 'Am I discovering or inventing, making or finding?' There is no point in dividing up the organisms' interaction with the environment in this way. Consider an example. We normally say that a bank account is a social construction rather than an object in the natural world, whereas a giraffe is an object in the natural world rather than a social construction. Bank accounts are made, giraffes are found. Now the truth in this view is simply that if there had been no human beings there would still have been giraffes, whereas there would have been no bank accounts. But this causal independence of giraffes from humans does not mean that giraffes are what they are apart from human needs and interests.

On the contrary, we describe giraffes in the way we do, *as* giraffes, because of our needs and interests. We speak a language which includes the word 'giraffe' because it suits our purposes to do so. The same goes for words like 'organ', 'cell', 'atom', and so on—the names of the parts out of which giraffes are made, so to speak. All the descriptions we give of things are descriptions suited to our purposes. No sense can be made, we pragmatists argue, of the claim that some of these descriptions pick out 'natural kinds'—that they cut nature at the joints. The line between a giraffe and the surrounding air is clear enough if you are a human being interested in hunting for meat. If you are a language-using ant or amoeba, or a space voyager observing us from far above, that line is not so clear, and it is not clear that you would need or have a word for 'giraffe' in your language. More generally, it is not clear that any of the millions of ways of describing the piece of space time occupied by what we call a giraffe is any closer to the way things are in themselves than any of the others. Just as it seems pointless to ask whether a giraffe is really a collection of atoms, or really a collection of actual and possible sensations in human sense organs, or really something else, so the question, 'Are we describing it as it really is?' seems one we never need to ask. All we need to know is whether some competing description might be more useful for some of our purposes.

The relativity of descriptions to purposes is the pragmatist's principal argument for his antirepresentational view of knowledge—the view that inquiry aims at utility for us rather than an accurate account of how things are in themselves. Because every belief we have must be formulated in some language or other, and because languages are not attempts to copy what is out there, but rather tools for dealing with what is out there, there is no way to divide off 'the contribution to our knowledge made by the object' from 'the contribution to our knowledge made by our subjectivity'. Both the words we use and our willingness to affirm certain sentences using those words and not others are the products of fantastically complex causal connections between human organisms and the rest of the universe. There is no way to divide up this web of causal connections so as to compare the relative amount of subjectivity and of objectivity in a given belief. There is no way, as

Wittgenstein has said, to come between language and its object, to divide the giraffe in itself from our ways of talking about giraffes. As Hilary Putnam, the leading contemporary pragmatist, has put it: 'elements of what we call "language" or "mind" penetrate so deeply into reality that the very project of representing ourselves as being "mappers" of something "language-independent" is fatally compromised from the start'.

The Platonist dream of perfect knowledge is the dream of stripping ourselves clean of everything that comes from inside us and opening ourselves without reservation to what is outside us. But this distinction between inside and outside, as I have said earlier, is one which cannot be made once we adopt a biologistic view. If the Platonist is going to insist on that distinction, he has got to have an epistemology which does not link up in any interesting way with other disciplines. He will end up with an account of knowledge which turns its back on the rest of science. This amounts to making knowledge into something supernatural, a kind of miracle.

The suggestion that everything we say and do and believe is a matter of fulfilling human needs and interests might seem simply a way of formulating the secularism of the Enlightenment—a way of saying that human beings are on their own, and have no supernatural light to guide them to the Truth. But of course the Enlightenment replaced the idea of such supernatural guidance with the idea of a quasi-divine faculty called 'reason'. It is this idea which American pragmatists and post-Nietzschean European philosophers are attacking. What seems most shocking about their criticisms of this idea is not their description of natural science as an attempt to manage reality rather than to represent it.

Rather, it is their description of moral choice as always a matter of compromise between competing goods, rather than as a choice between the absolutely right and the absolutely wrong.

Controversies between foundationalists and antifoundationalists on the theory of knowledge look like the sort of merely scholastic quarrels which can safely be left to the philosophy professors. But quarrels about the character of moral choice look more important. We stake our sense of who we are on the outcome of such choices. So we do not like to be told that our choices are between alternative goods rather than between good and evil. When philosophy professors start saying that there is nothing either absolutely wrong or absolutely right, the topic of relativism begins to get interesting. The debates between the pragmatists and their opponents, or the Nietzscheans and theirs, begin to look too important to be left to philosophy professors. Everybody wants to get in on the act.

This is why philosophers like myself find ourselves denounced in magazines and newspapers which one might have thought oblivious of our existence. These denunciations claim that unless the youth is raised to believe in moral absolutes, and in objective truth, civilization is doomed. Unless the younger generation has the same attachment to firm moral principles as we have, these magazine and newspaper articles say, the struggle for human freedom and human decency will be over. When we philosophy teachers read this sort of article, we find ourselves being told that we have enormous power over the future of mankind. For all it will take to overturn centuries of moral progress, these articles suggest, is a generation which accepts the doctrines of moral relativism, accepts the views common to Nietzsche and Dewey....

Critics of moral relativism think that unless there is something absolute, something which shares God's implacable refusal to yield to human weakness, we have no reason to go on resisting evil. If evil is merely a lesser good, if all moral choice is a compromise between conflicting goods, then, they say, there is no point in moral struggle. The lives of those who have died resisting injustice become pointless. But to us pragmatists moral struggle is continuous with the struggle for existence, and no sharp break divides the unjust from the imprudent, the evil from the inexpedient. What matters for pragmatists is devising ways of diminishing human suffering and increasing human equality, increasing the ability of all human children to start life with an equal chance of happiness. This goal is not written in the stars, and is no more an expression of what Kant called 'pure practical reason' than it is of the Will of God. It is a goal worth dying for, but it does not require backup from supernatural forces.

The pragmatist view of what opponents of pragmatism call 'firm moral principles' is that such principles are abbreviations of past practices—way of summing up the habits of the ancestors we most admire. For example, Mill's greater-happiness principle and Kant's categorical imperative are ways of reminding ourselves of certain social customs—those of certain parts of the Christian West, the culture which has been, at least in words if not in deeds, more egalitarian than any other. The Christian doctrine that all members of the species are brothers and sisters is the religious way of saying what Mill and Kant said in non-religious terms: that considerations of family membership, sex, race, religious creed and the like should not prevent us from trying to do unto others as we would have them do to us—should not prevent us from thinking of them as people like ourselves, deserving the respect which we ourselves hope to enjoy.

But there are other firm moral principles than those which epitomize egalitarianism. One such principle is that dishonour brought to a woman of one's family must be paid for with blood. Another is that it would be better to have no son than to have one who is homosexual. Those of us who would like to put a stop to the blood feuds and the gaybashing produced by these firm moral principles call such principles 'prejudices' rather than 'insights'. It would be nice if philosophers could give us assurance that the principles which we approve of, like Mill's and Kant's, are 'rational' in a way that the principles of the blood-revengers and the gaybashers are not. But to say that they are more rational is just another way of saying that they are more universalistic—that they treat the differences between women of one's own family and other women, and the difference between gays and straights, as relatively insignificant. But it is not clear that failure to mention particular groups of people is a mark of rationality.

To see this last point, consider the principle 'Thou shalt not kill'. This is admirably universal, but is it more or less rational than the principle 'Do not kill unless one is a soldier defending his or her country, or is preventing a murder, or is a state executioner, or a merciful practitioner of euthanasia'? I have no idea whether it is more or less rational, and so do not find the term 'rational' useful in this area. If I am told that a controversial action which I have taken has to be defended by being subsumed under a universal, rational principle, I may be able to dream up such a principle to fit the occasion, but sometimes I may only be able to say, 'Well, it seemed like the best thing to do at the time, all things considered.' It is not clear that the latter defence is less rational than some universal-sounding principle which I have dreamed up *ad hoc* to justify my action. It is not clear that all the moral dilemmas to do with population control, the rationing of health care, and the like—should wait upon the formulation of principles for their solution.

As we pragmatists see it, the idea that there must be such a legitimating principle lurking behind every right action amounts to the idea that there is something like a universal, super-national court of law before which we stand. We know that the best societies are those which are governed by laws rather than by the whim of tyrants or mobs. Without the rule of law, we say, human life is turned over to emotion and to violence. This makes us think that there must be a sort of invisible tribunal of reason administering laws which we all, somewhere deep down inside, recognize as binding upon us. Something like this was Kant's understanding of moral obligation. But, once again, the Kantian picture of what human beings are like cannot be reconciled with history or with biology. Both teach us that the development of societies ruled by laws rather than men was a slow, late, fragile, contingent, evolutionary achievement....

Someone who adopts the anti-Kantian stance... and is asked to defend the thick morality of the society with which she identifies herself will not be able to do so by talking about the rationality of her moral views. Rather, she will have to talk about the various concrete advantages of her society's practices over those of other societies. Discussion of the relative advantages of different thick moralities will, obviously, be as inconclusive as discussion of the relative superiority of a beloved book or person over another person's beloved book or person.

The idea of a universally shared source of truth called 'reason' or 'human nature' is, for us pragmatists, just the idea that such discussion *ought* to be capable of being made conclusive. We see this idea as a misleading way of expressing the hope, which we share, that the human race as a whole should gradually come together in a global community, a community which incorporates most of the thick morality of the European industrialized democracies. It is misleading because it suggests that the aspiration to such a community is somehow built into every member of the biological species. This seems to us pragmatists like the suggestion that the aspiration to be an anaconda is somehow built into all reptiles, or that the aspiration to be an anthropoid is somehow built into all mammals. This is why we pragmatists see the charge of relativism as simply the charge that we see luck where our critics insist on seeing destiny. We think that the utopian world community envisaged by the Charter of the United Nations and the Helsinki Declaration of Human Rights is no more the *destiny* of humanity than is an atomic holocaust or the replacement of democratic governments by feuding warlords. If either of the latter is what the future holds, our species will have been unlucky, but it will not have been irra-

tional. It will not have failed to live up to its moral obligations. It will simply have missed a chance to be happy.

I do not know how to argue the question of whether it is better to see human beings in this biologistic way or to see them in a way more like Plato's or Kant's. So I do not know how to give anything like a conclusive argument for the view which my critics call 'relativism' and which I prefer to call 'antifoundationalism' or 'antidualism'. It is certainly not enough for my side to appeal to Darwin and ask our opponents how they can avoid an appeal to the supernatural. That way of stating the issue begs many questions. It is certainly not enough for my opponents to say that a biologistic view strips human beings of their dignity and their self-respect. That too begs most of the questions at issue. I suspect that all that either side can do is to restate its case over and over again, in context after context. The controversy between those who see both our species and our society as a lucky accident, and those who find an immanent teleology in both, is too radical to permit of being judged from some neutral standpoint.

There Are Truths About Values

HILARY PUTNAM

A DEWEYAN VIEW OF VALUATION

My own answer to the question, "Are values made or discovered," is the one that I believe John Dewey would have given, namely that we make ways of dealing with problematical situations and we discover which ones are better and which worse. Obviously a good deal has to be said about what this means and why and how it is responsive to the question.

It will seem unresponsive to the question if one supposes that the judgment that one way of solving a problem is better than another must always be a purely "instrumental" judgment in the classical sense, that is, must be no more than a judgment to the effect that putative solution A is more efficient than proposed solution B with respect to values and goals already assumed (with respect to what Dewey calls "ends in view"). But this is not the way that Dewey sees matters. For him "inquiry" in the widest sense, that is human dealings with problematical situations, involves incessant reconsideration of both means *and* ends; it is not the case that each person's goals are cast in concrete in the form of a "rational preference function" that is somehow mysteriously imbedded in his or her individual mind, or that all we are allowed to do as long as we are "rational" is look for more efficient means to these immutable but idiosyncratic goals or values. Any inquiry has both "factual" presuppositions, including presuppositions as to the efficiency of various means to various ends, and "value" presuppositions, and if resolving our

problem is difficult, then we may well want to reconsider both our "factual" assumptions and our goals. In short, changing one's values is not only a legitimate way of solving a problem, but frequently the only way of solving a problem.

The claim has, of course, been advanced that what seems phenomenologically to be a decision to change one's values is "really" only a case of discovering new means to some still more fundamental (and higher-ranked) values that were "there" all along; this is not only armchair psychology; but (the worst form of armchair psychology), a priori psychology.

Dewey, then, is not just talking about finding better means to preexisting ends-in-view.... Dewey is really talking about learning through experimentation and discussion how to increase the amount of *good* in our lives. Once we see that this is what Dewey means and that he is serious about this, then very different objections arise.

Those objections can be divided into two classes. Objections of one kind I will call "Rortian objections," and I will consider those objections immediately; objections of the other kind I will call "reductionist objections," and I will consider them in a few minutes.

RORTY AND DEWEY

Readers of Rorty are well aware that Dewey is one of his heroes. Rorty hails Dewey's rejection of any supposedly fundamental fact/value dichotomy, either ontological or epistemological, and he thoroughly agrees with Dewey that serious inquiry in difficult situations results as often in a revision or redefinition of our "values" as in an improvement of our "factual knowledge." Yet Ralph Sleeper's accurate description of what he calls Dewey's "objective realism," while it contains much that Rorty would agree with, points to a side of Dewey that Rorty regards as lamentably metaphysical. Sleeper writes:

> Objects of knowledge, he [Dewey] wants to show, may be instrumental to satisfaction, but their warrant does not consist in that instrumentality. Dewey takes great pains to demonstrate that "warranted assertions" are the reliable means of obtaining desired results, that they function in controlled activity designed to resolve problematical situations and produce valued consequences. But he also takes pains to demonstrate that those valued consequences are reliable only when the means employed to obtain them are causally related to objective reality. He wants to show not merely that matters of fact *have* value as instrumental to satisfaction, but that they *are* values. He wants to demonstrate not only that there is no conceptually valid basis for the distinction between factual judgment and value judgment, but that there is no basis for an ontological distinction either. He seeks to attain by means of an objective realism and a logic of scientific method what James despaired of achieving except by the method of tenacity, and what Peirce thought could be reached only through objective idealism.

What Rorty would disagree with (not in Sleeper's account of Dewey's position, but in the position itself) are the references to "objective reality"—what Sleeper calls Dewey's "objective realism." Again and again, Rorty argues that the notion of "objective reality" is empty since we cannot stand outside of our skins and compare our notions with (supposed) objective reality as it is "in itself."

The idea of reality as it is "in itself," that is, as we would describe it if we knew the terms that describe its *intrinsic* nature, is apparently the only possible meaning that Rorty sees for the notion of "objective reality:" If the metaphysical sort of realism that posits "things in themselves" with an "intrinsic nature" makes no sense, then Rorty supposes, neither does the notion of objectivity. We should drop all talk of objectivity and talk of "solidarity" instead. The solutions or resolutions we find to our problematical situations are at best solutions or resolutions by the standards of our culture (which Rorty takes to be liberal, democratic, Whiggish, and European) and not by some supposed further standard or standards of "objectivity."

There is something I find very strange about this reaction of Rorty's. Although I join Rorty in rejecting certain traditional metaphysical notions, I do not believe that giving up these notions (finding them, in the end, quite empty) requires us to draw the conclusions that he does. What I agree with is that the idea of comparing my thoughts and beliefs, on the one hand, with things "as they are in themselves," on the other, makes no sense; but I do not agree that this idea is a necessary presupposition of the everyday thought that there are objects that are not parts of thought or language, or of the equally everyday thought that what we say about those objects sometimes *gets the facts right.* Perhaps I can bring out what I find unsatisfying about the conclusion Rorty draws by means of an analogy. Even though I cannot stand outside my own skin and compare the future as it will be after my death with my thoughts and ideas about that future, I do not for that reason stop supposing that there are events that will happen after I die, and I take out life insurance in order to affect the course of those events. Or, to take another example, even though I would agree with Rorty that I cannot step outside of my own skin and compare my friends' experiences "as they are in themselves" with my thoughts and ideas about them, I continue to sympathize with my friends and share their joys and worry about their troubles. I agree with Rorty that the metaphysical assumption that there is a fundamental dichotomy between "intrinsic" properties of things and "relational" properties of things makes no sense; but that does not lead me to view the thoughts and experiences of my friends as *just* the intentional objects of beliefs that help me "cope." If I did, what sense would it make to talk of "solidarity"? The very notion of solidarity requires commonsense realism about the objective existence of the people one is in "solidarity" with. What these examples show I think, is that it is important not to confuse one or another metaphysical interpretation of the notion of objectivity (for example, the idea that we can make sense of talk of things "as they are in themselves") with the ordinary idea that our thoughts and beliefs refer to things in the world.

The diagnosis that I have suggested of Rorty's predicament is that he is so troubled by the lack of a *guarantee* that our words represent things outside themselves that, finding a guarantee of the only kind he envisages to be "impossible," he feels that he has no alternative but to reject the very idea of representation as a mistake. (Here we also see that Rorty is a disappointed metaphysical realist.) The problem, it seems to me, is that Rorty has failed to explore the sort of "impossibility"

that is at issue when he concludes that such a guarantee is impossible. Rorty is right in saying that it makes no sense to think of standing outside of one's thoughts and concepts and comparing "reality as it is in itself" with those thoughts and concepts. How could *that* idea make sense? What Rorty has done is to move from the unintelligibility of this sort of guarantee to a skepticism about the possibility of representation in a perfectly everyday sense. He leaves us with the conclusion that there is no metaphysically innocent way to say that our words represent things outside themselves. By having failed to inquire into the character of the unintelligibility that vitiates the metaphysical sort of realism he attacks, Rorty remains blind to the way in which his own rejection of metaphysical realism partakes of the *same* unintelligibility I say, "partakes of the same unintelligibility"; for if it is unintelligible to say that we *sometimes* succeed in representing things as they are in themselves, then it is equally unintelligible to say that we never succeed in representing things as they are in themselves. The way in which skepticism is the flip side of the craving for an unintelligible kind of certainty is illustrated by Rorty's willingness to give up the perfectly obvious fact that language can represent something that is itself outside of language. The true task of philosophy here is to illuminate the ordinary notion of representation (and of a world of things to be represented), not to rest frozen in a gesture of repudiation that is as empty as what it repudiates.

SOME REDUCTIONIST OBJECTIONS TO DEWEY'S VALUE THEORY

By "reductionist" objections to Dewey's position I mean not simply criticisms of Dewey's own views, but more generally defenses of a sharp fact/value dichotomy as something inseparable from modern scientific sophistication. These defenses of the fact/value dichotomy are of two kinds: epistemological and ontological, or more simply, metaphysical. The oldest and crudest of the epistemological defenses of the fact/value dichotomy I have seen put forward like this: "How could there be 'value facts'? After all, we have no sense organ for detecting them. We can say how we detect *yellow* since we have eyes, but what sense organ do we have for detecting value?"

The weakness of this argument lies in its naiveté about perception. Perceptions of yellow may, indeed, be minimally conceptually informed, although even color perception seems to presuppose a process of acquiring the ability to discriminate the colors from one another and not just the possession of eyes. But consider the parallel question: "How could we come to tell that people are *elated?* After all, we have no sense organ for detecting elation." The fact is that we can tell that other people are elated, and sometimes we can even see that other people are elated. But we can only do so after we have acquired the *concept* of elation. Perception is not innocent; it is an exercise of our concepts, an exercise of what Kant called our "spontaneity." Once I have acquired the concept of elation, I can see that someone is elated, and similarly, once I have acquired the concept of a friendly person, or a malicious person, or a kind person, I can sometimes see that someone is friendly, or malicious, or kind. To be sure, such judgments are fallible, but pragmatists have never believed in infallibility either in perception or anywhere else. As Peirce once put it, in science we do not have or need a firm foundation; we are on swampy ground, but that is what keeps us moving.

Connected with the idea that to know that there are values we would need to

have a special sense organ is the empiricist phenomenology according to which perceptual experience (as opposed to "emotion") is value neutral and values are added to experience by "association." (In a variant of this idea—one equally wedded to separate mental "faculties"—"perception" supplies "reason" with neutral facts, and values come from a faculty called "the will.") This phenomenology (or empiricist psychology), too, has been sharply criticized by a number of authors, not all of them pragmatists by any means. But pragmatists in particular have always emphasized that experience *isn't* "neutral," that it comes to us screaming with values. In infancy we experience food and drink and cuddling and warmth as "good" and pain and deprivation and loneliness as "bad"; as our experiences multiply and become more sophisticated, the tinges and shades of value also multiply and become more sophisticated. Think, for example, of the fantastic combinations of fact and value in a wine taster's description of a wine.

However, Dewey does not make the error of supposing that merely being valued, as a matter of experiential fact, suffices to make something *valuable.* Indeed, no distinction is more insistent in Dewey's writing than the distinction between the *valued* and the valu*able.* Dewey's answer to the question, "What makes something valu*able* as opposed to merely being valued?" in a word, is *criticism.* Objective value arises, not from a special "sense organ," but from the *criticism of our valuations.* Valuations are incessant and inseparable from all of our activities, including our "scientific" ones; but it is by intelligent reflection on our valuations, intelligent reflection of the kind that Dewey calls "criticism," that we conclude that some of them are warranted while others are unwarranted. (Philosophy, by the way, is described by Dewey as *criticism of criticism!*)

This leads to the next question: "By what criteria do we decide that some valuations are warranted and some are unwarranted?" With this question, we enter more sophisticated levels of the epistemological issue. It is convenient to distinguish three parts to Dewey's answer:

(1) In judging the outcome of an inquiry, whether it be an inquiry into what are conventionally considered to be "facts" or into what are conventionally considered to be "values," we always bring to bear a large stock of both valuations and descriptions *that are not in question in that inquiry.* We are never in the position imagined by the positivists, of having a large stock of factual beliefs and no value judgments, and having to decide whether our first value judgment is "warranted," of having to infer our very first "ought" from a whole lot of "ises."

(2) We neither have nor require one single "criterion" for judging warranted assertibility in ethics (or the law) any more than we do in any other area. In particular, the authority of philosophy is not the authority of a field vested with knowledge of such a criterion or set of criteria. As Dewey himself put it, "As philosophy has no private store of knowledge or methods for attaining truth, so it has no private access to good. As it accepts knowledge and principles from those competent in science and inquiry it accepts the goods that are diffused in human experience. It has no Mosaic or Pauline authority of revelation entrusted to it. But it has the authority of intelligence, of criticism of these common and natural goods."

(3) With the appearance of the term, "intelligence," we come to the last part of Dewey's answer to the "By what criteria" question. If Dewey does not believe that inquiry requires "criteria," in the sense of

algorithms or decision procedures, either in the sciences or in daily life, he does believe that there are some things that we have *learned* about inquiry in general *from* the conduct of inquiry. Writing on Dewey, Ruth Anna Putnam and I have insisted that if one thing distinguishes Dewey as an ethicist or a meta-ethicist (the whole normative ethics/metaethics distinction tends to collapse for pragmatists), it is his emphasis on the importance of and his consistent application of the idea that *what holds good for inquiry in general holds for value inquiry in particular.*

But what does hold good for inquiry in general? We have learned, Deweyans insist, that inquiry that is to make full use of human intelligence has to have certain characteristics, including the characteristics that I have referred to by the phrase "the democratization of inquiry." For example, intelligent inquiry obeys the principles of what Habermasians call "discourse ethics"; it does not "block the paths of inquiry" by preventing the raising of questions and objections or by obstructing the formulation of hypotheses and criticism of the hypotheses of others. At its best, it avoids relations of hierarchy and dependence; it insists upon experimentation where possible, and observation and close analysis of observation where experiment is not possible. By appeal to these and kindred standards, we can often *tell* that views are irresponsibly defended in ethics and the law as well as in science.

Not everyone will be convinced, I know. Some of the undergraduates in a class I taught have suggested that belief in giving reasons and actually observing how various ways of life have functioned in practice, what the consequences have been, discussing objections, and so on, is just "another form of fundamentalism"! The experience of these students with *real* fundamentalism must be rather limited.

Anyone who has seen real fundamentalists in action knows the difference between insisting on observation and discussion and the repressive and suppressive mode of conducting discussion that is characteristic of fundamentalism. But, in any case, I think that this objection was both anticipated and adequately responded to by the founder of pragmatism, Charles Sanders Peirce, in "The Fixation of Belief." The discovery that inquiry that is to be successful in the long run requires both experimentation and public discussion of the results of that experimentation is not something a priori, but is itself something that we learned from observation and experimentation with different modes of conducting inquiry: from the failure of such methods as the method of tenacity, the method of authority, and the method of appeal to allegedly a priori reason.

In recent years, however, there has been a curious turn in the discussion. The sorts of epistemological issues that I have been dealing with were almost the only ones that figured in debates concerning the fact/value dichotomy, at least in Anglo-American philosophy, until the late 1960s. In recent decades, however, a different issue has come to the fore; more and more frequently we encounter the claim that *even if it is true that we can distinguish between an intelligent discussion in ethics and discussion that is prejudiced, closed-minded, and so on, still there cannot really be such a thing as warranted assertability in ethics, because there can only be warranted assertability where there is objective truth, and* (according to a number of recent thinkers) *there are good metaphysical grounds for saying that there cannot be such a thing as objective truth in ethics.* The grounds in a nutshell are that the only truly objective truths there are are the truths of physics, and the alleged truths of ethics simply do not "fit" into the world picture of physics.

This move fails, however, because (to use Kantian language) one thing physics cannot do is account for its own possibility. If the only facts there are are indeed the facts of physics, then there cannot be semantical facts. For example, semantical facts have proved as resistant to physicalist treatments as have ethical and legal facts. While British philosophers in particular have recently been entranced by the question of what does and what does not fit into the "absolute conception of the world" (a currently popular way of referring to future completed physics), I do not think that this particular intellectual temptation is one that this audience is likely to feel very strongly, and I shall not deal with it further here.

TRUTH AND WARRANTED ASSERTIBILITY

With this last metaphysical issue, however, I come to the topic, truth and justification in the law. I have just said something about warranted assertibility in ethics and the law. I have said that we can apply standards of inquiry that we have learned from experience are necessary to the intelligent prosecution of inquiry in *any* area, and that, since we are never in the position of starting *ex nihilo* in ethics any more than anywhere else, or in the law any more than anywhere else, there is no reason that it should be impossible to discover in individual problematical situations—however fallibly—that one putative resolution is superior to another. But what is the relation of *truth* to this sort of warranted assertability?

The question is enormously difficult and delicate. At one time, I myself believed that truth could be defined as warranted assertability under "ideal" (that is to say *good enough*) conditions, where what are good enough conditions is itself something that we are able to determine in the course of inquiry. I no longer think that this works, or indeed that one need define truth at all, although I think there is a great deal philosophically to be said about the use of the word "true" and the complex relations between truth and the various semantical and epistemological notions we have. But here I want to make just one point: even if one believes that truth sometimes transcends warranted assertibility (even warranted assertibility under ideal conditions, it would be a great mistake to suppose that truth can always transcend warranted assertibility under "ideal" (or good enough) conditions.

It may be the case, for example, that some statements about the cosmological universe are such that they could be true, but there are no conditions under which we could verify that they are true; the very notion of "ideal conditions" for verifying them may not make sense. For example, it may be true that there do not happen to be any intelligent extraterrestrials anywhere, but it may be impossible to verify that this is the case. On the other hand, if the statement that there are chairs in this room is true, then of course that is something that can be verified if conditions are good enough. In fact, on the occasion of my giving the lecture from which this chapter is taken, the conditions were good enough and the statement was verified. The supposition that truth, even in such a familiar case, might in principle be impossible to verify, that we might all be "brains in a vat," or in Descartes's version, that we might all be deceived by an evil demon, has only the appearance of sense. For the supposition in question has the (usually unnoticed) feature that if we were really out of touch with the world in one of these ways, then the assumption (which is, of course, an essential part of the supposition in question) that our referential powers extend so far as to enable us to understand

the conjecture that we are all brains in a vat or disembodied minds deceived by an evil demon would be false. The ability to refer to things is not something that is guaranteed by the very nature of the mind, as Descartes mistakenly supposed; reference to things requires information-carrying interaction with those things, and that is enough to rule out the possibility that truth is in all cases radically independent of what we can verify. Truth cannot be so radically non-epistemic.

These are dark issues. But it is not necessary to take a position on the question as to whether truth can ever be totally recognition transcendent in order to recognize that in such familiar cases as talk about the furniture in the room truth is not recognition transcendent, that truth does entail warranted assertibility if conditions are sufficiently good. This is even more the case, I believe, when the subject matter is ethics or when the subject matter is the law. Even a hard-line metaphysical realist must agree that some subject matters are such that their very nature entails that if the statement in question is true, then the statement can, under certain conditions, be verified. This is the case, for example, with predications of intelligibility. If I say that a text is intelligible, then part of what I mean is that it can be understood, and if one understands a text then, *pace* Derrida, one can know that one understands it. (*Perfect* understanding, whatever that might be, is not, of course, at issue here.) It does not involve any version of idealism to hold that for the predicate "intelligible," truth does not transcend warranted assertibility under good enough conditions. But in the same way, I argue, there is no reason to suppose that one cannot be what is called a "moral realist" in metaethics, that is, hold that some "value judgments" are true as a matter of objective fact, without holding that moral facts are or can be recognition transcendent facts. If something is a good solution to a problematical human situation, then part of the very notion of its being a good solution is that human beings can recognize that it is. We need not entertain the idea that something could be a good solution although human beings are *in principle unable to recognize that it is.* That sort of rampant Platonism is incoherent.

Moral realism should not become what I just called "rampant Platonism," in addition, it need not and should not represent a commitment to the idea that there is some final set of moral truths (or, for that matter, legal truths), all of which can be expressed in some fixed moral or legal vocabulary. An essential part of the "language games" that we play in science, in morals, and in the law is the invention of new concepts, and their introduction into general use; new concepts carry in their wake the possibility of formulating new truths. If the idea of a frozen "final truth" does not make sense in science, it is even more the case that it does not make sense in ethics and the law. But in contrast to most of the familiar forms of postmodernism, pragmatists do not conclude that therefore we cannot speak of truth or warranted assertability or even of objectivity.

SUMMING UP

Before I close, it may be well to sum up some of the conclusions that I have reached. I have argued that both in the case of ethics and in the law we are non-mysteriously able to observe that certain things have certain value properties: that a wine is "full bodied" and has a "rich bouquet," that a person is "refreshingly spontaneous" or "compassionate," that a legal brief is "sloppily put together." This is not perception that is based simply on hardwired groups of neurons, as color perception has sometimes been supposed to be

(there is still a lot of debate going on about this), but that involves the application of concepts; I have argued that all perception is of this kind. In addition, from the fact that all perception involves concepts, and concepts are always subject to criticism, it follows that perception itself is not an incorrigible "given" but subject to criticism. Inquiry does not end with perception, but the fact that perception sometimes turns out to be wrong doesn't mean that we are never justified in trusting it. Pragmatists believe that doubt requires justification just as much as belief, and there are many perceptions that we have no real reason to doubt. (This combination of fallibilism with anti-skepticism is, indeed, one of the chief characteristics of American pragmatism.) By Dewey's account, the judgment that something is valuable, in particular, requires not just an experience of the kind that he calls a valuing, but also requires the activity that he calls "criticism" (Dewey also uses the term "appraisal"). Furthermore, I have argued that in criticism the question "But how should we proceed?" is not the "stumper" it is sometimes supposed to be. We do know something about how inquiry should be conducted, and the principle that what is valid for inquiry in general is valid for value inquiry in particular is a powerful one. In this connection, I mentioned the principle of *fallibilism* (do not regard the product of any inquiry as immune from criticism), the principle of *experimentalism* (try out different ways of resolving problematical situations, or if that is not feasible, observe those who have tried other ways, and reflect carefully on the consequences), and the principles that together make up what I called "the democratization of inquiry." I have suggested that, in our actual lives, we are able to distinguish between warranted and unwarranted judgments (including judgments of value) at least some of the time—of course there are hard cases and controversial cases, and will continue to be—and the fact that we can distinguish between warranted and unwarranted judgments is enough. (As John Austin famously remarked, "Enough is enough; enough isn't everything.") There is no recognition transcendent truth here; we need no better ground for treating "value judgments" as capable of truth and falsity than the fact that we can and do treat them as capable of warranted assertibility and warranted deniability.

THE CONTINUING DEBATE:
Pragmatism and the Dispute Over Value Objectivity

What Is New

Pragmatism and feminist philosophy have obvious affinities: Both emphasize attention to particulars and details (and less focus on universals and abstract principles),
both have great interest in the cultural and social development of ideas and institutions, and both favor an experimentalist approach to knowledge (knowledge develops
through practice and experiment rather than from rationally derived principle). Thus
it is not surprising that there has been recent important work on pragmatist feminism
that expands perspectives in both areas, with new work emerging in ethics, political
philosophy, epistemology, and philosophy of education.

Where to Find More

Hilary Putnam is a leading figure in contemporary pragmatism. Among his many
influential books are *The Many Faces of Realism* (LaSalle, IL: Open Court, 1987);
Realism with a Human Face (Cambridge, MA: Harvard University Press, 1990);
Renewing Philosophy (Cambridge, MA: Harvard University Press, 1992); and *The
Collapse of the Fact-Value Dichotomy and Other Essays* (Cambridge, MA: Harvard
University Press, 2002).

The views of Richard Rorty are provocative and controversial. His most philosophically famous book is probably *Philosophy and the Mirror of Nature* (Princeton,
NJ: Princeton University Press, 1979), which includes only a brief discussion of
ethics. *Consequences of Pragmatism* (Minneapolis, MN: University of Minnesota
Press, 1982) contains interesting work on pragmatism and its social and political implications. *Contingency, Irony, and Solidarity* (Cambridge: Cambridge University
Press, 1989) is a very readable book that ranges through literature, social theory, and
philosophy (Chapter 9, "Solidarity," contains very interesting remarks on ethics).
Truth and Progress: Philosophical Papers, Volume 3 (Cambridge: Cambridge University
Press, 1998) and *Philosophy and Social Hope* (London: Penguin Books, 1999) are excellent collections of his essays.

The pragmatist view was developed by Charles S. Peirce, William James, and
John Dewey (among others) early in the twentieth century. It remains one of the
leading schools of philosophical thought—though its boundaries are not altogether
clear, and there is often dispute about who should be considered a pragmatist. For
classic pragmatic views of ethics, see William James, *Pragmatism* (originally given as a
series of lectures in 1907, it is available in a number of editions); John Dewey, *The
Quest for Certainty* (originally given as the Gifford Lectures in 1929, it was published
by G. P. Putnam's Sons, New York, in a paperback edition in 1960); John Dewey, *Reconstruction in Philosophy* (NY: Henry Holt, 1920); and John Dewey, *Human Nature
and Conduct* (NY: Henry Holt and Company, 1922). For contemporary work on
pragmatic ethics, see (in addition to the Rorty and Putnam citations above) Stanley
Cavell, *In Quest of the Ordinary* (Chicago: University of Chicago Press, 1988); an excellent brief history and development of the view in Hugh LaFollette's "Pragmatic
Ethics," in Hugh LaFollette, ed., *The Blackwell Guide to Ethical Theory* (Oxford:
Blackwell Publishers, 2000), as well as LaFollette's "The Truth In Ethical Relativism,"

Journal of Social Philosophy, volume 20 (1991): 146–154; two books by Joseph Margolis: *Pragmatism without Foundations: Reconciling Realism and Relativism* (Oxford: Blackwell Publishers, 1986), and *Life Without Principles* (Oxford: Blackwell Publishers, 1996); and the fascinating "prophetic pragmatism" of Cornel West, in *The American Evasion of Philosophy: A Genealogy of Pragmatism* (Madison, WI: University of Wisconsin Press, 1987).

The article by Judy Whipps on "Pragmatist Feminism" in the *Stanford Encyclopedia of Philosophy* is excellent, and the historical material is particularly interesting; it is available at *http://plato.stanford.edu/entries/femapproach-pragmatism*. Among the many interesting works in the intersection of pragmatism and feminism that are particularly relevant to ethics, see Beth J. Singer, *Pragmatisim, Rights, and Democracy* (NY: Fordham University Press, 1999); Erin McKenna, *The Task Of Utopia: A Pragmatist and Feminist Perspective* (Lanham, MD: Rowman and Littlefield Publishers, 2001); Charlene Haddock Seigfried, *Pragmatism and Feminism: Reweaving the Social Fabric* (Chicago: The University of Chicago Press, 1996); and the special issue of *Hypatia* on feminism and pragmatism, volume 8, number 2 (Spring 1993).

13   IS MORALITY RELATIVE TO CULTURE *OR* OBJECTIVELY AND UNIVERSALLY TRUE?

MORALITY IS RELATIVE

ADVOCATE: Gilbert Harman, Stewart Professor of Philosophy at Princeton University; author of *The Nature of Morality* (NY: Oxford University Press, 1977), *Reasoning, Meaning, and Mind* (Oxford: Oxford University Press, 1999), and *Explaining Value and Other Essays in Moral Philosophy* (Oxford: Oxford University Press, 2000).

SOURCE: "Is There a Single True Morality?" in David Copp and David Zimmerman, eds., *Morality, Reason, and Truth* (Totawa, NJ: Rowman & Allanheld, 1984).

MORALITY IS OBJECTIVELY TRUE

ADVOCATE: Carol Rovane, Professor of Philosophy at Columbia University; author of *The Bounds of Metaphysics* (Princeton: Princeton University Press, 1998).

SOURCE: "Earning the Right to Realism or Relativism in Ethics," *Philosophical Issues*, volume 12, Realism and Relativism (2002): 264–285.

In its popular *normative cultural relativism* form, the arguments for ethical relativism are weak and the opposing arguments powerful. *Descriptive* relativism points out that different cultures often have different values: the values of a Hasidic Jewish culture in New York City are distinctly different from the rural Irish culture of Country Mayo. *Normative* cultural relativists appeal to cultural diversity of values, but then jump from the descriptive fact that different cultures manifest different value systems to the *normative* claim that the values that prevail within each culture are *morally right* within that culture. Another popular argument in favor of normative cultural relativism is that it appears tolerant and open-minded. But some cultures are brutally intolerant—intolerant of racial and ethnic and religious minorities within their midst, for example—and normative cultural relativism implies that (at least within such intolerant cultures) intolerance is a virtue. And there are other problems for normative cultural relativism. One, it rules out all possibility of legitimate challenge to the prevailing values of the culture; thus within the racist culture of apartheid South Africa, the courageous reform movement led by such people as Nelson Mandela was—by the principles of normative cultural relativism—morally wrong. Second, while normative cultural relativism may seem culturally sophisticated, in fact it is culturally naive: it treats each culture as distinct, when in fact cultures overlap. All of us are members of many different cultures (you remain part of the rural farm culture of your childhood, you are now part of the urban culture where your university is located, you participate in American culture, you may distinctly identify with a specific ethnic or tribal culture, and perhaps you are also part of a culture connected with a religion or internet group), and the values of each culture may be quite different (the cultural values of your internet group are not the values of your rural farm culture). So when those values conflict, what *should* you do (by normative cultural relativist lights)? And finally, normative cultural relativism seems to assume—contrary to its basic premise—the existence of at least one universal ethical truth: For all cultures, the values of each culture are right within that culture.

While crude and popular forms of ethical relativism are easily refuted, Gilbert Harman's version is neither crude nor an easy target. Harman starts from the perspective of scientific naturalism, and uses that as a standard for successful explanation and for choosing among competing hypotheses. Harman's view is that at the level of basic ethical commitments, there is (in contrast to the situation within scientific naturalism) no rational objective way of choosing among basic principles or of refuting opposing views. That doesn't mean you must accept or approve of opposing views; to the contrary, you may vehemently oppose them. If you *really* favor brutal imperialism, even when you recognize all its harsh and painful effects—including the brutalizing effects on the imperialists as well as on those who are conquered—then there is no rational means of refuting you; but that doesn't mean I (as a relativist) must approve of your values.

Harman presents relativist ethics as an extension of the scientific *naturalist* approach to the world, and suggests that opposition to relativism stems from a position that treats ethics as an *autonomous* enterprise distinctly different from science. Carol Rovane defends an ambitious ethical *realist* view that includes a wide variety of ethical truths. Both devote considerable effort and skill to giving a clear account of what is really at stake between ethical relativists and realists.

POINTS TO PONDER

➤ *If* Harman is correct in his characterization of naturalist ethics and autonomous ethics, is there any way the debate between the two views might be settled? That is, would it ever be possible for one side to offer arguments that convince the other side?

➤ Are there any key points at which defenders of autonomous ethics might dispute the way Harman describes their position?

➤ Carol Rovane accepts that our ethical concepts (such as fairness) may have started as part of an assumed bargaining position, but she maintains that because we have the critical capacity to "make comparative judgments *about* moral agreements," we can thus evaluate a variety of agreements and initial bargaining positions from a larger "*single* ethical perspective," and that takes us down the path of ethical realism. How would Harman respond to that argument?

Morality Is Relative

Gilbert Harman

The question whether there is a single true morality is an unresolved issue in moral philosophy. On one side are relativists, skeptics, nihilists, and noncognitivists. On the other side are those who believe in absolute values and a moral law that applies to everyone. Strangely, only a few people seem to be undecided. Almost everyone seems to be firmly on one side or the other, and almost everyone seems to think his or her side is obviously right, the other side representing a kind of ridiculous folly. This is strange since everyone knows, or ought to know, that many intelligent people are on each side of this issue.

Two Approaches

In this essay I want to suggest that part of the explanation for this mutual incomprehension is that there are two different ways to do moral philosophy. If one approach is taken, moral relativism, noncognitivism, or skepticism may seem obviously correct and moral absolutism may seem foolish. If the other approach is taken, absolutism may seem clearly right and skepticism, relativism, and noncognitivism may seem foolish.

The difference in approaches is, to put it crudely, a difference in attitude toward science. One side says we must concentrate on finding the place of value and obligation in the world of facts as revealed by science. The other side says we must ignore that problem and concentrate on ethics proper....

I will use the term "naturalism" for an approach to ethics that is... dominated by a concern with the place of values in the natural world. I will call any approach that is not so dominated an instance of "autonomous ethics," since such an approach allows us to pursue ethics internally. Of course, autonomous ethics allows that science is relevant to ethics in as much as ethical assessment depends on the facts of the case. But unlike naturalism, autonomous ethics does not take the main question of ethics to be the naturalistic status of values and obligations.

Naturalism

I hope the terms "naturalism" and "autonomous ethics" will not be too misleading. The term "naturalism" is sometimes reserved for the thesis that moral judgments can be analyzed into or reduced to factual statements of a sort clearly compatible with the scientific world view. I am using the term "naturalism" more broadly in a more traditional and accurate sense. Naturalism in this sense does not have to lead to naturalistic reduction, although that is one possibility. Another possibility is that there is no way in which ethics could fit into the scientific conception of the world. In that case naturalism leads to moral nihilism....

Naturalism can also lead one to a noncognitive analysis of moral judgments. In this view, moral judgments do not function to describe the world, but to do something else—to express one's attitudes for and against things... or to recommend one or another course of action or general policy. Or a naturalist may decide that moral judgments do make factual claims that fit in with the claims of science. This can be illustrated by some sort of naturalistic reduction. One example would be an analysis that takes moral claims to be claims about the reactions of a hypothetical impartial observer....

Autonomous Ethics

Naturalism tends toward relativism. What I am calling autonomous ethics, on the other hand, can have a very different tendency. In this approach, science is relevant, since our moral judgments depend on what we take the facts to be; but we attach no special importance to saying how obligations and values can be part of the world revealed by science. Rather, we do ethics internally. We begin with our initial moral beliefs and search for general principles. Our initial opinions can be changed to some extent so as to come into agreement with appealing general principles and our beliefs about the facts, but an important aspect of the appeal of such principles will be the way in which they account for what we already accept.

This approach normally (but not always) involves an initial assumption of moral absolutism, which in this context is of course not the thesis that there are simple moral principles that hold absolutely without exceptions, but rather the thesis that there are basic moral demands that apply to all moral agents. Autonomous ethics tends to retain that absolutist thesis. It may also involve some sort of intuitionism, claiming that each of us has immediate insight into the truths of certain moral principles. It sometimes leads to a fairly conservative morality, not much different from one's initial starting point. That is not surprising given the privileged position assigned to our initial moral beliefs....

WHY DO WE BELIEVE WHAT WE BELIEVE?

Autonomous ethics and naturalism represent very different attitudes toward the relation between science and ethics. Consider, for example, the question of what explains our believing what we in fact believe. Naturalists see an important difference between our factual beliefs and our moral beliefs. Our ordinary factual beliefs provide us with evidence that there is an independent world of objects because our having those beliefs cannot be plausibly explained without assuming we interact with an independent world of objects external to ourselves, objects we perceive and manipulate. But our having the moral beliefs we have can be explained entirely in terms of our upbringing and our psychology, without any appeal to an independent realm of values and obligations. So our moral beliefs do not provide us with evidence for such an independent realm of values and obligations, and we must choose between skepticism, noncognitivism, and relativism.

Autonomists disagree with this. They claim we often believe that something is good or right or obligatory in part because it is good or right or obligatory. They accuse naturalists of begging the question. When naturalists say that a belief cannot be explained by virtue of something's being right, unless that thing's being right consists in some psychological or sociological fact, they simply assume that all explanatory factors are part of the world revealed by science. But this is the point at issue. Autonomists argue that it is more obvious that we sometimes recognize what is right than that naturalism is correct. True, we may be unable to say how a given "moral fact" and someone's recognition of it fit into the world of facts as revealed by science. But there are always unanswered questions. To jump from our current inability to answer this question to skepticism, relativism, or noncognitivism is to make a more drastic move than this puzzle warrants, from the point of view of autonomous ethics.

Explanation and Reduction

The naturalist seeks to locate the place of value, justice, right, and wrong, and so forth in the world in a way that makes clear how they might explain what we take them to explain. A naturalist cannot understand how value, justice, right, and wrong might figure in explanations without having some sense of their "location" in the world.... What a naturalist wants is to be able to locate value, justice, right, wrong, and so forth in the world in the way that tables, colors, genes, temperatures, and so on can be located in the world.

What is at issue here is understanding *how* moral facts might explain something, how the badness of someone's character might explain why that person acts in a certain way.... It is not sufficient that one be prepared to accept the counterfactual judgment that the person would not have acted in that way if the person had not had a bad character, if one does not see how the *badness* of the person's character could have such an effect. A naturalist believes one can see that only by locating badness of character in aspects of the world which one sees can have that effect.

Notice that a "naturalist" as I am here using the term is not just someone who supposes that all aspects of the world have a naturalistic location in this way, but rather someone who takes it to be of overriding importance in doing moral philosophy actually to attempt to locate moral properties. My claim is that, when one takes this attempt seriously, one will tend to become skeptical or relativistic....

MORAL ABSOLUTISM DEFINED

I now want to be more specific about what is to count as moral absolutism. Various things might be meant by the claim that there are absolute values and one true morality. Moral absolutists in one sense might not be moral absolutists in other senses. We must be careful not to mix up real issues with purely verbal issues. So let me stipulate that I will take moral absolutism to be a view about the moral reasons people have to do things and to want or hope for things. I will understand a belief about absolute values to be a belief that there are things that everyone has a reason to hope or wish for. To say that there is a moral law that "applies to everyone" is, I hereby stipulate, to say that everyone has sufficient reasons to follow that law....

DOES A SINGLE MORAL LAW APPLY TO EVERYONE?

Consider the issue between absolutism and relativism concerning reasons people have for doing things. According to moral absolutism about this, there is a single moral law that applies to everyone; in other words, there are moral demands that everyone has sufficient reasons to follow, and these demands are the source of all moral reasons. Moral relativism denies that there are universal basic moral demands and says different people are subject to different basic moral demands depending on the social customs, practices, conventions, values, and principles that they accept.

For example, a moral absolutist might suppose there is a basic moral prohibition on causing harm or injury to other people. This prohibition is in one sense not absolute, since it can be overridden by more compelling considerations and since it allows exceptions in order to punish criminals, for instance. But the prohibition is supposed to be universal in the sense that it applies to absolutely all agents and not just to those who happen to participate in certain conventions. The absolutist claims that absolutely everyone has sufficient reasons to observe this prohibition and to act as it and other basic moral requirements dictate.

A moral relativist denies this and claims that many people have no reasons to observe this prohibition. Many people participate in moralities that sharply distinguish insiders and outsiders and do not prohibit harm or injury to outsiders, except perhaps as this is likely to lead to retaliation against insiders. A person participating in such a morality has no reason to avoid harm or injury to outsiders, according to the relativist, and so the general prohibition does not apply to that person. Such a person may be a member of some primitive tribal group, but he or she need not be. He or she might also be part of contemporary society, a successful professional criminal, say, who recognizes various obligations to other members of a criminal organization but not to those on the outside. According to the moral relativist, the successful criminal may well have no reason at all not to harm his or her victims.

An Argument for Relativism

Let us concentrate on this case. The moral absolutist says the demands of the one true morality apply as much to this successful criminal as to anyone else, so this criminal does have a reason not to harm a given victim. The relativist denies the criminal has any such reason and so denies the relevant moral demand is a universal demand that applies to everyone. Here naturalism tends to support relativism in the following way.

Consider what it is for someone to have a sufficient reason to do something. Naturalism requires that this should be explained in terms congenial to science. We cannot simply treat this as irreducibly normative, saying, for example, that someone

has a sufficient reason to do something if and only if he or she ought to do it. Now, presumably, someone has a sufficient reason to do something if and only if there is warranted reasoning that person could do which would lead him or her to decide to do that thing. A naturalist will suppose that a person with a sufficient reason to do something might fail to reason in this way to such a decision only because of some sort of empirically discoverable failure, due to inattention, or lack of time, or failure to consider or appreciate certain arguments, or ignorance of certain available evidence, or an error in reasoning, or some sort of irrationality or unreasonableness, or weakness of will. If the person does not intend to do something and that is not because he or she has failed in some such empirically discoverable way to reason to a decision to do that thing, then, according to the naturalist, that person cannot have a sufficient reason to do that thing. This is the first premise in a naturalistic argument in support of the relativist.

The other premise is that there are people, such as certain professional criminals, who do not act in accordance with the alleged requirement not to harm or injure others, where this is not due to inattention or failure to consider or appreciate certain arguments, or ignorance of certain evidence, or any errors in reasoning, or any sort of irrationality or unreasonableness, or weakness of will. The argument for this is simply that there clearly are people who do not adhere to the requirement in question and who do not *seem* to have failed in any of these ways. So, in the absence of special theoretical reasons, deriving, say, from psychology, to think these people must have failed in one of the specified ways, we can conclude they have not done so.

From these two premises it follows that there are people who do not have sufficient reasons, and therefore do not have sufficient moral reasons, to adhere to the general prohibition against harming or injuring others. In particular, a successful criminal may not have a sufficient reason not to harm his or her victims. The moral prohibition against harming others may simply fail to apply to such a person. It may fail to apply in the relevant sense, which is of course not to say that the principle makes an explicit exception for criminals, allowing them but not others to injure and harm people without restraint. Rather, the principle may fail to apply in the sense that the criminal in question may fail to have sufficient reason to act in accordance with the principle.

An Absolutist Reply

Moral absolutism must reject this argument. It can do so by invoking autonomous ethics at the place at which moral relativism invokes naturalism. Autonomous ethics does not suppose that we must give some sort of naturalistic account of having a sufficient reason to do something, nor does it suppose that only a science like psychology can discover the conditions under which someone has failed to reason in a certain way because of inattention, irrationality, unreasonableness, or any of the other causes of failure mentioned in the relativistic argument.

Autonomous ethics approaches this issue in the following way. We begin with certain beliefs. Presumably these imply that everyone has a sufficient reason to observe the prohibition against harm to others, including, in particular, the successful criminal who does not participate in or accept any practice of observing this general prohibition. At the start we therefore believe that the criminal does have sufficient reason not to harm his or her victims. Following autonomous ethics, then, we should continue to believe this unless such

continued belief conflicts with generalizations or other theoretical principles internal to ethics that we find attractive because they do a better job at making sense of most of the things we originally believe. Taking this approach, the absolutist must claim that the relativistic argument does not provide sufficient reason to abandon our original absolutism. It is more plausible, according to the absolutist, that at least one of the premises of the relativistic argument is false than that its conclusion is true.

Assessing the First Premise

The first premise of the relativistic argument is that for someone to have a sufficient reason to do something there must be warranted reasoning available to that person that leads to a decision to do that thing, so that if the person fails to intend to do that thing it must be because of inattention, lack of time, failure to consider or appreciate certain arguments, ignorance of relevant evidence, an error in reasoning, irrationality, unreasonableness, or weakness of will. The absolutist might object that this is oversimplified. If a person with sufficient reason to do something does not do it, then something has gone wrong, and it might be one of the things the relativist mentions, but it might be something else as well. There might be something wrong with the *person* in question. That person might be bad, immoral. The failure might simply be a failure not to care enough about other people. A person ought to care about others and there is something wrong with a person who does not care, even if that person is not inattentive, ignorant, rushed, or defective in any other of the particular ways the relativist mentions. So, even if some people fail to observe the prohibition against harming others not because of inattention, lack of time, and so forth, but simply because of lack of concern and respect for others, such people still do have sufficient reason not to harm others....

This response to the relativistic argument is a response within autonomous ethics. It does not explain having a sufficient reason to do something in terms that are acceptably factual from a naturalistic perspective. It appeals also to the notion of something's being wrong with someone, where what might be wrong is simply that the person is bad or immoral. It is like saying one has a sufficient reason to do something if and only if one ought to do it, or if and only if it would be wrong not to do it.

The relativist claims that the only plausible accounts of these normative notions are relativistic ones. There is no prohibition on harm to outsiders in the criminals' morality. There is such a prohibition only in some other morality. In that other morality something is wrong with a person who has no compunction about injuring someone else; but nothing is wrong with such a person with respect to the criminal morality, as long as those injured are outsiders. But how can it be a sufficient reason for the criminal not to harm his or her victims that this is prohibited by somebody else's morality? How can its being bad, immoral, or wrong in this other morality not to care about and respect others give the criminal, who does not accept that morality, a sufficient reason to do anything?

The absolutist's answer is that failure to respect others is not just wrong according to some morality the criminal does not accept, it is also wrong, period. Something is really wrong with lack of respect and concern for others. It is not just wrong in relation to one or another morality. Of course, the relativist will not be satisfied with this answer and, appealing to naturalism, will ask what it is for

something to be wrong in this way. The absolutist supposes that the failure to care about and respect others does involve something the absolutist points to by saying this failure is wrong. But what is this thing that is true of such a failure to care and that can give the criminal a sufficient reason not to harm and injure others? The relativist can see no aspect of such a failure that could provide such a reason. This of course is because the relativist, as a naturalist, considers only aspects of the failure that are clearly compatible with a scientific world view. The relativist disregards putative aspects that can be specified only in normative terms. But the absolutist, as an autonomist, can specify the relevant aspect of such a failure to care about others: It is bad, immoral, wrong not to care; the criminal ought to have this concern and respect and so ought not to harm and injure others, and therefore has a sufficient reason not to harm and injure them.

Assessing the Second Premise

We have been discussing an argument for relativism concerning moral reasons. We have seen that naturalism supports the first premise of this argument and that autonomous ethics allows the rejection of this premise. The same thing is true of the second premise, which says that there are people, such as the successful criminal, who do not observe the alleged requirement not to harm or injure others and this is not due to inattention, failure to consider or appreciate certain arguments, ignorance of relevant evidence, errors in reasoning, irrationality unreasonableness, or weakness of will. Naturalism supports this because there do seem to be such people, and no scientifically acceptable grounds exist for thinking this is an illusion. On the other hand, autonomous ethics allows other grounds, not reducible to scientific grounds, for thinking this is an illusion. In autonomous ethics we begin by supposing that we recognize the wrongness of harming others, where this is to recognize a sufficient reason not to harm others. If that is something we recognize, then it must be there to be recognized, so the successful criminal in question must be failing to recognize and appreciate something that is there.

The absolutist might argue that the criminal must be irrational or at least unreasonable. Seeing that a proposed course of action will probably cause serious injury to some outsider, the criminal does not treat this as a reason not to undertake that course of action. This must be irrational or unreasonable, because such a consideration simply is such a reason and indeed is an obvious reason, a basic reason, not one that has to be derived in some complex way through arcane reasoning. But then it must be irrational or at least unreasonable for the criminal not to care sufficiently about others, since the criminal's lack of concern for others is what is responsible for the criminal's not taking the likelihood of harm to an outsider to be a reason against a proposed course of action. This is one way an absolutist might argue.

The relativist's reply to such an argument is that, on any plausible characterization of reasonableness and unreasonableness (or rationality and irrationality) as notions that can be part of the scientific conception of the world, the absolutist's claim is just false. Someone can be completely rational without feeling concern and respect for outsiders. But of course this reply appeals to naturalism. The absolutist who rejects naturalism in favor of autonomous ethics relies on an unreduced normative characterization of rationality and irrationality (or reasonableness and unreasonableness).

Now the argument continues as before. The relativist argues that, if rationality and irrationality (or reasonableness and unreasonableness) are conceived normatively, they become relative notions. What one morality counts as irrational or unreasonable, another does not. The criminal is not irrational or unreasonable in relation to criminal morality, but only in relation to a morality the criminal rejects. But the fact that it is irrational or unreasonable in relation to this other morality not to have concern and respect for others does not give the criminal who rejects that morality any reason to avoid harming or injuring others. The absolutist replies that relative irrationality or unreasonableness is not what is in question. The criminal is irrational or at least unreasonable, period. Not just irrational or unreasonable in relation to a morality he or she does not accept. Since it is irrational or unreasonable for anyone not to care sufficiently about others, everyone has a sufficient reason not to injure others, whether he or she recognizes this reason or, through irrationality or unreasonableness, does not recognize it.

The naturalist is unconvinced by this because the naturalist can find no aspect of the criminal the absolutist might be referring to in saying the criminal is "irrational" or "unreasonable," if this aspect is to give the criminal any reason to care about others. This of course is because the naturalist is considering only naturalistic aspects of the criminal, whereas the absolutist, as an autonomist, is thinking about an unreduced normative aspect, something the naturalist cannot appeal to.

So, as was true of the first premise of the relativistic argument about reasons, the second premise depends on an assumption of naturalism. By appealing to autonomous ethics, an absolutist can reject this premise.

An absolutist may in fact actually accept one or the other of the premises of the relativistic argument (although of course not both). A given absolutist might reject either the first premise or the second or both premises....

ARE THERE ABSOLUTE MORAL VALUES?

The situation is similar in the theory of value. Naturalism tends to support the conclusion that all value is relative and that something is always good for one or another person or group of people or in relation to a specified set of purposes or interests or aims. Autonomous ethics allows also for absolute values, things that are good, period, and not just good for someone or some group or for some purpose....

Now it can be argued that there is... a kind of absolute value. The claim is that states of affairs can be good or bad, period, and not merely good or bad for someone or in relation to given purposes or interests. On hearing of pointless painful experiments on laboratory animals, for example, one immediately reacts with the thought that this is bad and it would be good to eliminate such practices. Clearly, one does not simply mean that these tortures are bad for the animals involved and that these animals would benefit if such experiments were ended. A heartless experimenter might agree that what he does is bad for the animals without having to agree that it would be a good thing to eliminate this sort of experimentation. Similarly, it seems intelligible to suppose that it would be better if there were no inequalities of wealth and income in the world even though this would not be better for everyone, not for those who are now relatively wealthy, for instance. And this seems to say more, for example, than that the average person would be bet-

ter off if there were no such inequalities, since an elitist might agree with that but not agree that the envisioned state of affairs would be better, period, than our present situation.... It may seem, then, that we can consider the absolute value of a possible state of affairs.

Skepticism about Absolute Values

The relative value of a possible state of affairs in relation to given purposes and interests is a measure of the extent to which someone with those purposes and interests has a reason to try to bring about, or want, or hope for that state of affairs. The absolute value of a possible state of affairs is a measure of the extent to which anyone, apart from having a personal stake in the matter, has a reason to try to bring about, or want, or hope for that state of affairs. Naturalism leads to skepticism at this point. How could we ever be aware of absolute values? How could we ever know that everyone has a reason to want a certain possible state of affairs?

Further reflection along naturalistic lines suggests that apparent absolute values are often illusory projections of one's personal values onto the world. Sometimes this sort of projection yields plausible results, but usually it does not. To begin with the most plausible sort of case, in hearing about the pain involved in animal experimentation, our sympathies are immediately and vividly engaged; we immediately side with the animals against the experimenters. In saying "That is awful!" we are not just saying "That is awful for the animals," since our remark expresses our sympathetic identification with the point of view of the animals. We do not merely state a fact, we express our feelings and we expect an awareness of this state of affairs to call forth the same feelings of dismay in everyone. This expectation seems reasonable enough in this case, since it may well be, as Brandt argues, that everyone has a sympathetic reaction to suffering.

But plausibility vanishes as soon as the case becomes even a little complex. Suppose the animal experiments are not pointless but are an essential part of a kind of medical research that promises to alleviate a certain amount of human suffering. Or suppose that, although the experiments promise no practical benefit of this sort, they are relevant to a theoretical issue in psychology. A given person may still feel that it is bad that the experiments should occur and that it would be good if they were not done, the gain not being worth the cost. Again, the person is not just saying that the experiments are bad for the animals, something to which everyone would agree. He or she is also expressing overall disapproval of the experiments, expecting others also to disapprove if they consider the issue in an impartial way. The trouble is that people react differently to these cases.

Consider the question whether it is good or bad to experiment painfully on animals in order to resolve certain theoretical issues in psychology. The extent to which this is (absolutely) good is the extent to which everyone (apart from any personal stake in the matter) has a reason to try to bring it about that such experiments are done, or to want them to be done, or hope that they are done. The extent to which this is (absolutely) bad is the extent to which everyone (apart from any personal stake) has a reason to try to end the experiments, or want them to end, or hope they end. But naturalism suggests that there is no unique answer here and that what a person has a reason to want will depend on the relative value he or she attaches to animal suffering, to using animals as means, and to theoretical progress in psychology. Different people attach different values to these things without having overlooked something, without being irrational or unreasonable, and so on. So it seems that some people will have reason to be in favor of the experiments and others will have reason to be opposed to the experiments, where this is determined by the personal values of those people. If we suppose that our answer is the right answer, we are merely projecting our own values onto the world.

The Issue Joined

... Clearly the controversy over absolute values parallels the controversy about reasons to do things. The argument against absolute values has the same structure as the relativistic argument about reasons to do things. Its first premise is that a person has a reason to want or hope for or try to bring about a particular state of affairs only to the extent that he or she would be irrational or unreasonable not to want that state of affairs unless he or she was unaware of some relevant consideration, was confused, or had some other specified defect. Its second premise is that, except for the simplest cases, a person can fail to want a given state of affairs without being irrational or unreasonable or ignorant or whatever. The conclusion is that, except possibly for simple cases, where, for example, the only thing relevant is that a creature suffers, there are no reasons everyone has to want or hope for or try to bring about a given state of affairs. So there are no nontrivial absolute values.

As before, the two premises are defended in each case by an appeal to naturalism: We must give a naturalistic account of reasons and we must give empirical grounds for supposing someone to be irrational or unreasonable. The absolutist rejects the argument as before by invoking autonomous ethics, perhaps by rejecting the naturalistic account of reasons, perhaps by rejecting the requirement that scientific grounds must be given for a judgment of irrationality or unreasonableness, possibly remaining undecided between these alternatives.

NATURALISM VERSUS AUTONOMOUS ETHICS

So the issue between relativism and absolutism comes down to the dispute between naturalism and autonomous ethics. Which is the best approach in moral philosophy? Should we concentrate on the place of values and reasons in the world of scientific fact, as naturalism recommends, or should we start with our initial moral beliefs and look for general principles and moral theories that will eventually yield a reflective equilibrium, not putting too much weight on the question of the place of value in the world of facts....

Ethics

Defenders of autonomous ethics argue that their approach represents the only undogmatic way to proceed. They say that naturalism begs the question in supposing that everything true must fit into a scientific account of the world and by supposing that the central question about morality is how, if at all, morality fits into such a scientific account.

Defenders of naturalism reply that... autonomous ethics begs the question by assigning a specially protected status to initial moral beliefs as compared, say, with initial beliefs about the flatness of the earth or the influence of the stars on human history. Naturalists say that, starting with our initial beliefs, we are led to develop a scientific conception of the world as an account of everything there is. In doing so, we also acquire beliefs about how

we learn about the world and about how errors can arise in our thinking. We come to see how superstition arises. We begin to worry about our moral views: Are they mere superstitions? We note certain sorts of disagreement in morality and extreme differences in moral customs. We observe that some people are not much influenced by what we consider important moral considerations. All this leads us to raise as a central question about morality how morality fits in with our scientific conception of the world. Naturalism is no mere prejudice in favor of science; it is an inevitable consequence of intelligent thought. This, at least, is what a defender of naturalism will say.

A defender of autonomous ethics will reply that moral disagreements, differences in custom, and the behavior of criminals prove nothing. All these things are compatible with moral absolutism.

The naturalist retorts that any view can be made *compatible* with the evidence; astrology, for example, is perfectly compatible with the evidence. The issue is not what is compatible with the evidence, but what best accounts for it. The naturalist argues that relativism accounts for the evidence better than absolutism does, since relativism is able to say how reasons and values are part of the world science describes, whereas absolutism is not able to do that....

I see no knockdown argument for either side. A question of judgment is involved, "Which view is more plausible, all things considered?" To me, the relativistic naturalist position seems more plausible. Others find the absolutist position of autonomous ethics more plausible. I have not tried to show that one side is correct. I have tried to bring out the central issue.

Morality Is Objectively True

CAROL ROVANE

For some twenty hundred years, the disjunction between realism and relativism has had Philosophy in its grip. It may be that we simply can't prove either realism or relativism, at least not if that means keeping to the high standard of providing a proof that could not possibly be regarded as question-begging by the other side.

Consider, for example, the following argument against relativism, which is likely to get raised early on in any discussion of the issue. The argument points out that we cannot state that all truths are relative without making the statement itself an exception, thereby repudiating relativism and supporting realism after all. The thought behind this argument seems to be the following one: unless we intend our statement of relativism to be true in the realist sense, we will have failed to express the fact that relativism stands opposed to realism. Prima facie, the thought seems a good one. But before we draw a realist conclusion, we need to view the thought from the relativist's perspective. The relativist will insist that the statement of her thesis should not be interpreted along realist lines, on the ground that doing so would beg the question against her. Apparently, the only way not to beg the question here is to allow that the statement of relativism itself is only relatively true. The realist may try to turn this allowance against relativism, by pointing out that it leaves us free, even by the relativist's lights, to re-assert realism. But a determined relativist can grant this point without regarding herself as refuted. By

her lights, the realist's assertion of realism is only relatively true and, so, can hardly serve to rule out relativism. In response, the realist may echo the response that the relativist had earlier made to her, and insist that her statement of realism should not be interpreted along relativist lines—on the ground that doing so would just as clearly beg the question against her as she had earlier done against the relativist. And so on and on.

If these are the only terms in which we can argue about realism vs. relativism, the issue begins to look like a stand-off in which everyone must ultimately beg the question. Realists may want to point out that their position accords better with a classically conceived logic and with ordinary discourse. But it doesn't follow that they have more right to beg the question on their side. For, insofar as relativists can successfully beg the question on the other side, it is fair to ask that realists do more in order to earn the right to realism than just claim default status.

My aim in this paper is to explore the prospects of earning the right to realism or relativism in the ethical domain, insofar as reasons can be offered on either side that, though they do beg the question, don't *merely* beg the question. In section 1 I'll develop a positive conception of realism that I think is especially well suited to the ethical domain. The heart of this conception is a certain *realist ideal*, according to which there is a single and complete body of truths. I'll be arguing that this ideal constitutes the single most basic dividing point between realists and relativists. Regardless of how else they might want to characterize their respective positions and differences, realists are bound to embrace, while relativists are bound to reject, this realist ideal of a single and complete body of truths. If nothing else, identifying this basic dividing issue should help to clarify the terms of debate. But I will show that the realist ideal also points the way to a *pragmatic conception of realism*. So conceived, realism is a *practical stance* that we can bring to bear in *inquiry*. What makes this an essentially realist stance within an essentially realist project of inquiry is precisely that it is guided by the realist ideal of a single and complete body of truths. What I'm proposing, then, is this: that we frame the issue of realism vs. relativism in ethics in terms of the feasibility and point of this realist ideal, which would motivate a form of ethical inquiry that ethical relativists are fundamentally committed to rejecting. I'll elaborate and defend this proposal in section 1.

My proposal has the effect of transposing the metaphysical issue about realism into one that is also practical, more an issue about how inquirers should proceed, and less about the nature of reality and whether it is or is not epistemically constrained. As I see it, this transposition represents the best hope for realism in ethics. But I'm sure that many philosophers will disagree because, in their view, no position deserves to be called "realist" unless it provides for a conception of the world as it is in itself, independently of how we might take it to be. Bernard Williams calls this the "absolute conception of reality," Thomas Nagel calls it "the view from nowhere," and it is often called "metaphysical realism." On the metaphysical realist view, beliefs and judgments are true just in case they capture the ways things really are—that is, just in case they 'correspond' to the mind-independent facts.

From this metaphysical realist perspective, no view deserves to be counted as a realist view unless it provides a positive account of these "truth-makers."

Let me briefly indicate at the start some of the reasons why I'm going to set aside the doctrine of metaphysical realism.

It is well known that the doctrine invites skepticism. Frankly, I don't see any point in going to the trouble of earning the right to realism in ethics if skepticism is the destination.

Not all metaphysical realists are skeptics. The best example we have of an attempt to earn the right to metaphysical realism without skepticism is scientific realism....

It stands to reason that scientific realism is a poor model for ethical realism. After all, the aims of ethics are very different from the aims of science. While the aims of science are explanatory, the aims of ethics are evaluative. What one wants from an ethical theory is some sort of guidance concerning how one ought to conduct oneself, especially in relation to other people and, more broadly, in relation to anything that has a point of view from which it could be said to matter how we treat it. These different aims bring in train different approaches to the task of theoretical justification. In accordance with the explanatory aims of science, the task of justification there is primarily one of establishing the explanatory adequacy of a given theory with respect to various empirical data that stand in need of such explanation, where this task is closely associated with correct prediction. In contrast, ethical theories tend to look for "foundations" of certain ethical values. Although it could be said that these foundations "explain" why certain ethical values ought to be given priority in our lives, it is a quite different sense of explanation than we find in science. The task is not to predict or otherwise account for empirical data but, rather, to justify certain reasons for action, often in the form of a normative ideal of which our actions fall short.

The favorite candidates for such a foundation in ethics are reason and human nature. The former has been claimed to ground Kantian ethics and some versions of utilitarianism, while the latter has been claimed to ground virtue ethics. Anyone who is convinced of any of these foundationalist ethical theories is thereby bound to regard ethical relativism as untenable. This is especially clear in the case of the rationalist theories proposed by Kantians and utilitarians. Each of these theories provides a single ethical principle that is supposed to determine the truth-value of all of our more specific judgments about what is ethically right or wrong, good or bad. That leaves no room for relativism. I want to urge, therefore, that the proponents of these theories be counted as ethical realists even if they can't satisfy the demands of metaphysical realists to provide a positive account of what the mind-independent ethical "truth-makers" are. However, I'm not going to assume that either Kantian ethics or utilitarianism—or, indeed, anything like these ethical theories—is true. This is partly because they are controversial. But it's also because I'm inclined to take value pluralism seriously. And ethical theories of the sort that would automatically vindicate ethical realism don't typically recognize a significant plurality of ethical values. Obviously, virtue ethics recognizes a greater plurality of ethical values than the Kantian and utilitarian theories do. But virtue ethics will not automatically rule out relativism unless it seeks a foundation for the virtues in human nature. And such a foundation would have a constricting effect on the number and range of virtues that it recognizes. The sort of value pluralism that I'm inclined to take

seriously would be more broad-ranging than that. It would countenance virtues and other values that cannot be said to have a foundation in either reason or human nature. So I would not propose to earn the right to realism in ethics by defending any of the major ethical theories. It may seem that my determination to leave room for a broad-ranging value pluralism stacks the deck against ethical realism. But I don't see why this should be so. I don't see why there couldn't be just as much objectivity in connection with a plurality as there can be in connection with a unity. The evident plurality of natural facts all around us does nothing to undermine the idea that they are objective.

So far, I've explained that I'll be setting aside two strategies for earning the right to realism in ethics: the strategy of modeling ethical realism on scientific realism, and the strategy of establishing the truth of any foundationalist ethical theory....

By setting aside these... strategies, I'm left with the following point of departure. On the one hand, I've improved the prospects for earning the right to realism in ethics by relinquishing the metaphysical ambitions of scientific realism in the ethical domain. But, on the other hand, that gain has been offset by my decision to recognize both a significant plurality of ethical values and a significant diversity of ethical opinion.... It may seem that there is no route from this point of departure to a realist conclusion. But this isn't so. The realist stance that I described above—that is, the commitment to a realist project of ethical inquiry in the light of the realist ideal of a single and complete body of ethical truths—is compatible with both a significant plurality of ethical values and a significant diversity of ethical opinion. And we shall see that it is highly resilient in the face of various arguments for ethical relativism.

In particular, the realist stance is not undermined by Gilbert Harman's argument for moral relativism. His argument rests on a particular account of the foundations of morality, in terms of what self-interested individuals have reason to agree to on the basis of moral bargaining. Harman is certainly right that this account provides for a certain kind of relativity in the ethical domain: some moral judgments have force only relative to specific moral agreements. But, at the same time, the account also provides scope for the sort of ethical inquiry that goes together with the realist stance. In fact, we can get a very clear picture of what a realist project of ethical inquiry might consist in by seeing how it could and should be conducted within Harman's framework. So, not only is it the case that Harman's argument does not undermine the realist stance; it positively invites it....

1. Realism as a Practical Stance

It seems to me that we ought to step back and ask: What is the most basic and minimal commitment that is held in common by different sorts of realists, and that all relativists are committed to denying? If we could identify this basic and minimal realist commitment, then we could formulate a new strategy for settling the issue of realism vs. relativism. We could consider what reasons there are to embrace or reject this basic and minimal realist commitment.

I've already stated what I take this commitment to be, which most fundamentally distinguishes realists from relativists. It is their commitment to the realist ideal of a single and complete body of truths.

Let me now clarify what I take this ideal to consist in. When I say that a body of truths is *complete* I mean: for every well-formed proposition, either it or its negation figures in that body.... I mean well-formed in a very broad sense, according to which a proposition is well formed just in case it is capable of having a truth value. Thus, a body of truths is complete just in case, for every proposition that is capable of having a truth value, either it or its negation figures in it. This idea of completeness can be further qualified by restricting it to specific domains. For example, we can think of a complete body of truths within the domain of facts or within the domain of values, or within the more restricted domains of physical facts, psychological facts, mathematical facts, ethical values, aesthetic values, and so on. If we are prepared to distinguish domains, then we can raise the issue of realism vs. relativism separately in each domain. To embrace realism with respect to a given domain is to hold that there is a single and complete body of truths in that domain. And, if we embrace realism in more than one domain, then the various bodies of truths associated, respectively, with each domain, would together constitute a single and complete body of truths. In other words, they would not be *many* bodies of truths in the sense that interests the relativist. The whole point of relativism is to allow that there can be many bodies of truths that *cannot* be conjoined in accord with the realist ideal of a single and complete body of truths.

I've introduced the idea of a realist *stance*, because I want to draw attention to the fact that the realist ideal is something we can actively embrace and that, when we do so, we must *act* in accord with it. There are two fronts on which its practical implications need to be recognized, namely, inquiry and interpersonal relations.

Inquiring realists hold that there is a single and complete body of truths in the domain (or domains) into which they are inquiring. It follows that there is no well-formed proposition in that domain (or domains) concerning which the question of its truth value does not arise. Any such proposition is, therefore, an appropriate target of investigation. However, it would be wrong to infer that the realist ideal constitutes the proper goal of inquiry. For one thing, it is probably an incoherent goal, since it is probably impossible for finite beings like us to know all of the truths. But even if it were not an incoherent goal, there are many reasons why we might not embrace it. Take the domain of facts. There are certainly truths about the facts that it would be quite useless to know (how many grains of sand are there).... All that the realist stance *per se* commits us to is the idea that there is a single and complete body of truths. And, in most domains, we can retain this commitment even if we happen not to be interested in knowing all of the truths in those domains. Yet even when this is our attitude, the commitment still has practical import. If we do embrace the realist ideal, we shall have to conceive inquiry—the business of acquiring knowledge of the truths in which we *are* interested—in relation to it. It will remain true that there is no well-formed proposition (in the domain of our inquiry) concerning which the question of its truth does not arise. And, insofar as we think our beliefs are true, we must think of them in accord with the realist ideal. That is, we must think of them as figuring in the single and complete body of truths. Likewise whenever we change our minds. Whenever we acquire new beliefs or correct mistaken beliefs, we must think of these epistemic activities as bringing us closer to that ideal.

The practical implications of the realist stance for interpersonal relations are as follows. Once we adopt the stance, we cannot ever be *wholly* indifferent to the views of others. We must always take a stand. If we find that others' views are not conjoinable with ours, then we must either reject theirs as false or change our own minds. (When we change our minds we have two options. Either we can reject our own view as false, or we can suspend belief on the matter. The point is that we are constrained by the realist ideal to do one of these things whenever we are unwilling to reject a conflicting view as false.) And if we find that others' views are different from ours but conjoinable, then we must allow that we may have something to learn from them. Of course, there is no presumption that others are right when they believe a proposition we haven't yet considered. There isn't, any more than there is a presumption that others are right when we disagree. Nor is there any general presumption that we should always be interested in the propositions that others believe but we don't (though, as I've already indicated, there may be reason to presume this in the specific case of ethics). What is presumed—actually that's too weak: what is *built into* the realist stance—is that there is a single ideal in the light of which all of the differences among believers could in principle be sorted out, namely, the one complete body of truths. The realist stance does not exhort us to actually resolve our differences with others (any more than it exhorts us to learn all of the truths). It only requires that we view our differences with others in the light of the realist ideal. As realists, we must hold that whenever disagreements do arise, at most one party can be right. And this, of course, is precisely what the relativist wants to deny.

It should already be clear that relativism can also be characterized as a stance that has significant practical implications. When I adopt the relativist stance, I am free to disregard epistemic differences between me and others in the deepest possible way: I can regard others as neither right nor wrong by my lights. And this is not because I regard myself as ignorant about whether they are right or wrong. It is rather because the sense in which they might be right or wrong has absolutely nothing to do with my own inquiry into what's true. I can view others as seeking something else, namely, *their* truths. Their truths are not conjoinable with mine at all. But I need not, for that reason, reject them as false. They are altogether out of the loop of consideration.

I want to emphasize that it is important not to exaggerate the practical implications of these stances. One very common mistake is to think that relativism instructs us to be tolerant of the views of others, while realism instructs us to be intolerant. But this is not so. Realism does provide the resources for one very common argument in favor of intolerance, which I'll call the argument from righteousness. This argument says that there is one truth and, if I take myself to know that truth, then I have a duty to spread it to everyone else whether they want it or not. But the realist stance doesn't require such an intolerant attitude toward the views of others. It is coherent to embrace the realist ideal of a single and complete body of truths and yet, also, embrace the sorts of moral values that would entail an obligation to be tolerant—values like self-determination and freedom from oppression. Similarly, it is coherent to adopt the relativist stance according to which different people may have different truths and yet, also, embrace the project of trying to stamp out alternative viewpoints. What is clear is that relativism lacks the resources to mount the righteous argument for intolerance that is available to realists. But, nevertheless, relativists have available less righteous grounds for intolerance, such as zeal to get everyone to be just like me.

I hope it is clear, then, that the practical differences between the realist and relativist stances cannot be cashed out in terms of the issue of tolerance. The difference turns on a less morally loaded and more purely epistemic issue. When I adopt the relativist stance, I am free to disregard the views of others as lying completely outside my pursuit of truth. They are utterly irrelevant—so irrelevant that even if they conflict with mine I needn't, for that reason, regard them as false. As I put it earlier, the views of others are simply out of the loop of consideration. But this is not so when I adopt the realist stance. If I'm pursuing truth in the sense that goes together with the realist ideal, then no one's views are ever wholly irrelevant. And this is so even if I am not particularly interested in them. Even so, my critical perspective on my own views must somehow comprehend theirs as well. If their views conflict with mine, I can't hold mine without deeming theirs false. Or, to put the point in its full generality, I must view myself and others as subject to a single standard in the light of which all of our epistemic differences could in principle be sorted out—the single and complete body of truths.

So, my proposal is that we address the issue of realism vs. relativism in the ethical domain by considering the respective merits of these two practical stances in that domain. This is why I call it a pragmatic approach to the issue....

My concern is to see whether we can earn the right to a position in ethics that stands opposed to ethical relativism because it insists that, in all cases of ethical conflict, at most one party is right. It would be very reassuring to get that much objectivity in the ethical domain, even if we couldn't satisfy the metaphysical ambitions that enter into some philosophers' conception of realism. And, in any case, there is at least one good reason to call this sort of objectivist position in ethics a kind of realism. It incorporates the idea that there is something to inquire *about* in the ethical domain—something to get right or wrong, something to know.

2. Harman's Defense of Moral Relativism

I want next to consider whether Gilbert Harman's defense of moral relativism gives us reason to abandon the realist stance in ethics in favor of the relativist stance. We shall see that the reverse is true. Harman's conception of the foundations of morality positively invites the realist stance, along with all of its practical implications for ethical inquiry and interpersonal relations.

On Harman's account, moral rules are the result of moral bargaining. Such rules arise when individuals find self-interested reasons to enter into agreements with others to abide by certain common moral rules. It is undeniable that there are moral agreements in Harman's sense. And he is absolutely right that they provide an occasion for adopting the relativist stance. When we observe that other people subscribe to a different agreement, as outsiders to that agreement we are free to regard what's right or wrong within it as irrelevant to the question what would it be right or wrong for us to do. We can say to ourselves, that's just what they agreed to do and their agreement doesn't bind us in any way. Harman captures this relativist attitude with his notion of an "inner moral judgment," which he defines as a judgment about what it is right or wrong to do in the light of a specific moral agreement. Once we've mastered this notion, we're supposed to recognize that our inner moral judgments can't properly be extended to those who stand outside of the moral agreement(s) to which we are party. And, of course, we know that the same

goes for parties to other agreements; they too must recognize that their inner moral judgments do not extend beyond their agreements. Harman illustrates this relativity of inner moral judgments with a rather unwinning example, in which he points out that it sounds odd to say that Hitler was "wrong" to do the various things he did. It doesn't sound nearly so odd to me as it apparently sounds to him. But I think I see what he means. Hitler does seem to be beyond the reach of a certain *sort* of moral judgment, namely, the sort of inner moral judgment that presupposes that he and we subscribe to the same moral agreement. It is not Harman's aim, however, to show that Hitler is immune from all ethical evaluation on our part. He allows that we can say of him that he was evil.

This allowance should give us pause. If we are capable of ethical responses that are *not* confined to our moral agreements, that should make us wonder whether Harman is right to locate the foundations of morality in such agreements, rather than in our capacity for such wider ethical responses. But, for the sake of argument, I'll assume that he is right to do so. For it will prove instructive to see what does and doesn't follow. It follows that every ethical concept that is now available to us began its life as a by-product of moral bargaining. (Self-interest is the one exception, for obvious reasons.) It also follows that the initial meaning of any given ethical concept incorporates a kind of implicit relativization to the specific moral agreement in which it was first introduced. However, no interesting form of relativism follows unless it can be shown that our ethical concepts are forever confined to their original contexts. And I don't see how this can be shown. More specifically, I don't see how we can rule out the possibility of extending the application of ethical concepts beyond the confines of the moral agreements that originally gave rise to them. It seems obvious to me that this has actually happened. It happened, for example, when we took notions of rights that were originally introduced in the context of the specific moral agreement that is articulated in the U.S. Constitution and, then, used those same notions as a standard for criticizing agreements arrived at in quite different political contexts. A defender of Harman-style relativism might point out that it is always within the rights of those who stand outside our moral agreements to protest that they should not be subjected to the standards of our agreements. This is certainly true; the relativist stance is always available. But that doesn't end the matter. For, as I shall now argue, Harman's highly rationalistic account of the foundations of morality invites us to frame and pursue a project of ethical inquiry that is essentially realist in spirit.

Agents who have the requisite rational capacities to devise and implement moral agreements in Harman's sense must surely also have general capacities for critical reflection. And, so, even if they begin by uncritically accepting the ethical concepts that figure in their own moral agreements, there is no reason why they couldn't or shouldn't subject them to critical scrutiny. Of course, within Harman's framework the only possible source of such critical insight is other moral agreements to which one is not a party. But this is a perfectly good source. There is nothing to stop us from learning about other moral agreements to which we are not a party, and thereby acquiring conceptual resources for adopting a critical perspective on our own moral agreements. And it is important to see that such a critical perspective would not coincide with the moral perspective that is supplied by the particular moral agreement to which one is a party. It is a

more comprehensive critical perspective from which one can make comparative judgements about whether one's own moral agreement is better or worse than some others. It is also important to see that this more comprehensive critical perspective need not coincide with the perspective of self-interest that one occupies while contemplating whether to enter into a given moral agreement. I can certainly ask whether someone else's agreement would be better for me than the one to which I am a party. But there are other critical issues I can raise as well. To take a realistic example, consider a woman who is party to a moral agreement that systematically oppresses women. It is in her self-interest to abide by this agreement not because it serves her interests so very well, but because she has no better option. After having made the agreement and lived by it, she comes to learn about a different moral agreement in which women are given the same rights to education, property and self-determination as men. And she thinks to herself, that's a better agreement. Perhaps this thought begins as a self-interested wish that her agreement were more like that one, or that she were a party to that one rather than her own. But she also has the conceptual resources to think that that agreement is simply fairer. I've assumed for the sake of argument that the notion of fairness is itself a by-product of moral bargaining and, so, must have begun its life relativized to a particular moral agreement. But the point remains that it can also provide a perfectly reasonable standard by which we can make comparative judgments *about* moral agreements. When we make these comparative judgments, we are taking conceptual resources that, by assumption, have been supplied by *different* agreements and we are incorporating them into a *single* critical perspective. This constitutes a move away from the relativist stance, toward the sort of ethical inquiry that would go together with the realist stance.

It might be objected that this sort of ethical inquiry needn't be fully committed to the realist ideal according to which *all* ethical differences could in principle be sorted out. Perhaps it needn't be. But, once we've begun the task of critical reflection, it is unclear why we should ever bring it to a halt. That is, it is unclear why, once we've begun the process of comparative evaluation of different moral agreements and their different terms, we should regard any of the ethical differences we find as falling outside the constraints that are imposed by the realist ideal. Either they are the sorts of differences that are conjoinable, or they are conflicts that need to be resolved. We needn't be committed to the idea that we will always know how to resolve such conflicts in order to cleave to the realist stance. We need only be committed to the idea that there is something to resolve. And, it should be borne in mind that there are more ways to resolve conflicts among evaluative attitudes than among beliefs. Instead of giving up one or other of the conflicting values, we can resolve the conflict by ranking them in relative importance. It should also be borne in mind that some ethical conflicts aren't really significant from the point of view of the realist ideal. I'm thinking of the sort of conflict that arises when we rank several ethical values as equally important and yet, due to contingent practical limitations, we find that we can't pursue them all together. The fact that we must choose among them for this reason does not signify that they wouldn't all figure in the single and complete body of ethical truths. And, more generally, the fact that there are all of these ways to interpret and cope with ethical conflict should help to strengthen our confidence

in the feasibility of the realist project of ethical inquiry.

The specific approach to this project that I've proposed as a response to Harman is not the only possible approach. I think that anyone working in the contractarian tradition of moral and political philosophy who doesn't share Harman's relativism is carrying out what is, essentially, a realist project of ethical inquiry. These contractarians seek an answer to the very same question that would guide the inquiry I just described, namely, what is the best moral agreement? The main difference is that they tend to give a narrow interpretation to the term "best" as meaning something like "serves everyone's interests in the most optimal way," and they tend to take a highly rationalistic approach to establishing what is best in this narrow sense. It is important to see that this familiar contractarian endeavor qualifies as ethical inquiry in the realist mode. But it is also important to see that the alternative approach that I've described here is also available. On this approach, ethical inquiry can be far more empirical, insofar as it undertakes to make many specific and substantive comparisons between actual moral agreements using their own terms....

We're bound to come across ethical difference. And I don't see how we could possibly respond without adopting one stance or the other, the realist or the relativist. We will have to choose. Furthermore, when we choose, we should want to do more than *merely* beg the question on the side we prefer. We should want to earn the right to our chosen stance. Obviously, we can't do this without addressing the question on which I've recommended that we suspend belief: is our actual condition the condition in which the relativist stance would be warranted? This is an empirical question. And the only way to answer it is by pursuing the realist project of ethical inquiry. We need to learn about values that figure in other forms of life and try to make comparative evaluations. Of course, what the ethical realist hopes to gain from these comparisons is ethical illumination, perhaps in the form of learning about new practical possibilities that we might pursue, or in the form of a deeper understanding of (or even correction of) our evaluative commitments. But it may be that ethical inquiry will fail to deliver such illumination. If a sustained attempt at such inquiry failed to deliver anything of ethical interest, then we could in retrospect say that the realist stance had, after all, been pointless. This is important. It shows that the realist stance does not prejudge the central issue on which its warrant would ultimately depend. In contrast, the relativist stance does prejudge the issue—at least in fact, if not in intention. It would foreclose the realist project of ethical inquiry. And that would prevent us from discovering the extent to which the project does or does not have a point. This is something we need to discover and know. Because this is so, we have reason, at least at the present time, to prefer the realist stance in ethics over the relativist stance.

I have tried to transpose the virtues of realism as being those of the nature of inquiry rather than directly of a certain conception of epistemically unconstrained reality, and I have tried to do so in a way that, unlike Peirce, does not make any idealized end point of inquiry the licit surrogate of the idea of such an unconstrained conception of reality. It's not as if, by stressing inquiry and having criticized the contractarian tradition, I have tried to find a licit surrogate for their notion of a discoverable, contractable ideal in some Whiggish *consummation* of the *progress* that the path of ethical inquiry might take. No notions of progress, and no ideal consummation inform the realist project of ethical inquiry that I have tried to formulate. Nevertheless it is in inquiry, and its pursuit under the realist stance that I have elaborated and defended, that the doctrine of ethical realism will flourish, if it does.

THE CONTINUING DEBATE:
Is Morality Relative to Culture *or* Objectively and Universally True?

What Is New

Recent issues in medical ethics raise important questions concerning cultural relativity. Although beneficent paternalism was standard practice until recent decades, the doctrine of individual informed consent is now central to contemporary Western medical ethics: Every competent adult patient has the right to make his or her own informed and uncoerced choice concerning what treatment to have (or not to have). But the principle is not universally accepted, and in some cultures it is regarded as wrong to inform people of bad prognoses: Patients must always be told they will get better, and detailed information is kept by the physician (or perhaps is given to a tribal or community leader or to the patient's family) who makes the decision on behalf of the patient. With patients from throughout the world arriving at major Western hospitals daily, these issues of cultural relativism have immediate consequences.

Where to Find More

The anthropologist Ruth Benedict was a major advocate of cultural relativism; see her *Patterns of Culture* (NY: Penguin, 1934). Mary Midgley offers a well-crafted critique of cultural relativism in *Heart and Mind* (NY: St. Martin's Press,1981).

More on Gilbert Harman's relativism can be found in his "Moral Relativism Defended," *The Philosophical Review*, volume 84 (1975); *The Nature of Morality: An Introduction to Ethics* (NY: Oxford University Press, 1977); and in *Explaining Value and Other Essays in Moral Philosophy* (Oxford: Clarendon Press, 2000). Steven Darwall critiques Harman's relativism in "Harman and Moral Relativism," *The Personalist*, volume 58 (1977). Hugh LaFollette, "The Truth in Ethical Relativism," *Journal of Social Philosophy*, volume 22, number 1 (Spring, 1991), offers a spirited defense of "rational relativist ethics." Gilbert Harman and Judith Jarvis Thomson debate moral relativism vs. moral objectivism in *Moral Relativism and Moral Objectivity* (Oxford: Blackwell, 1996).

Nicholas Sturgeon criticizes the "argument from disagreement" (the argument that cultural disagreement provides support for *normative* cultural relativism) in "Moral Disagreement and Moral Relativism," *Social Philosophy and Policy*, volume 20 (1994). James A. Ryan recasts the argument and defends it from Sturgeon's criticisms in "Moral Relativism and the Argument from Disagreement," *Social Philosophy and Policy*, volume 34 (2003).

Herbert Feigl presents a strong argument that our most basic value principles are "relative," in the sense that no real argument can be given for or against them, and disagreements at that level cannot be rationally resolved; see his "Validation and Vindication," in C. Sellars and J. Hospers, eds., *Readings in Ethical Theory* (NY: Appleton-Century-Crofts, 1952); and "'De Principiis non Disputandum...?' On the Meaning and the Limits of Justification," in Max Black, ed., *Philosophical Analysis* (Ithaca, NY: Cornell University Press, 1950).

A good anthology—containing works by both philosophers and anthropologists—is Michael Krausz, editor, *Relativism: Interpretation and Conflict* (Notre Dame:

University of Notre Dame Press, 1989). Another excellent collection is by Paul K. Moser and Thomas L. Carson, editors, *Moral Relativism: A Reader* (NY: Oxford University Press, 2001).

A review of recent work on moral relativism, primarily examining work by philosophers, is Robert M. Stewart and Lynn L. Thomas, "Recent Work on Ethical Relativism," *American Philosophical Quarterly*, volume 28 (April, 1991).

The extensive bioethical literature on cross-cultural issues includes A. Surbone, "Letter from Italy: Truth Telling to the Patient," *Journal of the American Medical Association*, volume 268 (1992); N. S. Jecker, J. A. Carrese, and R. A. Pearlman, "Caring for Patients in Cross-Cultural Settings," *Hastings Center Report*, volume 25 (1995); and Bernard Freedman, "Offering Truth: One Ethical Approach to the Uninformed Cancer Patient," in G. E. Henderson, N. M. P. King, R. P., Strauss, S. E. Estroff, and L. R. Churchill, editors, *The Social Medicine Reader* (Durham, NC: Duke University Press, 1997).

The debate over relativism in anthropology (debate 14) is obviously closely connected to the present debate, and the readings cited there should be examined; and Richard Rorty, though he himself rejects the classification of relativist, is often considered a relativist, and the issues raised in debate 12 are relevant to this debate over relativism. The "autonomous ethics" position that Harman opposes is championed by Virginia Held in debate 10 (though of course Held might not accept Harman's detailed characterization of autonomous ethics).

14   IS CULTURAL RELATIVISM
A HELPFUL APPROACH TO ETHICS?

ETHICAL CULTURAL RELATIVISM SHOULD BE REJECTED

ADVOCATE: Ruth Macklin, Professor and Head of the Division of Philosophy and History of Medicine, Department of Epidemiology and Population Health, Albert Einstein College of Medicine; member of many important national and international advisory boards and committees; author of *Double Standards in Medical Research in Developing Countries* (Cambridge: Cambridge University Press, 2005), and *Enemies of Patients* (NY: Oxford University Press, 1993).

SOURCE: *Against Relativism: Cultural Diversity and the Search for Ethical Universals in Medicine* (NY: Oxford University Press, 1999)

ETHICAL CULTURAL RELATIVISM HAS SOME ADVANTAGES

ADVOCATE: Elvin Hatch, Department of Anthropology, University of California Santa Barbara, specializes in the history and theory of cultural anthropology and the study of small communities; among his many works are *Culture and Morality: The Relativity of Values in Anthropology* (NY: Columbia University Press, 1983).

SOURCE: "The Good Side of Relativism," *Journal of Anthropological Research*, volume 53, 1997: 371–381.

Cultural relativism is a major research principle in contemporary anthropology. That is, cultural anthropologists start from the working assumption that their role is not to judge or reform cultures and communities, but instead to understand their relations and structures: it is impossible to act as an accurate and unobtrusive and accepted observer while simultaneously pushing for fundamental cultural changes. Closely connected is the recognition that careful nonjudgmental study of cultures may reveal that elements of the culture initially perceived as cruel and callous take on new meaning when the larger cultural context is better understood. The classic example was the apparently cruel abandonment of the elderly among nomadic arctic tribes; understood in the larger context of a culture adapted to survival in the severe conditions of the Arctic environment, this is understood as the deeply grieved leaving of tribal members who cannot successfully travel with the group, a sadly necessary cultural strategy to prevent the starvation death of the entire tribe.

    The benefits to anthropology of the cultural relativism methodology notwithstanding, the process has obvious limits when recommended as a broader ethical principle. If torture or the abuse of women or a rigid caste system are part of a cultural tradition, then the culture must be questioned. Nor can we justify the brutal racist apartheid practices of South Africa or the American South on grounds of cultural relativism. Of course such cultural practices are often challenged and changed from within the culture: Gandhi led the struggle against the caste system of India, and Nelson Mandela and Bishop Tutu and many other South Africans showed great courage in their fight against apartheid. But pressure from outside can also be beneficial in facilitating reform, and that support is often welcomed by the internal reformers. During the American civil rights movement of the 1950's and 60's, Southern defenders of racial discrimination and racist injustice condemned Northern civil rights workers as "outside agitators," who had no business interfering with the "traditional Southern culture"; but cultural relativism cannot legitimize such practices, and efforts by "outsiders" to correct such wrongs is often justified, and perhaps sometimes morally mandatory.

However, some people believe that the pendulum has now swung too far in the other direction. Thus while not actually defending cultural relativism, they may dispute some of the stronger claims of those who condemn cultural relativism; that is (in the phrase of the distinguished anthropologist Clifford Geertz), rather than pro-cultural relativism, they are anti-anti-relativism. They counsel that understanding evolving cultures is a complicated process, and that—while some cultural practices are certainly worthy of condemnation—the strong temptation to condemn any practice different from our own should be resisted. While changing cultural practices that involve mistreatment of women, for example, is a positive development, too often the "reform" agenda also includes imposing a radically individualist Western economic pattern that undercuts social support systems, destroys effective subsistence economic practices, and leaves people—particularly the poorest indigenous groups—vulnerable to economic exploitation. Thus the recognition of universal human rights is in itself a positive good—and a facile "relativism" that blocks such recognition can impede important reforms—but it is also important to recognize the genuine and enormously complicated problems that are involved in transforming cultures and cultural practices.

POINTS TO PONDER

➢ Ruth Macklin considers the possibility that in cultures where violence against women is approved, such violence "is a telling example of exploitation of the powerful over the less powerful, but it does not represent a *cultural* tradition in the true sense of the term." Macklin rejects that claim, arguing that it depends on an "intuitive grasp" of what is cultural and "intuition is a notoriously poor guide to anything." Could there be better evidence for a distinction between what is *cultural* and what is merely opportunistic exploitation?

➢ Macklin believes that while some values may be relative to culture, practices that violate human rights are objectively and universally wrong. Elvin Hatch promotes a more skeptical position, but does he *deny* Macklin's view?

➢ Elvin Hatch asserts that "the very search for universal human rights today rests upon a relativistic position." Could Macklin accept that claim? Does Hatch's claim *undercut* or *support* the effort to establish universal human rights?

➢ Execution of juveniles is almost universally condemned as a severe violation of basic human rights: it is legally permitted only in Somalia and the United States. Would it be legitimate for other countries to exert pressure on the United States to reform its cultural practice of capital punishment of juveniles? Would such pressure be effective?

Ethical Cultural Relativism Should Be Rejected

RUTH MACKLIN

A long-standing debate surrounds the question whether ethics are relative to time and place. One side argues that there is no obvious source of a universal morality and that ethical rightness and wrongness are products of their cultural and historical setting. Opponents claim that even if a universal set of ethical norms has not yet been articulated or agreed upon, ethical relativism is a pernicious doctrine that must be rejected. The first group replies that the search for universal ethical precepts is a quest for the Holy Grail. The second group responds with the telling charge: If ethics were relative to time, place, and culture, then what the Nazis did was "right" for them, and there is no basis for moral criticism by anyone outside the Nazi society.

Both sides of this unsophisticated version of the debate appear to capture a kernel of truth. There is no denying that different cultures and historical eras exhibit a variety of moral beliefs and practices. The empirical facts revealed by anthropological research yield the descriptive thesis known as *cultural relativity*. But even if we grant that cultural relativity is an accurate description of the world's diversity, whether anything follows for normative ethics is an entirely different question. Do the facts of cultural relativity compel the conclusion that what is right or wrong can be determined only by the beliefs and practices within a particular culture or subculture? Does it mean that there can be no overarching ethical principles that could be used to assess the rightness or wrong-

ness of actions or practices in different places or at different times?...

Consider the following practices: female genital mutilation; requirement of husbands' permission for their wives to participate in research; self-immolation of widows in India. Female genital mutilation (politely but misleadingly termed "female circumcision" or "surgery") is a ritual practiced in some African countries. Its defenders dismiss Western condemnation as a misplaced failure to show respect for African traditions. Spousal authorization for medical procedures is a commonly accepted custom in many developing countries, and its defenders contend that the custom embodies the traditional marital roles of husband and wife. Self-immolation of widows in India is also defended by an appeal to the significance of the marital bond in Hindu religion and morality (however, there is no corresponding tradition of self-immolation of widowers). In addition, apologists contend that it is a genuinely voluntary act on the part of a newly widowed woman. A defender of any of these customs can point to cultural significance, tradition, or religion. But even if such customs can be distinguished from raw exercise of power or exploitation by the strong over the weak, why should the defense that they are religious or cultural traditions render them immune from moral criticism by outsiders to the culture?...

People make cross-cultural ethical judgments all the time. Westerners criticize authoritarian nations that prohibit political dissent and imprison political opponents. International moral outrage followed the reports of ethnic cleansing in Bosnia and the rape of Muslim women by soldiers as a deliberate weapon of war during that bloody conflict. Women and men throughout the world contend that female circumcision both harms and wrongs the girls and women who are subjected to it, and even defenders of women's right to abortion affirm their opposition to forced abortions that have occurred in China. Although defenders of each of these practices can be found within the culture or country where the conduct occurs, there is something about these actions that prompts almost universal condemnation. The justifications that underlie these ethical judgments rely on fundamental principles that I maintain can be universally applied. And those principles are the underpinnings of at least some of what are recognized today as human rights.

It is sometimes hard to tell whether a rejection of cross-cultural judgments stems from a postmodern challenge to ethical universality or from a concern for politically oppressed minorities. There is often a tendency to defend the actions of marginalized groups even if those same actions would be condemned if carried out by the dominant or more powerful group. I participated in a meeting in Chile in which a young woman told a story that shocked my Western (or "Northern," to use the currently preferred term) ethical sensibilities. The majority of Chileans are of European origin, but there remain a few scattered indigenous groups outside the large cities. One such group continues to practice a traditional ritual in which newborn infants are sacrificed. The government of Chile forbade this practice by law and succeeded in bringing it to a halt. But when the region where the indigenous group dwelt experienced a severe drought, causing suffering and hardship to the peo-

ple, they contended that the gods were punishing them for their failure to carry on the ritual sacrifices required by their religion and blamed the state for its prohibition of human sacrifice.

The woman who recounted this story defended the stance of this ethnic group and condemned the government for imposing its power and authority on the weaker indigenous group. I countered by saying that the group was doing something ethically unacceptable in killing babies and, further, that there was no scientific validity to their belief that human sacrifice could prevent drought or that to resume the sacrifice would end the drought. In reply, the woman who had told the story scorned my ethical concerns and considered me an unenlightened victim of narrow Western (Northern) scientific and ethical dogmatism. "That is their belief; the belief in modem science is your belief. Both are simply beliefs." Scientific notions of causality have no more validity than ethical judgments. Both are up for grabs. This position illustrates a form of "epistemological" relativism, distinct from yet related to ethical relativism. Epistemological relativism is the view that systems of belief about the natural world differ from one culture to another and so, too, do the ways of justifying beliefs about "matters of fact." No one belief system can be held to be more valid than the next. Beliefs based on modern science are no more true than beliefs based on myth or superstition.

Although it is indisputable that different nations, cultures, and religious and ethnic groups adhere to different norms of behavior, it is possible to analyze individual conduct and social practices by seeing how they conform to fundamental ethical principles. Whether those principles are universal, applicable to all societies at all times in history, is a matter of ongoing debate. Whether general ethical principles are so vague and indeterminate as to be useless is another point of contention. It is certainly the case that general principles are open to a variety of particular interpretations, and these have evolved over time.

Consider, for example, one of the leading principles in bioethics, "respect for persons." This general principle is open to interpretations that depart from the most common Western version that focuses on individual autonomy. Even the idea that there is a single "Western" concept of autonomy has been challenged....

I define *autonomy* as "the human capacity for self-rule or self-determination." Following from this definition is the moral principle that *the autonomy of persons ought to be respected.*

This, in turn, poses the further challenge of understanding the concept of a "person," a task that has occupied philosophers throughout the ages. While I recognize that certain metaphysical assumptions underlie the position I develop, I have chosen to avoid a digression into metaphysics in this book. Nevertheless, it is critically important to distinguish between the claim that the concept of a "person" does not have a single, unequivocal meaning (which may be true even within a single culture) and the quite different claim that the *value* accorded the individual person varies from one society or culture to another. It is undeniable that some societies place the interests of the community or group over the interests of the individual person, whereas it is often noted that the United States is a country in which the individual "reigns supreme." When the interests of the larger group ought to take precedence over those of the individual is an important question of normative ethics, and the answer may vary from one place to another. But it would be an uncritical concession to ethical relativism to say that whatever value a particular society accords to individuals is therefore morally right.

The contrast between the Western world and the East is frequently noted in this connection. A Chinese colleague mentioned that "respect for persons" has a long history in China and is part of the Confucian heritage. He acknowledged, however, that the traditional Chinese interpretation of the "respect for persons" principle did not include autonomy. It is also unlikely that the principle in China has traditionally been understood to include *equal* respect for persons, which would grant full status to women. Analogously, Islamic scholars contend that the Koran contains many points of Islamic law that require respect for women as persons, but that respect does not extend to granting women decision-making autonomy. Historically, of course, the interpretation that mandates equal respect for women has not prevailed in the West either. This poses the related question of historical ethical relativism: Is ethics relative to the historical time in which actions and practices that are today considered unethical were widely practiced and considered to be right?...

Within cultures as well as across cultures, some ethical values have greater importance than others. Some ethical matters deal with basic ways human beings treat each other, whereas others shade into what is more like etiquette. The recognition of different levels of ethical significance enables a case to be made for a modified form of ethical relativism. To reject an ethically unacceptable brand of relativism—the extreme version—does not require us to accept the view that no ethical values whatsoever can be relative to a culture or region. An example of this middle ground between ethical universalism and ethical relativism is the difference in how privacy and confidentiality are viewed in China and elsewhere in Asia in contrast to in the West.

In daily life the traditional Chinese culture has not recognized or respected either informational privacy or physical privacy. A rather trivial yet amusing example, recounted by a North American woman who was living in China, was an experience she had in the workplace. As in many countries, people often bring their lunch to work. My colleague was surprised to find her coworkers opening up each others' lunch bags (including her own) to find out their contents. In the United States, the contents of a lunch bag are normally not viewed as something intimate or intrinsically private. When lunchtime rolls around, coworkers sit at a table and display for all to see what they have brought for lunch. But it would surely violate a cultural norm for someone in this country to peer into the lunchbag of another without asking permission. Would it be an ethical transgression? It would surely be less of an invasion of privacy than reading another person's diary or looking through the contents of someone's desk drawers. But in our culture, to peer into a coworker's lunchbag without permission would be a transgression of someone's personal property and therefore, an invasion of privacy. We value informational privacy and spatial privacy, and place a high value on personal property. In the West, we elevate the protection of these forms of privacy to a "right"; but surely a glimpse into a coworker's lunchbag is not a violation of a basic right. It involves a social norm—something a bit more serious than mere etiquette, yet surely not approaching the level of a violation of a universal ethical principle.

Although respect for privacy is much more a Western value, even in China and other Eastern cultures some respect for boundaries is an accepted norm. A Chinese colleague recounted this next example during a visit I made to China. Patients who were unclothed or partially clothed were subjected to a medical examination in full view of a group of visitors to the hospital. Despite their manifest discomfort, they submitted to this indignity without complaint because their physicians told them that visitors were to observe the medical exams. Physicians in China are so revered and respected that patients almost always comply with their orders. But the discomfort of the patients demonstrated that bodily privacy is a boundary that would not be overstepped even in China were it not for the authority commanded by the physician.

However, embarrassment over intrusions of bodily privacy might not extend to other realms. In the early 1970s an American colleague visited China to study the health care delivery system there. When he saw the names of patients, along with their diagnoses, displayed in a public place, he inquired through his interpreter whether the people did not consider this an invasion of their privacy. The interpreter replied that he could not properly translate the question because there was no word for privacy in Mandarin Chinese. If the language lacks a word for privacy, it is a foregone conclusion that ethical prohibitions relating to privacy will be similarly lacking. Yet it does not follow that there is no way of describing and ultimately condemning the Chinese doctor's action of ordering his patients to undergo medical examinations in front of strangers. Perhaps the Confucian version of the principle "respect for persons" could justify moral condemnation of the physician's behavior. It is the Western version of the same principle that provides a basis for making ethical judgments relating to privacy in our own culture....

Cultural relativity is apparent in other situations concerning informational privacy. Breaches of confidentiality that would be viewed as wrong in the West are taken for granted and widely accepted in China. One example is the public postings of women's menstrual cycles, not only in the hospital or clinic but also in the workplace. The factory or work unit is frequently the site of various forms of health care monitoring and delivery. This arrangement accounts, in part, for the well-developed health infrastructure in China. In this typical circumstance, disclosure of personal or intimate information about health status is expected and does not, as a rule, have harmful consequences to the individual whose data are made public. According to Western values, however, individuals would be wronged, even if they are not harmed, in these situations of disclosure of personal health-related information.

Nevertheless, in China as in the West, some breaches of confidentiality could harm the individual and would then be regarded as wrong. An example that came out in a meeting with researchers on human sexuality and AIDS was that of disclosure to the work unit leader that a worker was HIV positive. This resulted in the worker's dismissal from his job and possible inability to obtain another job. Even though the Chinese government and employers defend the requirement that physicians report to employers any individuals tested for HIV and found to be positive, the breach of confidentiality is considered ethically unacceptable by the Chinese academics with whom I spoke because of the social and economic harm it typically produces for the affected individuals and possibly also their families.

In a culture like China's, where there is no recognized right to privacy or confidentiality, to invade an individual's privacy or to breach confidentiality would not automatically be viewed as wrong. This is partly because of norms that have prevailed for centuries, reflecting the different status of the individual in Western and Eastern cultures. Even in our Western philosophical tradition, privacy seems to be a middle-level concept rather than a fundamental ethical value like liberty. Privacy does appear to be a culturally relative value, one that can vary from one culture to the next without violating a fundamental ethical principle. However, when the invasion of privacy or breach of confidentiality causes demonstrable physical, psychological, or social harm to the individual, as in the examples given earlier, then it can be judged ethically wrong because of these harms and not because it is a violation of a fundamental right to privacy....

To determine whether cross-cultural judgments are sound requires taking a step beyond the type of ethical analysis used for moral judgments normally made within a cultural context. In the intracultural situation, we begin with a description of the act or practice under scrutiny. The analysis starts with a value-neutral description, insofar as that is possible. (Some may argue that value-neutral descriptions are never possible, but I think that view is mistaken.) The analysis proceeds by identifying relevant facts and background circumstances, including an account of why this information is morally relevant. What counts as a justification will depend on which ethical theory, principles, perspective, or approach one takes when conducting an ethical analysis. Adherents of ethical principles employ one or more of the well-known quartet in bioethics; a rights theorist looks to see which, if any, rights have been violated; a casuist presumably begins without principles or theories, but those elements often lurk in the background and come to the fore at the point of final justification. Feminists use one of the approaches that have come to be associated with the various versions of feminist ethics: examining power relations between men and women and oppression of women, making the notion of "caring" central to the analysis or emphasizing "gender awareness" and "gender sensitivity."

What all these approaches have in common is the presumption that, given a shared cultural background, ethical judgments are both meaningful and valid. A moral nihilist rejects the possibility of ethical judgments altogether, as does the radical subjectivist. If the subjectivist's views can be characterized as "What's right for me is right for me, what's right for you is right for you," then criticisms of another's actions always lack validity or, worse, are altogether meaningless. There is no point to even talking about ethics. But if we begin with the assumption that making moral judgments of other people's actions is a legitimate enterprise, then the task is to justify such judgments by appealing to some shared values.

We have to start somewhere. If shared moral values do exist within cultures, what is the source of moral disagreement when that occurs? At least three obvious sources of disagreement are evident when controversies exist within a country or culture. The first lies in disagreement about facts or probabilities in the situation under analysis. Ethical debates that rely on assessments of the consequences of an action or policy typically illustrate this sort of disagreement. For example, opponents in recent debates concerning the acceptability of physician-assisted suicide dispute what would happen if physicians were legally permitted to help their patients to die. One side argues that physicians would be all too willing to save time and money caring for chronically ill patients and would write lethal prescriptions for vulnerable, elderly patients whose suffering could be relieved by more attention to palliative care. The other side envisions a different set of consequences, whereby only those patients suffering untreatable pain would be given the lethal prescriptions, and careful safeguards would prevent abuse.

The second type of disagreement surrounds the moral status of entities central to the case or situation. The abortion controversy is one case in point, where the moral status of embryonic or fetal life is disputed. Another example is that of anencephalic infants as a source of organs for transplantation. One side argues that anencephalic infants lack a brain and will inevitably die in a short while and therefore have a "lower" moral status that can permit taking their organs to save the lives of other infants. Opponents claim that the anencephalic is still a human infant and deserves the same respect as other living beings, from whom organs may not be removed until after death.

The third source of disagreement occurs when people place different priorities on values or principles that conflict in a particular situation. An example is the controversy about overriding Jehovah's Witnesses parents' refusal of a blood transfusion for their child and other cases in which parents refuse to consent to a treatment. One side argues that parents' rights over their minor children extend to refusal of medical treatments—even those deemed necessary to preserve life, while the other side places limits on parental decision-making. Both sides recognize parental rights of decision-making in general, but they disagree over whether the value of preserving a child's life or health may override that of respect for parental authority.

One or more of these sources of disagreement may be present in any ethical controversy. Sometimes an ethical resolution is possible in these different types of intracultural disagreement, and sometimes it is not. The contribution that a clear ethical analysis can make is to identify the source or sources of disagreement and thereby determine whether a resolution can be forthcoming. In cross-cultural ethical judgments, an additional step is necessary. That is the task of showing that ethical concepts or perspectives from outside the culture's accepted value framework are (or ought to be) relevant and applicable to the culture's traditions and practices. One way this could be done is to demonstrate that the culture already recognizes this particular ethical value in another sphere of activity but has so far neglected to apply that ethical concept to the practice under scrutiny, as the following example from our own history demonstrates.

The subsequent granting of rights to groups that were initially denied those rights illustrates the evolution of this moral concept. The Constitution and the Bill of Rights established the centrality of individual rights under the U.S. legal system. But amendments were needed before basic constitutional provisions, such as the right to liberty, were held to be applicable to black as well as to white Americans and the right to vote was applied to women and to former slaves as well as to white men. People from other cultures with a very different history contend that individualism is taken to an extreme in the United States and that this excessive individualism is unique to our culture. Critics from Asian and African countries claim that their cultures have legitimate values that depart from American individualism.

Their lack of recognition of all of the rights embedded in American society is not an ethical deficiency, they claim, but a cultural difference.

Of course it is hard, if not impossible, to escape one's own cultural biases. At the same time, changes take place within cultures when a visionary or courageous group seeks to alter the status quo. The women's movement in developing countries around the world today demonstrates how groups within a culture can come to recognize as injustice behavior that the majority in the culture takes for granted as "natural," inevitable, or part of its traditional heritage. Examples from two different countries are illustrative.

In the Philippines, many people perceive diseases that afflict them as "natural" and, therefore, not subject to control. This perception exists on the part of people who use the services of traditional healers as well as the healers themselves. This is one manifestation of a tendency toward "fatalism" as a general cultural trait. Many Filipinos believe that "God will take care of things," an attitude reflected in the broader cultural phenomenon of lack of planning for the future. A fatalistic attitude or a resigned acceptance of the status quo extends to human affairs as well as to natural phenomena like the periodic eruptions of Mount Pinatubo, the volcano. People's perceptions of what is not subject to control or change also includes violence women experience at the hands of men. Battering of women is a serious and widespread problem. Yet because it has been a long-standing practice in Filipino culture, it is viewed as "natural." Interestingly, during the period surrounding the birth of a child women are granted special "concessions" by men. Uncharacteristically, men perform household chores during this period. Also during this period they refrain from beating their wives. However, these special concessions do not last beyond the postpartum period.

As in many other developing countries, women's health activists in the Philippines are seeking to change the traditional healers' view that violence against women is "natural" and that efforts to change this pattern would be futile. Women's health advocates also work at the grassroots level directly with women, trying to empower women within the family and the community. But first they must tackle the fundamental belief that underlies an acceptance of violence against women, the belief that such behavior is "natural" and therefore cannot be changed. If non-Filipinos were to propose attempts to change such beliefs and the violence that flows from them, the outsiders might be criticized for trying to impose alien beliefs and to change cultural traditions. That has been the response in Africa—including by some African women—to the concerns of Western feminists about female genital mutilation.

A popular stereotype holds that Mexican and other Latin cultures are traditionally *macho* in their attitude toward women. Accounts by women activists in Mexico depict the dominant value of *machismo* that creates in men a desire to prove their masculinity by having many children. Whether it is their wives or their mistresses who bear the children, credit goes to the men for fathering numerous offspring. A Mexican social anthropologist notes that the prevalent values of patriarchal Mexican culture make the roles of motherhood and fatherhood central elements in the gender construction of masculinity and femininity: "Until recent years, popular sayings included: 'To be a man is to be the father of more than four.'" A saying pertaining to women is considerably less charitable: "Women... were to be kept 'like shotguns, loaded and

in the corner.' That is to say, pregnant and marginalized when it came to important matters."

In both the Filipino and Mexican situations, dominant cultural beliefs and practices have perpetuated violence or other forms of coercion directed at women. If dominant cultural patterns deserve respect and continued adherence, as ethical relativism would appear to dictate, what can be the basis for an ethical critique of those practices? Must we conclude that violence against women is ethically permissible as an expression of dominant cultural values? A defender of "respect for tradition" might reply that these are not genuine examples of cultural traditions. Not every attitude or practice within a culture embodies a tradition in the way that religious and other rituals do. Violence against and domination of women in Mexico and the Philippines is a telling example of exploitation of the powerful over the less powerful, but it does not represent a *cultural* tradition in the true sense of the term. Violence against women exists in every culture, even in societies that profess gender equality and strive through laws and other reforms to achieve gender justice.

This reply is reasonable, but it relies on the intuitive ability to grasp the difference between treatment of women that embodies a genuine cultural tradition of distribution of gender roles, on the one hand, and the abuse by men of their greater power and authority, on the other. However, intuition is a notoriously poor guide to anything. Consider the following example from China, a country that retains a strong Confucian tradition despite the overlay of a half-century of Communist rule. This example demonstrates the power of the mother-in-law in an alliance with her son. At a meeting of Chinese reproductive health professionals and policymakers, a physician described the case as "an old example from years ago."

A woman in a village had three children, all girls. She did not want more children, but her husband and mother-in-law did not want her to be sterilized. They wanted her to continue having children. The ethical issue was presented as a dilemma for the physician: Should she sterilize the woman or follow the wishes of the patient's husband and mother-in-law? The physician tried to persuade the mother-in-law and husband to agree to the woman's sterilization, but that attempt failed.

What would be the consequences for the woman if the physician counseled her to go ahead with the sterilization? Everyone at the meeting concurred that the consequence would be that the husband would divorce her. Because the husband and mother-in-law wanted sons in the family, the husband would have to divorce a sterilized wife and get himself a new wife who might bear him sons.

What then would be the consequence to the woman following a divorce? She would be rejected from the family and lose whatever possessions she had, including custody of her own children, who would remain with their father and his family. Although this woman could remarry, she did not want to divorce the husband. She loves the family, and she especially did not want to lose custody of her daughters.

One participant intervened when this story was being told and asked, "What about her rights? Doesn't she have a right to decide for herself?" This rare use of "rights" language in China was seen as acceptable when it pertained to the right of a woman against her husband. There was no corresponding use of rights language to identify the rights of women or couples vis-à-vis the government.

This case was presented as having happened a long time ago. I asked whether it could still happen today and was told "yes, in some remote mountainous areas." Remote mountainous areas are ostensibly the places where traditional Chinese values respecting the authority of husbands and mothers-in-law still rule in the family. My guess is that the speaker did not want to admit to a visitor from the United States that similar things could occur in urban areas, as well, in modernized China.

Whether general principles are necessary or even useful is a topic of hot dispute among scholars in the field of bioethics. My own view is that without ethical principles as part of a framework, there can be no systematic way to justify ethical judgments. Opponents would reply that these principles are Western in origin and therefore cannot be used for justification across cultures. I maintain that without principles to serve as an ideal to strive for, there could be no concept of moral progress. Opponents would argue that the very notion of progress is a Western invention. To argue at length here for the relevance and importance of ethical principles would require endless digressions into the scholarly literature of bioethics. I plan to avoid such scholarly excursions and try to make my point with illustrative examples.

What I intend to show is that some things are relative, others are not. A convincing argument against ethical relativism need not conclude that *nothing* is relative, only that certain types of actions or practices—chiefly, those that violate human rights—are not. Because I reject the extremist version of ethical relativism, the task before me is to construct a plausible argument by way of rebuttal. One strategy toward that end will be to distinguish between explanation and justification. It is one thing to provide an explanation of why an individual or an entire culture holds certain beliefs and acts in certain ways. It is quite another thing to provide a justification for those beliefs and actions. Another strategy is to ask whether the consequences of traditional practices provide an objective basis for making ethical judgments. If a cultural practice produces manifest suffering or produces lifelong physical disability, there are good grounds for judging that practice to be ethically wrong. A well-known example is the historical practice in China of foot-binding women.

Ethical relativists question whether cross-cultural value judgments can ever be valid. If ethical norms are relative to time and place, it is a conceptual mistake, as well as a moral transgression, to pass judgments on other cultures. An even more radical step than making cross-cultural ethical judgments is for those outside a culture to seek to bring about changes in internal customs or traditions. Such actions were common among European colonial powers and Christian missionaries who saw themselves as undertaking the "white man's burden." These efforts eventually fell into disrepute as benighted attempts to "civilize the natives." The legitimacy of outside interference into the cultural or religious traditions of other societies today raises as much a political question as it does an ethical one. Not surprisingly, it is condemned as a new form of cultural imperialism or as an ethical version of "neocolonialism."

So we need to separate the question of whether cross-cultural ethical judgments are legitimate and how they can be justified from the very different question of whether it is ethically permissible for outsiders to actively interfere with a culture's or nation's traditional practices. Even if there are some universal ethical principles capable of yielding transcultural moral judgments about a particular culture's traditional or religious practices, when, if ever, is it legitimate for outsiders to seek to change those practices? Defenders of ethical relativism use the term *ethical imperialism* to refer to situations in which one culture—usually Anglo-American or Western European—seeks to impose its ethical requirements on a less-developed country. If all such efforts are ethically suspect, then *ethical imperialism* is an apt term. But if ethical judgments of better or worse, more or less humane, can have cross-cultural validity, then *imperialism* is not a correct way to describe the transcultural imposition of values. A more accurate description would be *reform*. If the allegedly "superior" values express what are widely held to be human rights, there may exist an ethical obligation to try to bring about changes in countries or cultures where violations of those rights are occurring. The best way to do this—strategically as well as ethically—is to form alliances with people within those cultures who are seeking to bring about such changes.

The trouble is, the charge that something is a human rights violation has become so common and widespread that the term is in danger of losing its meaning and import. It is a mistake to assimilate all ethical values to the level of human rights. As the term implies, *human* rights are universal precisely because they are held to be fundamental moral requirements for treating all members of the species *Homo sapiens*. But to accept this view we must first agree that, in relevant respects, human beings everywhere are fundamentally alike. The view that all aspects of social life and culture are socially constructed must ultimately reject the idea that human beings everywhere are fundamentally alike and, with it, the notion that there are any human rights.

Ethical Cultural Relativism Has Some Advantages

ELVIN HATCH

The efflorescence of ethical relativism among American anthropologists took place in the 1930s and 1940s, when Benedict and Herskovits were its most notable proponents. Their relativism combined two principles. The first was an attitude of skepticism in relation to Western values, for they held that Western standards with respect to such matters as sexuality and work are historically conditioned and do not warrant elevation to the status of universal principles. The second was the value of tolerance, inasmuch as they held that people everywhere ought to be free to live as they choose.

Opposition to this form of relativism was evident almost from the start, however, and by the 1950s some of the leading anthropologists in this country were speaking out against it. World War II stimulated some of this reaction, for it was difficult for people in the United States not to think in terms of universal or ultimate values in the face of the events taking place then. The intellectual climate for nearly two decades following the war also included a number of powerful images which seemed to speak against relativism. These were images about the end of colonialism, opportunities for economic development in underdeveloped countries, and the seemingly universal desirability of Western technology. Thus during the postwar years, such leading figures in anthropology as Ralph Linton, Robert Redfield, and Alfred Kroeber were critical of moral relativism, while a variety of philosophers underlined the flaws in the ethical reasoning of Benedict and Herskovits. Strong opposition has continued to the present, and today ethical relativism is more often attacked than embraced; I am not sure that anyone now is willing fully to endorse the version of relativism that was articulated by its major proponents in American anthropology in the 1930s.

It is in this context that I want to offer a defense of ethical relativism. This will be a very limited defense, and I do not propose reinstating the theories of either Benedict or Herskovits. But I believe that in our rush to distance ourselves from the moral and philosophical difficulties of their ideas, we may give up too much, and, indeed, we may fail to see the legacy of their thought continuing in other ethical theories today. In any event, it is important for us to keep sight of the issues that they were concerned with.

I need to be clear that I accept that there are situations in which ethical relativism is untenable, for it may lead to moral neutrality and inaction in situations that are intolerable. Ethical relativism is mistaken when it calls for us to be nonjudgmental in relation to such issues as political executions, genocide, genital mutilations, honor killings, and the like. The recent executions of Ken Saro-Wiwa and others in Nigeria, which received international attention at the time this essay was first drafted, are a case in point. A strict relativist might argue that a moral response by the West is ethically unwarranted, yet how can we not respond? Again, how can we not express value judgments in regard to the reports of rape and mass killing in parts of the former Yugoslavia? But ethical relativism is not a simple, unitary scheme that can be dismissed by a single argument, for it is a complex notion made up of a variety of features which need to be evaluated individually. A corollary is that most anthropologists are ethical relativists in some respects and nonrelativists in others.

Underlying my defense of relativism—or my interest in looking on its good side—is my recognition that at the time of writing, the United States seems to be experiencing a cultural shift to the right, or at least the cultural right has gained significant ground in the national political arena. We see concerted attacks on multiculturalism in the schools and universities, for example, and on multilingualism, immigrants, and affirmative action. These pressures—which have never been absent in the United States, but which appear to be stronger now than they have been in recent memory—stimulate us to take another look at relativism. The philosophical questions raised by it do not exist independently of a context of real-world affairs, and as those affairs change, we see the elements making up that complex of features called relativism in a different light. Put simply, our judgments about ethical relativism are historically situated.

THE PARADOX OF ETHICAL RELATIVISM

The place to begin is with what I will call the paradox of ethical relativism. On one hand, the theory is mistaken to the extent that it denies the very possibility of making moral judgments across cultures or of developing a framework of human rights; but on the other hand, the problems that the relativists of the Boasian tradition were concerned with have not gone away. One of these is the problem of establishing reasonable and general grounds for making moral judgments about the actions of others, and another is a strong tendency among the more powerful peoples of the world to use their own standards, or standards favorable to them, in their relations with others. What standards are appropriate for us to use, how do we defend them, and how can we know that they will hold up to the scrutiny of those who do not share our perspective, now or in the future? No moral theory that has been advanced in opposition to relativism has been sufficiently convincing that it clearly stands above the rest as the winning alternative; consequently we cannot forge ahead with confidence in making moral judgments or establishing universal standards and a body of human rights. Whenever a set of standards is proposed, I feel myself being pulled back by a nagging sense of doubt. I have yet to see a general ethical theory that I personally find convincing. The paradox of ethical relativism is that we can't live with it, but it isn't clear how to avoid the skepticism which underlies it.

This paradox has helped structure the debate over the question of moral judgments and human rights, which is suggested by the fact that ethical relativism occupies such a prominent place in the literature on universal standards. Much of this literature takes relativism as its starting point or as its main foil.... It is as if we cannot conceive the one—the search for general moral principles or human rights (whether they are based on utilitarian principles, Kantian rights-based theory, or any other ground)—outside the context of the other. Adapting a Derridian argument, the question of human rights and general standards of ethical judgment are never a mere "presence," something to be established in their own right, but exist only in relation to their opposite, which is relativism.

I have mentioned my sense of skepticism about attempts to establish general moral standards, and the ethical relativism that underlies the paradox that I cite *is* a form of skepticism. What is more, the moral theories of such Boasians as Benedict and Herskovits had an important skeptical component, although not all forms of relativism in the anthropological literature did so. For example, skepticism seems to have played no part in the relativism of Malinowski, whose position rested on the principle that other cultures are successful or functional, which in turn assumed a universal standard of good. For example, his analysis of magic contained the message that missionaries and colonial administrators should not undermine the magical beliefs of other peoples because these rituals enabled the individual to cope with his or her anxieties and therefore to be more effective with the task at hand. Malinowski's relativism rested not on a form of skepticism, but on a version of utilitarian theory whereby the practical benefits of institutions served as a standard for making value judgments. For Malinowski, the institutions of non-Western societies are appropriate given the conditions in which those peoples live, and Western values regarding such matters as sexuality and marriage do not constitute universal standards.

The relativism that was incubated in Boasian anthropology adopted a skeptical attitude toward cross-cultural standards of all kinds, including Malinowski's utilitarianism. The Boasians would have been justified in accusing Malinowski of accepting this standard uncritically: it needed better philosophical grounding than he provided, and one even wonders how much care he gave to these matters. And this problem is still with us: the failure to arrive at a moral theory that is generally accepted and that will serve as an intellectual basis for universal human rights is notable.

I disagree with Benedict and Herskovits to the extent that they held that warrantable judgments across cultural boundaries can never be made, if only because the failure to act is itself an action that may have unacceptable consequences for other people—consequences which are unacceptable to us. But I agree with Benedict's and Herskovits's version of relativism on several other counts. The first is their basic skepticism: we do not have a set of moral principles that are rationally warranted, generally acceptable among those who are informed on these issues, and universally applicable. While there are situations in which we are compelled to take a moral stand, the grounds which warrant our doing so will necessarily be ad hoc and limited. I also agree with the connection that they made between skepticism and tolerance: when we do not find good reason to make judgments about the actions or ways of life of other people, we ought to show tolerance toward them, and we should do so on the basis of the moral principles that people ought to be free to live as they choose. One might argue that any ethical theory might call for tolerance in situations in which it lacks adequate reasons to respond otherwise. And it seems to me that, to the extent that it does, that theory *incorporates* relativism. Ethical relativism is espoused even among the ethical theorists who reject it. But my argument goes even further, for I am suggesting that, at this point at least, no ethical theory which seeks to establish general standards of value is fully compelling. Consequently we are faced with the paradox of relativism: we have no moral theory to replace it with, yet there are situations in which the failure to take a moral stand other than tolerance is clearly unacceptable.

THE ISSUE OF CULPABILITY

Relativism may have at least a tacit presence even in cases in which we decide that moral judgments are warranted, for to judge that the actions of the Other are intolerable is to raise the additional question of what went wrong: who or what was responsible for the actions that we find objectionable? To put this another way, moral judgments may take place at two levels. The first concerns the events that we want to evaluate, and here the issue is to find adequate grounds for making value judgments about those events; the second concerns the human agents involved, and here the question is their responsibility for these matters. It is important that relativism is an issue at both levels. I turn here to the second level, the question of culpability, and the work of Edward Tylor is illustrative.

Tylor was not a relativist at the first level, of course, for he ranked human societies by reference to degrees of moral perfection, and, in principle, evaluations were to be made on the basis of how effective the institutions were in promoting human happiness and physical well-being. Yet a form of relativism appeared at the second level, for he argued that savage societies should not be judged according to European standards of thought. Savages were not as intelligent as Europeans—they did not have the intellectual capacity to draw the same moral conclusions from experience that Europeans did; hence their institutions should be understood according to their standards of reason and not one's own. The implication was that the people of the lower societies were not culpable for their moral mistakes. Like children, they didn't know better. This was a form of relativism in that a society's standards of justice, say, were relative to the level of the people's intelligence, and institutions

that were appropriate for societies at one level, that of the Tasmanians, say, were not appropriate for societies at another level, such as Britain. To state this another way, while Tylor faulted the institutions of lower societies, he held that the individual's actions should not be judged by reference the standards of a higher civilization.

We find a similar division between the two levels of moral judgment in the work of Ruth Benedict. What stimulated Elgin Williams's criticism of her *Patterns of Culture* in 1947 was that Penguin had just issued a new, twenty-five-cent edition of her book, making it readily accessible, as Williams said, to the common man. The book was now available on book racks in drug stores and dime stores across the country. Williams showed that while the formal argument of Benedict's book was one of relativism and tolerance—she explicitly argued that all cultures were equally valid—in another sense the book was profoundly nonrelativistic, for it offered a plethora of value judgments. And Williams applauded her for it. For example, Benedict described war as an asocial, destructive trait; she preferred the nonviolent marital relations of the Zuni to the jealous outbursts of the Plains; and she favored the lack of a sense of sin among the Zuni to the guilt complexes that were associated with Puritanism.

We find similar departures from relativism elsewhere in Benedict's work, including her discussions of what she called the bereavement situation, or the cultural patterns associated with a person's death. She distinguished between realistic and nonrealistic ways of handling death and grief. The Pueblo peoples of the Southwest, she said, handled death in a realistic fashion, for the individual's behavior was directed toward the loss itself and toward getting past the trauma with as little disruption as possible. By contrast. the Navajo were nonrealistically preoccupied with contamination. They had a strong fear of pollution from the dead and of the dangers posed by the possibility of the ghost's return.

These cases reveal Benedict abandoning her relativism, but it reappeared at another level. For example, while she looked unfavorably on Plains warfare and while she regarded Navajo reactions to death as nonrealistic, an implicit message was that the people themselves should not be faulted. Yet her grounds for denying their culpability were different from those that underlay Tylor's thinking. It was not that the people didn't know better, but that they adhered to cultural traditions which largely governed their lives: to a significant degree, the individual's actions were a product of cultural conditioning. While Tylor granted agency to other peoples but absolved them of culpability because of their low intelligence, Benedict held that all people were equally intelligent but denied their blameworthiness on the grounds of enculturation. In other words, the individual's culpability should not be judged by reference to standards that derive from outside his or her culture.

This reveals how our assumptions about culture, society, and human behavior influence the kinds of value judgments we make, and it suggests the critical importance of being clear about these matters in our own minds when developing moral judgments. This also reveals the importance of separating the two levels of moral evaluation. Consider the recent executions in Nigeria. It is one thing to condemn the Nigerian government's actions, but quite another to assign moral responsibility. Ethical, political, and legal judgments may be made at both levels, but the reasoning is different in the two cases, and the paradox of relativism applies to both. It is conceivable that one could favor the imposition of sanctions against the Nigerian government in order to bring about a change in its policies, while still accepting that the people who were behind the executions were not morally culpable since they were acting reasonably given the cultural meanings that underlay their behavior.

It is not only ethical relativism that operates at both levels, for other ethical theories do so as well, such as when they take into account, say, what Benedict referred to as cultural conditioning. And when they absolve the individual of blame on these grounds, then they are employing the relativistic principle whereby the individual's actions should be judged by reference to the historically variable standards within the culture, not by external ones.

TOLERANCE AND SKEPTICISM

The Boasian relativists may be faulted for being less critical than they should have been with regard to the question of making moral arguments. First, they were patently inconsistent. On one hand, they held that moral standards are historically conditioned, the same as pottery designs or folk tales—like all cultural features, values differ from society to society, and therefore we are not justified in making cross-cultural judgments. But on the other hand, the Boasians proceeded to do exactly what they asserted should not be done, which was to advance a universal moral standard. This was the standard of tolerance, whereby we ought not be judgmental about cultural differences; we ought to allow people to live as they choose.

Second, it was a mistake for them to assume that the means for arriving at universally valid moral principles should be by a comparative study of cultures. The question of values is a philosophical matter and not an empirical one. True, judgments of reality (as distinct from judgments of value) do enter legitimately into the application of value standards, inasmuch as the empirical facts of the case need to be understood before a standard of value may be applied to a given situation. But the process of arriving at value standards is a rational and not an empirical matter and cannot be approached by a comparative study of cultures. Indeed, if the Boasians had been consistent about using the comparative method, then surely they would have had to give up the call for tolerance, since intolerance is more likely the norm around the world.

Yet in spite of its difficulties, there is something to recommend the call for tolerance, which is grounded on the notion that people ought to be free to live as they choose. But the idea needs to be framed differently from the way the Boasians conceptualized it. In place of the straightforward principle that we ought to be tolerant of other ways of life, we should substitute the more limited principle that we ought to do so in the absence of persuasive arguments that would enable us to make moral judgments. Tolerance ought to constitute the default mode of thought governing our ethical judgments today. For example, we ought to be nonjudgmental in relation to culinary styles and modes of dress and about people's life goals and their treatment of one another—we should, that is, unless we see persuasive reasons to react otherwise. If we are not tolerant in such situations, then our actions necessarily will be arbitrary and will contravene the moral principle of freedom, whereby people should be able to live as they choose. This notion of relativism as default is crucial: the nonjudgmentalism that we associate with relativism is an attitude that does not come easily to most Americans, perhaps to most people throughout the world. Certainly it does not come easily to the religious right in

the United States or to many members of the present U.S. Congress.

If we retain the Boasian call for tolerance as our default, what about Boasian skepticism? How may we fit that into our thinking? The Boasian relativists were not as consistently skeptical as it might appear, as Elgin Williams's criticisms of Benedict reveal. The principle that we should extract from Benedict—a principle that she herself was not very careful with, as Williams has shown—is the importance of maintaining a highly critical attitude in relation to the standards that we use in making value judgments. We need not remain skeptical to the point of denying the possibility of making any valid judgments, but we should submit our evaluations to severe scrutiny. And we do not need to resort to such obvious examples as the moral beliefs of the religious right to make this case, for anthropology itself provides illustrations. This point is crucial: even well-meaning, sympathetic, and informed people may be faulted for their failure to be as cautiously skeptical as they should.

I appreciate that it doesn't take relativism to make us aware of unwarranted judgments about other people, for surely any scholarly ethical theory today recognizes the subtleties of ethnocentrism. Yet the limited form of relativism that I urge suggests that an attitude of skepticism should be our first reflex in the face of moral judgments.

I want to illustrate the subtleties of ethnocentrism and the importance of a basic skepticism in relation to moral judgments by examining the work of the late Ernest Gellner. His *Reason and Culture* is about rationality, not ethics, but the central argument of the book has important implications for ethical relativism. At one level, he rejected universal rationality, for he accepted that reason does not stand outside of culture. And he held that in an important sense, modern science is an irrational endeavor, as criticisms of the Popperian philosophy of science have shown. But Gellner accepted universal rationality at another level, for Western thought, he argued, is demonstrably better than that of other peoples. What sets Western rationality apart is that it gets better results, regardless of its truth-value. He wrote,

> The astonishing and unquestionable power of the [Western] technology born of [Western] rational inquiry is such that the majority of mankind— and in particular those men eager to increase their wealth and/or power— are eager to emulate it.

What are the characteristics of this new, Western form of thought, this rationally unwarranted rationality which is conquering the world? It is a fusion of two seemingly contradictory philosophical theories, Western rationalism and Western empiricism. This form of thought is empiricist in that it takes experience as the arbiter of competing ideas, but this empiricism is under the control of rationalism.

Drawing on Weber's analysis of the history of Western society, Gellner went on to describe Western rationality as a way of life, or lifestyle, which permeates much of Western society and culture. For example, it is manifest in the modern economy, which operates according to judgments about efficiency and cost-effectiveness. Gellner is clear that not all spheres of society or culture are fully dominated by the rationalist ideal, for in many spheres— etiquette might be one example—rules "have no rhyme or reason". Even more to the point, morality itself, he said, cannot be justified by pragmatic considerations the way science and economic production can.

Gellner's valorization of Western rationality stopped short of defending Western values in general, but I suggest that his

privileging of Western rationality helps to normalize certain forms of thinking, and in doing so may have harmful ethical consequences. An example would be the use of highly rational, highly empirical, but highly value-laden economic models derived from the West for development programs in other parts of the world. Gellner's response to this criticism might be that it ignores a key part of his argument, which is the importance of the judgments of non-Western peoples. It is *their* demand for the products of Western rationality—medicines, new crop forms, tape recorders, television, rifles, missiles— that confirms the universality of Western forms of thought. And if an economic order is imposed on them that they do not want, then their judgments should be respected. Yet it is extremely difficult to circumscribe those things which are genuinely desired by the Other and to distinguish them from the things that are forced upon them because of asymmetries of privilege, prestige, and power. Gellner's thinking was insufficiently skeptical.

Consider the case of Appalachia. The Tennessee Valley Authority was created by an act of Congress in 1933, and its initial purpose was the planning and development of the entire Tennessee River Basin, which was considered underdeveloped and poverty-stricken. Dams would be built to improve navigation and flood control and to produce hydroelectric power, conservation programs would be implemented, and both agricultural and industrial development would be introduced. According to David Whisnant, the TVA began as a progressive, idealistic, democratic, comprehensive effort to improve the region. Its idealistic goals were soon subverted by powerful business interests, particularly after the dams were completed in 1944. But even if the original goals had not been subverted, Whisnant argues, the TVA would have been destructive. The leading figures in the organization believed that by instituting rational, apolitical, disinterested economic and social engineering, the project would succeed in improving the lives of these backward people. In brief, the project was founded on a set of cultural assumptions of the dominant society, assumptions about development and the virtues of bringing a people with an aberrant way of life into the mainstream. Whisnant writes,

> Beneath the vast technological superstructure of TVA I perceived a substructure of cultural values and assumptions that controlled the agency more surely than the geomorphology of the Tennessee River Valley itself.

This kind of normalization is manifest in another characteristic of the relationship between Appalachia and the larger society, which is the tendency of the latter to perceive the Appalachian people as backward and impoverished. It is unquestionable that the people of that region do suffer impoverishment, which is evident, for example, in the figures on health care and education. But granting that, nevertheless, the *perception*, by mainstream, middle-class Americans, of the Appalachians' backwardness and impoverishment is a result of something else as well. For one thing, there has been a "systematic denigration" of the local population as a way to justify such programs as the TVA. The portrayal of Appalachia as backward has served the interests of certain individuals and agencies of the dominant society. For another, and more to the point here, some Appalachian patterns are seen as backward from the point of view of mainstream, middle-class America. The emotional forms of religious service among the congregations that proliferate in Appalachia

are illustrative. These are perceived by the dominant society as manifestations of a gullible people. Similarly, one Appalachian pattern is a form of economic life whereby the people depend heavily on the informal economic sector (such as subsistence gardening and labor and food exchanges); they are jacks of all trades, and they tend to avoid long-term job commitments and regular employment. Tom Plaut argues that while there are many studies of the culture of Appalachia, very little work has been done on the "rationalist, achievement-oriented, 'scientific' culture" that is overwhelming the region. This "scientific" culture "has levelled, bleached, and bled out a rich variety of human ways of being that have stood in its path". Plaut sees the way of life of the Appalachians as meritorious in its own right.

Earlier I said that it is sometimes difficult to distinguish between those features of Western society which the Other truly wants and those which are forced on them. I suggest that one aspect of this problem is that mainstream Westerners tend to engage in a kind of metonymic thinking in conceiving the relationship between Us and the Other, for technology sees as a trope for representing a more general relationship among societies. For example, the success of such Western forms of technology as tape recorders, electric guitars, and rifles provides a model for thinking about the relationship between the Western economy and that of the Other. We tend to elide the distinction between specific forms of technology and, say, the value of economic efficiency and the work ethic. The theme of skepticism that we find in the work of Benedict and Herskovits retains its significance today.

CONCLUSION

The emergence of relativism at about the turn of this century was associated with a

Copernican shift in both the Western worldview and the Western sense of self-identity. Western thought about where our civilization stood in the total gamut of human societies underwent profound change, and this took place in part in the context of Boasian anthropology and was one aspect of the emerging relativistic perspective. Whereas earlier, anthropologists imagined their own societies to be at the pinnacle of development, the Boasian worldview had it that the West occupied a very equivocal position, for while it may have enjoyed greater material power than other peoples, it did not enjoy moral superiority. This facet of relativism was crucial, and it remains a central legacy, regardless of how we may feel about the possibility of establishing general ethical standards or universal human rights. What is more, the efforts today to develop a warranted body of human rights are framed by this principle, for we now assume that the views of non-Western peoples ought to weigh as heavily as the views of Westerners in establishing general standards. So the very search for universal human rights today rests upon a relativistic foundation. Even the ethical theories which reject relativism reflect the Copernican shift that the Boasians helped to achieve.

THE CONTINUING DEBATE:
Is Cultural Relativism a Helpful Approach to Ethics?

What Is New

While the integrity and cohesiveness of culture and cultural identity is an important value, problems arise when the values of local cultures violate what many regard as fundamental and universal human rights. This conflict has often focused on the tension between the rights of women to self-determination and control of their own reproductive lives, and the strong cultural and religious traditions that reject such rights; more recent has been recognition of the conflict between cultural condemnation and persecution of homosexuality and the basic rights of individual homosexuals. These difficult issues cannot be resolved by simple pronouncements, but require careful anthropological study of how various customs fit into a culture and whether the customs are vital to community cultural survival (for example, some anthropologists have argued that many customs that treat women as subordinate are not essential cultural elements).

Where to Find More

Ruth Macklin's related work includes "After Helsinki: Unresolved Issues in International Research," *Kennedy Institute of Ethics Journal*, volume 11, number 1 (2001); and "Justice in International Research," in *Beyond Consent: Seeking Justice in Research*, edited by Jeffrey Kahn, Anna Mastroianni, and Jeremy Sugarman (NY: Oxford University Press, 1998).

Elvin Hatch takes up related issues in *Theories of Man and Culture* (NY: Columbia University Press, 1973), and *Culture and Morality: The Relativity of Values in Anthropology* (NY: Columbia University Press, 1983).

The arguments of Clifford Geertz are in "Anti Anti-Relativism," *American Anthropologist*, volume 86, number 2 (June, 1984); reprinted in Michael Krausz, editor, *Relativism: Interpretation and Conflict* (Notre Dame: University of Notre Dame Press, 1989). See also Clifford Geertz, *Available Light: Anthropological Reflections on Philosophical Topics* (Princeton, NJ: Princeton University Press, 2000).

Merrilee H. Salmon, "Ethical Considerations in Anthropology and Archaeology, or Relativism and Justice for All," *Journal of Anthropological Research*, volume 53 (1997), argues that anthropologists' respect for other cultures should not lead them to ethical relativism, and that values promoted by anthropologists—such as the value of preserving archaeological sites—indicate belief in values that go beyond the values of individual cultures. John J. Tilley, in "Cultural Relativism," *Human Rights Quarterly*, volume 22 (2000), critiques a number of arguments for normative cultural relativism, and argues in favor of ethical universalism.

One issue of the *Journal of Anthropological Research*, volume 53 (1997)—the issue that contains the reading by Elvin Hatch—is devoted to relativism, pluralism, and human rights. Several significant articles are included in the special issue: Elizabeth M. Zechenter's "In the Name of Culture: Cultural Relativism and the Abuse of the Individual," is a trenchant critic of ethical cultural relativism. She describes in detail some of the "cultural practices" that have resulted in "a long history of abysmal treatment of women" and argues that cultural relativist ethics undermines the movement toward basic human rights and thus contributes to enormous suffering. Carole Nagengast, "Women, Minorities, and Indigenous Peoples: Universalism and Cultural Relativity," fully recognizes the genuine difficulties in dealing with both cultural practices and individual rights, and her thoughtful and informative essay scrupulously avoids shallow slogans and inadequate solutions. Ellen Messer, "Pluralist Approaches to Human Rights," combines broad and insightful knowledge of both anthropology and ethics in her argument for a pluralist approach to human rights that avoids both ethical relativism and the simplistic universalization of Western individualist values. See also Ellen Messer, "Anthropology and Human Rights," *Annual Review of Anthropology*, volume 22 (1993).

The readings cited with debate 13 are also relevant here.

IS MORALITY AN IDEOLOGICAL ILLUSION?

CLOSE EXAMINATION OF MORALITY REVEALS ITS IDEOLOGICAL NATURE

ADVOCATE: Anthony Skillen, Reader in Philosophy at the University of Kent at Canterbury; author of *Ruling Illusions* (Hussocks, Sussex: Harvester Press, 1977).

SOURCE: "Is Morality a Ruling Illusion?" in *Morality, Reflection and Ideology*, edited by Edward Harcourt (Oxford: Oxford University Press, 2000): 44–63.

THE OBJECTIVITY OF MORALITY REMAINS AN OPEN POSSIBILITY

ADVOCATE: Peter Railton, Nelson Professor of Philosophy at the University of Michigan, Ann Arbor; a leader in the development of contemporary moral realism

SOURCE: "Morality, Ideology, and Reflection; or, The Duck Sits Yet," in *Morality, Reflection and Ideology*, edited by Edward Harcourt (Oxford: Oxford University Press, 2000): 113–147.

Is morality an ideology? That is, is morality just something dreamed up by some group in order to control or shape or exploit others? Or does morality have some objective basis?

The suggestion that morality is merely an ideology—imposed by the rulers on the ruled, for the benefit of the powerful—goes back at least to Plato. In the *Republic*, Thrasymachus boldly asserts that "the just is nothing other than the advantage of the stronger." And of course when the stronger call it "justice" rather than "power," it becomes easier to keep the weak under control.

But to be a genuine "ideology," the scam must ultimately fool the scammers themselves. After all, it's difficult consistently to fool the masses into believing something that the privileged rulers reject; the process is much easier when the rulers themselves actually believe the ideology. So it becomes a genuine ideology when *both* those who benefit from the "system of justice" *and* those who are exploited by it genuinely believe that the system is just. ("It's true, I have a lot more wealth than most people; but it's fair because I *deserve*—or earned, or inherited—it.") As Karl Mannheim maintained, an ideology results when a "ruling group becomes so interest-bound that they cannot see facts which would undermine their sense of domination; they obscure the real condition of society to themselves and others and thereby stabilize it."

The modern ideological analysis of morality (that is, the attempt to give an ideological account of morality that would *debunk* morality by exposing its ideological origins) primarily stems from two very different sources: Karl Marx and Friedrich

15 Nietzsche. In the Marxist view, ideology mystifies economic processes, hiding the reality of an economic structure that exploits the workers for the benefit of the wealthy; and morality (as well as religion) is enlisted in its cause. For Nietzsche, the "slave morality" (or "herd morality") which enables the weak to control the strong is an ideology and Nietzsche aims to expose and overthrow it. Thus for Nietzsche, the use of ideology is still for control, but it is used for the binding of the strong by the weak, whereas for Marx it is for the exploitation of the economically weak by the economically powerful.

Anthony Skillen rejects rule-governed moral systems as ideologies that justify harsh judgments and obscure the basic feelings and affections that are the foundation of friendship, good will, and decent humane relationships. Following our natural humane feeling responses to our fellow humans guides us to reject harmful systems and mistreatment of others, and allows us to live well with one another without ideological distortions.

In opposing the suggestion that morality is ideological, Peter Railton draws on his belief in *moral realism*: the view that there are genuine objective moral facts that can be known in a manner analogous to the way in which we know scientific facts, and that knowledge of such facts can support legitimate moral systems that are not ideologically imposed distortions.

POINTS TO PONDER

➤ Anthony Skillen condemns the systems of moral education and moral conditioning that—from his perspective—lock people into the dominant ethical ideology of rules and obligations and blame and punishment; but what does he regard as a better alternative?

➤ Skillen considers the bad morality that (almost) leads Huck Finn to betray his friend Jim, the escaped slave, to the slave catchers; and ethical rules that treat people as property are a clear example of a profoundly bad moral system. In this case (as Jonathan Bennett notes) we are glad that Huck's feelings of friendship overcame his "moral obligation" to turn in an escaped slave. But consider another case: I am tallying the votes, and I have an opportunity to stuff the ballot box in favor of my friend, who is running for mayor. Friendship might suggest I boost my friend's vote total, but my moral commitment to fair play prevents me from manipulating the vote count. This *seems* to be a case in which ethical rules are beneficial; would Skillen agree?

➤ Peter Railton maintains that our subjective sentiments and feelings need not be arbitrary; rather, they can be reflectively and rationally approved (a condition Railton characterizes as "objective subjectuality"). How would Skillen respond to Railton's claim that subjective feelings may be *objectively* evaluated? *If* Skillen agreed that was possible, would he find it *desirable?*

Close Examination of Morality Reveals
Its Ideological Nature

ANTHONY SKILLEN

Ideologies represent orders of society as inevitable or as the best possible order, given the nature of things. In *The Communist Manifesto* Marx and Engels seem to have thought the capitalist system so transparently transitional that the workers' movements would see through it and, through their necessary self-organization, discover the power to smash it. There was no need to educate, let alone to preach morality to those who were not only combining and resisting out of self-interest, but were, through that struggle, discovering a new interest, that of human association itself. Thus did Marx come to think his youthful battles with 'the German Ideology' of largely biographical interest compared with the project of ruthlessly organizing to build the Party and proving the evolutionary mortality of capital through the inevitable decline of the rate of profit. Yet just because he so misjudged the durability of bad things and the fragility of good ones, his debunking critique of ideologies remains central to our self-understanding in a world that remains Marx's nightmare of barbarism.

Though his weapons were those of the intellectual and many of his targets fellow members of that class, it is, at least from a Marxian perspective, wrong to see ideology predominantly in terms of the productions of such ideologues or even of the function their works play in reinforcing regimes through rationalizing them. Sages, prophets, and intellectuals work up into doctrines, albeit to return them with interest to the soil that nourished them, discourses, vocabularies, modes of understanding, outlooks, that are already present in everyday social practice. That is a condition both of the production of these discourses and of their reception as intelligible reflective accounts of any way of life. When, therefore, as philosophers we look at Bentham, Kant, Hegel, or for that matter Marx or Nietzsche, it is idealistic to think of them as cultural constitutors whose ideas were embodied in social practice. Rather, to the extent that they are ideologues, they articulate explicitly ideas already implicit in the world of which they make their sense. Kant and Bentham, for example, were in many ways antithetical, but shared a view of the natural teleology and menace of desire or inclination. Both presented the subject as naturally isolated, naturally selfish, and naturally short-sighted—as a domain to be ruled over, a beast to be tamed. In the eyes of both, morality was opposite to and complementary with Political Economy's self-interest. Morality, in the absence of direct surveillance and tangible sanctions, is what ensures that the rules of market exchange, whether of worker and capitalist or among bourgeois owners, hold sway. Thus in both we find a debasing ideology of natural desire on the one hand and an aggrandizingly sublimated account of that which regulates desire on the other. Thus do their philosophies interweave with bourgeois ideology's 'construction of the self', mirroring common sense and ramifying its hegemony. Thus does each legitimize what survives of the Church's gift to capitalism in the form of the notion of the sinfulness of man and the certain fear of everlasting life. And thus does each survive a thousand refutations. What else could we expect in a world where life teaches us daily both that we must look after ourselves and at the same time that this protégé is so worthless?

I argued in *Ruling Illusions* that an authoritarian and reductive model of human life dominated and philosophically legitimized actually existing institutions of state, law, education, punishment, work, and, pervasively, morality. Attacking these interlocking ideologies, I claimed a Marxian inheritance. Marx was said to laugh whenever the name of Morality was invoked, while retaining, as we have seen, a rich, uneccentric, and sometimes deep ethical vocabulary. I argued that Marx was consistent here and, moreover, broadly right: not only is Morality—with its abstract laws to be obeyed, for duty's sake, by equally abstract individual moral subjects—in Marx's view an 'illusion'. It is an oppressive illusion, to be rejected by the parties both of Reality and of Humanity. Marx, in the main, had a quite specific conception of morality, not a generic one embracing the norms and values of all societies. For him, morality was a historically determinate ideological institution consisting of internalized commandments functioning to mystify and discipline people in accordance with the oppressive needs of class society. To describe an institution as ideological is to describe it as the expression of a restrictive perspective and as occlusive of actualities and possibilities liable, but for it, to be discerned and acted on. The concept of ideology is at once epistemic and ethical in so far as it implies concealment and thwarting, and sociological in so far as it implies determinations, functions, and mechanisms. In the spirit of this understanding, I argued along the following lines:

> Our society divides people up and presents this atomisation as the human condition; it pits them into competition with each other and calls this human nature; it demands the suppression of impulses and calls these humanity's enemy.... If the State is God's march on earth, Morality is his parade on the spirit. In the absence of positive cooperative ties and positive motives to work and create, the capitalist system requires 'specialist' forces of control, armed men and harsh consciences, bullies, to make us do what money alone cannot bribe us to do.

Formulating a more positive account of morality, I wrote:

> To talk of morality in [a] 'non-moralistic' way, it seems to me, would be to talk in terms, not of a higher power, an authoritative voice, controlling our inclinations, but rather of the relation among our activities (dispositions, impulses, feelings, passions, values) as they are formed and expressed in our ways of life.... And 'socialist' restraint would be the preponderance of communal, productive, loving and communicative activities and motives over invidiously divisive (including moralistic) activities and motives.

Moralism sets up rules, requirements, and duties as that which controls, inhibits, or overrides desires, inclinations, and affections. The non-moralistic philosophy I am advancing prefers to talk of morality as forms of, cultivations of, such passions or inclinations.

Something similar, I think, is implicit in Philippa Foot's 'Morality as a System of Hypothetical Imperatives'. By her account, the moral 'volunteer' acts well out of intelligent care for the good of others, for truth, liberty, and for a life open and in good faith with his neighbours. No need here for a 'categorical imperative'. Lay people and philosophers alike adhere to the 'moral conscript' notion of the 'categorical imperative' thanks to the standard form of moral inculcation: 'moral rules are often enforced'... 'relative stringency of our moral teaching'... 'must do'... 'have to do'... 'the non-hypothetical moral "ought" by which society is apt to voice its demands'... Such 'psychological conditions of the learning of moral behaviour' explain for Foot the feelings of inescapability accompanying the 'magic illusion' of a peculiar bindingness in the moral 'ought'. What I am inclined to say, agreeing that obligation is not by itself reason-giving, is that her critical account is more than a 'clarification' of moral thought: it is foundational to the defence of a clear-eyed moral life against an obscurantist and authoritarian one that rules in everyday language and practice in the name of 'Morality'.... Foot offers us a picture of suffering, need, tyranny, and injustice as being in their distinctive ways themselves reasons for response and action in so far as appropriately situated people care about such things. Such caring constitutes their individual or collective (Foot instances the defence of Leningrad) 'moral' character— their virtues.

I find other fellow travellers. More recently, Bernard Williams, in *Ethics and the Limits of Philosophy*, has targeted as a 'particular development of the ethical' the 'Peculiar Institution' of 'Morality'. It is, he says, something we would be better off without. As a way of clarifying my own thinking of where this consensus leaves us, I want to attend to some of the things Williams says here and in his *Shame and Necessity*. There is not very much in the critique of 'the morality system' and of the meanly imperialistic spirit that Williams takes as its core that I would want to dispute; in particular I think Williams is

right to see the philosophical illusions of the freely willing moral subject helping to underpin the moralistic stand's empirical and practical isolation of the blamed individual as a sort of ultimate originator of sin. And he is right too to see a decolonized future for notions of obligation and responsibility, independent of moralistic mythology, 'as merely one kind of ethical consideration among others.' But I have two worries with Williams's outlook which will serve to introduce larger issues.

The first has to do with moral blame. Williams denies that moral considerations are necessarily reasons for a person to do things. Moral blame, he says, is a piece of 'machinery' which involves the 'fiction' that the individual is necessarily susceptible to moral reasons, ascribing moral reasons to its target in such a way that 'this may help him to be such a person'. Thus, despite its dangers, it is a 'positive achievement' of the 'blame system' that it fosters 'recruitment into the deliberative community', the community who share ethical dispositions. But what constitutes this 'recruitment'? Anything more than the disposition to avoid (these people's) blame? For what reasons? Now, as a critic of moralistic blaming and as one who looks forward to our disembarking from the moral guilt-trip in general, Williams himself adumbrates such questions. But whereas an Old Left Footian like me might grant that a condemnatory attack on somebody just might have the consequence that they came to see the error of their ways independently of the attack— 'How didn't I see that?'—Williams wants to see this part of the 'ethical system' demoted to a 'pragmatic blame' surrounded by other 'practices of encouragement and discouragement, acceptance and rejection, which work on desire and character to shape them into the requirements and possibilities of ethical life'. What eludes me here is a sense of such social processes as anything other than 'recruitment', socialization into particular 'deliberative communities' on pain of rejection, blame, and exclusion. Minus moral metaphysics, I am not clear that we have really left behind the discourse of requirements and permissions.

The second worry has to do with Guilt, Victims, Enforcers. In *Shame and Necessity* Williams devotes a seminal endnote to 'Mechanisms of Shame and Guilt', giving a naturalistic social-psychological account of them as involving distinct 'internalised figures'. (I take it that this rooting is intended not merely to trace origins, but to characterize the nature of these sentiments.) Whereas shame internalizes the 'watcher or witness', guilt internalizes the 'victim or enforcer'. My worry is over this account of guilt.... Williams runs victim and enforcer together. As I take it that guilt as constructed by the morality system is or involves rule-transgression, I find this hard to understand. Surely it is not 'primitively' the case that these two roles are, let alone have to be, identical; for surely the aggression in guilt as constructed by the morality system is internalized, broadly speaking, from the primitive enforcer of transgressed requirements. Retaliation implies power, and the victim, who may not even be hostile, may, if hostile, be unthreatening. Sorrow towards someone one has wronged seems to me something that the punitive recriminations of the Morality System get in the way of by focusing attention on the self—imagine the victim ignored as the parent turns on the offending child: 'Say sorry!' Thus I do not agree with Williams's claim, contrasting guilt with the 'narcissism' of shame, that 'the victims and their feelings' are at the core of the guilt system. That connection is contingent on the presence of victims in the content of the prohibitions and sanc-

tions. Still less, since it is the victim's hostile feelings, not their sufferings, that Williams highlights, do I see why focusing fearful attention on such feelings should be seen as 'an inherent virtue of guilt as opposed to shame'.

Williams looks forward to the erosion of the Peculiar Institution of Morality: its machinery carries too much untenable baggage and wreaks too much damage to wider concerns, ethical and otherwise. It might be thought that emancipation from it would leave us with a better chance of clear-eyed ethical vision. But Williams is inclined to think an undimmed, perhaps even enlightened, capacity to be in touch with ethical realities an illusion: 'ethical thought has no chance of being everything that it seems'. One such false appearance, as I understand Williams, is that of the possibility of full-blooded ethical truth. This appearance is undermined not only by the fact of disagreement within as well as among societies but by the fact that were such disagreements to dissolve and the world to converge in what Williams has more recently called 'one homogeneous ethical language', this would not be because people's ethical outlooks had come to be guided by how things ethically are. Disagreements do not entail failure in any party, for any reason, to appreciate a truth that is there independently to be agreed upon; their existence will be best, if not sufficiently, explained sociologically, maybe by cultural imperialism—unlike purely sociological accounts of scientific disagreement which are hopelessly deaf to the way scientific inquiry is responsive to reality. Within the territory constituted by an ethical outlook, there will be a range of 'thick' concepts, picking out kinds of situation, disposition, and so on that are sufficiently stable and have sufficiently salient features in terms of that value-outlook to merit a label. But 'the question of what your repertoire of thick concepts is reveals your own or your society's attitude'. Nothing 'in the situation' can 'recruit' people into using such concepts for, being a 'cultural' function, their being employed is determined not by the situation but by attitudes to situations.

Williams gives the example of boys who torture a cat for fun, saying that if an observer uses the concept 'cruel' at all, she will have to think that this is cruel. But the thought that this is cruel, as I understand Williams's view, no more has to be taken on board by the boys than an old-fashioned bystander's criticism of a bare-footed girl as 'immodest' would have to be taken on board by her—if she doesn't use that concept. The boys simply may not be disposed to view their actions in this light. Having such a concept, then, is having 'a disposition that expresses itself in categorising the world in those terms', and gaining or losing a concept is a matter of disposition, hence not of discovery. So, for Williams, as I understand him, it is not the case that, getting away from a narrowly 'moralistic' understanding of, say, cruelty or bullying, we might be able to move towards a richer, sociologically and psychologically sophisticated understanding of such truly bad things; the ethical in general is as much a social construct as its metaphysically deformed subspecies, the moral. Thus, though there may be no independently describable interests disguised behind its posturings, of the sort which Williams takes to nourish the metaphysical claims of the morality system, ethical life will be 'ideological' at least in the epistemic sense that any basis in the transcultural nature of things will be illusory. There are, on Williams's account, cultural realities, but no ethical realities in so far as these would be more than facts of valuings. Or at least their existence is strongly doubted. However, it is one thing

to say that only some ethical values can survive the transparency of reflective scrutiny, but if it is also conceded that the value of reflective scrutiny, as part of modern liberalism, is itself a cultural option, we are left with a darkness at enlightenment's noon.

It seems to me that some of the preoccupations of *Shame and Necessity* might be partly explained in terms of their complementarity with what I'll risk calling the subjectivist and cultural relativist drift that I've tried to catch in the above account of Williams's views. For the 'mechanisms' of guilt and shame depicted throughout *Shame and Necessity*'s terrific and restorative account of Homer and the Greek tragedians and analysed in the endnote are sociological or social-psychological mechanisms *par excellence*, with their internalizations of Significant Others and their implication that character formation progresses with such internalizations. Such mechanisms are compatible with just about any substantial content. A view of ethical learning, therefore, which was thus confined would be one of a learning to admire and obey what is laid down by the terms of any given society. This confinement, I suggest, remains despite Williams's successful rescuing of the ethical culture of shame from the reductive alienizings of the anthropologists. Lacking determination by their targets, ethical responses emerge on this account as socially constructed; and what is at the subject's end 'internalization' is at the other end 'recruitment', 'instilling'—the socialization process we keep hearing about from our students of sociology. Dumping the illusory autonomy of the moral, we seem to have jumped into the real heteronomy of the social, hanging by our bootstraps at the mercy of conventional prestige and its conditionings....

My question is this: if we let shame supplant guilt, what exactly do we gain in the critique of oppressive and deceitful institutions and the struggle for an ethical life capable through its transparency of winning our 'unprejudiced assent', the dampened but undoused liberal aspiration of Williams's postscript to *Ethics and the Limits of Philosophy*? As Williams himself suggests, honour and shame presuppose not just an authoritative identity-conferring and -confirming 'honours system' but the formatively habitual face-to-face visibility of communal ethical life. Maybe these could have their electronic surrogates, but that is scarcely the direction of transparency we, with Williams, are after.

I have suggested that Williams is left with no more than recruitment machinery partly by his scepticism about the possibility of ethical knowledge that transcends the inwardness of a given way of life. This seems to imply that an objectivist would offer a different account of moral education: of what they will see as practical processes of coming to recognize, say, bullying, cruelty, exploitativeness, or servility for what they are—of judgements and responses best explained (even when not rationalized as such) as caring awarenesses of what is the case rather than simply as internalizations of socially accredited valorizations. I am inclined to go that way and to contrast good moral education through experience and reflection with moralistic and other forms of conditioning inculcation.

But although relativism is a sufficient condition of assimilating education to conditioning, it is not a necessary one. For some non-relativists are content to think of the unreflective masses acquiring true opinion by what amounts to social conditioning: the compelling force of external socialization mechanisms is often assumed to be acceptable by naturalistic philosophers of an objectivist cast too. (See, for an ancestor, Hume's objectivistic defence

of feminine modesty and the modes he thought appropriate for its inculcation in the 'ductile' minds of girls.) Rationalists for whom the existence of moral reasons is independent of individuals' or even cultures' grasp or disposition and for whom moral thought is the bloodless computation of a rational fish sometimes leave me mystified on behalf of the person-in-the-street, whose best hope is to have been so socialized as unreflectively to accord with norms elaborated over her head. How, socially, interpersonally, do such people see the normatively desirable getting 'internalized' as the formation of motivating desire? How is 'co-ordination' achieved? What instils 'mutually beneficent attitudes'? Kant himself wanted the educator to rely on the pupil's fear of his contemptuous tongue. Are we not left with a Benthamite split between the educated officers and the trained troopers, notoriously illustrated by Sidgwick's doctrine that Utility would be best served by its doctrines being the object of general revulsion? Peter Railton, who proposes a rich eudaimonistic objectivism, says something along those lines: 'My sort of naturalist reduces moral properties to complex social-psychological phenomena; not to extra-human Nature. At least since Durkheim there has been a naturalistic way of understanding how social phenomena may bring into individuals a notion of obligatoriness that will present itself to them as objective and independent of their personal inclinations.' But this is a shaky hitching-post; it makes it hard, in my view, to develop a conception of moral education as something tying content to mode of becoming aware of content, in which the explanation of judgements vindicates them. Durkheim's model of moral education is basically one in which an official ideology, what Talcott Parsons was to call the 'central value system', is imposed through the orchestrated double whammy of guilt and shame. Whether such an ideology would accord with Railton's 'content' criteria of the moral is a contingent matter. Durkheim says, for example:

> It is through the practice of school discipline that we can inculcate the spirit of discipline in the child.... The principal form of punishment has always consisted in putting the guilty on the index, ostracising him, making a void around him and separating him from decent people.

> If we renounce the option of calling upon a divine power, then we must seek another which can play the same role... This power is of course society.... For, in effect society stands in relation to its members as a god stands to his followers.

Psychologically, I see Durkheim as offering as a model of moral education what amounts to something dangerously like the sort of school bullying that produces identification with the aggressor. But the main point I am making is this: relativists may see cultures as internally vindicated structures of conventionally constituted meaning; 'ideologies' on this picture would just be regimes of understanding. Some non-relativists, on the contrary, see cultural structures as open to criticism or theoretical vindication in terms of functional coherence and utility. In either case there is a tendency to see them, in effect, as ideologies in at least the sense of a way of thinking, feeling, and seeing things, whose explanation at the individual level makes only derivative reference to the things such mindsets are, apparently, focused on. There is, that is, a division between the rationale of the system and the reason for individuals' thought and action within the system. There is a tendency, then, not to see the ethical in terms of modes of being alive or dead, perceptive or blind, to situations, but as conventional modes of framing or defining situations in such a way that they are constituted as requiring this or that of us.

But consider the time in *Huckleberry Finn*, chapter 16, when the narrator's conscience fails to get him to hand over the 'nigger' slave to be returned to Miss Watson, his owner. All the moral arguments voiced in Huck's internal soliloquy line up against protecting Jim: the Guilt Mechanism, the Shame Mechanism, even the God Mechanism. All conspire to define Huck as a conspirator in criminal outrage. But, try as he does, Huck cannot live up to the commands his conscience is shouting at him. Brilliantly he deceives the slave-hunters, judging himself to be a spunkless backslider. In his discussion of it, Jonathan Bennett says that this is a case where all the reasons are on the wrong side, being defeated by 'unreasoned moral pulls'. But this is surely not right; Huck's saving Jim is intelligible, is best explained, as a response to a grasped situation: that 'nigger' is his human companion, Jim. Emotional intelligence, nourished by the experiences Huck has been through with Jim, carries the day against the System. Had his generous mind not been darkened by ideology, Huck would have seen that there was nothing else to do than what, for at least some of the very best of reasons, he does do. Being good-natured and knowing more about life than he thinks, Huck can see more clearly, roundly, and subtly than, for example, Tom Sawyer, even though Huckleberry nearly always defers to Sawyer's judgement.

Williams rescues Homer, for all humankind, from the exoticizing archaeologists. But there is an aspect of Homer's 'humanity' that seems to me to get sidelined in the status-focused emphasis on shame-identity and in the tendency to write off anything that smacks of Christianity. I am thinking about themes of human pity and inhuman pitilessness.... Throughout his portrayal of the mayhem, pitiably used for the gods' sport, Homer reminds us that each member of the to-be-devastated masses has, not just a status but a life, home, and loved ones, all soon to be lost. Here we are talking about a kind of recognition that is not expressed in a citizenly nod among the members of a Hegelian community of mutual regard. Plato thought Homer shamefully, 'womanishly', indulgent in pity. Can't we say that something was missing from Plato's sensibility, something of which his Guardians' orphanage was symptomatic? I complained earlier about the central place Williams ascribes to the victim in the morality system's version of guilt. I think victims and our capacity to respond to them belong somewhere else, more fundamental and more directly connected with our response to them than as the sources of retaliatory threat.

At one point in *Ethics and the Limits of Philosophy* Williams talks about 'the basic issue of what people should be able to rely on', and that sounds pretty fundamental and unrelativist: 'People must rely as far as possible on not being killed or used as a resource, and on having some space and objects and relations with other people they can count as their own. It also serves their interests if, to some extent at least, they can count on not being lied to.' To some extent at least: what modesty with the truth! Williams then says that 'one way, perhaps the only way' in which these basic interests can be served is 'by some kind of ethical life' and again that 'one way' of achieving this is by 'instilling certain motivations'. Again, 'one way', one way, of securing these non-maleficent reli-

abilities is by constituting and instilling them as obligations with virtually absolute priority corresponding to basic rights. Perhaps an alternative might be for the interested parties' mutual interests to be protected by the police. But if that was all there was to it, as Williams himself says, you wouldn't have an ethical life here: 'certainly, if there is to be ethical life, these ends have to be served by it and within it'. But not only is ethical life in fact a condition of such minimum goods; we would get off to the wrong start if we wheeled in obligations and rights as our primary constitutive and protective 'mechanism' for securing reliabilities in this area.

If rights and obligations, permissions and requirements, are to have a character other than that of social demands and allowances, they must express and guide something that is in a different and more vulgar register. I think we are here on ground which needs to be understood in terms of basic or common humanity—of care, nurture, trust in and uptake of each others' responses, compassion, love, fair-mindedness, acknowledgement of the other in gesture, speech, and action—of patterns and structures of attention and failures of attention. This was the warmest wisdom of the eighteenth century, best articulated perhaps in Henry Fielding's novels. And Plato and Aristotle are deviant, as maybe a lot of the philosophers were, certainly Bentham and the elder Mill, in their extrusion or ignoring of these foundationally and seminally virtuous sentiments and dispositions—and of their destructive and ugly opposites.

Much of this reductive extrusion is achieved by an amnesic rhetoric that insults our passions and inclinations by representing them as psychic ephemera: inherently capricious and contingent bubbles on the stream of consciousness; alternatively, as wantons waylaying our unguarded selves. Such sabbatarian imagery, blind and deaf to the richness and depth of the working value vocabulary of everyday life, belongs to the ideological ensemble that constitutes moralism's vision of its redemptively policing role. But if we think of 'culture' generally in the imperative mood and correlatively of acculturation as a process of subjection rather than of structuring nurture—cultivation—we imagine we are only kept together by interest corrected by duty. That is why the term 'humanity', which points beyond and beneath our stature as 'rational beings', is invoked here, not as an essentialist slogan so much as a reminder of a family neglected by theory.

Certainly humane virtues (whose warm guise is taken on in the affected cheerfulness of even the most duty-bound acts) have their consequential utilities: they serve interests. But they entail responses in which others are more than a set of rivals whose rights oblige us to police our own usurping inclinations. That prohibition-fenced, 'bourgeois' model of life was of course one of the reasons why Marx was so hyperbolically hostile to the claims of 'rights' discourse and averse to recognizing its back-up functions. Thoughtlessly, he seems to have imagined a time beyond scarcity when interests would not seriously conflict. That said, however, it is not through recruitment and control mechanisms that the reliabilities of ethical life exist; rather, its taken-for-granted reliabilities are conditions of the elaboration, for good or ill, of such mechanisms. Not all virtues are artificial virtues.

I am attempting to question the adequacy of what I will call the Durkheimian model of socialization and of moral education, and at the same time to suggest that the concept of humanity brings with it a notion of naturally appropriate understanding responses to individuals, which

are social and communicative without being the activity of 'Society' or 'the Community'. Cultures build on this and also articulate it so that there are many ways of being human. Cultural practices do represent themselves as ways of being human: as appropriate to the specific and individual nature of its members. Putatively, children everywhere are brought up, not just under. But not all cultural practices constitute equibrilliant contributions to life's rich tapestry; some but not all are sustainable only through ideological illusion. We recognize what it is to find criticism or defence, of our own and others' practices and responses, more or less understandable, sound, or wise. I am thinking of racist hatred and contempt, of child slavery and prostitution, of the ritual mutilation of girls' genitals and also of the dumping of elderly people into drugged isolation, young people into what is called 'care', and the banging up of the criminally convicted in institutions that make them worse people. These things hardly bear thinking about or looking, clear-eyed, at. If they are looked at, they need special stories to render them tolerable within an otherwise humane mind. It is a modern nervousness that, behind the ideology of cultural relativism, stills the voice of, or blocks the ears to, criticism. Valued qualities tend to flourish in structured syndromes and to need to be understood as part of situated patterns; some goods come at a price of other goods risked, damaged, or forgone. But that pluralist truth does not entail that any more or less coherent pattern is as good as another.

A child's shin is painfully bruised. This is a bad thing. It turns out that he is a newcomer, picked on because of his unusual accent. In a more complex but no more extraordinary or suspicious way, this is a bad thing too. Maybe the best explanation is in terms of the individual bully, maybe in terms of fairly stable patterns of such treatment. Ethical features of situations—summarized in terms of bullying, cruelty, cowardice, destructiveness, callousness, meanness—seem to be a part of everyday causal stories, and to play that part even under more sophisticated ethical descriptions. This consequentiality and importance for human harm and good perhaps distinguishes ethical attributes from those that Hume talks about that, in artworks, are the objects of aesthetic 'taste'. For there, the 'beauties fitted by nature to excite agreeable sentiments' exist only to be appreciated. They are created to excite and to be, given human responsiveness across 'nations and ages', the best explanation—as against prejudice, provincialism, partiality, and other candidates—of the sound judge's thereby sound appreciation....

Since it is not a nihilism, a Marxian outlook seems to me to presuppose some such humanist naturalism. Otherwise we are left with a pan-ideological scepticism often accompanied by some arbitrary notion of 'commitment'. Stunting, distorting, and fragmenting divisions, penetrating to the heart of domestic life, Marx traced predominantly to the social mode of production, to whose reproduction he saw ideologies as functional. His 'historicism', his own 'illusions of progress' as Georges Sorel put it, disposed him to miss the contemporary trees for the future wood. But this long-sightedness, which brought with it an obsession with attacking what he thought of as a sentimental

nostalgia for the present, was consistent with an ethically rich and passionate grasp of that present. The eighteenth-century or even Dickensian notion of humanity that I have been advancing as a multi-piled foundation of ethical life and ethical consciousness might seem a long way from a historical materialist vision. But Marx's perception of capitalism's meanly malign neglect for its participants, its victims if you like, is not only continuous with but dependent on the more rudimentary sense of humanity and inhumanity. For the sense of violation of an infant, or an elderly man or woman, is under the aspect of maturational potentialities, possibilities, and powers thwarted, damaged, or destroyed. Marx's account of capitalism's havoc is, at a macro level, akin to a story of the depredations of a vicious children's home: in each case we have a picture of limitation and of damage, of survival and natural resistance. In each case we have a picture of 'alienation', the twisting into a destructive chain of that whose nature is to be a creative communication. In each case too we have a sort of epistemic privileging of those without privilege, as those best if still precariously placed unreflectively to grasp the ethical reality of their oppression. And, although, certainly in the abstract, it makes little sense to think there is a determinate answer to the question what would be the best realization of such possibilities, within our ignorances and disagreements we have some that we would, truly, rank lower, and some that we would reject....

The Objectivity of Morality Remains an Open Possibility

Peter Railton

Should we see morality as an ideology? And, if so, what are we to conclude?

Morality *does* make an almost irresistible target, a sitting duck, for *Ideologiekritik*. For it presents itself as a set of evaluations and commands of lofty impartiality or universal validity; yet a glance at history shows instead a succession of norms—all at one point or other widely viewed as moral—that have sanctioned slavery, the subjugation of women, and a host of other purported rights and duties that seem to us in retrospect to correspond more closely to the prevailing distribution of power, privilege, and interests than to conditions of absolute value or universal reason.

None the less, we seem to have a soft spot for morality and moral theorizing. Professional philosophers and historians not excepted, we by and large continue to think of our own morality as something possessing considerable authority (with allowance for the usual slippage between what we practise and what we preach). This social and cultural deference has inspired some of our most incisive intellects—Marx and Nietzsche, to take an interesting pair—to critique morality mercilessly.

'The ideas of the ruling class are in every epoch the ruling ideas,' Marx wrote, and are 'nothing more than the "ideal expression" of the dominant material relationships.' Every ruling class will 'represent its interest as the common interest' and 'give its ideas the form of universality, and represent them as the only rational, universally valid ones'....

Nietzsche, for his part, did not doubt that interests far from universal underlie existing morality, though he hardly thought of them as élite interests. In morality 'high and independent spirituality, the will to stand alone, even a powerful reason are experienced as dangers; everything that elevates an individual above the herd and intimidates the neighbor is henceforth called *evil*, and the fair, modest, conforming mentality, the *mediocrity* of desires attains moral designations and honors'.

Many elements of the full critiques Marx and Nietzsche have lodged against morality are uncomfortably convincing....

Even shot full of holes, however, the duck sits yet. What are we to make of this situation? I will venture the suggestion that this situation is, in a sense, as it should be. But I do so with some awareness of the paradox this appears to involve....

In recent years the term *ideology* has once again acquired currency....

An ideology is in the first instance a set of beliefs or values held by individuals or groups, not a set of propositions considered in itself. The same descriptive or evaluative proposition could be held for quite diverse reasons, and this points us to a key element: whether a belief or value (as held by someone) is ideological will depend upon the nature of the explanation of why he or she has it.

A given set of descriptive or evaluative propositions as held by a certain individual or group might be more or less questionable, but it will count as ideological only if there is an explanation of these beliefs and other attitudes according to which their prevalence is attributed (to a significant degree) to the fact that holding them serves certain non-epistemic interests—especially, perhaps, interests in *legitimation*. The interests in question need not be the interests of all of those holding the beliefs. They may, for example, be the interests of the socially or culturally dominant class. An *ideological diagnosis* (as we might call it) of why certain attitudes are held typically involves showing that they serve a legitimizing function because they represent particular institutions, practices, or norms as good—or as obligatory, natural, universal, or necessary. Equally, they may represent alternative institutions, practices, or norms as bad—or as unnatural, impermissible, foreign, or, especially, impossible.

Although this diagnostic notion of ideology is at root explanatory in ambition, it has a potential normative relevance that has been salient throughout its career. For example, to attribute the currency of a belief chiefly to *non*-epistemic interests is hardly a form of epistemic endorsement.... It is evident that beliefs can satisfy various sorts of interests without being true or well warranted—indeed, in certain contexts true or well-warranted belief might be antithetical to an individual's or group's strongest interests.

Now it cannot be the whole of ideological critique to claim that there is a contrariety between a belief's functioning ideologically and the belief's truth or warrant. For there are many cases in which epistemic and non-epistemic interests point in the same direction: often our non-epistemic interests will be advanced more effectively by true belief or reliable belief-forming practices than by error or

arbitrariness. A belief's truth or a belief-forming mechanism's reliability can be part of an explanation of why I get so much out of it, and it sometimes seems quite possible for me to 'see through' a largely non-epistemic explanation of my belief to an epistemically vindicatory picture of why that non-epistemic story works.

However, we also find cases in which the attempt to 'see through' to the non-epistemic explanation is naturally destabilizing of belief. Suppose that, like most automobile drivers, I consider myself well above average (on a 0 to 10 scale, I have heard it said, drivers on average rate themselves about 7.5). This belief not only feeds my vanity and legitimizes my conduct—it also gives me the nerve to venture out on the roads, to trust my children to my hands, and so on. Let us suppose that I could be shown rather quickly that this belief of mine really stems almost entirely from these non-epistemic interests—e.g. that I have been grossly selective in my attention to evidence and highly biased towards my own case in interpreting what evidence I do notice. Can I 'see through' this non-epistemic explanation of my belief to an 'epistemic explanation' that would provide reasonable warrant? No. Neither can I attribute the effectiveness of the belief in advancing my interests to its truth. (The main contribution of the belief is to enhance my mobility and confidence. Even as a below-average driver I may well benefit on the whole from this.) This sort of non-epistemic explanation invokes a mechanism that depends to some extent on its lack of transparency. The belief is therefore more likely to be destabilized than reinforced on reflection....

Thus far we have been speaking primarily of belief in general. What, then, of *morality?*...

Can we identify certain core elements that serve to distinguish moral evaluation from other species? We can then ask whether these elements might be vulnerable to critique as ideological.

Here, then, are some central truisms of various philosophically self-aware traditions within modern thought. Moral evaluation is:

(a) *impartial* (or, as I would prefer to say, non-partial)—it takes into account all those potentially affected;

(b) *universal* (or, as I would prefer to say, non-indexical)—it claims a legitimacy and scope of application that goes beyond any particular set of social boundaries or convention;

(c) *beneficent*—it assigns prima facie positive deliberative weight to the well-being of those potentially affected, negative deliberative weight to their suffering....

(d) Morality is *practical*—it purports to provide answers to the agent's questions 'What ought I to do?' or 'How best to live?'....

We will come back to morality shortly, but first let us pick up the thread of our discussion of ideology and belief. We had briefly discussed how a philosophical explanation of the destabilization of belief under reflection might go: in the relevant cases, reflection on the ideological origins of belief will be destabilizing not merely by some quirk, but because belief by its nature 'aims at' truth. The fact of destabilization thus seems to possess a kind of normative relevance *internal* to epistemology, even if it is not in itself normatively determinative (it is, after all, just a fact). Might there be an analogue on the moral side, such that if ideological criticism in fact tends to undermine moral commitment, this is more than a mere curiosity but rather possesses internal normative relevance to morality?

To be sure, ordinary, 'descriptive' belief has a central place in moral thought and practice. It is easy to say a priori that moral evaluation 'floats free' of descriptive belief so that people could have all the same descriptive beliefs yet differ arbitrarily much in their moral evaluations, but in fact this is seldom or never the case. Historically, beliefs about the nature of action, the psychology of motivation, the likely causes and outcomes of acts and practices, the teleological structure (or lack of it) of the world, the distribution of human differences and similarities, and so on, tend to be found clustered with particular moral points of view, rather than distributed arbitrarily across the moral landscape. Arguably, some of the most profound historical changes in moral opinion have been precipitated precisely by changes—seemingly very 'normatively relevant', if not 'logically compelling'—in underlying descriptive beliefs about the existence of natural hierarchies, human variability, cosmological origins, and so on. And much of ideological critique is focused directly on these areas of belief....

To grasp the nettle, however, we need to ask explicitly whether the effect of the 'reflection test' in changing moral opinion can be underwritten in a way *normatively internal* to morality. After all, some quite humane values might as a matter of fact fail to survive a ruthless preoccupation with personal failings or with the loss of national prestige suffered as a colonial empire crumbles. How would this tend to disqualify these values morally?

We need, then, to locate a path of disqualification that is relevant according to distinctively moral standards of relevance. We began in the case of belief with the *attitude* of belief, and the norms said to be 'internal' to it. Let us proceed similarly with the attitude of valuing, and moral valuing in particular.

The attitude of valuing typically involves some sort of desiring, it seems, but is distinct from *mere* desiring, much as believing that p typically involves some sort of 'finding oneself drawn to believe that p', but also involves something more. Belief that p characteristically involves various commitments and claims of authority, usually tacit: one accords p a degree of confidence in one's actions and interactions; one gives p a certain weight in assessing one's own beliefs, new evidence, or the beliefs of others; one seeks to render p, and one's commitment to it, consistent with one's other beliefs; one is inclined to feel defensive about one's attitude towards p and to be disquieted by learning that the explanation of why one believes that p is not truth-related—that one's belief that p cannot be seen as *attuned to* evidence for p. At this point one may freely recognize that one still is drawn as strongly as ever to believe that p, but one's attitudes of epistemic commitment to p and claimed authority regarding p will not comfortably remain undiminished. Putting things the other way around, one might find that one is not much 'drawn to believe' this uncomfortable explanation of one's belief that p, but that, given the evidence, one is none the less inclined to accord it epistemic authority.

Similarly, I can desire A without the sorts of commitments or claims of authority that valuing A characteristically—and, again, usually tacitly—involves. When I value A, other things equal: I am inclined to accord A some weight in regulating my deliberation and choice, and also my judgements of others and recommendations to them; I seek to reconcile my plans, goals, and ends with A; I am inclined to invoke A to justify or defend myself, and to treat it as in turn justified and

defensible; thus I typically feel uneasy when I perceive A to be threatened, and defensive when I take A to be challenged. One way in which A might be challenged is by an explanation of my valuing A that removes any element that I would count as an appropriate ground of value, such that my valuing could not be seen as an *attunement* to relevant value-making features. In the absence of any other backing for A, I could still acknowledge that my desire for A is undiminished, even as I will no longer be easy in according A the same regulative role in running my life or judging myself and others. Put the other way around, I may come to see the taking of not-A as an end as appropriate—as attuned to value-making features—even though I do not now much desire not-A at all.

An example of this 'internal' purport of the attitude of valuing might help, and for our purposes the relevant domain of evaluation is the moral. Given the amount of content in conditions (a)–(c), above, and the regulative practical role (d), we can see how moral evaluation cannot 'float free' of other attitudes and beliefs. Consider someone brought up in a racial or caste system, who initially deemed it morally appropriate to keep 'higher' and 'lower' groups from mixing. Were he ever to be attracted to a member of a 'lower' group, this individual would likely find that attraction 'unclean', 'intrinsically degrading'—an appropriate source of guilt, and not to be permitted to regulate his choice of social relations. Were he to learn that his sister had formed a romantic relationship with a 'lower' group member, he would think her 'disgraced' and 'for ever stained', and be very ashamed for himself and his family. Suppose now that this individual learns that the supposed historical and biological basis of the caste or racial distinctions is bogus: the groups are virtually indistinguishable genetically and the actual origin of the subordination-superordination relationship is a brutal conquest unrelated to any moral concerns. This individual might well continue irresistibly to *feel* that there is something in itself 'off' or 'shameful' when members of the different castes or races intermix, but would be unlikely to think that moral 'righteousness' lies in reinforcing this feeling to prevent any intercaste or interracial attraction from having a regulative role in action. He might still find himself acutely uncomfortable when his sister presents her new spouse, but he would feel quite differently about whether or why she now should be driven from the family.

Moral evaluation, then, finds its place in a complex constellation of non-moral beliefs and attitudes, and indeed *supervenes* upon them, yielding the final element of the moral point of view to be mentioned here:

(e) one is committed to defend one's moral evaluations by citing non-moral but morally relevant value-making features.

This sort of supervenience has been seen by moral philosophers of all stripes as a conceptual, a priori, or otherwise fundamental truth about valuation—one would simply not grasp the idea of value if one thought that values could simply be 'added' to a state of affairs or 'pasted' to them (such that two states of affairs could be identical in all non-moral characteristics, yet, properly, receive different moral evaluations). When allied with elements (a)–(d), the result is that moral evaluation hardly 'floats free' of our best account of how the world works, why we believe what we do, and so on. Thus, while these various constraints are logically consistent with the persistence of moral disagreement in the face of many factual agree-ments, factual agreements that concern matters within the scope of (a)–(e)—such as learning that there is no difference between the races and castes of a given society that could affect characteristics relevant to well-being, capacity for rational action, etc.—impinge forcibly on moral opinion, not as a psychological curiosity, but by the nature of the moral attitude itself....

We now are in a position to begin to apply our characterization of what (at least in part) makes a set of views an ideology to our account of what (at least in part) makes a set of views a morality. It is already easy to see why it is so tempting to apply an ideological critique to morality. But spelling this out a bit will help us to say something about a quite general question, 'What is the nature of ideological critique itself?' It will also enable us to pose a more particular question, 'Does the weight of ideological critique, such as it is, fall uniformly upon moral notions, or are there some elements that are much more vulnerable than others?'

Marx spoke of ideologies as standing things on their heads: representing the particular as general, the local as universal, the contingent as necessary, the profane as sacred, the effect as cause. Although he diagnoses ideologies as in fact expressing a particular standpoint in a contingent and historically evolving world, he insists that they do not—indeed, cannot—represent themselves as such. A given class (for example) will 'represent its interest as the common interest' and 'give its ideas the form of universality, and represent them as the only rational, universally valid ones'. It is essential to a functional ideology that those holding it and passing it along to others by and large take it to heart. That is, if (say) partial, conventional, contingent norms are to be reified as disinterested, natural, and necessary, then this reification must have a deep grip on the ideologues themselves....

We have identified both passive and active elements in our philosophical understanding of morality. Each is at risk, in its own way, from ideological criticism. But to the same degree?

Shared risks first. The passive, evaluative component (comprising (*a*)–(*c*) and (*e*)) claims to perceive things comprehensively and coherently, from a point of view that is not merely descriptive, and yet is not the point of view of anyone or any time in particular—no individual, group, or society. This seems not only grandiose, but potentially nonsensical. Points of view do not need to be perfectly coherent, but surely they cannot be as incoherent as the jumble that would result from simply aggregating individuals and their ends across time and space. A point of view is by its nature selective, offering a perspective on the landscape rather than the landscape as such. The moral point of view *is* supposed to be selective, glimpsing only that which is relevant to moral evaluation—typically, philosophers have spoken of the general interest and the intrinsically good. Yet Marx and Nietzsche each argued in his own way that actual societies are scenes of conflicting interests, and that actual goods have their value not inherently, but in virtue of their relation to subjects. Without subjects, nothing would be of value. Not because there would be no one to see or appreciate it, but because, without subjects, there would be nothing that could *constitute* value. Absolute or non-relational value, value that stands apart from subjects and calls forth their pursuit, is a *fetish*.

One can, of course, readily see the legitimizing function of a claim made on behalf of a particular standpoint that it is universal, impartial, attuned to objective, intrinsic value-making features. Such a claim privileges a particular standpoint, and privileging is the secular equivalent of canonization. Yet it is altogether too easy in retrospect to see past claims of universal validity as unwarranted projections of the local and particular into the eternal and sacred, and thus supposedly beyond question or challenge. Philosophical conceptions of the good, too, seem in retrospect expressive of their context. Not much imagination is required to see in the Aristotelian notion of proper function a reflection of the Greek caste system. Or to see in medieval notions of noble and base, or honour, the reflection of an aristocratic warrior society. Or to see in the utilitarian ideas of happiness as individual desire-satisfaction and of a universal metric of value the reflection of modern bourgeois commodification and market society.

The issue here is not, or at any rate not yet, whether this constitutes a telling reason for rejecting these notions. And it would take an altogether different level of engagement with history to say anything about the credibility of these claims. But at the moment our concern is merely hypothetical: since previous conceptions of the good bear some of the superficial marks of ideologies, we should ask whether and to what extent this diagnosis, if borne out, would disqualify them. Before investigating further, we need to have a similarly preliminary look at the active element in morality's alchemy.

The active side of morality has characteristically found expression during the modern period in the notion of *obligation*, which in turn has been voiced in two terminologies. First, a terminology familiar from emergent civil society: rights, laws, duties, requirements, contracts. Of course, however much they resemble civil notions, moral rights and laws are, according to this conception, natural or rational rather than conventional. We understand the 'force' of these notions in civil society to lie in their civil embodiment: mechanisms for verifying and enforcing contracts, advantages of mutual trust, the institutionalization of property, etc. As natural or rational notions, we must see these as owing their force to something else, such as the abstract notion of respect for others, reasonableness, or fairness.

Secondly, we find a terminology of religious and, ultimately, I suppose, familial origin: a language of commands and imperatives issued from some authoritative source. This language we understand tolerably well if attached to an actual (presumptively authoritative) issuing subject using the imperative voice. And we can grasp its 'action-guiding' force if we imagine that the issuer is someone we wish, or are constrained by some interest or incentive, to please. But moral commands or categorical imperatives are supposed not to be issued by a lesser force than Reason itself, or rather, that part of each of us which embodies Reason.

It is, again, not difficult to see the potential contribution to legitimation of such 'denatured' notions of obligation or imperative. Yet as philosophers since Hobbes and Hume have urged, it is problematic whether these notions can really have application apart from a background of actual institutions, sanctions, etc. Kant's critical philosophy sought to move from a metaphysical conception of the ground of obligation to a 'practical' one, but even for him a background teleology of reward and sanction remained in place as a necessary postulate of practical reason. Historical perspective may well convince us that what is in fact going on is less an expression of divine teleology than of local social circumstances. The distinctive notion of natural property rights as individual entitlements that demand respect, which gains ascendancy in early modern moral philosophy, seems to have a great deal to do with the emergent forms and conflicts of modern civil society, but it hardly affords the *only* or *natural* condition under which humans have lived together with some semblance of peace and flourishing, or mutual respect.

So has the mainstream moral philosophy of Hobbes and Hume already done the work of ideological critique for it? Not the whole job, surely. For the philosophical critique of 'naturalizing' obligation and property has made use of its own 'naturalizing', which Marx and others have deemed to be equally dubious: a theory not of Reason but of Human Nature (and allied theories of 'natural appetites' or 'sentiments')....

On the surface at least, modern moral philosophy—even modern critical moral philosophy—is grist to the mill of ideological analysis. The particular character or content of the reifications involved varies between passive and active elements in morality, and with the evolution of the various schools of moral thought. But in general it is possible to begin to tell a story in which the particular is being taken as universal, the conditioned or relational as absolute, the contingent as necessary, and the socially and historically local as natural. And in all cases we can see how these stories could have a legitimizing function, at the least by turning back certain challenges to legitimacy.

But what are we to do with these bald claims? Let us simply suppose for the moment that something like them is true.

Ideological (self-)criticism is normally understood to involve posing to ourselves the question: Can our commitment to particular views and practices be (sincerely, and with awareness) sustained in light of a full social-historical understanding of where those views, practices, and commitments come from, how they operate within us (e.g. their psychological or psychodynamic mechanism), and what their actual or likely consequences are (e.g. which interests they effectively promote or hinder)?

At the outset I mentioned the remarkable degree to which even philosophers critical of past moral theorizing or practice have defended continuing commitment to morality. One usually has to look outside mainstream philosophy—to Marx or Nietzsche, say—to find attitudes more openly dismissive of the core of conventional morality. Suppose, as I just did, that the ideological diagnosis is largely true. Which response—the sceptical or the defensive—seems more appropriate?

Asking this question seems, however, to be stepping outside the framework of ideological critique. For it suggests that we have a *second* sort of test in mind. In the first test we ask whether or to what extent our convictions do in fact survive critical self-awareness. In the second test we ask what to make of that—whether this response on our part is or is not appropriate. When put this way, it seems as if the second test is the locus of all the *epistemic* action—the first test is just one more piece of empirical psychology, which might figure in the second as a kind of evidence but which lacks normative standing in its own right.

Or is the 'second test' really separate? Deeming one's responses *appropriate* appears to be just one more normative conviction. Are we now asking whether this conviction itself will in fact be retained when we are fully aware?...

Bernard Williams, in his influential book *Ethics and the Limits of Philosophy,* raises what I take to be a similar concern about the easy supposition that a distanced perspective destroys prejudice but nothing of real epistemic looks like a normative issue, for it requires us to ask not 'What is *altered* by reflection?' but 'What of *epistemic value* is at peril?' or 'What do we have *epistemic reason* to make of this alteration?' It begins to look, therefore, as if we can normatively problematize ideological critique itself by a reflective process that asks where our confidence in the authority of changes wrought by such critique might come from....

Now let us... suppose that existing moral practices in our home country are highly appropriate from a moral point of view, but we have become uneasy about relying upon them owing to reflective awareness of their arbitrary origins and of the extent to which social practices in general are variable or arbitrary. Can our pre-anthropological moral knowledge be rewon? Moral inquiry can no longer for us take the form of asking with great care, 'Is tradition being followed?', even if this question did occupy the centre of pre-anthropological debates over a practice's wisdom or fairness. We must be able to see established moral practices as yielding certain regular outcomes—contingently, relationally—in our evolving context. And we perhaps must also have some idea of how it could be that practices of arbitrary origin whose surface appearance or formal features do not as such distinguish them from other, morally unreliable practices might none the less, in a given social and historical setting, be robustly dependable morally. Of course, our participation in any such reflective, vindicatory process may now have tainted us or our society: we have lost the innocence that was a key ingredient or a saving grace, and an ideally full self-understanding that would overcome this could be for ever out of reach in practice. But even this unfortunate result need not preclude our knowing that the pre-anthropological practices were good. So normative moral knowledge perhaps need not be an altogether closed book to the cosmopolitan mind.

We are working here with the idea of a *vindicatory explanation* of a practice, as opposed to a debunking explanation. Vindication may take many forms. The explanation can be 'direct': we might show that, though the origins are arbitrary in various ways, the practice (or artefact, phenomenon, etc.) has certain features which, in its context, make it robustly reliable in particular respects. Or, the explanation can be 'indirect': the practice (artefact, etc.) exists as it does and where it does (or plays the role in people's lives that it does) because of a *selection mechanism* that favours reliability of the relevant sort. The explanation can also combine the two.... Direct explanations are often of the 'existentially quantified' form: we have reason to think there is *something* about this practice (or artefact, etc.) in this setting that yields reliability. Indirect explanations are often highly speculative: we have reason to think this practice (or artefact, etc.) wouldn't continue to be used if it didn't play such-and-such a role at least as well as salient, available competitors.

Not much is clear about *how much* vindicatory explanation one must possess once a practice (artefact, etc.) has become as deeply problematized as talk of objective moral knowledge has been for us moderns. No doubt the answer is pragmatic in the sense that how much vindication we need depends upon the centrality of a practice (artefact, etc.) to our lives and the seriousness and specificity of the problematization....

We might think that telling time is of little direct relevance to the moral case be-cause of the existence of objective indicators to check correlations independently. And we might also think that, in the story of the pre-anthropological home society, the real issue for moral epistemology has just been assumed away—the practices are described as if they unproblematically bore identifiably moral properties. This, too, would yield the possibility of objective indicators and independent ways of checking, but only because we have fixed the moral criteria. What if our concern—what has been problematized by the ideological critique of a Marx or a Nietzsche—is with the criteria themselves, or their very possibility? Where then is the objective indicator or independent check?

To move further along in answering such questions we need to be more self-aware in thinking about the critical reflection test itself. How well does *it* survive critical reflection?...

What sorts of ambition must a theory of belief or value have in order to underwrite talk of warrant or objectivity? These are very large and contentious questions, and we will have to content ourselves with looking only at one aspect: how *rationalistic* must the ambition be? Hume famously argued at the end of part 1 of the *Treatise of Human Nature* that a strict rationalistic project failed even in its own terms: 'understanding, when it acts alone, and according to its most general principles, entirely subverts itself, and leaves not the lowest degree of evidence in any proposition, either in philosophy or in common life'. Kant, coming along behind Hume, attempted to rescue rationalism by rendering it *critical* rather than dogmatic, grounding claims of objectivity and warrant in a priori necessities inherent in thought and action rather than metaphysical necessities inherent in the world.

Many in the tradition of *Ideologiekritik* can be thought of as pressing this critical rationalist project beyond Kant, situating it socially and historically. But it would appear to sustain after all a commitment to the attainability of objectivity and warrant through an operation of reflective understanding.... In a word, a faith in *reason*....

In any event, the crucial step lies in repudiating such thoughts as those equating subjectivity or contingency with arbitrariness. Subjects are parts of the world, possessing at a given time more or less definite properties, as well as the capacity to remake themselves in various ways. Sentiments as well as reasoning are products of a long-term interaction between organism and the natural and social world, and both sentiment and reasoning may be more or less impartial and object-oriented. When critical reflection brings them together, it may accomplish something neither could accomplish on its own. If we call that which relates to subjects *subjectual*—as we now call that which relates to objects *objectual*—we can see at once how misleading the equation of subjectual with arbitrary can be. Ideological criticism draws upon this very thought: while the subjectual cannot simply be reified as merely objectual—subjects have ways of seeing themselves that then contribute to the explanation of how they behave—subjects none the less are implicated in the world and interactive with it in ways that may make them more or less capable of seeing themselves or the world as things are. We might call this *objective subjectuality*, a condition that requires effort and good fortune, to shake the complacency of our ordinary self-conceptions, but is in no way incoherent. Ideological analyses contribute to the shaking of our complacency by indicating how deeply things might not be as they seem.

There is a remarkable similarity between the critical machinery of ideological analysis, Hume's 'accurate proof' of his ethics, and Rawls's notion of (wide) reflective equilibrium as a form of justification. All three operate with the thought that we concede normative authority to conclusions which show a certain kind of stability in the light of fuller information, greater sensitivity and awareness, and movement away from various kinds of parochialism. Such a picture presents the appearance of illicit movement, from... brute fact to normative authority. But the fact isn't very brute (it is reflective, critical) and the authority isn't absolute (it is provisional, and dependent upon rationally optional natures and purposes).

We do of course start off with what we believe and value, and where we end up may depend more or less heavily upon that. But rationality in belief—as philosophers of science have long emphasized—must be a matter of *where one goes from here*. For surely neither alternative is rational: to go nowhere (because one cannot start anywhere) or to start from where we aren't (with what we *don't* believe).

If morality, the sitting duck for ideological critique, is still afloat, that is because we have been able both to criticize and to rebuild it—as we have rebuilt scientific belief—from normatively available materials to meet the empirical onslaught of experience. Moral thought itself furnished the essential ingredients to give rise to challenges of partiality, false factual assumptions, or parochialism about the good life. These have been recognized grounds of criticism within moral practice, stemming from its objective purport. But moral thought has also evolved under these criticisms, becoming less partial, less factually benighted, less parochial. As criticisms have become normatively intelligible (e.g. charges of parochialism of various kinds), so has a morality rebuilt in response to them.

We ask a lot of morality for it to be in good standing because we grant moral assessment a good deal of authority. Perhaps this will be vindicated over time to a significant degree. Further knowledge and reflection do seem unlikely to unsettle altogether such ideas as these: that lives can go better or worse for those who will live them; that institutions and attitudes can be less or more partial; and that practices can be more or less widely, reciprocally, or equally beneficial to those affected by them. Perhaps the reluctance of philosophers in the modern epoch to consign morality to the depths where notions of honour, divine order, and natural teleology now repose reflects their sense that morality has proven remarkably adaptive, remarkably effective at co-opting its critics....

THE CONTINUING DEBATE:
Is Morality an Ideological Illusion?

What Is New

Though it is hardly a new idea, the issue of whether ideology and ideological influence has ended (or whether its demise is near) remains a much debated topic. Daniel Bell launched much of the discussion in 1960, arguing that the wonders of democracy and capitalism would make all the machinations of government transparent to citizens, and spell the end of ideology. Though Bell's perspective now seems rather dated, the issue continues to draw attention. For example, Richard Rorty (who has a very different perspective than Bell's) has recently argued that contemporary liberal societies share widespread principles concerning fairness, justice, and injustice; but they *consciously* and knowingly fail to follow those principles, so the problems of our culture do not stem from ideological deception, but from failure to recognize genuine new possibilities for structuring behavior and society. Thus whether one rejects or accepts the importance of ideological influence on our ethical thinking and behavior, the issue of ideology remains an important question.

Where to Find More

Many of Peter Railton's major papers, including "Morality, Ideology, and Reflection; or, The Duck Sits Yet", from which the foregoing selection was taken, are collected in his *Facts, Values and Norms: Essays Toward a Morality of Consequence* (Cambridge: Cambridge University Press, 2003).

Karl Mannheim's views on ideology can be found in *Ideology and Utopia*, L. Worth and E. Shils, trans. (NY: Harcourt Brace, 1936). Karl Popper's critique of Mannheim's position can be found in *The Open Society and its Enemies* (London-Princeton, NJ: Princeton University Press, 1966).

The Marxist view of ideology can be found in Karl Marx and Friedrich Engels, *The German Ideology*, edited by C. J. Arthur (London: Longman, 1994); and Friedrich Engels, *Ludwig Feuerbach and the End of Classical German Philosophy* (1888). For comments, see Martin Seliger, *The Marxist Conception of Ideology: A Critical Essay* (Cambridge: Cambridge University Press, 1977; R. G. Peffer, *Marxism, Morality, and Social Justice* (Princeton, NJ: Princeton University Press, 1990); Allen Wood, *Karl Marx* (London: Routledge & Kegal Paul, 1981); and Allen Wood, "Marx Against Morality," in Peter Singer, editor, *A Companion to Ethics* (Oxford: Blackwell Publishers, 1991). Friedrich Nietzsche's account of ideology can be found in *Toward a Genealogy of Morals* and *Beyond Good and Evil*, available in several editions.

Daniel Bell's case for the end of ideology is presented in *The End of Ideology: On the Exhaustion of Political Ideas in the Fifties* (NY: The Free Press, 1960). For a discussion of the "end of ideology," see Richard Rorty, "Feminism, Ideology, and Deconstruction: A Pragmatist's View," in Slavoj Zizek, *Mapping Ideology* (NY: Verson, 1996). Terence Kelly, "The Unhappy Liberal: Critical Theory without Cultural Dopes," in *Constellations*, volume 7, number 3 (2000): 372–381, responds to Rorty, and also applies his own account of ideology to the behavior of contemporary American college students.

A recent book on ideology (generally critical of the theory of ideology) is Michael Rosen, *On Voluntary Servitude* (Cambridge: Polity Press and Cambridge, MA: Harvard University Press, 1966). Rosen responds to criticisms of the book and makes further comments in "On Voluntary Servitude and the Theory of Ideology," *Constellations*, volume 7, number 3 (2000): 393–407.

An excellent set of essays on ideology is *Morality, Reflection and Ideology*, edited by Edward Harcourt (Oxford: Oxford University Press, 2000) Another good collection of articles concerning ideology is T. Eagleton, editor, *Ideology* (NY: Verso, 1991); still another is Slavoj Zizek, *Mapping Ideology* (NY: Verson, 1996).

A very readable and informative websource on the topic is "Ethics and Ideology," by Sandra A. LaFave, found at *http://instruct.westvalley.edu/lafave/IDEOLOGY.html*.

Further information issues related to this debate can be found in debate 2.

CREDITS

Baier, Annette. "What Do Women Want in a Moral Theory?" from *Moral Prejudices: Essays on Ethics, Nous,* 19, (March 1985) reprinted by permission of Blackwell Publishing.

Card, Claudia. "Particular Justice and General Care," from James P. Sterba, ed., *Controversies in Feminism.* Lanham, MD: Rowman & Littlefield, 2001.

Copp, David and David Sobel. "Morality and Virtue: An Assessment of Some Recent Work in Virtue Ethics," *Ethics,* vol. 114 (April 2004).

Friedman, Marilyn. "Beyond Caring: The De-Moralization of Gender," from M. Hanen and K. Nielsen, eds., *Science, Morality, and Feminist Theory.* Calgary, B.C.: *Canadian Journal of Philosophy,* 1987.

Gauthier, David, "Why Contractarianism?" from Peter Vallentyne, ed., *Contractarianism and Rational Choice: Essays on David Gauthier's Morals By Agreement.* NY: Cambridge University Press, 1991.

Hampton Jean. "Two Faces of Contractarian Thought," from Peter Vallentyne, ed., *Contractarianism and Rational Choice: Essays on David Gauthier's Morals by Agreement.* NY: Cambridge University Press.

Harman, Gilbert. "Is There a Single True Morality?" from David Copp and David Zimmerman, eds., *Morality, Reason, and Truth.* Totawa, NJ: Rowman & Allanheld, 1984.

Harman. Gilbert. "Moral Philosophy Meets Social Psychology: Virtue Ethics and the Fundamental Attribution Error," *Proceedings of the Aristotelian Society,* vol. 99 (1999) Reprinted by courtesy of the Editor of the Aristotelian Society: ©2006

Hatch, Elvin. "The Good Side of Relativism," *Journal of Anthropological Research,* vol. 53, 1997

Held, Virginia. "Caring Relations and Principles of Justice," from James P. Sterba, ed., *Controversies in Feminism.* Lanham. MD: Rowman & Littlefield, 2001.

Held, Virginia. "Whose Agenda? Ethics Versus Cognitive Science," from Larry May, Marilyn Freidman, and Andy Clark, eds., *Mind and Morals: Essays on Cognitive Science.* Cambridge, MA: MIT Press, 1996.

Hursthouse, Rosalind. *On Virtue Ethics.* London: Oxford University Press, 1999.

Johnson, Mark L. "How Moral Psychology Changes Moral Theory," from Larry May, Marilyn Freidman, and Andy Clark, eds., *Mind and Morals: Essays on Cognitive Science.* Cambridge, MA: MIT Press, 1996.

Krebs, Dennis. "As Moral as We Need to Be," *Journal of Consciousness Studies,* vol. 7, no. 102, 2000.

Macklin, Ruth. *Against Relativism: Cultural Diversity and the Search for Ethical Universals in Medicine.* Copyright ©1999 by Oxford University Press, Inc. Used by permission of Oxford University Press, Inc.

Montmarquet, James. "Moral Character and Social Science Research," *Philosophy,* vol. 78 (2003). By permission of Cambridge University Press.

Nagel, Thomas. "Chapter 6: Ethics," from *The Last Word* by Thomas Nagel. Copyright © 1997 by Thomas Nagel. Used by permission of Oxford University Press.

Putnam, Hilary. "Are Values Made or Discovered?" in *The Collapse of the Fact-Value Dichotomy and Other Essays,* Cambridge, MA: Harvard University Press, 2002.

Rachels, James. "God and Human Experience," from S. M. Cahn and D. Shatz, eds. *Contemporary Philosophy of Religion.* NY: Cambridge University Press, 1982.

Railton, Peter. "Alienation, Consequentialism, and the Demands of Morality," *Philosophy and Public Affairs*, vol. 13. no. 2 (1984).

Railton, Peter. "Morality, Ideology, and Reflection; or, The Duck Sits Yet," from Edward Harcourt, ed., *Morality, Reflection, and Ideology.* Oxford: Oxford University Press, 2000.

Rorty. Richard. "Relativism: Finding and Making," from Jozef Niznik and John T. Sanders, eds., *Debating the State of Philosophy: Habermas, Rorty, and Kolokowski.* Westport, CT: Preager, 1996.

Rovane, Carol. "Earning the Right to Realism or Relativism in Ethics," *Philosophical Issues*, vol. 12, Realism and Relativism (2002). By permission of Blackwell Publishing.

Schlesinger, George N. *New Perspectives on Old-Time Religion.* Oxford: Oxford University Press, 1988.

Skillen, Anthony. "Is Morality a Ruling Illusion?" from Edward Harcourt, ed., *Morality, Reflection, and Ideology.* Oxford: Oxford University Press, 2000.

Stocker, Michael. "The Schizophrenia of Modern Ethical Theories." *Journal of Philosophy*, LXXIII (1976).

Williams, Bernard. "Foundations: Practical Reason" reprinted by permission of the publisher from *Ethics and the Limits of Philosophy* by Bernard Williams, pp. 54–70, Cambridge, Mass.: Harvard University Press, Copyright © 1985 by Bernard Williams.

Wilson, Catherine. "On Some Alleged Limitation to Moral Endeavor," *Journal of Philosophy*, XC, 6 (June 1993).

Wolf, Susan. "Moral Saints," *Journal of Philosophy*, LXXIX, 8, (August 1982).